White Collar Skid Row

Melissa Ann Bell
by Melissa Ann Bell

The Quilldriver
WORKS WITH WORDS
Clarksville, Ark.

White Collar Skid Row
by Melissa Ann Bell
copyright © 2012 The Quilldriver, Clarksville, Ark., U.S.A.

ISBN 978-0-9791639-6-8

Publisher's Cataloging-in-Publication data

Bell, Melissa Ann.
   White collar skid row / by Melissa Ann Bell.
   p. cm.
   ISBN 978-0-9791639-6-8
1. Bell, Melissa Ann. 2. Alcoholics --Biography. 3. Substance abuse --United States --Biography. 4. Ozark Mountains Region --Biography. 5. Dysfunctional families --United States --Biography. 6. Christian biography --United States. I. Title.

HV5060 .B45 2012
362.292092--dc22   2011934347

Printed in the United States of America

IN LOVING MEMORY
OF JAKE
MY PARENTS
AND AUNT ROXENA

ACKNOWLEDGMENTS

I have been working on this manuscript for over 37 years, and from the very beginning, I've had the encouragement of friends and family, some of whom are now gone. I am delighted for the opportunity to say "Thank you!" and acknowledge some by name.

Roxena Lynne: You heard me say I was going to write a book for the first time when you were just eight years old. I wrote it twice and then waited several years more, until you were grown—now a wife and mother—to ask if you would type this story for me, if I were to once again try to write it down. You said, "Sure, Mother. You need to tell our story." You typed and typed, one time all night, calling me when the pain of reliving the story hurt so badly. You never complained about the many changes and stops along the way. Your encouragement kept me going. I can't imagine not having you for a daughter.

L.J.: My, what a patient, loving guy you are. All the long hours Roxena Lynne was typing, you never complained. You saw the strain it really was but never suggested that I find someone else. You always helped when needed and were very encouraging.

Cooper: You were very patient all the time your mom was working on Grandma's book. You are great.

Karen: You gave me the same kind of encouragement about the book through the years as you did during the time your siblings were growing up. Your steady kindness has always been a blessing to me.

Candy and Wendy: You both spent a lot of time reading and writing about your memories of growing up with alcoholism. Your kindness, honesty and insight have helped me very much.

Jacob: Your insights helped as well! Your letter helped me understand your thoughts concerning our life and how we were all affected.

Neil: You were available to help when I needed you most. You did last-minute research and took care of lots of little jobs that mounted up to a lot of time. Your comments and approval after reading the book did my heart good.

Zach: You've been a great encouragement to me in the writing of this book, just as you are in everyday life and have been for 48 years. You and Lynne were always my best supporters. I miss her too.

Anita: You kept me from quitting when I didn't think I would finish.

Marilyn: You always believed in me.

Ellen: You traveled fifty miles each week in 1974 to help me sort stacks of notes I had written and stored in boxes. When I was discouraged, you kept me from burning the whole thing. You spent many hours typing all that I had written. Thirty-seven years later, you are still there for me in many other ways.

Marian Scheirman: You spent many hours typing, asking me questions and pulling out thoughts and experiences I wanted to keep buried. Had it not been for the injury you received from a fall on the ice in 1983, I'm sure we would have been coauthors in the mid-1980s.

Juli Ginn: You believed in my story. Your wisdom in what the story needed and how to get the point across was the best. It was a sad day when we both saw there wasn't enough time in your life to continue our work. You and James were there when I needed you—always.

Jan Brooks: When I had gone as far as I could in writing the book, you came to meet me at my friend's house and knew as soon as you read it what needed to be taken out. Then you spent a lot of time working on it. I was very pleased with the result.

Jean and Tom: Thank you for your help each time I needed you.

Evon: The first time our late pastor and your husband, Donn, brought you to meet us, we became friends and prayer partners. During all these years, you always asked, "How's the book coming?" In the beginning of the third writing of this story, I was thrilled to be invited to your vacation home in Palm Springs. It was at the card table you set up for me there that my writing started to gain momentum.

Dr. Faye: What good talks we had into the nights when I traveled to the city to work on the book. My room in your home was always waiting.

Doris: Your wisdom has helped me to stay on track.

Ginger: You put so much time into reading and advising through the years. Whenever I got worried about the book, I always called you.

Loretta, my newest friend since moving: You seem to know just when I need encouragement.

To Dani Helm and all my teammates in Live Ministries: You have given me much encouragement and love.

To all the ladies of my last two Christian Women Connection groups: Though most of you didn't know about my writing, when I was not there you always carried my load without complaint. Your love to me is wonderful!

To my pastors and their wives through the years of my writing: Your wisdom, time and confidence were always an encouragement to me.

Shirley, my hair dresser for twenty years: You always asked with excitement about my book. I always left your place believing I'd get it done.

Ann, my high school classmate: Even though I've seen you very few times in the past 57 years, when I called and asked you to read my book, you agreed to do so, graciously.

Chris and Gerry: The door of your office was always open for me.

Mason, Andrew and Adam: When I had more jobs than I could get done, your dad would say, "The boys will help." When I was discouraged, your mom would say, "The boys and I pray for you each morning on our way to school." Now you are young men and very important to me.

To Nan, my friend and prayer partner: When I started rewriting my story you said, "You'll get it done, Mel, I'll help." Help you did. When I got worried that I wouldn't get done, you'd think of a way and did many jobs yourself with joy. Most of all, you introduced me to the publisher. You are wonderful.

My editor and publisher at The Quilldriver, Donna Lee Schillinger: Your availability and willingness to please never ceases to amaze me. Working with you has been a wonderful experience. You will go far in the publishing business.

Most of all, I thank the Lord. You were always there just in time to help me cross all my rivers and tunnel though all my mountains. I truly give you praise!

TABLE OF CONTENTS

Preface   7

Prologue: One Evening in January 1974   8

1961: Boy Meets Girl (in Rehab)   9

1962: In Six Months, I'll Have You   33

1963: I Feel Like Cinderella   55

1964: Where's My Bottle?   87

1965: Jake's Been Hurt   103

1966: And Baby Makes Eight   117

1967: Dr. Searchbrains   129

1968: I Will Not Live with Drugs   141

1969: A Back-Breaking Job   157

1970: Jake Agrees to be Admitted   169

1971: Now the Kids?   181

1972: It's the Life I Chose   197

1973: Reading and Growing   233

1974: A Plan to Break Free   259

1975: The Final Accident   283

Epilogue   299

PREFACE

When I first heard the words "skid row" in 1943, I lived in a farming community in the Ozarks. Our big social events were gatherings at Grandma's—and there was no drinking. "Skid row" later became a highly relevant concept when I worked at Wolfe's Clinic, an addiction treatment hospital.

Other concepts relevant to my life were not so easy to articulate. I never heard the word "dyslexia" during the years it was haunting me as I walked through "the hollers" and across the creek on a swing bridge to the country school with my brother and sisters. And even though the concepts of "enabler," "tough love" and "intervention" were profoundly affecting my life, I was not to discover these words until toward the end of my struggle with an alcoholic spouse. I could have benefitted from knowing them sooner.

Though I've not used any new words for today's readers, I have put some together in ways they might not have been used before. (And I'm not referring to the infusion of Ozark slang in my writing.) I have juxtaposed "white collar" and "skid row" to describe the alcoholic and drug dependent, upper-middle-class patients, many of whom were doctors, that I cared for at Wolfe's Clinic. And it aptly describes the man I fell in love with and married.

Jake was a respected radiologist and his patients loved him. He was the kindest man I ever knew, and even though we loved and genuinely liked each other, our household was far from normal. Jake's drinking caused our children to struggle in school and socially, and I had health problems as a result of the stress. Jake hated what he was doing to his family, yet there was always another binge.

How alcoholism affected our lives remains a delicate subject for a few of the key characters in our life story, so it was important that I change most of the names and our place of residence in this otherwise true story. Also, as such, I have not censored the curse words that were occasionally used.

I offer my story out of concern for families living with alcoholism. My heart goes out to the spouses and children who are looking out the window today, wondering, "Will he be drunk when he comes home? Will he even come home?" Or, "What if she's been in a wreck? What if she hurts someone else?"

Though my husband was the alcoholic, I made a generous share of mistakes too. If my recounting them will help one other spouse, parent, family member or friend to learn to believe in him or herself and lean on the Lord as he or she daily faces the truth, then the pain of my own struggles in living and writing this story will have been worthwhile. The reader will gain a great deal of perspective on alcoholism and its effects on friends and family. However, if I there is only one thing about alcoholism that you remember from this story, it should be that a person is responsible for only his or her own actions. I hope this story will help all those who have a loved one who is an alcoholic to realize that controlling circumstances to prevent binges, regardless of how well you do it, is not going to change your loved one.

PROLOGUE
ONE EVENING IN JANUARY 1974

I lifted the phone to my ear. There was a familiar silence, and then, "Hello there. I've stopped for a drink. I won't be long, but don't wait for me."

I glanced at Wendy who was mashing potatoes. "Just go right ahead and drink to your heart's content," I said, with none of the anger and dread that I had lived with for eleven years. "I'll see you when you get here."

"I won't be long."

"Okay. Bye."

Wendy had her potato masher in mid-air over the pan, a soft smile on her face. "Boy, I never thought I'd hear you say that, especially with such a soft tone in your voice."

"I know. I'm surprised myself," I said to our high school senior.

"Mama," our seven-year-old daughter Roxena Lynne asked, "Where was Daddy?"

"Down by the high school in a bar," I said as I set the chicken on the table. "I don't want you to be worried about your daddy, Honey; I'm not."

"Well, that's because you're big, but I'm little, and I'm worried about my daddy."

"I think he'll be home soon. Honey, why don't you put your coloring up; it's time to eat," I said.

We were just finishing dinner when Jake drove up. Usually when he stopped for a drink, he'd also bring home a bottle and drink in the car before he came in. He came in quicker than we expected, and looked and sounded like he had not had more than one drink.

I am glad I didn't yell or cry and beg him to not drink. Wendy and Neil will be in college soon, I thought. *As soon as they are settled, I can put the bottle behind me. If he chooses to continue drinking, I can manage with just Roxie and me.*

That night I lay in bed for a long time thinking how my life with Jake had started, and that night I decided I needed to share my story.

1961
BOY MEETS GIRL (IN REHAB)

It was a Monday afternoon, January 1961. I was living with Aunt Roxena and Uncle Jesse. They were actually a friend's aunt and uncle, but they treated me just like their niece. I was relaxing in Uncle Jesse's chair in front of the fireplace. The annual week-long, citywide youth services of the Church of God would be starting in a few hours.

The phone interrupted my thoughts. *Maybe it's an answer to the ad I placed for a job as a private duty nurse.*

"Hello?"

"Hello, I'd like to speak with Miss Jenkins, please."

"This is Melissa Jenkins."

"Miss Jenkins, I'm Alta Gwynn, nursing supervisor at Wolfe's Clinic, a private hospital for alcoholism and drug addiction, here in the city. Are you looking for a job?"

"Yes, I am."

"I understand that you just got off a case working with one of Dr. Martin's patients and that you worked in a nursing home where he saw patients."

"That is correct, but private duty is what I do best."

"When Dr. Martin learned we needed a charge nurse for the 11:00 p.m. to 7:00 a.m. shift, he recommended you."

"I appreciate Dr. Martin's confidence, but I've had no schooling and I don't think I could handle that much responsibility."

"Miss Jenkins, I'm very interested in talking with you. Would you come over tomorrow afternoon at 1:00 for an interview?"

How am I going to handle this, Lord, with my reading problem? And I know nothing about alcoholics.

"Miss Jenkins, could you come?"

"Oh, wow! This makes me a little nervous, but I'll come."

Why in the world did I agree to do that? With my reading problem, I'll never be able to handle it. There will be reports to write, orders to read, charting and no telling what else. Oh well, going for the interview would be a learning experience. So I'll show up and act like I have "good sense."

The next day I walked up the front steps of an elegant, old, three-story brick building, opened the heavy front door and walked into a large hall with dark woodwork and an Oriental rug. Sunshine came through stained glass windows and fell on a wide stairway with a curved banister that led to the second floor.

Just then, a sharply dressed gentleman, about sixty-five, came from another room with a folder in his hand. He had a friendly smile. "You must be Miss Jenkins."

"Yes, sir."

"I'm Dr. Frank Wolfe."

"Hello, Dr. Wolfe," I said as we shook hands. "It's nice meeting you."

Just then a nurse came from another wide stairway.

Alta Gwynn was a lovely lady in her late thirties. Her dark eyes and complexion were a perfect contrast to her heavily starched, snow white uniform. Her white cap with a black stripe looked perfectly professional with her salt and pepper hair. I liked her right away.

She showed me the clinic. Women occupied the first floor; men were on the second and third floors. The hospital could accommodate twenty-three patients. At the top of the steps, Mrs. Gwynn opened a locked door. There were three patient rooms, a kitchen, two bathrooms and a small room referred to as the chart room. This room housed the nurses' station, with a cabinet for the patients' medicine and liquor. As we left the locked area to go to the third floor, I noticed two fully-dressed patients visiting in the hallway and three or four others in the library.

By the time we got back downstairs and into Mrs. Gwynn's office, I had a lot of worries. I was excited about the prospect of working in such a nice, relaxed hospital, but how was I going to do this without telling her about my reading problem? "Mrs. Gwynn, I love caring for patients. I like challenges but don't do as well at keeping records."

"Our record keeping here isn't that much. I understand you've had experience giving medication. Do you know the medical abbreviations?"

"Yes."

"I'll work with you on the day shift a week before I turn the night shift over to you."

What if I can't learn this all in a week? "I'm not sure I can do it, but I could try. If I can't handle it, I'll tell you."

"Can you start in the morning?"

"Yes."

I arrived at 6:45 a.m. the next day. There were a lot of details to remember. Patients were to be referred to as "sick" instead of "drunk," and nurses said, "Yes, sir," "No, sir," "Yes, ma'am" and "No, ma'am" to both doctors and patients at all times. As one of my duties, I would chart the medication. On the night shift, the charge nurse would also have to log incoming and outgoing calls in a record book. I checked it and found the details were brief.

"Alcoholism is a disease," Mrs. Gwynn said before she explained the procedure of caring for the patients. When a patient came in "sick," he or she was put in one of the rooms in the locked area for twenty-four hours and tapered off of drinking. They could have a drink every four hours for the first twelve hours and every six hours for the next twelve hours. After the twenty-four hours were up, they were not given any more alcohol; instead, for the next forty-eight hours, they could have a teaspoon of liquid Delvinol. The patients called it "the brown medicine." After that, they received no alcohol and no Delvinol. They stayed at the clinic for ten days, which gave them a full week without medication.

Some of the patients were admitted under an alias. Some would request that if they got a call, we should say they hadn't been admitted to the hospital. I voiced my reservations to Mrs. Gwynn about lying, but she didn't think I would have many calls on the night shift.

I was surprised to see the caliber of people who came in for treatment. I had been expecting drunks like the old man I remembered from my childhood. His name was Woodrow Thomas and every one called him "Woody Tom." I wondered what Woody Tom would have thought about this place. Regardless of how brilliant, well dressed or their status in life, the patients were just as drunk as Woody Tom when they came in.

I thought a lot about Woody Tom during that first week at the clinic. The summer when I was eight years old, I spent a few days with my Aunt Vergie and Uncle Elic. They ran a country store. They lived next door to it and my bedroom window was close to the back of the store building. There was a large crawl space under the store. One night I was awakened by a loud noise. I looked out the window and saw some men in front of their car lights carrying a man over to the crawl space. They put him down and dragged him up under the back of the store. That sight worried me all night long. I could not imagine what could be wrong with him.

Early the next morning, Aunt Vergie and I went to the store. When we were alone I said, "Aunt Vergie, who was the man that stayed under the store last night?"

"That was Woody Tom."

"Why couldn't he walk straight?"

"Because he was drunk."

"Why was he drunk?"

"Because he had too much liquor. Melissa, if he lived in the city, they'd say he was on skid row."

"What's skid row, Aunt Vergie?"

"I've got to go put some gas in the car that just drove up. You ask too many questions."

"Oh! Let me pump the gas, Aunt Vergie, please!"

While I pumped the gas, I kept looking across to the crawl space, wondering if Woody Tom was okay.

All these years later, I still wondered about Woody Tom. As I drove home from the clinic, I wondered if he was still alive. I remembered seeing him in my teen years. It was common knowledge that on weekends, he drank and slept away from home.

The people that came to the clinic were so much different from Woody Tom; yet, when they are drunk, they seemed the same.

Winter was harsh that year and the clinic was busy. I was surprised to see people of all walks of life come to the clinic: a service station owner, mortician, large trucking company president, factory workers, school superintendent, doctors, lawyers, wives of well-known business men, and a famous female athlete.

"I'm beginning to understand that alcoholism is no respecter of persons," I told my friend Betty, as she set a plate of pancakes in front of me one morning when I stopped by her house after work.

"Do you still like your job?"

"I love working at the clinic. I liked working at the nursing home. I remember when you came to look at it for your mother. I'd begun to wish I was back on private duty so I could have quality time with the patient. When you called and offered me the job of taking care of your mother, I was delighted. I loved everything about the job. Not to mention your pancakes and Leo's dinners."

"You were here almost a year. I'm so glad we were able to keep her at home as long as she lived. We'll always fix you pancakes and dinners when you have time for us," Betty said with a smile.

"Both you and Aunt Roxena spoil me with your good meals and waiting on me hand and foot."

"How are you doing with record keeping?"

"Okay, I guess. One written report was really long. You know how I have trouble with long paragraphs? I hadn't taken the time to break the paragraph down sentence by sentence and I missed something."

"What did your supervisor say?"

"She said not to worry about it. The other morning I reported to Dr. Wolfe by phone that I'd found some pills that a patient had hidden. In the written report, I explained how I found them. I wrote, 'I was him walking away from his light switch with a table knife.' Mrs. Gwynn just laughed and said I must've been tired because I'd written 'saw' backwards. I've never told a soul, except you, that I never see that it's backwards until someone points it out."

"I'll find a tutor for you if you'll agree to it."

"No, Betty, I don't think I'm ready to do that."

"Well, when you are, you call me."

"Thanks, Betty, I've got to go and get to bed. Aunt Roxena stayed here in St. Louis while Uncle Jesse went to check on business in Omaha. She's taking me to the game tonight. I've never been to a major league game."

"That's wonderful. You're off tonight, aren't you?"

"Yes, two nights, thank the Lord! It's been a busy week."

"I'll see you next week," she said as she walked me to the door.

"I'll be here, same time, same kitchen that puts out those wonderful pancakes," I said as we hugged.

On my way home, I kept thinking about what Betty said about a tutor. *Could there be a way to overcome my reading and other learning problems?* I headed toward Aunt Roxena's house with just a glimmer of hope.

Aunt Roxena was waiting. "Just having my devotions, Honey. Sit down and I'll read some in Psalms before you go up." The last Psalm she read was 121. I had memorized part of it from hearing it quoted often. When I was young, I used to go down by the spring, sit on a big rock, and look over on the hill to a tall sycamore tree and recite the first two verses. "I will lift mine eyes unto the hills, from whence cometh my help. My help cometh from the Lord, which made heaven and earth."

When she was finished, I asked her what time we'd leave for the game. "We'll leave about 6:00 p.m. Why don't you come down about 5:00 and we'll eat."

My alarm sounded all too soon. I went downstairs and turned the corner to the kitchen. I gasped as I saw the doorway between the dining room and kitchen filled with all seven of my white uniforms. "Aunt Roxena! You washed, starched and ironed all of my uniforms! Oh my, I don't know what to say!"

We sat down at the table and I looked at her with love in my heart and said, "Thank you, Aunt Roxena. I told Betty this morning that you spoil me."

"You're welcome. Would you ask the blessing?" She reached for my hand. I was so overcome with emotion; it took me a minute before I could start.

We left a little early for the game. She had bought the tickets ahead of time and we had excellent seats. *I wonder if I'll see anyone from the clinic* had just come to mind, when one row in front of us I saw a young mother who had been a patient at the clinic about a week before. Mrs. Gwynn told me on my first day at the clinic that if this ever happened to let the patient speak first and never to mention to anyone that I'd seen one of the patients. I handled it by not looking in her direction.

At the end of the game, Aunt Roxena said how glad she was our team had won, since it was my first major league game.

When I arrived back to work, I saw that the 3:00-11:00 p.m. nurse I was relieving looked unusually tired as she opened the door to the locked area. As the door opened, I could see that we had three very "sick" patients.

"I see you've been busy admitting new patients," I said as I sat down by the desk for her report.

"We couldn't get them all in here, so one is in number eighteen. We only have one empty bed on second floor if you have to admit a new patient." During her report I learned three of the new patients were doctors. She gave me an update on the patients in the locked area first, and then on number eighteen. "He is a radiologist from here in the city. His name is Dr. Jacob Bell. Dr. Wolfe has known him since he was young. He's thirty-nine years old, has five children and is in the middle of a divorce. He has been drinking and not showing up for work. His medical partners insisted he come for help. I think his brother, Dr. Zach Bell, who is also one of his partners, called, but the patient drove himself here."

"Hope you're rested and ready to work," she said, as I put the key in the door of the locked area and bid her a good night.

"I like to be busy. That and coffee keep me awake." *I like the challenge of working here*, I thought as I started up the steps.

When I got to the third floor, I checked the patients who were awake first. Number eighteen was just at the head of the stairs. I decided to check on him last, because his room was dark. When I was finished checking the other patients I quietly opened the door and turned on my flashlight. I shined it to the floor. He was asleep; his respirations and pulse were steady, so I made my way back to the chart room.

The next morning at 5:00, I admitted another patient, filling the last vacant room. I then took a quick check upstairs to see about the new patient in number eighteen. He wasn't in his room, but I heard the shower. *Pearl can check on him before we go off duty*, I thought, and I went to check on the women patients.

I hurried to finish my last chart just as the office bell rang. I thought the day nurses were there already, so I grabbed the keys, and unlocked the door, pulling it back so they could enter.

It was by no means who I expected. Before me stood a very handsome, intelligent looking, impeccable man about six feet tall. His brown eyes were very alert, his hair was combed and a little damp, he was fully dressed in a brown and tan plaid shirt and brown slacks. He didn't look at all like he'd been admitted less than twelve hours before; he looked in perfect shape. Somehow I knew instantly that it was Dr. Bell.

"Good morning, I'm Miss Jenkins."

"Good morning, Miss Jenkins. I'm Dr. Jacob Bell. I've come down for my spirits." All the patients called it "spirits," and although I had never thought of questioning them, "spirits" seemed wrong for this particular new patient.

"Doctor, do you want a drink?"

"Yes, please, Miss Jenkins."

He remembered my name. Most of the patients remember Jim Beam or Jack Daniel's, but never Miss Jenkins, I thought as I got his drink.

When I got home, I was totally exhausted. I let Aunt Roxena's dog Jitter outside, had a bowl of cereal, and some quiet time. There were so many people to pray for. For the first time in the six months that I'd worked at the clinic, I felt completely drained. I was grateful when Jitter barked at the back door. As soon as he came in, we headed upstairs.

When I fell into bed, my mind started going over all the events that had happened on my shift. A female patient, whose family owned a large department store in the state capitol, had been up most of the night worrying about her family. The three men in the locked area were awake off and on. One of them wanted to use the phone to call his family to come get him. He had taken off his watch and offered it to me if I would put the call through. "I've got to get out of here, Miss Jenkins. I've got to get out of here. Take this watch and make the call."

"Dr. Barnes, I can't do that. I'd have your watch and you wouldn't know the time of day." *When Dr. Wolfe sees my report he'll keep him in the locked area to make sure he doesn't leave when the outside door is unlocked.*

Mid-afternoon came and I hadn't slept a wink. *It's starting to get to me, working nights so long, seeing so much trouble and not being properly trained. It's hard to settle down when I'm off duty.* I reset my alarm clock from 7:00 p.m. to 9:30 and finally went to sleep.

No new patients had been admitted when I took my chair for report at 10:45 p.m. that night. Two of the old patients had been dismissed and two of the patients in the locked area had been moved to the third floor. I wanted to check them first to make sure they were adjusting.

When I got to the top of the steps, number eighteen was sitting at a small round table in the middle of his spacious room reading the paper.

"Hello, Dr. Bell," I said as I entered his room. "I'm Miss Jenkins. I met you this morning."

"Yes, ma'am," he answered as he laid his paper aside and stood.

"I have several snack orders on this floor. Would you like for me to bring you some hot Ovaltine or a glass of milk? I also have some fancy crackers and a variety of cookies."

"I'll take a glass of milk, Miss Jenkins, please."

"After I check the lower floors, I'll be back."

"Thank you."

"Yes, sir, you're welcome."

He was standing at his door when I started down the steps.

I wonder if anyone ever said "Yes, sir" to Woody Tom.

I stopped by the chart room to give the orders from third floor to Pearl, and then checked the first and second floors. All the ladies on first were asleep and there was only one order from second floor. The snacks for third floor were ready and on the dumbwaiter. Since all the patients' rooms in the back of third floor were close to the dumbwaiter, they were waiting when I went back to unload it. They took their snacks and thanked me.

I told them good night and took the tray and milk to Dr. Bell. He took it from the tray, thanked me and set it on the table. I was about to say good night and turn to go when he said, "Miss Jenkins, where did you train?"

Oh dear, I wasn't expecting that. I hate to tell him I've never been to training, but I have to be honest. "I didn't, Doctor. I worked in a small hospital for a while. I came to the city three years ago to do private duty and I worked in a nursing home for a while. Then I got a call from Alta Gwynn, asking if I'd come to work here; I thought I'd give it a try." He was silent and just looked at me and picked up his milk. *I guess he wasn't impressed with that. If Betty were here, she'd say, "Oh heavens, Melissa what difference does it make? Why would you want to impress him?"*

"How long have you worked here?"

"Almost six months." He didn't comment, just looked at me. I told him to let me know if he needed anything and went to the chart room, anxious for a cup of coffee since I'd slept so little.

Visiting with the patients was part of the job. There was a lot on their minds, mainly their families. During his stay, number eighteen always waited in his doorway while I checked the other patients. He talked a lot about his five children and how much he missed them. When his ten days were up, he went back to work, but Dr. Wolfe suggested that he stay the entire month at the clinic at night. Surprisingly, he agreed to do that.

"Good evening, Doctor." I said one night as I walked in his room and handed him his regular glass of milk.

"Miss Jenkins, I'd like to ask you a question, if I may."

"I don't know if I can answer it, but you may ask."

"When you have overwhelming problems, what do you do?"

"I take them to the Lord in prayer. The Scripture says, 'He is an ever present help in time of need.'" Dr. Bell was silent. *Should I say more, Lord, or just answer his questions*?

"Do you live close to the clinic?"

"It's about five miles. I live at my aunt and uncle's house here in the city." He didn't comment and I had lots to do. I told him if he needed anything to let us know. Pearl made the rest of the trips to third floor that night.

When I came back on duty the next night, number eighteen had been dismissed. *My, I hope he overcomes the drinking problem for himself as well as his family*.

I was anxious to have the weekend off. Betty, her husband Leo, and the boys were having me over for my twenty-sixth birthday on Sunday. She always made a big deal about it. Also, I was to have my second date with a guy I'd met through a friend.

"Happy birthday, Melissa!" Betty said, as she met me around back by her patio Sunday after church.

"Oh, wow! We're having steaks. Just look at the size of those things," I said, standing by Leo while he turned them.

"This is a special day, Melissa. You're twenty-six."

We went in and made the salad then Leo and the four boys came in with the steaks and we gathered around the dining table. A beautiful cake was in the middle with twenty-six candles.

Jeffrey, who was five said, "That's a lot of candles!" We all laughed.

"That's just what I was thinking, Jeffrey." *Thank you, Lord, for this family that I've been a big part of for three years. I feel so loved*, I prayed, as I blew out the candles.

Back at work, it felt good to be making the rounds. I visited awhile with a ninety-three year old male patient, who had been admitted while I was gone, then had a small snack with Pearl while we stood in the kitchen and chatted.

"It's time for me to do charts, Pearl." I said as I carried a cup of coffee toward the chart desk. "I wish we could visit all night."

"There's your phone," she said, just as I sat my coffee on the desk. "I have a feeling, Melissa, that we'll fill the last empty room before morning."

I lifted the receiver of the heavy, black phone. "This is Miss Jenkins, may I help you?" There was silence for just a second.

"Miss Jenkins, this is Dr. Jacob Bell speaking."

"Yes, sir?" *That's the patient that was in number eighteen so long. His voice is strong, but I bet he's started drinking again*. There was a silence before he spoke, like I remembered from when he was in number eighteen.

"How are you, Miss Jenkins?

"Fine, thank you. How are you doing?" *There's that silence again. He's probably slipped and knows he needs to come in so he won't get on a binge*.

"Doctor, if you need to come into the clinic, I have a room for you."

"No, Miss Jenkins, I don't need to come in. I called Wolfe's Clinic to talk to you."

"I'm flattered. How may I help you?"

"I want your church address."

"Oh, okay. Let me look it up. I can get to the church, but I only know the street name." *This is a switch, for one of these patients to be interested in church. Maybe it's a start for him to turn his life around. This brilliant, handsome, impeccable doctor needs help from the Lord.* I gave him the address and said, "You'll be most welcome, Doctor. I'll introduce you to the pastor."

"When do you go?" he asked.

"When I work on Saturday nights, I go Sunday night at 7:00."

"Then that's when I'll come." He thanked me and said he'd see me Sunday night.

For crying out loud! I never thought I'd get a call like that, I thought as I picked up my coffee cup and slowly took a drink. *What is going on with that patient? There's such a similarity to Woody Tom and yet such a difference.*

All night I kept thinking off and on about the phone call. *That is so strange that he'd call here about church.* Then I remembered the conversation we'd had about the Lord being my help in trouble. *That's it! He wants to think about going that direction so he can get his life straightened out. That's great!*

That Sunday night, I sat up front with the youth, as I usually did, since I worked with the youth. When the service was over, I started to the back to see if Dr. Bell was there. Sure enough, he was.

"Good evening, Doctor."

"Good evening, Miss Jenkins." he said as he started walking toward the door with me. I introduced him to Dean and Vonda, the pastor and his wife. As soon as we got outside, he said, "Would you like to go for a cup of coffee?"

"Sure. I'll drive my car home, just follow me." *Maybe he wants to talk about how to accept help from the Lord. He should talk to Pastor Dean, though. When he asks me more questions, I'll suggest that. Dean will be glad to help him. Lord, help Dr. Bell to find you.*

I parked my car on the street beside the house, since I'd be leaving again soon for work. As I got out, he drove up behind me. We drove to a nearby A&W drive-in and ordered coffee in the car. Conversation came easily. He told me about his medical practice with his brother and three other partners. He asked if I wanted to drive by and see his office. I thought that was okay. On the way home, I asked, "Where were you raised, Doctor?"

"Here in the city, not far from the office. My dad started the practice. He was a pioneer in the field of radiology. He's been gone several years. My mother remarried and lives close to here. By the way, let's drop the 'Doctor' and 'Miss Jenkins.' I'm Jake."

How strange that he wants to be on a first-name basis; he must want to talk more informally. I'll take it slow and not push. I've witnessed to people before, and this conversation should be no different. "I'm Melissa," I said as we stopped at a light.

"Melissa, how old are you?" he asked, looking over at me.

"What would you guess?"

"I'd say twenty-six." He looked so confident about his guess.

"Yes! I just had a birthday in July."

"I just turned forty last week," he said as the light changed. "When is your next night off?"

"This week it's Wednesday. I just have one night off since I took an extra day last week to go home."

"I'd like to have some more time to visit. Do you have plans for Wednesday night?"

"I usually go to mid-week service, but there is a business meeting this week and I hadn't planned to go."

We were pulling in my drive when he said, "What time could I call you Wednesday to see if it's convenient for another visit?"

"Oh, mid-afternoon. I don't sleep as long when I have a night off."

When he stopped the car, I said, "Thanks for the coffee," and hurried to open my car door.

"You're most welcome," he said, and I noticed he had his hand on his door handle. That made me a little uncomfortable.

"It's getting late, I'd better run. Good night."

"Good night, Melissa."

He waited in his car until I went inside.

Surely he didn't intend to walk me to the door, but he's so polite, he'd do it out of habit, I'm sure. I'll call Dean tomorrow and tell him about Dr. Bell. He needs a man to talk to.

I drove to work thinking about him. "Lord, he needs You so badly," I said aloud. I was impressed with Jake's manners and sense of humor, but didn't think of him as being interested in me. *Could tonight be the start of Dr. Bell turning his life around? Going to church is a good step forward.*

The next three nights were very busy and I thought they would never end. Both Pearl and I were running up and down the steps all night. When Wednesday morning came, I hurried home and fell into bed. I didn't set my alarm and slept most of the day.

I was just waking up as the phone rang.

"Hello?" Silence. I knew it was Dr. Bell.

"Hello, there. Is your evening still free?"

"Yes, just Jitter and me here."

"Who's Jitter?"

"Aunt Roxena's dog."

"What kind is it?"

"I have no idea."

He laughed. "I'm going to be at the office for a while. I'll grab a bite to eat on the way over. By the way, I always take Thursday afternoons off and I'm going to see a friend who's in the state hospital tomorrow. He's in AA with me. I'll only be there about thirty minutes, and I thought you might like to ride along; you could take a book. The ride there and back would give us a lot of time to visit."

"How would you like to go to my brother's for dinner? We won't be far from him," I said, excited about any excuse to get to see my brother Stan and his wife, Anita. It had been six months since our last visit.

"That would be fine. I'll see you around seven tonight."

I decided to bake one of my Cousin Ellen's oatmeal cakes. I'd watched her enough to know just how she did it, so I wouldn't have to worry trying to read a recipe.

Jitter barked at 6:55 p.m. to let me know Dr. Bell had arrived.

"Come on in. I'm just ready to pour some lemonade."

He followed me into the kitchen. "This is a nice place," he said, looking around.

"I call it Aunt Roxena's cottage. Her home in the country is twice this size."

"Do they come home much?"

"Very little since her country house was finished. Uncle Jesse travels a lot. He checks on his businesses in Dallas, Tulsa and other cities, so he's not here much either." I handed him a glass of lemonade and led the way to the front porch.

We sat down in the swing, drinking our lemonade and chatting comfortably. Before we knew it, it was dark and the streetlight came on. We talked non-stop. He told me about his family's farm that he and his brother now owned. His great-grandfather had bought it from Native Americans in 1863 for a dollar an acre. He and his brother Zach had spent a lot of time at the farm with their grandparents when they were growing up. He told me all about each of his children. There was pain in his voice when he talked about them.

I shared about being raised in the Ozarks, the youngest of six, with two brothers and three sisters. He didn't seem a bit shocked to hear there had been no inside plumbing for years and that my favorite toy when I was a little girl was a rock that I had imagined to be a beautiful doll.

It was almost 11:30 p.m. when I finally asked him if he wanted some cake and coffee. We went in, I poured the coffee and cut the cake. We sat down at the table—I had remembered to put on the tablecloth as Aunt Roxena always did.

"I miss Aunt Roxena. I had to iron this tablecloth myself."

"Does she iron all of her linens?"

"Oh my, yes, and my seven uniforms. I miss her since she's gone most of the time. I have to do my own ironing and everything."

He laughed, asked about my youth group, then said before I could answer, "Do you call your hair red or strawberry blonde?"

"Strawberry blonde, I guess. I don't think much about it," but I was flattered that he did.

"There's a lot of red in it."

"My grandmother has red hair. Her middle name is Melissa."

"I'm amazed," he said.

"What about?"

"You're twenty-six and have never been married. Why?"

"Well, where I come from, you fall in love first and I've never fallen. I don't worry about it. I don't need to. Everyone else worries for me. You can't believe some of the characters my friends try to match me up with."

"Tell me about the characters that your friends fix you up with."

"Well, for one thing, they aren't gentlemen. They take you out for a ten cent coke and try to squeeze it out of you on the way home." I took a bite of cake and looked at him. He was smiling from ear to ear. *That might have sounded a little silly,* I thought, my face reddening. "That's not original. Dr. Wolfe's secretary, Georgia, came up with it."

"Do you know Georgia very well?"

"Yes. She has me over to have dinner with her and her teenage daughter quite often. She is a very polished lady and I think it's her mission to put a little of her polish on me. I wish her luck. You can take the girl out of the country, but you can't take the country out of the girl. You've heard that, haven't you?"

"Yes, I've heard that," he said, still smiling.

He's such a good listener. He acts like he enjoys hearing what I have to say.

"I called my brother Stan. He and Anita are looking for us tomorrow. He's ten years older than I, but he didn't marry until he was twenty-seven. All the other kids were gone when I was eleven. He always came home on weekends. I guess I'm extra close to Stan. He's always been there for me. You're close to your brother, too, aren't you?"

"Yes, we are ten months and three weeks apart. I'm the eldest."

"Like another piece of cake?" I said, getting up to get it.

"Oh, I shouldn't. I've had two pieces. It's very good. I've never had it before." He had another piece.

"Do you like your job at the clinic?" he asked.

"Yes, but not as well as private duty." I said as I sat down across from him.

"You have a lot of responsibility, don't you?"

"I do, and I'm not trained for it." I shifted uncomfortably and picked up my coffee cup.

"Did you ever think about going to school?"

"Yes."

He put down his fork and just looked at me. "Why don't you?"

"I have a reading problem." *Oh dear, why did I do that? I wish he wouldn't look at me like that. I'm afraid I'm going to cry.*

"You can get help with that. Did you ever apply for nursing school?" he said, picking up his fork again.

"No," I said, "but do you remember Margaret Jackson, an R.N. who worked at the hospital until last year? She left for the mission field."

"Yes. She went to Africa."

"That's right."

"How do you know her?"

"She's a close friend from church. She had everything lined up for me to apply before she left. She had told the mission board about me, and one of its representatives interviewed me. He said they had a place for me if I were a registered nurse. I was heartsick. I couldn't bring myself to tell them about my reading problem. I knew if I started nurse's training, I'd have to quit. All my high school teachers thought I didn't apply myself. What I did learn was from memorization. In the two-room school where I went through the eighth grade, I'd heard the work three or four years before I reached that grade, and so I could do it from memory."

"Tell me about your reading problem."

"If it's more than a sentence, I don't know what I've read. I can't spell very well. Plus, I write a lot of my words backwards. My teachers thought I was careless. I didn't know I did it until they pointed it out, and then I couldn't explain why. But if I hear a paragraph read out loud at least three times, I can quote it and not miss a word. If it's written simply enough, I can read it out loud three times and quote it, but I can't explain to you what I've just quoted." He looked at me and didn't say anything for a while. *Oh, I've blown it. I shouldn't have said all that.*

"That's amazing." He moved his chair and leaned back still looking at me.

"That I can't understand what I read?"

"No. That you can hear something three times and quote it. I have never known anyone with that kind of memory."

I didn't really believe him, it was such a way of life for me, but it sounded good.

I don't condemn him for having a drinking problem. He doesn't condemn me for having a reading problem.

The clock in the living room struck midnight. He got up to go. "It's been great, Melissa. Thank you. What time should I call you tomorrow?"

"I'll sleep until about noon since I work tomorrow night."

"I'll call you about two."

Having him here seems so natural. I feel flattered that he has sought me out as a friend.

"Jake, I'm looking forward to riding with you tomorrow. I love visiting with you." I paused and unplugged the white and blue Corning Ware coffeepot and leaned up against the cabinet. "But don't you think you should have a man to talk to? My pastor is very non-judgmental. I haven't told him where I met you—just that you were working through some problems. He'd be glad to help."

"I'll call you tomorrow." We were silent as we walked to the door. "Good night, Melissa."

"Good night."

"Come on, Jitter," I said as I locked up and made my way upstairs. I couldn't sleep at first. I thought about how Jake needed help so he could get his family back. He talked of his children so fondly. Around 1:30 a.m., I had a strange last thought: *I don't remember when I've ever enjoyed myself that much.*

The next day, Jake picked me up at 2:00 p.m. I took a walk while he visited his friend at the hospital. On the way to Stan's he told me that he visited his AA friend in hopes he could help him. He said, "It helps me to help someone else."

"Jake, real help comes from the Lord."

"I suppose. When I talk about God to another AA member, I'm talking to myself, too."

I didn't think he really felt it for himself, so I said, "Jake, this is something you can know for yourself. In order to turn your life around and get your family back together, you must know Jesus Christ on a personal level."

"Melissa, I've never heard anything like that before."

"That's why you need to talk to my pastor. He could help you understand just how much God loves you. He'd be glad to visit with you. He's real easy to talk to and he and his wife are very good friends of mine."

"I may want to do that sometime. It's been good today just to know I would be going with you to visit your brother. Oh, by the way, your dog is a Manchester Terrier."

"Thanks! I always did want to know what kind of dog Jitter is."

"Does your brother know you're bringing someone you met at Wolfe's Clinic?"

"No. I told Anita you were a doctor and a friend. They are used to my bringing people by, so they'll think nothing of it. Since I called, we'll get a better dinner. But we could have come unannounced and they would have been pleased to have us. They're a relaxed, loving couple and their home is always open."

"I'll be honored to meet them."

"It's just around the corner." As we came to the corner lot, I pointed to the right and said, "That's the back of the house just up there. See that tall blonde out at the grill?" I felt such pride and excitement.

Stan saw us and came toward the car. We got out and went to meet him.

"I sure can tell he's your brother. If he were younger, you could pass as twins," Jake said as we walked toward Stan.

We hugged and before I got a chance to introduce them, Stan released me and reached for Jake's hand. "Hello there. I'm Stan Jenkins."

"Hello, Stan. Jake Bell."

"You're just in time. I just put the steaks on the grill. Come in, Jake, and meet Anita."

I could tell Jake felt very relaxed with Stan and Anita. The evening went much too quickly for me, but we had to leave shortly after dinner so I wouldn't be late for work. Stan and Anita walked to the car with us and stood waving when we left.

"You are really close. I could see that," Jake said as he pulled out onto the street.

"Yes. Stan had a girlfriend who used to refer to us as Stan and his little shadow."

As we got on the interstate, Jake asked, "Do you want to take a nap so you won't go to sleep on the job?"

"I won't go to sleep. I'll drink coffee and fly up and down those steps all night."

"You do go fast up and down the steps," Jake smiled. "By the way, I take it that your brother is religious, too. When he returned thanks, it seemed like he really thought he was talking to someone."

Does Jake just think I'm religious? I hate that word. I could hear the hum of the tires on the pavement of the interstate; other than that, a silence hung between us. Finally, I looked over at him. "We were never religious. In fact, we lived in a community with no church until the late forties. I still don't want to be religious. I gave my heart to Jesus Christ in 1950 and was baptized in a creek on December seventeenth. Stan and Anita gave their hearts to the Lord in 1957. Stan really has a wonderful relationship with the Lord. He reads and memorizes the Word of God and daily talks to the Lord in prayer. What you heard was really what it sounded like. He was really talking to Someone."

"That's amazing."

Lord, I don't think he wants to talk to Dean. Help me to know how to give him the plan of salvation without talking too much.

"Jake, when I was fifteen, I was a very angry teenager. I felt unloved and alone. That wasn't the case, but that's the way I felt. I was at a revival meeting and the minister read John 3:16: 'For God so loved the world that He gave His only begotten Son, that whosoever believeth in Him should not perish, but have everlasting life.' I knew it by heart, but that night when he said, 'God so loved the world that He gave His Son that whosoever believed on Him might be saved,' suddenly I realized that was for me!

"The minister kept talking, but I didn't hear him. Verses that I'd heard often kept coming to my mind, like Romans 3:23: 'For all have sinned, and come short of the glory of God.' And another verse about sin seemed to speak to me, Romans 6:23: 'For the wages of sin is death; but the gift of God is eternal life through Jesus Christ our Lord.' I realized that night that if I died, I'd be eternally lost.

"I thought of a picture I'd seen with Jesus knocking on a door, and the verse I'd learned in Sunday School, Revelations 3:20: 'Behold, I stand at the door and knock: if any man hear my voice, and open the door, I will come in to him, and will sup with him, and he with me.' It was that night that I opened the door of my heart and let the Lord come in. I knew that I was loved, and I could start a new life.

"Jake, the Lord wants you to have the same attitude that David did. In Psalms 51:10, he said, 'Create in me a clean heart, O God; and renew a right spirit within me.' We all have to face that we are sinners. I was burdened down with anger, guilt and sin, but I found rest through Jesus Christ, who loved me so much that He gave His life for me. God loves you that much, Jake. He wants to forgive you of your sins and take your heavy burden on Himself."

I've given the basics to him, Lord, by giving him the scriptures that mean so much to me. I don't know what to do next, so I need to let You work.

A deafening silence hung between us. At last Jake said, "It's amazing you just learned all those scriptures by hearing them."

Is he trying to change the subject?

"The main thing, Jake, is that I responded to the Lord of the Scripture. He wants to make a difference in your life."

We drove in silence for a while, so I changed the subject and began asking him questions about his childhood. He told me about growing up in a neighborhood with seventeen boys. He and his brother had horses and were in several horse shows. He talked about his love for his grandparents. He and his brother had spent a lot of time with them on the farm.

Then he said, "I had my first drink when I was fourteen. Alcoholism is in my blood. My grandfather and my uncle on my mother's side were alcoholics. I worry about my kids."

His life is too complicated for me, Lord. He needs a Christian man to be a friend and lead him to You. Then he could get his life in order and his family back together.

We turned off the interstate into the city. It wasn't far to my house.

"Here we are. I got you home before you turned into a pumpkin."

"Yes, I can get to work in forty-five minutes. Jake, I loved taking you up to Stan's. I wish you could know him as a friend."

"Thank you for taking me. I liked your brother." Jake's last words were, "I'll see you at church Sunday night."

Wow! He's coming! He must be sincere about wanting help, I thought, naively.

On Saturday, I went to the mailbox and found a letter from my brother. *He never writes to me. What has brought this on?*

I tore the letter open and sat down in Uncle Jesse's chair. Stan got right to the point. "You are my little sister and I can't stand by and see you date this older man. He doesn't seem to be walking with the Lord, and he has children and a broken home. You must not see him."

He's crazy. I'm not dating this "older man." Suddenly, I had never been so angry in my entire life. *He always lets Anita do all the writing, but all of sudden when he wants to set me straight about something, he decides to write. He should know by now what kind of life I live. How could he think I would be dating Jake!* I immediately went to the kitchen, got some paper and started writing: "First of all," I reminded Stan, "it has been years since you've written. If you can't trust me, stay out of my business!"

⌒

I was getting good at making oatmeal cakes. One Sunday night I had one ready just in case Jake came by. Sure enough, he called and said he'd pick me up for church. "Come a little early and we'll have some cake," I said.

We sat down at the table for coffee and cake. He looked at me and said, "Melissa, you are real good for me. When I'm around you, I don't think as much about drinking."

All of a sudden something my mother said when I was about sixteen popped into my head. Mama and I were in the kitchen canning blackberries and she was standing near the wood cook stove, spooning berries into a jar. I don't remember what prompted it, but she said, "Melissa, always remember an older man knows just what to say to a younger woman." I dismissed the thought as having nothing to do with Jake.

Jake sat with his hand on the handle of his cup looking at me. He took a sip of coffee then said, "I'm going to a three-day meeting in Colorado Springs during the same week as your vacation."

"Oh, you are? Are you going to drive?"

"No. I'm going by train. Melissa, I know you're a very proper young woman. If you'd like to go, I'll arrange a room for you and try to show you a good time."

"Oh my, Jake, I can't do that." I took my last bite of cake then looked at him. *Surely he isn't serious. I can't believe he'd want me to go along. Stan would really have a fit.*

"You think about it, and I'll check with you in a few days."

"I'll think about it, but that's not my style."

"I understand your style and have great admiration for the way you think and live, but I'd really enjoy having you along."

Doctor, you are so charming, so easy to talk to, so educated, I'd love spending that time with you, I thought, as I got up and refilled the coffee cups. I looked at the clock and said, "We have time for you to have another piece of cake."

"I'll never turn down a piece of your cake," he said smiling.

"Jake, I don't think I'll go, but if I do, I'd insist on paying for my own room."

"We'll see about that."

After church, we stopped by the hospital. Jake turned off the car and said, "I won't be long. I just need to check a film and call the patient's doctor. Melissa, you know that I'm waiting to go to court for a divorce, I just wanted to tell you that. I don't know if I could go back if I wanted to. And even if I could, I will never go back. It's important to me that you know that." We looked at each other in silence. "I'll be right back."

I'm not sure what to think about his wanting me to know that he would never go back to his wife. We've kept this relationship strictly as friends, and I've often told him the Lord could put his home back together. I don't know what to think.

In just a few minutes, he was bounding down the hospital steps. When he got in the car, he said, "It's wonderful having you here in the car waiting for me."

"Jake, I've loved being your friend and having you as mine, but does your not wanting to go back to your wife have anything to do with me?"

"No, Melissa. I'd already decided that before I ever met you. I just wanted you to know."

I feel so confused. I had wanted Jake to go back to his family, but now that he isn't going, what should I do from here? Stan was so definite in his letter about my not seeing Jake—but Stan is too protective.

"I'd like to know the thoughts that are going on behind those blue eyes," he said as he pulled out of the parking lot.

"I'm not sure myself."

We rode around a while. He showed me some of the better homes in the city. Some of the owners' names I recognized from businesses and the clinic, but I said nothing about that. He was impressed with the landscaping and architecture. He seemed interested in every detail. Other than being disturbed by the news of him not going back to his family, it was turning out to be a pleasant evening.

We pulled in my drive about thirty minutes before I needed to leave for work.

He waited, holding the screen as I unlocked the door.

"You think about it," he said as I stepped inside and turned around. "I'd really like you to go to Colorado with me. I'll make sure that the whole trip will meet with your approval."

"When do you have to know?"

"I could make the reservations, and if I have to, I can cancel your room. The trains aren't that crowded anymore, so that will be no problem."

"Will you agree that I pay for my own room?"

"That's not necessary, Melissa. I'll pay for it."

"Maybe I'm old fashioned, but I won't be comfortable doing it any other way. I've never done anything like this."

"I understand. We'll do what you're comfortable with, but I'll still try to talk you out of it."

I'm so confused that he just might be able to do that. "Okay. You may make the reservations."

"I'm real glad you're going. We'll leave Thursday morning and come back Monday night."

"That works out great. My vacation is Wednesday to Friday of the next week."

Maybe I should have said no, but I can't think of anything I'd rather do than to spend several hours on the train visiting with that most intelligent and educated man. I never tire of his vocabulary, even though I don't know the meaning of some of the words. When I ask him to explain, he never acts surprised or condemning. I really want to go on that trip. First, I've got to get the idea past Betty. I sure hope she thinks it's okay. I trust Betty's judgment.

My Wednesday morning pancake date finally came. Betty was waiting for me with her beautiful smile.

"Betty, I have some exciting news."

"Good, Melissa, I'm glad. You deserve some excitement. Let me hear it," she said as she put pancakes on the griddle.

I got the coffeepot and poured our coffee. "Jake wants me to go with him on a trip to Colorado." She looked over at me. "Are you surprised?"

"Not a bit," she said casually, as she took the syrup from a pan of hot water and placed it on the table then went to turn the pancakes.

"I was."

"Why wouldn't he want you along?" she asked, as she picked up her coffee cup.

"I'm a country girl. I know none of the social graces. I'm not educated. I can think of all kinds of reasons."

"Well, I can think of all kinds of reasons why he'd want you."

"Like what?" Trying to be equally casual, I said, "Boy, these are good pancakes."

"In the first place, he doesn't care that you're a country girl and uneducated. A man doesn't care that much about those things. He has lots of problems and you are free of problems. His life is all messed up; yours isn't. You're fun, you're young, your life's not complicated and, Melissa, you're a little naïve."

I was shocked. "For crying out loud, Betty, it's not like we're sharing a room. From the beginning, I said I'd pay for my own room because I thought that was proper. I'm not naïve!" I lowered my voice, "This is my first week-long vacation on this job. I've never been anywhere since I came to the city, except a church convention in Indiana and a trip to Mississippi. It would be so good just to be on vacation and do fun things, see new places. What's wrong with that?"

She leaned across the table, took my hand and looked me in the eyes, "You mean to do nothing wrong. You do work hard and have very little time for fun. You are happy because of your beliefs and the standards you hold. I know you're not planning to go off and live recklessly, but you're in love with that man, and you'll be away from all of us who love you. Your conscience won't be as strong. When you come back from that trip some of your standards will have been compromised."

I can't be hearing right, I thought. *I would never sacrifice my standards for any man, and being in love has never crossed my mind. How could she think that?*

She got up from the table and took the butter to the refrigerator. As she put her hand on the door, she turned around and looked at me. "Melissa, you are not going on that trip with that doctor." I sat there stunned. She placed the butter on the shelf, closed the door and went to the sink to load the dishwasher.

I got up and said, "Well, I'd better go. Jitter will be waiting. Thanks for the pancakes, Betty."

"You're welcome, Melissa. On your next free morning, I'll make you some more."

Oh no you won't, I thought angrily, but I could not let her know how mad I was because of how great a friend she was to me.

She followed me to the door. "Tell Leo and the boys hello," I said as calmly as I could.

"I will. You get some rest."

I hurried to my car. Betty's words haunted me throughout the day. "You're in love with that man and you'll be away from all of us who love you." I couldn't rest for thinking of those words. I was to leave the next day. Yet, I knew Betty always told me the truth, and I always went to her because I trusted her judgment. *I know I think about him a lot and am glad for his visits. Maybe I should listen to her. When I pray, I can't get peace. Maybe I should just go home instead of going on vacation with Jake.*

It was 9:00 p.m. I had packed my suitcase and was giving Jitter a bath at the foot of the basement steps when the phone rang. I ran up the steps and answered, "Hello?"

"Hello, there. What have you been doing to start your vacation week?" Jake sounded happy.

"I was giving Jitter a bath and just finished packing my bag."

"You're early. I haven't even started that."

"Jake, I think I should go home to see the folks. When I had my quiet time this morning, I prayed about it. I don't think it's proper for me to go on the trip to Colorado."

"I certainly understand. I'm not surprised. You are an outstanding young woman."

"Thank you."

We wished each other a pleasant trip and he said he'd call the day I was to return. I found myself wishing that day was much sooner than a week.

The folks were surprised to see me drive up. It was a beautiful fall day. They were out front under the oak tree. We visited about an hour and Daddy said, "You haven't said anything about that doctor that you took to your brother's."

"Not much to tell." *Oh boy. They've heard from Stan.*

"I understand he's a lot older than you and has children."

"Sounds like you already know a lot about him."

"You need to think about this. Your mama married someone a lot older. Look at her. She has this old man on her hands and all the work to do."

"Daddy, Dr. Jake Bell is a friend. And is Mama complaining?"

"No, she's not complaining. You shouldn't get mad at your brother. He's always been there for you and he always will be. You've been awful quiet since you got home. One way to get your mama's and my attention is for you to be quiet. Right now, you're just busting to cry."

I got up and hurried into the house.

Mama came inside later and said, "Melissa, I was going to tell you that Stan and Anita were home for a long weekend and told us about your visit and your letter. They are really worried about you. Stan thinks you're mad at him. He doesn't know what to do."

"Did they come home to report on me, Mama?"

"No. They had an extra day off."

"Mama, that man hasn't done anything improper. Stan doesn't trust me; that's what upsets me."

"Oh, yes, your brother trusts you."

"Then he thinks I'm dumb." *Maybe I am. Betty thinks I'm naïve.*

"Stan doesn't want you to get hurt, but I'm afraid it's too late. An older man always knows what to say to a younger woman. Just be careful, Honey, and don't let anything destroy the love you have for your brother."

"I won't, but I just wish he trusted me."

"He does. You just do what's right. We don't want to see you hurt."

"Thanks, Mama." I reached up and got a green, barrel-shaped glass from the cupboard.

"You're a good girl, Melissa. Just stay that way," Mama said as she got the cold water from the refrigerator.

"Mama, you have nothing to worry about."

We didn't discuss my private life for the remainder of my visit, which was a relief. They said what they thought they should and let it rest. I was grateful.

When my week was up, I headed back to the city. I was an hour away, sitting at a stop light, wondering if Jake would call, when suddenly a truck crashed into the back of my car. I couldn't believe it. I got out and looked at my beautiful red and white Plymouth. As I moaned in grief, I thought, *This is the only thing that I own, completely paid off. Now it's gone, just as a friendship with a wonderful man soon will be.* Life was falling apart. Tears filled my eyes.

The back of the car was smashed. The trunk lid was demolished, part of it was dragging and some of the chrome looked like it would fall off. I could drive the car into the city, the officer said, if I'd go slowly. The one-hour drive took two hours.

Jake had returned from his trip two days before and was expecting me to be home. He called shortly after I arrived and came right over. He said he would help me find a car. My insurance agent started working with the other driver's insurance company the next morning, while Jake and I looked at cars. I decided on a beautiful late model, two-tone green Buick.

As soon as the car problem was solved, I made a trip to see my pastor. Dean and Vonda were only a little older than I, and although we were very close friends, first and foremost, Dean was my pastor. He met me in the parking lot of the church to admire my car before we went to his office. When we were seated in his office, he said, "Your face tells me that we need to pray for your broken heart." I lost it! The tears burst forth, and for a long time, I couldn't speak. Dean leaned back in his chair and sat silently. I had shared with Vonda about my morning with Betty. Dean knew this was going to be tough.

"I'm sorry, Dean."

"That's okay. Let's pray." Dean's prayer was short and mostly for the Lord's love to engulf me.

"Vonda tells me you've had a hard couple of weeks. Why don't we just talk about the practical side of this for now, and if you feel that we need more time, we'll talk on your night off. You do have to sleep, and Vonda is thinking you're not doing much of that. She said you'd been to see your doctor and he'd given you some medication, but you still can't sleep."

"I don't know where to start. Jake and I have kept this a friendship, Dean."

"I know you have kept it on a friendship level, and you say you are not dating, but ask yourself these questions. One: If one of the youth group was seeing someone at set times and places, would I think they were dating?" He leaned forward and put out his arms on the desk, hands together, and looked me in the eye. "Two: Would I approve of one of the young people seeing someone who is in the middle of a divorce? And the final question I want you to ask yourself is: Can I talk openly with peace to the Lord about this friendship?"

We sat silent a moment. Finally, I looked up, "Do you want me to give up the youth group?"

"Not yet. Everyone in this church believes in you, Melissa." We were silent again.

"I should go."

"Call Vonda if you need us," he said, standing.

"I will. Thanks, Dean." I left his office immediately.

I got very little sleep that day for thinking of my conversation with Dean. *Can I openly talk to the Lord about this friendship with peace? I guess not. I haven't slept well in a long time, and I can think of nothing else.* I finally got about two hours sleep.

Jake called about 9:00 p.m. I asked him if he would come over, so we could talk. I hurried to get ready for work. He came about 9:30.

"I'm going to let you take me for a hamburger while we talk. I haven't had time to eat." We went to the drive-in near the house, ordered hamburgers and coffee and visited casually while we ate.

Driving out onto the street, I said, "Jake, I want to tell you something. This morning I went to see my pastor. He suggested I ask myself some questions. One was 'Can I talk openly with peace to the Lord about this friendship?'"

After some silence, Jake spoke: "Mel, I've never known anyone like you. We are beginning to care too much. I have too many problems."

He'd never called me Mel before. No one had. It sounded so soft and tender. It was my undoing. I wilted. We drove into my drive. He stopped the car, put his hand on my shoulder and said, "Mel, I need to let you get on with your own life. You need to forget about me."

I kept looking down and said the best I could in a low voice, "Okay, I accept that. I won't be expecting your call." Hurt and angry, I jumped out of the car and hurried to my new car to go to the clinic. He backed out and waited for me to back out. When I did, I backed into the ditch. The twin, teen boys next door came running over to help Jake push the car out of the ditch. I hurried down the street without a wave or a thank you.

Lord, I just wish I could have You and Jake both, I admitted.

When I arrived at work it was obvious that I'd been crying. Pearl was kind, offering to do any extra thing that would help. Since I was just two blocks off the main street, she offered to pick me up each night, to which I agreed.

We were coming home one morning and Pearl said, "Melissa, you are so pale."

"I'm exhausted, but the pills that my doctor gave me don't help me sleep. I'm not sick, Pearl, trust me."

I went in and sat down by the phone to call Vonda and Betty, but I was so tired. It was just too much effort to make the calls. I started shaking.

The phone rang and it was Vonda. "What's wrong, Melissa?"

"I'm exhausted, and I've started shaking a little."

"I'll be right there." She put me to bed and called my doctor. His office scheduled me as his first patient in the afternoon. His diagnosis was total exhaustion. I wasn't to work for a week. He was afraid I was letting the patients' problems get to me. He thought that's why I couldn't sleep.

I did improve, but sleeping was still a problem after I returned to work. It was close to youth convention time and I was busy with the kids. Uncle Jesse and Aunt Roxena came to the city for the winter, leaving a caretaker with their house in the country. When Aunt Roxena got on the scene, she pampered and cared for me in style. She read to me from the Psalms every morning and prayed with me, and made special foods for me.

One afternoon, I came downstairs early. Aunt Roxena was cleaning carrots at the sink. She looked so pretty in a soft blue dress. "Well, I'll declare, Melissa. What are you doing up so early?"

"I couldn't sleep, thinking of the tapioca pudding you are going to make for me."

She started laughing, and before I knew it, I was laughing too. She got a big yellow mixing bowl out of the refrigerator. It was full of pudding. I ate two helpings. She sat with me while I ate and told me a joke she'd heard. We laughed more. It was about 3:00 p.m. when I went back up to bed. I reset my clock to 9:00 p.m. and slept—the most I'd slept in months.

When I told Aunt Roxena about my good sleep, she said, "Melissa, it looks like I have to come to town to look after you. I'm glad you aren't seeing your friend Jake anymore. Mr. Right will come along."

After waiting twenty-six years, Mr. Right came along and he wasn't right. I just need to accept that.

"Just make me tapioca pudding, and I won't need Mr. Right," I said as I polished off another helping.

I had arranged to have Wednesday through Saturday off to take the kids to the youth convention. The keynote speaker was the president from a Christian college in Portland, Oregon. In the last service on Saturday morning, he invited the young people with struggles to come to the altar and give those struggles to the Lord. I was among several at the altar that morning. It was wonderful to have the freedom of an open altar. It was the first time I admitted that I was in love with Jake. I didn't know how to pray about it; I just knew I was doing the right thing by not seeing him.

My heart was also heavy because of my relationship with Stan. It was like missing an arm not to have contact with him. *Lord, I don't know what to do about Stan and Anita. I need to ask him to forgive me for my answer to his letter. I have a car full of kids, but I'd love to see him on the way home.*

After the service, I said, "We're four hours from home, kids, let's go eat." However, all six of the kids were broke, and I was short of cash because I'd helped some of them out the day before. *These kids will never last four hours in the car with nothing to eat. I'll call Stan. Wow! Such a wonderful feeling.*

I went to the church office and made the call. I heard Stan say, "Hello?"

"Will you accept a collect call from Melissa?" The operator asked.

"I sure will."

Oh wow! I believe his voice has a ring to it. "Stan?"

"Yes! Where are you?"

"I'm at the youth convention. We are leaving for home. Stan, the kids are all hungry and broke, and I don't think I can buy gas and feed them, too."

"You bring them by here. Anita and I will feed you."

"Just sandwiches, Stan."

"Good! You'll be here in about two hours, so we'll have time to go to the store."

"Thanks, Stan."

"Melissa, you're my sister."

What could I say to that! I never doubted that Stan and Anita would be there for us.

Stan and Anita had a huge, round tray loaded with sandwiches, chips and dip. There was soda of all kinds. When we saw all the food, one of the youth blurted out, "I'm starved."

Stan laughed, and putting his hand on his shoulder, said, "Well, we'll pray and dig in."

After lunch, the kids piled in the car and Stan put his big arms around me and held me just long enough for me to remember the time he came home on furlough from the Navy in 1943. It was early spring. I wasn't eight yet. Everyone was around him, hugging him. I couldn't get to him, so I crawled through the crowd and put my arms around his Navy blue, bell-bottom trouser legs. He reached down and picked me up. I felt so loved and special with him.

I looked up at him there in his yard, nineteen years later, and I felt just as safe and accepted. "I'm sorry I got mad at you, Stan."

"Don't you worry," he said, as he and Anita walked around to the driver's side with me.

"I'm not seeing Dr. Bell anymore," I said in a low tone.

Anita said, "Good." Stan gave me another hug.

⁓

The Christmas season brought a full house to the clinic. We were busy almost constantly. Dr. Wolfe, his secretary and the two younger physicians on staff were very concerned about my lack of sleep. I feared that one night I'd go to work and find Jake there. I had confided in Pearl that it was Dr. Bell that I'd been so disturbed about. There were no rules about the nurses being friends with the patients, but I felt it was better kept quiet. It was the beginning of secrets that would dominate my life for years.

1962
In Six Months, I'll Have You

January 1962 was another busy month both at work and with the youth group. We were to have our annual, week-long citywide youth meeting. One of the ministers called and asked me if I could speak on alcoholism. Next to taking care of patients, my favorite thing was speaking to youth. I loved the challenge of getting their attention.

The next morning, after my daily phone report to Dr. Wolfe, I told him I'd been asked to speak. "Doctor, would you have time within the next week to give me some information on alcoholism for my speech?"

"Sure, Melissa. I'll have my secretary get it together for you today. It will be in the chart room tonight."

I thanked him but thought, *Oh dear, it will be a lot of reading. I'll never be able to sort it out.* When I got home, I called Betty and made arrangements to meet the next day for pancakes and help with the information.

"I never dreamed there'd be so much stuff on this subject," I said as I laid it on her table the next morning. "Betty, are you sure you want to wade into all this?"

"It will be no trouble. Everyone needs to know about this."

I left it with her and after breakfast hurried home to Jitter and sleep. *I'll go back on my night off and Betty will go over everything I need to know for my speech. Betty never mentions Jake,* I thought as I closed my eyes. I had told her our decision and she let the subject drop. She didn't always agree with me, and was quick to say so, but she was always there for me, and I never hesitated to go to her.

On one of my nights off, I went to Betty and Leo's for dinner. Betty had gone through all the flyers and written out all the statistics. "In a room of sixty people, four will be alcoholics." She had short sentences and skipped a line after each one, so I could get the full meaning before I went on.

"Betty, you've worked so hard," I said.

"Melissa, I'm so proud that you're going to make this speech!" She was so enthusiastic that I could hardly wait to get started on it.

I worked hard on the speech during both of my nights off, and I felt I understood the subject well enough to speak without notes, weaving in my experiences at the clinic, some sad, some funny, but using no real names.

My last morning at work before the speech, Dr. Wolfe had all kinds of suggestions when I called him for report. "Melissa, I'm so glad you're going to do this. Be sure those young people know that the only sure way they will not be alcoholics is to never take the first drink, and let them know it is a disease." I gave him my main points and told him some of what I was going to say. He was as enthused as I.

The big night finally arrived. The pastor who had asked me if I would speak was waiting for Dean, Vonda and me in the narthex. He and Dean shook hands and exchanged a few words. Then we joined his wife on the front row just before the youth president went to the podium. Parents throughout the city had been encouraged to come hear the speech on alcoholism. The youth had a great service lined up. The music from the different youth groups was always excellent. A couple of kids from my group sang just before the pastor introduced me.

I thanked them for having me and asked, "Did you know that, according to statistics, one out of every fifteen of you in this audience is or will be an alcoholic?" *The eyeballs are looking my direction. They may think I'm crazy, but I have their attention.* "Most likely, whether you know it or not, someone close to you has a drinking problem."

I talked about alcoholism as a disease and told about Woody Tom in comparison with the polished people who were our patients. I explained that research showed that the disease could be inherited. I explained how a grandparent might have had a problem with alcohol and how it could affect children and grandchildren afterward. I told the young people that Dr. Wolfe had said to tell them the only way to be sure they'd not become alcoholics was to never take a drink and that if they started even drinking socially this could be the start of a tragic illness that would affect the whole family. I told about some of the patients and their heartbreaks—people from such different backgrounds and the unbelievable number of women patients.

The young people listened and responded when I asked for questions.

"Do any of the drunks say real bad words?" a teenage girl asked. "And if they do, how do you handle it?"

"Yes. While they are drinking, some say very bad words. How do I handle it?" I repeated. "I go on taking care of them as professionally as I know how and never comment about their language. However, most of the patients would never say a bad word in front of a lady after they become sober. I'd like to add that most of them have wonderful dispositions. Sometimes I wish the church people were as nice." The ministers laughed.

I fielded several more questions and then a boy of about fifteen said, "Do any of them ever ask you for a date?"

"Yes," I said, "and two of the patients asked me to marry them. One was eighty-one and one was ninety-three." The kids were laughing as I left the podium.

Although the kids had listened attentively to the entire program, they were visiting with one another after the service as if they'd been to a pep rally or ballgame. Several of the parents and ministers thanked me, but I got the impression that none of them thought it would ever happen to them or their families.

One night in mid-March, Pearl and I were walking up the steps to the second floor and several patients were standing or sitting in front of the door. One of the men was reading a newspaper. A man who owned a printing business close to Jake's office said, "Boy, that judge didn't leave the doctor much to live on. Ninety-four thousand dollars plus child support is quite a chunk."

Pearl and I looked at one another. We both suspected that it was Dr. Bell.

"Hey, Miss Jenkins," one of the patients said, "You wouldn't sue a man for $94,000 if you were to divorce him, would you?"

"It would depend on what kind of money he had and how mean he was," I said as I rang the doorbell to the locked area.

"Who has that kind of problem?" Pearl asked him just as the door opened.

The patient answered, "That radiologist that was here the last time I was."

Later, Pearl got the paper and read the article out loud to me.

"Oh, wow, Pearl, I just hope he doesn't show up here tonight. This thing's been going on nearly a year."

Jake wasn't the only one with problems. Dr. Wolfe asked me every day if I was getting any sleep, and my answer was the same: "Doctor, I only sleep two or three hours." What I didn't tell him was that when I went home, I stayed up worrying about if I had charted everything, spelled any words backwards and turned everything off I was supposed to. My list of worries was long. I realized more and more that I needed to be a registered nurse to do my job. On top of worrying about my job, I was always wondering what I would do if Jake showed up. I knew Dr. Wolfe wouldn't think it wise for me to be friends with any of the patients outside of work, and I feared Jake would say something to him while he was drunk.

Dr. Wolfe was so concerned that after one particularly difficult shift, he had me come back to the clinic and take an empty room. He gave me medication that he said should put me to sleep for several hours. Instead, I was wide awake all day. I'd think, *I should pray, but if I do, I'd need to ask the Lord what His will is, and I don't want to know.*

—

The youth group conducted the Easter sunrise service, reenacting the visits to the tomb. Our next project was Youth Sunday. The kids were to take charge of the entire service. I spent a lot of time working and praying with the kids. On Saturday morning before Youth Sunday, we met and one girl, Kathy, made notes that we thought we would need. Just before leaving for work on Saturday night, I put them in my uniform pocket. The notes were short and by reading them out loud several times during my shift, I knew by memory what we were to do.

I was so thankful for the notes as I placed them back in my uniform pocket right before I left work. *I'm not going to worry anymore about the program. Lord, it's up to you. Just help me to trust you with the program and the kids.*

I hurried in the door at home, let Jitter out and poured a bowl of cereal. The phone rang. *I hope that's not one of the kids calling to say they can't be there.* I left my cereal and walked over to the phone.

"Good morning."

Silence, then, "Good morning to you, Sunshine."

Now it was my time to be silent.

"Mel, this is Jake."

Sitting down by the phone, I thought, *Why is he calling me? I didn't think I'd hear from him again. I feel so confused. What if he wants to come over or asks me out? I want to see him, but I can't go through losing him again. And why does he have to be calling me now?*

"Mel, I need to talk to you."

"Okay," I said. "I have a few minutes before getting ready for church. The youth group has the service this morning."

"I need to talk to you because I'm so bitter. You always have answers from the scripture you know from memory. I really don't want all these bitter feelings."

Before I knew it, I was caught up in conversation. "Jake, the only thing I know to tell you is you've got to start with step number one. All have sinned. You've got to deal with just your sin. And as David did, ask the Lord to create a clean heart and renew a right spirit within you." I kept rattling off scripture, and then I looked at my watch and said, "Oh dear, the service starts in one hour. Jake, I must run. I'll pray for you. Take care."

"Good-bye, Mel."

"Bye."

Oh dear, what am I to do now? I'll be late for service. I ran upstairs and grabbed a dress, changed and hurried to the car.

I arrived at the church three minutes before the service was to start. The kids were waiting for me, and when I saw Kathy, I realized the notes she had so carefully written were still in my uniform pocket.

"Kids, the notes are in the pocket of my uniform. We have to go completely by memory. It's up to the Lord. Let's pray."

When we were finished praying Kathy said, "He'll take care of us, Melissa."

The youth group had chosen the theme "Peace." I watched as Mark, our youth president, led the congregation in singing. He was normally shy but he looked like he was enjoying the experience. The congregation never took their eyes off the kids. I could tell they were drinking in every word the kids had to say. The youth didn't make any mistakes. The scripture, the prayer and the offering were all done in quiet order. The youth trio had never done so well.

Why did I doubt you, Lord?

Then, it was my turn. According to my timing at home, my speech would be twenty minutes. *I feel so unsettled, Lord, but you've been with us so far. Then I heard myself start to speak. Do I believe all the scripture I'm quoting by memory*? When I finished I sat down and the pastor came to the front where I stood. I didn't hear what he said.

I had just pointed out to the congregation that Stephen had peace when he was stoned and that Paul had peace before King Agrippa. *But, I thought uncomfortably, after Dr. Jake Bell's call, I became a basket case. How could the Lord work something good out of this? I spoke of peace but I feel very unsettled.*

The clinic was filled throughout the spring. I kept dreading the night that Jake might be a patient. Betty's advice was, "Get away from that place."

I had told Vonda I needed to talk to her and Dean. She invited me for lunch on one of my days off. While we were fixing chicken salad sandwiches, I told her how disturbed I had been after Jake had called.

"Vonda, when the phone rings I'm afraid it will be Jake. I know Dean thinks it's a mistake, and I don't take that lightly. My parents wouldn't agree with my seeing Jake if they knew he has a drinking problem. My going with him is against all my teaching about being 'unequally yoked together with unbelievers.' That's why I dread to answer the phone. Then when I do, and it's not him, I'm disappointed."

"Melissa," she said as she was chopping an egg, "if you don't get that doctor off your brain and open your heart to some good Christian man, I'll have an old maid on my hands."

During lunch, I announced, "Dean, I'm considering moving to Columbia to a new job. I need to get away from the clinic and try to forget about Dr. Bell."

Dean took a bite of his sandwich and looked at me. We all three were silent a while, and then he said, "You don't have to run away. You can be strong right here where you are."

"Yes," Vonda spoke up, "but if she was in the middle of the highway and a big truck came along, she'd need to get out of the way. I think you need to go to Columbia."

"My vacation starts Saturday morning. I'm going home for a week, and then I'm to take the day shift while the supervisor goes on vacation. Maybe when I come back, I'll give my two weeks notice. I need to get off nights and I need to get away from Wolfe's. I've got so much responsibility and don't have the education for it. Plus, if that truck Vonda mentioned comes back on the road, I'll be completely smashed." We all laughed.

"I'd still like to see you go to school." Dean said encouragingly.

The week passed slowly and it was finally time for vacation. I packed my bag, loaded my car and made arrangements for Jitter. I started for work feeling ready to face the world. When I topped the hill, I saw Jake's white Rambler sitting beside the clinic.

Oh no! Now what do I do? As I got out of the car, I saw Pearl step out the back entrance to wait for me.

"Is he in bad shape?" I asked, as I put my keys in my purse.

"No. He drove himself here, but his partners say he can't come back to work until he goes for long-term treatment. That's all I know. I got here ten minutes ago and I didn't ask a lot of questions. He's not in the locked area."

Soon report was over and Pearl and I were left with a full house. Dr. Bell was on the third floor.

"My! I hate going up there," I said to Pearl.

"I'll go, Melissa."

"No, I'm to check on each of the patients when I come in, so I'll do that. After that, the third floor is yours. Oh, if he could have waited just one more day!"

All was quiet on the third floor. Jake was asleep. In report, we'd learned he'd been on a binge but he was sober when he came in. He was here to stay until Dr. Wolfe could get him into long-term treatment at Silver Hill in New Canaan, Connecticut, but there was a long waiting list.

When Pearl came down from the 2:00 a.m. rounds, she said, "Melissa, Dr. Bell asked if you were here. He wants to see you."

"I'm busy."

She set down her tray and put her hand on my shoulder and said, "That's what I told him, but if I'm any judge, he won't give up that easily."

I got up to go for a cup of coffee and stepped on Pearl's toe. "Oh, Pearl! I'm so sorry."

"That's okay. This room is much too small."

"I know. Down home we'd say, 'You couldn't cuss a cat in here without getting hair in your mouth.'" We were both so tired we started laughing and couldn't stop. I was afraid the patients would see or hear us. "Pearl, these patients will think we've been on the bottle."

After she made the last check on the third floor, she said, "Dr. Bell asked that you come up to see him, Melissa. I told him you were going on vacation and were in a hurry to get away. He'll be down here if you don't go."

It was 6:30 a.m. I was caught up on my charts and was ready for report. "I'll go up and check everyone and since he's new, I'll ask him if he wants to order the paper." I got the pad and put it in my uniform pocket with my pen and headed for the third floor. I visited with the patients as I went down the hall. Jake was at the far end of the third floor in number twenty-four. He had heard my voice and was standing at his door. "Hello, Dr. Bell," I said. "Did you have a good night?"

"Yes, ma'am." He lowered his voice, "Mel, I need to talk to you."

In an equally low voice, I said, "I'm on duty." Then I raised my voice to a professional tone and asked, "Doctor, would you like for me to order a paper for you?"

"Yes, please."

"Miss Jenkins," one of our regular patients, Mr. Wrinkle, said from the room across the hall, "would you come see me before you go back downstairs?"

"Yes, sir, I'll be right there." I wrote "paper for number twenty-four" on the pad and put it in my pocket to take to report. I turned to go.

"Melissa."

"I'll be right back."

I went into Mr. Wrinkle's room and he said, in a low tone, "Miss Jenkins, I just have to say something to you. That doctor came in here before noon yesterday. He has asked every nurse that comes to this floor about you. He asked for you all night long every time your assistant came up here. This is none of my business, but my Alice was a nurse here when I found her and she's had a life of hell. Every one of us patients would be heartbroken if you married one of these drunks."

I call them "sick;" Mr. Wrinkle calls them "drunk." I wonder which one of us is right.

"Don't you worry about that, Mr. Wrinkle. Oh, say, you'll be gone when I get back."

"Where're you going?"

"Home for a week. One of my brothers and his wife are going to be there."

"You have a good time and remember what I told you."

Jake was standing just inside of his room. *He heard Mr. Wrinkle's comment, I'm sure. I can't talk to him.* "Good luck, Doctor. I'm going home and won't be on duty for over a week. You'll be gone by then."

He was silent and I kept walking down the hall picking up speed as I walked. I could hardly wait to get out of there and on my way.

⁓

When I arrived home, everyone was sitting under the beautiful, big oak tree. I joined the conversation with my brother Doug and his wife, Marilyn.

Out of the blue, Doug commented, "Melissa, I thought you'd be married by now."

I wanted to cry. I got up to take my dishes inside and said, "I can't find anyone that will have me."

Later, Doug and I walked down to the spring and sat on a big rock and talked. He asked me all about "that doctor." None of my family knew he was also a patient. He asked me if I was still seeing him. I told him I wasn't, unless I ran into him unexpectedly. I shared with Doug that I'd been considering moving to Columbia.

"I'd be just as near to the folks as I am now, maybe a little closer. I'd hate to move away from my youth group, though."

"You don't need to be in a strange town by yourself. You're hurting right now, but you'll get over that doctor."

"Who told you I'm hurting?"

"No one needs to tell me, it just shows."

You sound like Daddy."

"Dad thinks you're completely gone on that man. He said, 'She's trying to forget but one of these days she'll drive up out there with that doctor. Now, you just mark my word.'"

"What does Mama say?"

"She's afraid you're going to get hurt and she's thinking about the possibility of your being a stepmother to five children. Can't you find some young guy who's never been married?"

"None of them is the gentleman that Jake is—or has his charm. He's why I need to take that other job," I admitted.

After church and dinner on Sunday, I headed back to the city. That night, I went to bed thinking how good it was going to be to go to work the next morning, knowing that Jake was as far away as Connecticut. Maybe he'd be away until I was settled in my new job in Columbia.

I really need to leave that job and get away from here. Lord. Help me to do a good job in this new role, I prayed, since this was my first time in charge of the day shift. *I must get there early to make rounds with Dr. Black without being pushed.*

At 6:00 a.m., I bounded out the back door and down the walk to my two-tone green Buick, excited and afraid of this new challenge. I turned the key, but there was no power. I tried again. The battery was dead. Dr. Black would be at the clinic shortly after 7:00. I ran in, called the clinic and a cab then waited for what seemed an eternity.

I arrived at the back door and hurried up the steps at 7:15. Dr. Black was at the desk in the chart room looking calm and collected. "You're late," he said with a teasing grin on his face.

"Don't remind me."

"What's the matter? Is that fancy Buick a piece of junk?"

"Maybe so. I must need a new battery."

He got up from the desk. I reached for all the things he'd need and we headed up the steps to check the third floor. I explained that I'd been gone a week; I wasn't here for the nurses' report and I had no idea what we were doing.

Dr. Black didn't seem concerned. "We'll go back at the end of the hall. Frank Lowe came in last night, so we'll need to check him first. All the others have been seen before, so we don't need to spend much time with them," he said. We walked in Mr. Lowe's room. I got the stethoscope and blood pressure cuff out of the case and waited while Dr. Black made small talk.

Then I heard his voice. *Oh no! Lord I can't do this. Jake is still here!*

"Let's take a look inside your mouth, Frank." I reached inside the case and handed Dr. Black a tongue depressor. I knew he saw my hand shaking. He looked up at me. I forced a smile and he continued. He visited with the patient a few minutes and started for the door. Next stop was the sitting room.

I stayed in the doorway. Jake's back was to me. Dr. Black spoke to everyone in general then walked over in front of Jake and said, "How are you, Jake?"

Jake stood and they shook hands. *Oh, don't turn around.*

A big, burly guy over in the corner spoke up and said, "Dr. Black, that little nurse you've got with you there is the best hand to sling that needle since Florence Nightingale."

Jake turned around and saw me.

"That's good. I'm leaving all that with her today," Dr. Black said.

As we went down the steps, Dr. Black looked at me and said, "Melissa, are you okay?"

"Yes. I feel a little rushed and unprepared for this shift, but I'll be fine once I get started."

How I missed Pearl! I could have let her cover the third floor, but I wasn't sure about the assistant on the day shift. I went upstairs twice to see about Frank.

On my way up, I met Jake in the hall. "How are you, Dr. Bell?"

"I'm fine, Mel. How are you?"

"Let's use 'Miss Jenkins' and 'Doctor,' if you will. I'm on duty," I said with a loud whisper.

"Yes, ma'am." Then in a low voice, "I need to talk to you."

"I'm on duty."

"I hear you're having car trouble. May I take you home?"

"No, sir, and no more conversations, please." I hurried on down the hall to see the patient.

Pearl had been on the night shift when I'd called that morning about my car. She called me back just before I went off duty. Her husband, who was retired, had gone to look at my car while I was working. It had needed a new battery, so he bought one and put it in. My car would be ready to drive when I got home.

"Thanks, Pearl. Dr. Wolfe wants me to drop by and visit with Mrs. Wolfe while her nurse is on an errand." Mrs. Wolfe had been ill for a while and needed round-the-clock care. I often went by to relieve her nurse when I was needed. "I'll tell him I can go since I'll have my car."

Mrs. Wolfe and I had a fun visit, but on my way home, I began to think about Jake again. I had wanted to ask Dr. Wolfe when he thought Jake would be going to Silver Hill, but decided against it. I'd learned at work that day that he would be with us until there was a place for him. He wasn't going back to work until after he came back from treatment. The day assistant said he'd been taking his kids swimming and different things during the days.

I hope he becomes a professional swimmer while I'm working days, I thought as I turned into my drive. Jake was in front of his white Rambler, blowing smoke in the air and holding his cigarette like a dignitary, but all I could think of was how one day he would probably end up with lung cancer. I got out of the car and walked toward the house. "What are you doing here?" I snapped, wishing I didn't have to deal with this.

"I came to see you."

"What if I hadn't come home for three or four hours?"

He met me as I came around the front of the car. "I was going to wait."

"You sound sure of yourself."

"Some things I'm not sure of."

"Like what?" I leaned backward on the front of the car.

"Like, why you are avoiding me?"

"We both agreed not to see one another or call."

"I know we did. That's been several months ago. Mel, I've missed you. I'm really going to try to be worthy of your company."

"Jake, I'm trying to sort things out. One thing I'm sure of," I raised my voice considerably, "I will quit my job before I become unprofessional at that clinic. It's got to be all business or I'll quit my job tomorrow and take a job in Columbia."

"You'll have no more problems with me. Tell me about the other job."

"I'm not sure what I'm going to do yet." I looked away.

"May I come up and sit in the swing?" His voice was softer than before, persuasive.

"I don't know what to say." We stood there silently, just looking at one another.

He turned on his charm and cocked his head to one side and said, "I'll tell you what, Miss Jenkins. I suggest you don't say anything and let's just walk up there and sit down."

I felt so helpless with him looking at me. I didn't know what to say, so I just started walking toward the swing with that most irresistible guy.

"I'm sorry if I made you feel uncomfortable at the clinic," he said, reaching for my hand and taking it in both of his. "I do understand your position there and I'll respect that." My heart was pounding faster than I'd ever known it to beat as I looked into his deep brown eyes. "With us not talking at the clinic, we'd better make our dates when I see you. I want to see you a lot, Melissa, and I'm willing to go to Dr. Wolfe and tell him, if that will ease your mind."

"No, don't do that. I'm not sure if I'm going to be there very long. I went to an interview for a job in Columbia," I said looking down.

He squeezed my hand. "I sure don't want you to do that."

I looked up at him. He was looking at me as though he was trying to read my mind. Even though I had reservations about seeing more of Jake and knew about his problems, he seemed larger than life to me.

"I want my kids to meet you. Let me know when you have a free day," he said, releasing my hand and putting his arm around me as he moved closer.

"You should have waited until I went to Columbia before coming back to the clinic," I said softly. I felt so helpless. *Lord, I love this man so much and he wants me to meet his kids!*

We both laughed a little and he said, "I should have been seeing you instead of misbehaving." Being with him was so natural, yet unsettling, so thrilling, yet worrisome. That was how it was to be involved with an alcoholic.

Jake and I started seeing one another again regularly, but I didn't want it known at the clinic. I wanted no one to disagree about my seeing Jake. Everyone who knew disapproved, but he was more overpowering than their concern and warnings.

Jake went to church with me most Sunday nights. Vonda and Dean, good friends that they were, didn't try to keep their disappointment secret. Stan and Anita backed off. I wrote to the folks and told them that I was seeing Jake again. I was sure they wished he were younger and didn't have a family, but they surely knew that no one had ever meant as much to me as Jake. What they didn't know was the whole truth—about the alcoholism—and hiding that from them weighed heavily on my conscience.

I decided not to go to Columbia.

Jake and I were busy each evening. Even after my temporary stay on the day shift was over and I started working nights again, he came each day. When I was at work, he stayed out of sight by my request. Pearl made most of the trips to the third floor. The only time I went up was at the beginning and end of each shift. There was no need for me to check on Jake because he was just boarding there, so to speak, until Silver Hill had a place for him.

In June, on my full weekend off, Jake asked if I'd like to go on a picnic to his farm on Saturday afternoon. I couldn't wait. I fried chicken in bacon grease, like Mama always did, and made potato salad the old fashioned way.

The farmhouse was white with a front porch. It had been rented out to a small family, Jake said, but we drove around the circle drive anyway. It looked like a place I could call home so easily. The trees were tall and beautiful. Two antique urns were in front. I commented on them.

"They were in the family for years. My great aunt lived across the street from James Whitcomb Riley's house. Those were her urns."

"You mean the poet that wrote 'The Ole' Swimming Hole'?"

"He's the one."

"I remember that from Hickory Grove School when I was a kid."

Down in the south pasture was an old pond that was partly filled in. Just west of it on a hill was the old home place where Jake's father and aunts had been born. All the buildings were gone, but the trees were magnificent. Just above the pond was a beautiful cottonwood tree. We parked on the lane and got the things out of the trunk. We climbed the fence and walked over to the tree. Jake spread out an old quilt and took off his hat. I got out one of Aunt Roxena's luncheon cloths, spread it out, placed the food on it while Jake opened the Cokes and we loaded our plates.

"I'd like to thank the Lord for the food," I said.

"Yes, ma'am." He bowed his head.

I thanked the Lord for the beautiful spring day, the food and His love for us. When I said "Amen," Jake did also.

After taking a bite of chicken, Jake said, "I have never tasted chicken as good as this before."

I wasn't about to tell that doctor that I fried it in bacon grease. "I just fried it like my mother always fries hers."

"Does she mash her potatoes for potato salad?"

"Sure. Is there another way?" I teased.

"Yes. Most people boil the potatoes and then cut them up."

"Well, I mash mine." I didn't tell him that I did know how to make the other kind. He was always curious about how I did things and I got the feeling he'd believe anything I told him.

We ate and talked, then put the food away. "When do you think you'll leave for Silver Hill?"

"It should be soon." He put his arms around me and drew me near to him. With a heart beating faster than any pulse I'd ever taken, I put my arms around him and laid my head on his chest. He smelled so clean and good and it felt so right to be there with his arms around me. *I've heard of being hopelessly in love*, I thought, just as he lifted my chin and tenderly kissed me for the first time. We sat there arm in arm, my head on his chest, his cheek against mine. *Oh Lord, what am I going to do? I've never been in love before and I love this man so very much. How can I have him and still have a close relationship with You?*

"Mel."

"Yes?"

"I've wanted to kiss you for a long time."

"I know, me too, but I want us to go slow." We sat there in silence and I thought, *We can't stay like this forever if we're going to go slow.* "Jake?"

"Yes?"

I didn't dare look up. "Could we walk over yonder and see the little spring?"

"Sure. I'll take you 'over yonder' to see the spring."

"You're making fun of the way I talk."

"No, I'm not. I love to hear you talk. There's something so wholesome about your country expressions."

My mother's words came to mind again as we walked hand in hand toward the spring: "Remember, Melissa, an older man always knows what to say to a younger woman."

~

I had Labor Day weekend off from work. It had been one year since Jake had come to church for the first time but now he was at Silver Hill. Vonda invited me over after church for hors d'oeuvres, and as she was an elegant hostess and great cook, I couldn't refuse. She served home-made pastries filled with seafood along with two other trays of goodies.

"I was starved, Vonda, and these are so good. I've also been starved to have time with you and Dean. I just wish I could sleep so I could do a few things besides work."

"Why can't you sleep, Melissa?" Dean asked.

"I just can't."

"Vonda tells me that you're exhausted again like you were almost a year ago. The Lord has rest for you, Melissa."

"I wish He'd give it to me." We were all silent as I picked up another pastry.

"Why do you think you aren't resting?"

"I don't know how to explain it."

"Try."

"It's almost like I feel guilty and yet, I really don't feel like I'm doing anything sinful. I've told Jake I want to take this slow. He understands that. He's a perfect gentleman, Dean. I've never been out with anyone more respectful."

"Vonda and I believe that. I suggest that you ask yourself, 'Am I totally in the will of God by dating a man who doesn't share my faith?' I think this is what is tearing you apart. You worry about your influence on the youth group. You worry about going against Dr. Wolfe's judgment by dating an alcoholic patient. I'd guess you feel guilty for not sharing the whole truth with your parents. Yes, the Lord can give you rest, or meet any other need that you have, but sometimes there's a price to pay."

That night, I lay in bed thinking of all we had talked about. I remembered being in an Old Testament history class and hearing that God gave the Israelites the desires of their hearts, but sent leanness to their souls. Then I remembered Dean saying, "Sometimes there's a price we have to pay." *Is my price giving up Jake? I just can't handle that.*

I was off on Labor Day. I was sleeping soundly then heard some noise. It kept coming and finally I realized it was the telephone. I sleepily answered it.

"Mel, did I wake you?"

"Yes, you did, but I'm glad." It was the first time Jake had called from Silver Hill. He didn't think it would be long before he'd be home. We talked for about thirty minutes. He was golfing a lot, which he loved to do. He worried that I wasn't sleeping and wished that I'd get off the night shift. When we hung up, I was wide awake and didn't go back to sleep until nearly daylight. I kept thinking about what Dean had said the night before.

At work the next night, I thought, *I know I'm trusted with the keys to the patients' records to use when the doctors ask for that information. I really do want to know how he's doing. Maybe I'd sleep better tomorrow if I read that he's doing well.*

As soon as I had caught up with my charts and checked the patients, I left the second floor and went down to check Jake's record. As I turned the key in the door, a scripture I'd heard many times came to mind. "To him that knoweth to do good and doeth it not, to him it is a sin." I knew all too well the right thing was to follow the rules and not check records when I hadn't been told to. *I know I'm wrong for doing this, but how will I ever know if he is really doing well unless I check the record? I just have to know he's okay. I can't wait until he gets back and I can't just ask Dr. Wolfe because he'd ask why I wanted to know.*

I opened Jake's file, and sure enough, I found a recent letter from his psychiatrist. I placed a card over the page and read one line at a time. As I moved the card down the page, studying each sentence so I wouldn't miss anything, I read, "The patient is beginning to respond to treatment." *Oh, it's so important for me to know that. Maybe I can start sleeping.* The letter continued, "If the patient continues to respond, we'll consider a time for his release." *Oh wow!*

At 3:00 a.m., Dr. Wolfe called to check on things.

"Everything is quiet, Doctor. It's a slow night." I felt so guilty when I hung up because we'd had some stealing at the clinic and his secretary, Georgia, told me Doctor Wolfe had said, "We don't have to worry about it being Miss Jenkins." My guilty conscience was screaming. I could hardly wait to get off duty. I knew that even though I felt guilty for checking Jake's record, I'd do it again.

Later, I phoned Betty about what I'd done: "It's like I can't stand it if I don't know all about him. I wouldn't look at anyone else's record but Jake's."

Betty sighed, "Melissa, alcoholics are always making excuses for their behavior and I see it happening to you now. Don't let yourself get into a life of deceit. No man is worth that. I'm going to find you a better job and get you away from that place. I don't like to see what's happening to you!"

When I hung up, I ate breakfast and sat down in front of the TV, which I seldom did. I sat there awhile but couldn't think about anything or anyone but Jake. Finally, I dragged myself up the steps to bed, and later in the afternoon, I went to sleep.

I was becoming so exhausted that I could hardly drag myself to the regular meetings at the church. To make matters more difficult, September was a busy time for the youth group. The youth convention was coming up in November, the Christmas program in December, then the citywide meeting in January. All my free time was taken with planning those activities. For the first time in my life, I felt like it was a burden. I found myself going into the meetings empty, with nothing to give.

Early one morning in the middle of October, I called Vonda. I asked if Dean would be in his office early or if I could come by the parsonage on my way home. She invited me to breakfast.

Vonda and Lisa, her two-year old, met me at the door. "Come in and sit at the table and visit while I fix breakfast."

Dean poured us coffee. Lisa climbed into my lap.

"Dean, the kids need more than I can give them. They can't learn from an empty shell. The youth convention and Christmas play are coming up, then the citywide meeting. I've been to no extra meetings for leaders for months. I am doing our kids a great disservice. We need to find someone else to lead the youth group."

"If you were working days and resting properly, I'd disagree with you, but I think you're going to get sick if you don't get out from under some of your pressure," Dean reasoned. "We'll find someone until you work through some things."

"Thank you, Dean."

I slept better that day after talking to Dean and having his and Vonda's total acceptance. They didn't approve of my seeing Jake, but they accepted me and they put no pressure on me about the youth group. They had wanted what was best for everyone.

That night, I read in Jake's record, "We've had a breakthrough with this patient. Probably in a month or six weeks, he'll be dismissed." *I wonder what the breakthrough is. It's October 17th, so he may not be here for Thanksgiving. If he is, he'll need to be with family. Oh, I can hardly wait to see him.* As I closed his file, I remembered Betty's words: "Don't get into a life of deceit."

When I got home the next morning, I called Betty. She was glad I'd slept five hours the day before, but didn't think that was very much. "Melissa, you've got to get off that night shift. I'm going to find you another job."

"You find it. I'll take it." I was ready for the change.

"That's a deal."

It was the twenty-first of November. Pearl had two nights off and a medical student worked in her place. After the first night, I was exhausted. An irate man had come to the door of the clinic demanding his wife be dismissed. The medical student handled the situation by talking to the man through the intercom, but Pearl would have known just what to do. Without her there, I had more running to do.

I got home, let Jitter out and sat down in Uncle Jesse's chair. I was too tired to fix breakfast, but I couldn't stand the thought of going to bed because I was expecting a letter from Jake. Sure enough, I was awake at noon to check the mail. I wasn't disappointed. As usual, I pored over one line at a time of Jake's letter.

Jake didn't know when he'd be home. "I hope for Thanksgiving, but I may not be there to see you much before youth convention." I hadn't told him I'd given up my youth group. To talk about it seemed to make it too much a reality, so I tried not to think about it. I was scheduled to work on Thanksgiving night, but I would have the two nights before Thanksgiving off.

By the time I went back to bed, I had the letter memorized. I always read and reread Jake's letters out loud.

It took a while to get to sleep. Then in the late afternoon, the phone awakened me.

"Hello?" Silence.

I jumped up and put my feet on the floor as Jake said, "Hello, Sunshine."

I could hear noise in the background. "Where are you?"

"I'm at the airport in New York changing planes. I was dismissed this morning. I haven't called anyone to meet me. I hoped you could."

Thank the Lord. Pearl is off tonight. She can work for me while I go get him. "I can," I answered joyfully. We just said a few words and he had to go. He'd be on TWA at 9:00 p.m. I looked at the clock. I'd have time to bake an oatmeal cake.

I dialed Pearl. "Oh Pearl, guess what?"

"Dr. Bell's coming home."

"Yes!"

"When?"

"9:00 p.m. on TWA."

"I'll work for you, and I'll call the supervisor."

"Thanks, Pearl. I'll work for you tomorrow night." I hung up without saying good-bye.

At the airport, I waited behind a man who was also waiting for someone. When Jake came in the terminal, I was just about to rush to him, when the man said, "Jake!" and reached for his hand and slapped him on the back.

"How did you know I was going to be in?" Jake asked.

Oh dear, I bet that's his brother. I won't even get to hug him, I thought as I tried to politely hang back.

Then the man explained he was there to meet someone else, but said, "I'll take you home."

"Oh no, that's not necessary." He walked over, took my hand and introduced me to his cousin.

I could hardly wait to get to the car. We put Jake's things in the trunk. I handed him the car keys. "You may drive my car that is paid for as of the first of this month."

He was silent. He opened my door and I got in. He went around and got in and closed his door. "I'm real glad you got your car paid for, but before I drive it, I want that greeting my cousin interfered with."

He took me in his arms and as he kissed me, there was only Jake. After our kiss, we sat with our cheeks pressed together. His whiskers felt good against my face. *Thank you for bringing him home, Lord. I love him so much.*

We came near his office on the way from the airport. A light was on in the window and he said, "The partners must be having their monthly meeting. I'm sure my brother, Zach, is there. Instead of our going out to get my car without him being there, I'd like to call first. Is it okay for us to stop by my place?"

"Sure, that's fine."

"Jake, this is lovely," I said as we walked into a small sitting room. The elegant Oriental rug with deep wine, blue and beige colors almost covered the floor. Pink and blue chairs, small antique tables and lamps tastefully filled the room. He placed his things in his bedroom and came back where I stood looking at an English painting.

"These were my mother's things. That painting and several of these other items were my great aunt's."

We went into the very small kitchen. "My mother has been here," he said as we spotted some bright red, polished apples in a cut glass bowl in the middle of the small kitchen table. He opened the refrigerator.

"She thought of everything," I said as I saw all the food anyone would want. "She must have known you were coming."

"I had told her it would be this week."

Oh, I'm glad he chose me to meet him.

"Zach should be home soon. I'll call and see." He indicated by her name that his sister-in-law Lynne answered. He explained he was home and said he'd come for his car as soon as Zach was home. "Miss Jenkins met me. She'll bring me out."

I wonder if they've ever heard about me before. Maybe someday, he won't be so proper and just say Melissa or even better, Mel.

"He's on his way home," Jake said, as he came and put his arm around me with the other hand on the doorknob.

"Jake, do Zach and Lynne know about me?"

"They do now."

"I hope they aren't disappointed."

"They'll think you're wonderful, the way I do."

That sounds good, but when they find out I work at the clinic, they're going to think I'm a little unstable for dating one of the patients.

Zach and Lynne were a lovely couple. What I noticed most about her was how her brown eyes seemed to sparkle when she showed me her three boys' pictures that were hanging by the door. We didn't stay long, but I saw in the short time we were there the comfortable relationship the two brothers had. They talked and laughed easily. I liked Lynne and Zach right away.

Jake followed me home in his car. He parked his car and met me at mine. We walked into the house with our arms around one another. The oatmeal cake was on the cabinet with a towel over it. I plugged in the coffee and he looked under the towel.

"Well, look here. I haven't had oatmeal cake since I left."

I laid my head on his shoulder as we put our arms around one another. "Jake, I'm so glad you're home."

He was silent.

Oh boy. Something's not right here.

We stood there making small talk. I got the dishes, cut the cake and put some in a container for him to take home. He poured the coffee into Aunt Roxena's china cups and we sat down at the table. *He has something he needs to say and I don't think it's what I want to hear.*

He hoped to see his children the next evening, which was Tuesday. I told him I worked Thanksgiving night but was supposed to have Tuesday and Wednesday off. Now I'd need to work for Pearl on Tuesday night. He suggested we go to dinner on Wednesday evening. I was thrilled.

He was looking down at his cup, holding to the handle. Then he looked at me and said, "Mel, I'm not going to ask you to marry me. It's too early. I have so many problems. It's not fair to you."

We held one another's gaze. "I think that's a good idea." *Now, why did I say that? That's not what I think, but what could I say?* Then a thought came in my head and I almost laughed out loud. *Just you wait, Doctor, in six months I'll have you.*

Wednesday night I was getting ready to go to dinner with Jake and I got a call from his sister-in-law, Lynne, inviting me to Thanksgiving dinner the next day. I had to work Thanksgiving night and declined the invitation. Lynne was very sweet and told me anytime Jake wanted me to come with him to their place, I'd be welcome.

Jake and I ate at a beautiful restaurant by candlelight. He looked so good and was so charming.

"You look very nice, Miss Jenkins."

"Thank you."

He broke his roll in half and buttered a piece then said, "Did Lynne call you?"

"Yes," I said, "but I'm not comfortable going to meet the rest of your family just yet. You need to spend time with them without worrying about getting me back home in time to get some sleep. You indicated last night that you needed time and I understand that. I want to see you as much as you want to see me, but maybe we should continue to go slow."

He was smiling as I talked. We became silent as we sat there looking at one another. He continued to smile then he said, "Yes, ma'am."

How could anyone keep from loving this man?

⁓

I had off of work Thursday and Friday of the following week. Mid-afternoon on Thursday, I had just ironed my seventh starched uniform when the phone rang. I sprang to answer it.

"That was a peppy hello."

"Oh. Hi, Betty, I thought you were Jake."

"Sorry to disappoint you, my dear, but no way could his phone call be as good as this one."

"Wow. It must be something."

"It is. A lady just called wanting your telephone number. She's going to call you. My cousin works for their company and told me they needed a private duty nurse. Their little boy, who's three, has had an operation on his hip. He has Perthes disease."

"I've never heard of it."

"I haven't either, but, man, Melissa, I was terrific. I told her how you had a good paying job with a lot of responsibility."

I laughed and said, "Does she know I'm not properly trained?"

"I told her you hadn't been to school, but you'd taken care of my mother and you were the best nurse I've ever seen."

"That's stretching it, Betty."

"No, it's not, and most important, she wants you really badly. I suggested that she meet with you and offer what she thought you'd be worth. Melissa, I want you out of that place and away from those drunks."

"She may not want me when she finds out I will work only days."

"She knows that. The family takes care of him in the evenings and she sleeps with him at night. Her husband wants someone with him during the day that they can trust, so she can get out and golf and go to luncheons and do things at the other kids' schools... those kinds of things."

Shortly after Betty and I hung up, Ruth Stone called to ask me if I'd be interested in coming over to meet her and her little son. She sounded very nervous.

"I'll be delighted to come. I need to get out. I've just ironed seven uniforms."

She laughed, "That would make you want to do something different."

Good, she's relaxed.

Mrs. Stone was a tall, striking blonde in her early forties, and Dicky was a beautiful little blonde boy with the deepest blue eyes I'd ever seen. He was sitting on the counter in the kitchen eating an Oreo cookie and had chocolate on his face. He stole my heart immediately. When we were ready to go in the other room, he let me wash his face and carry him. He lay with one of my arms around his upper back and my other arm under his knees. While his mother and I asked one another questions pertaining to the job, Dicky snuggled in my arms. He was taking no medication and was in no pain, but he had to stay off his feet and knees so his hip could heal. Sounded to me like a babysitter would be all they needed.

I no sooner than had the thought and Mrs. Stone said, "We don't want someone to sit with him that doesn't understand the seriousness of his staying off his feet and knees." She told me I'd need to lie down with him for his nap and keep my arms around him, so he wouldn't wake up and get on his knees.

"Oh, dear. I'd go to sleep for sure because I'm used to sleeping during the day."

"That's fine. I sleep with him at night and it will give me a break from constantly being there."

When she told me what she and her husband were willing to pay if I would take the job, I was surprised. *That's just a little less than the average RN is making,* I thought.

That same day Aunt Roxena and Uncle Jesse came home.

"Oh, Aunt Roxena," I said as she walked in the door, "you got here too late. I have all my uniforms ironed."

After we hugged, she said, "Well, Honey, you seem awfully happy about it. What's got you so excited?"

"Number one: Jake's home. Number two: He just called and we're going to dinner. Number three: I just got a new job, working days, that pays almost as much money as an RN makes."

She stood looking at me and said, "Well, Honey, I'm real happy about number three."

"Just wait until you meet Jake. You'll like him, I know you will."

"I may like him, but I want my girl to have a husband who loves the Lord like you do. Melissa, I don't like you going out with this man."

However, later that evening, I could tell that she was pleasantly surprised when she met Jake. They talked with ease, as each of them always did. When we left, she told us to have a nice time. I could tell she meant it. Had she not, she wouldn't have said anything. *Lord, I thank you for her. She's like Vonda, disappointed but always accepting.*

In the car, Jake said, "Mel, the renters just moved out of the farm house. I want to take you to see it."

This is great! I can hardly wait. He backed out of the drive and looked over at me. I was trying not to show how happy I was but I could tell he knew I was pleased. "Will the electricity still be on?"

"Yes, I asked my mother to keep everything turned on."

"Are you going to move out there?"

"Not yet."

I wonder what he means by that.

"There's a rustic restaurant out there near the farm called the Ranch Inn. We'll go look at the house and then go eat."

"Sounds wonderful."

We drove up into the circle drive. He got out and came around to open my door. We walked through a closed-in back porch. The minute I stepped onto that porch, I felt at home. I wasn't sure when, but someday before long, this would be home. He put the skeleton key in the kitchen door and we walked in. Jake said, "I can still smell ham and eggs in this kitchen."

I can fry ham and eggs and make biscuits.

The dining room had three south windows with a window seat where Grandma Bell had put her flowers. The living room was across the front with a fireplace and a stairway with a banister going to the second floor. Three bedrooms and a bath were upstairs. Two of the bedrooms were very small.

Oh, I can hardly wait to get out here. If I can talk Jake into moving into this house, he'll see how much better it would be if I were here.

"What do you think?"

"I love it."

"We'd better go eat," he said. We walked out on the back porch. I waited for him to lock the kitchen door.

As he held the screen for me to go out to the yard, I asked "Jake, why don't you move out here?"

"Oh, I don't know. My apartment is close to work. I'm fine there," he said as he locked the outside door. I let it drop.

During dinner at the Ranch Inn, Jake leaned back and said, "Melissa, I'm broke." He went on to tell about his obligations and that it would take a while to catch up. I wanted to tell him what he had or didn't have made no difference to me, but I just listened.

My first night back at work, I left my resignation on Mrs. Gwynn's desk. She had been a wonderful supervisor and I had learned a lot from her. I would miss her and Pearl, but I was glad to be getting off nights and away from the clinic.

Jake started worrying about Christmas. Not only would there be so much temptation to drink, but he was to have all his kids with him and his apartment was too small. One evening when he called, I said, "Jake, could you find enough furniture to use out at the farm just on weekends? If so, you could have your family there for Christmas."

"Yes. I have some extra furniture in storage."

"I'll do the baking for you just as soon as I get off nights."

He decided to move some things to the farm.

Mid-December 1962, I started my new job taking care of Dicky. I couldn't believe how enjoyable it was. Dicky and I played on the floor and we read many books that he knew by heart. I loved working with this sweet little boy. Another thing I couldn't believe was the way I was treated at the Stone's. Their maid served my meals and often asked if I needed anything. I never dreamed of a job like that. It was more like playtime.

The first two days, I tried not to sleep while Dicky was taking his nap, just because I didn't think I should while I was on duty. Finally, on the third day, I just gave it up. I was sleeping soundly with my arm around my patient when I heard Dicky's mother say, "Melissa, are you awake?"

"Yes."

"I'll watch Dicky," she said with a funny smile on her face. "Dr. Bell is on the phone. I told him you were taking a nap, and I asked him if he thought it would be okay if I woke you." She was smiling from ear to ear.

"Oh no! He'll know I'm sleeping while on duty." She was obviously enjoying the whole thing.

I went to the phone and said, "Hello," trying my best to sound awake.

"I understand you're taking a nap. Your employer wanted to know if I thought it would be okay to wake you." Then he laughed like he thought it was the funniest thing he'd ever heard. I tried to explain but I could see he was going to have a lot of fun with this.

"If you get your nap over in time, I'd like to take you to dinner tomorrow evening. We'll eat early at the Ranch Inn and then go out to the farm to hang curtains; everything I had in storage is moved in."

"Aunt Roxena didn't decorate for Christmas before she left. She wouldn't mind my using her decorations for your place. We'll get ready for your party." I was excited.

Jake arrived about 4:00 p.m. the next day. "What's in all these boxes?" He asked when he saw them by the front door.

"Christmas decorations. Can we stop for a small tree?"

"I think we can do that."

Oh, this seems so right. We found a nice tree and stand on the way to the restaurant. When we got to the farm, a Duncan Phyfe dining room suite was nicely arranged in the dining room. Jake had a large desk that almost filled one end of the living room. There was a small table, a TV and a few chairs. We decided to put the tree in front of two windows. We decorated it and put electric candles in the five windows in the living room. On the mantel, I put pinecones, a sleigh and reindeer. When we were done, we looked at it and Jake said, "Melissa, these are very nice decorations. I hope you will come to the party."

"I think not. You need time with your children and the rest of your family. No one needs to wonder where I fit in."

His children, mother and stepfather, Zach and Lynne and their three boys would all come over the Sunday before Christmas. I worked all day on Saturday baking cookies. When Jake came to pick them up on Sunday, I had made hot chocolate and had a little one-burner hot plate for him to heat it on. "Wish you would come," he said.

"Not yet. Ask me after Christmas and I'll go out while your children are there."

He came by on Christmas Eve just before going to Zach and Lynne's for dinner and brought me a beautiful gold billfold. My gift to him had been all the baked goods for his party.

He had lunch with me Christmas Day. I made noodles from scratch. The chicken turned out tender and tasty and the rolls tasted almost as good as Mama's. I took such care in making sure everything was just right. I set up a card table in front of the fireplace with a linen cloth and napkins. I used Aunt Roxena's china and sterling silver. "Mel, this is delicious and everything is elegant."

Good. Now he knows I can serve an elegant and delicious lunch. "I loved cooking for you, Doctor."

One evening after Christmas, Jake came over. He said there were lots of New Year's Eve parties we could go to but suggested we go to a movie instead. New Year's Eve he picked me up just before the movie and we went to eat afterward. He seemed quiet and didn't say anything about when we'd be seeing one another again.

1963
I Feel Like Cinderella

A week went by and I didn't hear from Jake. I knew I would see him again because I had to get Aunt Roxena's Christmas decorations. He finally called on Saturday.

"Hi, Mel."

I was silent. Then I said, "This is a pleasant surprise. I thought you'd left the country."

"No, I'm still around. I've been very busy. The kids and I will pick you up tomorrow and go to the farm. I want them to know you better."

"Jake, this isn't how I'd do things."

"How's that?"

"I haven't heard from you in ten days and you call out of the blue and say you and your children will pick me up so they can know me better."

"Mel, I really want you to go with me tomorrow." I finally agreed. He'd pick me up after church.

The next day, it was very cold with a big snow on the ground. Jake came with all five of his children to pick me up at about 1:00 p.m. I had met them all in the summer except Candice, a very sweet girl, full of life, with brown hair and brown eyes.

The children were polite, but their dad had just bought a new color TV. They spent most of the afternoon in front of it. The three younger children mixed chocolate milk in the pantry. Wendy, the cute six-year-old, spilled milk down the front of her blue and white dress. She went with me upstairs and let me clean her up the best I could, but never took her eyes off me.

Oh well, I'm being looked over by this one, that's for sure.

About 4:00 p.m., we took the children to the Ranch Inn and on our way to take the kids home, the oldest, Karen, said, "Daddy, let's take Melissa home first, so we'll have longer."

I heard Candy say, "Oh, no. That wouldn't be appropriate."

Jake had heard it, too, and we smiled. I said, "Are you going to church with me?"

"I don't think so."

"Then take me on home and you'll have more time with your kids."

He looked over at me and said, "You are a kind and gentle lady."

Is that what I am to him, a kind, gentle lady? Would I ever be something else? Well, we'll see how long before he calls again. Anyway, I "accidentally on purpose" forgot Aunt Roxena's Christmas decorations, so I know I will see him again!

The next week was the citywide youth meeting. The new youth director at our church asked me to help in transporting the kids. Going every night was no problem, since I worked days and got a nap while watching Dicky. I hadn't felt so rested in years.

Jake didn't call for almost a week. Then one morning he called me at work and said, "Melissa, I'm going to buy a kitchen stove for the farm today. Should I get gas or electric?"

"That's up to you, Jake. I don't know what kind of stove you want." *How dare he take his time about calling me, then call to ask what kind of stove to get!*

"I just thought you'd have an opinion. I'll go ahead and get electric."

"Whatever you think you'll be happy with." He asked about Dicky and kept the conversation light. After we hung up, I thought, *I spoke a little too soon because I'm mad at him. I really would prefer a gas stove.* I called him back and said, "Jake, I think you'll like the gas stove better. It may heat the kitchen faster on winter days."

"Thank you for calling me back, Mel. Gas is what I'll get."

It is so maddening dealing with that man, I thought after we hung up.

Aunt Roxena was gone for a few days, so each afternoon I made dinner for Uncle Jesse. He'd call and say, "Hello, Miss Melissa. I'm on my way home." I'd go open his garage door and have dinner on the table like Aunt Roxena always did. I was very well aware, however, that my dinners didn't taste as good as hers.

One night we were eating and Uncle Jesse said, "What's the matter with the doctor? I haven't seen much of him lately."

"I don't see much of him either. He wanted me to go to the farm again with the kids. I went. Then a few days went by. He called and said he was going to get a new stove for the kitchen. He wanted my opinion on whether to get electric or gas. I haven't heard from him since. So, I guess the only man I get to cook for, Uncle Jesse, is you when Aunt Roxena is gone."

He laughed and took a second helping of stew and said, "When he moves out to that farm full time, he'll need a cook. If your daddy isn't able to come, I'll walk you down the aisle."

Forget walking down the aisle. A trip to the church office or courthouse, and soon, is fine with me.

One evening, I decided I needed to at least let Jake know I was around and also give him something to think about. So I called. I was angry as the phone rang, but when I heard the silence and then his healthy greeting, I was ready to forget being mad at him.

I better hurry and tell him or I'll never say it. "Jake, this is Mel. I'd like to meet you out at your farm as soon as possible and get Aunt Roxena's Christmas decorations. I've been waiting around for you, but I need to get on with life. When I get the decorations, you won't hear from me again."

Silence. "Now that's not what I want to hear. I was getting ready to call you, Mel, and tell you that Lynne is going to get in touch with you soon. We're invited to Zach and Lynne's for dinner with several doctors and their wives."

"I'm not sure about this. I don't see or hear from you for two weeks, and then I show up at a party at your brother's with you. That doesn't make sense."

Silence again. "I'll call you at work tomorrow if you're sure your employer won't care if she has to wake you."

I was caught off guard and laughed. *Oh, he knew that would happen!*

I agreed to go and when I hung up I called Betty and told her about the call. "You see, Melissa, it's you he wants his kids to know. It's you he wants to take around his brother, sister-in-law and friends."

The day finally arrived for the dinner party. Aunt Roxena asked what I was going to wear. I showed her the dress. It was a beautiful lined beige dress, a gift from my sister, Shirley.

"Oh, Honey, that is beautiful." She looked at my shoes, and said she had some jewelry that would go with the outfit.

All of that day was spent making sure everything about me was going to look perfect. I didn't have to worry about a thing. Aunt Roxena thought of my hair, my nails and pressing my dress. She was having so much pleasure in helping me get ready that it was a joy to watch.

"Melissa, I missed so much not having a daughter to do these things for. You start getting ready, and when you're ready, call me and I'll come up and check you out."

About thirty minutes before Jake was to come, I called Aunt Roxena to come check me. I was standing in the middle of the room when she came up the steps. I looked at her when she turned the corner. She was carrying a shoebox in her hands. She opened the box and took out the most beautiful black suede shoes I'd ever seen.

"Honey, I'm glad I knew your shoe size. These are for you."

"Oh! Aunt Roxena."

"Now, Melissa, don't you start crying, you'll ruin your makeup."

Jake and I were the first couple to arrive at Zach and Lynne's. They were such a lovely couple and made me feel so much a part of everything. Lynne let me help her and when Jake and Zach came in the kitchen, Zach said, "Oh look, she's got on an apron."

I hope to be wearing one at the farm soon, I thought.

I could see right away that everyone at the party liked Jake and they were very friendly to me.

About 9:00 p.m., the phone rang. Lynne came in and said, "Dr. Jacob Bell, you're wanted on the phone. It's the hospital."

When he hung up, he said there had been a wreck and he came over and asked if I wanted to go with him. He said he'd take me home afterwards or I could stay at the party, if I wanted, until he got back. I had enjoyed myself, but I didn't want to stay without Jake, so we said our good-byes and thanked Lynne for the dinner. I went to the hospital with Jake and waited while he read films and talked to the other doctor about his findings.

When we got to my drive, Jake turned off the car, put his arm around me, drew me near to him and said, "Mel, I was so proud to show you off tonight."

I could feel my heart pounding as I sat there with my head on his shoulder. He lifted my chin and kissed me. I started to melt in his arms.

I love him so, but when will he call again? I need to take this more slowly. I pulled away and said, "I loved going to your brother's with you, Jake. I'm always proud to be with you. Thank you for asking me." We were silent for a few seconds, and then I said, "I need to go inside."

His last words at my door were, "I'll call you soon."

Jake called at work or in the evenings and we went out often, then all of a sudden he didn't call. I let a couple of weeks go by, then decided I'd call and say I needed to pick up Aunt Roxena's Christmas decorations.

When I called, Jake's usual beginning silence was missing, but the "Hello" sounded like his voice.

"Jake?"

"This is Dr. Zach Bell."

"Oh! Hello, Dr. Zach. This is Melissa Jenkins."

"Melissa, Jake's had an accident. I'm here to get some things he'll need at the hospital."

"Is he okay?" I had a feeling of dread in the pit of my stomach.

"Yes, but he's been drinking and he totaled his car. I've put him in the hospital for the night. I wanted to make sure nothing is broken. We should dismiss him tomorrow."

I had no idea this was the first of many times Zach and I would talk to each other about Jake's drinking problems.

Jake called me at work the next morning. "I'd like to come by tonight," he said as if nothing unusual had happened.

That evening after dinner I was home alone. When I opened the door, he was stamping snow off his shoes. "Hi, Jake. Come in."

He took off his hat and looked at me as he walked into the living room. "I've really blown it this time, Mel."

"Here, let me take your coat." He sat down in Uncle Jesse's chair as I put his coat away.

He said, "I haven't been calling you because I started drinking. I totaled my car. My partners are pressing me to quit. Zach always stands by me, but our senior partner says he'll leave if I don't. I can't let him do that just because I'm not behaving."

Uncle Jesse had left his paper neatly folded on the footstool. Jake picked it up. "I'll check a stock that I have. I've got to do something to get me out of this crack."

While he was checking the paper, I poured coffee and thought, *I can see he's sorry, but more because he's in a crack than because of all the trouble his drinking is causing.* I placed his cup and saucer on the table by his chair and took mine to Aunt Roxena's chair. I sat silently as he continued to talk.

"I'll sell this stock. I'll move the things from my apartment to the farm. This morning Zach told me you had called the apartment last night."

"I was calling about Aunt Roxena's Christmas decorations," I said, trying to act nonchalant.

"We'll get her Christmas decorations, but I want you calling my place often."

"I don't have a hang up about calling you, Jake, but it's really not my style."

He was silent as he sat and looked at me. "I know it's been hard on you wondering why I haven't called. Melissa, I want you to meet my mother."

"I'll be glad to do that, Jake, but I want to know ahead of time."

He arranged for me to meet his mother and stepfather, Mr. and Mrs. Fred Snow, on Saturday before going out to dinner.

That Saturday, as we got off the elevator on the second floor of their apartment building, a tall, white-haired southern gentleman came to the door. Behind him stood a perfectly groomed lady with silver hair and dressed in a rose-colored silk dress. She was smiling and responded to me warmly when Jake introduced us. I seemed to be the only one who was nervous, but I liked them both and our first visit together was perfect.

⁓

Dicky's parents made a trip to Florida a week later. I spent extra time in the evenings with Dicky and each night to make sure he didn't get on his feet or knees.

While Dicky's parents were away, the big day came for Dicky to go to the doctor to see if he could start walking some. The doctor had me put him down and then said, "Dicky, walk across the room to that door."

Dicky looked up at me but refused to move. I walked over to the door and held out my arms. He looked at me then to the doctor and all of a sudden he started running toward me! He was limping, but was enjoying every step. I picked him up. He laid his head on my shoulder and I didn't even care that tears came to my eyes. His doctor was equally happy.

When I got him in the car he asked, "Is Dr. Jake coming tonight?"

"Yes, he is."

"May I walk for him?"

"Yes. We'll let that be one of the times you can walk."

He was so excited that he would be able to walk for Dr. Jake.

The time ticked slowly away that evening, but Jake didn't come or call. Finally, I had to put a disappointed little boy to bed. His parents came home a few days later and I had some much needed time off.

⁓

Early one Sunday morning in late March, Pearl called. She was working the day shift. "Melissa, Dr. Bell is here. He asked if I would talk to you. He's in number twelve."

That's in the locked area. He must have been in bad shape when they brought him in. He's never been back there before, because he's always been able to drive himself over. I wonder who brought him. "I'll come to see him on my way to church," I told Pearl. Then I added hastily, "I'll go see Mr. Buttons, too." Mr. Buttons was a permanent resident because of an addiction to prescription drugs after a long illness and intensive surgery. "I'll visit with him a while and come see you while I'm there. I'll see Jake last. Before I leave, could you just write in the report book that I came by to see Mr. Buttons?" The deceit that went with loving an alcoholic was becoming so natural that I didn't hesitate to drag another into it.

Aunt Roxena had heard the conversation, and when I started toward the door, she said, "Melissa. I don't like this. You shouldn't go to that clinic." Her eyes were focused on mine. "You're not going to do this are you, Melissa?"

"Yes."

"Melissa, this is a big mistake. You shouldn't do this, Honey."

Avoiding her eyes, I said, "I love you, Aunt Roxena," grabbed my purse and Bible and walked out the door.

Mr. Buttons was happy to see me. He asked about my job. I asked him about the stock market and his grandchildren and told him I was on my way to church.

After I visited with Mr. Buttons, I rang the bell to the locked area. Pearl opened the door and said, "Hello, come in and visit." I walked toward the chart room and paused at number twelve to my right. Jake was sitting on the side of the bed eating breakfast. His face was red, his hair was a mess and he was in pajamas and a robe.

"I'm glad to see you. I've really done it now," he said. "I'm supposed to see the kids this afternoon. Will you call them for me and tell them I'm out of town?"

"No, Jake, I can't do that," I said as I walked over by his table.

He looked down at his plate. "Okay, I understand. I'm in another crack. My old truck from the farm is down by a bar on West Avenue. Will you call Zach and ask him to go get it?"

"Yes, I'll do that." And then I said, "Goodbye."

I stuck my head in the chart room door and thanked Pearl for calling me.

All the way to church I was so sorry I'd gone to see Jake. I worried about him. I was humiliated to have to call Zach and I felt guilty that I'd asked Pearl to write in the report book that I'd come to see Mr. Buttons. *I wouldn't lie to Jake's kids, but I really have lied and also had Pearl lie. What is happening to me? If only I'd listened to Aunt Roxena.*

Almost a week went by. Georgia, Dr. Wolfe's secretary, called me and told me that Jake had confided in Dr. Wolfe that he was seeing me.

"What did Dr. Wolfe say?" I asked her.

"He said, 'Georgia, I just wish she'd think this over.' Dr. and Mrs. Wolfe really care for you, Melissa."

The ten days Jake spent in the clinic passed slowly. Aunt Roxena and Uncle Jesse left for the country. During the day, Dicky and I would go see Betty, and at night I stayed busy helping one of the youth workers plan a program and visiting Vonda and Dean.

No sooner than Pearl had informed me that Jake had been dismissed from the clinic, I got a call from his AA friend, Jim, asking me to come out to the farm to see if I could help talk Jake into going back to the clinic. He'd already started drinking again. Jake didn't agree to that but he did agree to take a ride with me. Jim and Zach told me to take him to the clinic and they'd come behind me. Jake fell asleep as we drove. We were almost there and in heavy traffic when Jake woke up and saw where we were. I was stopped at a light with a lot of cars behind us.

"Oh, no! Mel, you tricked me!" He got out of the car. Jim jumped out and grabbed him. Jake yelled, "Oh, no you don't! I'm not going back to that clinic!" Jim got him over on the sidewalk while Zach and I got out of traffic.

Zach said, "Get back in the car with Melissa, Jake, and we'll go back to my place."

I stayed just a little while after taking Jake to Zach's.

The next day after work I could stand it no longer and called Lynne.

"He's back at the farm. He was determined to go for a bottle and I told Zach he couldn't be up with him all night, because he had to work. I told him he couldn't help Jake by trying to make him do something against his will. I suggested Zach let Jake go."

What Lynne said made sense. But as long as there is life, there's hope. Shouldn't we try?

I didn't hear from him or anyone for a few days. Early on Saturday morning, Dr. Wolfe called to ask if I'd go to the farm to see Jake with him. Jake's mother had gone out to help Zach try to get Jake to go into the clinic.

When we got out there, Jake was missing. They had all been in the living room; Jake went to the kitchen for coffee and didn't come back. They had looked all over the farm but hadn't found him, but his car was still there. Dr. Wolfe and I didn't stay long. As we were driving into Dr. Wolfe's drive, Mrs. Wolfe's nurse came out and said they had found Jake. He was hiding in a very short closet on the back porch where Grandfather Bell had kept his boots and chore coat. So we went back to the farm. When we arrived, Jake was standing in the kitchen with the others. I could tell he'd been drinking but he wasn't in bad shape.

Zach suggested we sit down. As the men started for the living room, Jake's mother said she had a pot of coffee made, indicating we should remain in the kitchen.

I'd never been alone with Mrs. Snow before and had only met her twice. I really didn't want to go in the living room, though, so I stayed in the kitchen. Mrs. Snow had a warm smile and I judged her to be someone who never met a stranger.

"Wonder if they'd like to have some coffee?" she asked.

"Yes, that sounds great. Dr. Wolfe takes his black." I reached above the sink for the cups. *Oh boy. She'll wonder how I know where things are. I hope she doesn't think I spend a lot of time out here.* She disappeared in the pantry and came back with a small tray of cookies. We took coffee to the men. Zach and

Dr. Wolfe were laughing about something, so I knew the conversation was light.

As soon as we served the coffee, I went back to the kitchen and poured Mrs. Snow and me each a cup. She had seen me one day when I was carrying Dicky into the doctor's office. She asked me about him. I explained about his hip and that he'd soon be completely on his own. She was so easy to talk to. Neither of us mentioned Jake.

Soon I heard the front door open. I knew Dr. Wolfe had decided it was time to talk to Jake in private. Mrs. Snow and I joined the other men in the living room.

When Jake and Dr. Wolfe came back inside, Dr. Wolfe said, "Jake isn't through drinking. He says if he goes to the clinic, he'll come back and start drinking again as soon as he gets out. So, I've told him we'll leave him alone. He told me when he makes up his mind to quit drinking, he'll call one of us. We should all go and respect his wishes. When he wants to hear from us, he'll contact us."

I got up and gathered the cups while Jake's mother got the cookie tray. I hurried back to the kitchen and started washing the cups. I knew Dr. Wolfe wouldn't leave until he had us all out of there.

He shook Jake's hand and said, "The ladies have your kitchen in order, Jake. We are going to all leave you now. You won't talk to any of us until you call." Then he said to us all, "It's important that we abide by his wishes."

He looked over at me with a defeated look and said, "Thanks for coming, Mel."

"You're welcome." I stepped out into the yard. We hurried to our cars. Dr. Wolfe and I left last, as Jake watched from the porch.

We were going down the country road toward the interstate when Dr. Wolfe said, "Melissa, are you going to be able to keep from calling him?"

"Oh yes, sir. Doctor, I don't make it a practice of calling him. As far as I'm concerned now, he's a patient. I wouldn't call unless you asked me to." *Now that he is drinking and Dr. Wolfe has asked for my help, I will try to be all business. I can keep from calling Jake and go about my own job of taking care of Dicky, but my thoughts will always be on Jake.*

Dr. Wolfe broke into my contemplation, "I thought that, but I wanted to know for sure. I suspect he'll call you first. I don't know when, but regardless of what time it is, I want to know it."

I assured Dr. Wolfe if I heard from him that I'd let him know.

"You're a very smart girl. I'd sure hate to see you make a mistake that you'd regret the rest of your life. I've seen you with these patients. You enjoy dealing with them and out thinking them, but taking care of one on the job and being married to one are two different things."

⌒

The next two weeks seemed like two months. Late Saturday night before Easter I was in the basement hanging up my uniforms that I'd starched. The kitchen phone rang and I flew up the steps knowing that no one but Jake would call me at eleven o'clock. I grabbed the phone.

"Hello," I said.

Silence.

Yes, that's Jake. I waited, more silence. "Jake, is that you?"

"Melissa, I'm trying to get off the bottle. I want to quit drinking." He wasn't slurring his words, but he sounded weak. "I'm at a hotel downtown."

"What kind of shape are you in? Do I need to come and get you?"

"I haven't had a drink for a while. I can drive to you. Then, I want to go to the farm."

"Come on, Jake, just don't take another drink. Can you keep from doing that?"

"Yes, I won't drink."

"I'll be waiting for you."

I called Dr. Wolfe. "Doctor, this is Melissa. Jake just called. He's been in a hotel downtown. He said he's trying to get off the bottle. He's on his way here, and then he intends to go to the farm."

"Go with him and don't let him out of your sight."

"Doctor, I agree he should have someone. Do you think it's wise for me, a single woman, to go out there? He has neighbors across the road that may see me. I don't want to go against your wishes, but this isn't my style."

"I understand, but he mustn't go by himself and you're the only one he'll accept. If you wear your uniform they'll see you're taking care of someone."

"All right, I'll go."

"You know what to do. See how sick you think he is when he gets there. Taper him off like we do at the clinic. If he has trouble and needs the 'brown medicine,' come by my house and I'll give you some."

Jitter barked when he drove up. I went to the door to see if he needed help. He was walking straight, but I could tell he was weak. His head was bobbing up and down. He was trying to hold it with his hands when he came up on the porch. If I didn't do something quick, he would go into convulsions.

"Come in and sit down, Jake. How long has it been since you had a drink?"

"Four or five hours."

"Do you have a bottle in the car?"

"Yes, in the trunk."

By now he was shaking all over.

"Where are the keys?"

"In the car."

"Hang on, I'll be back."

I ran out and got a fifth of Jim Beam that was in the car. As I would have done in the clinic when tapering a patient off the bottle, I poured him a drink. He was shaking so badly, I had to hold the glass to his mouth. I got him a glass of water and said, "Jake, drink a little of this for me."

"Okay." He drank some water, again with my holding the glass.

"How long has it been since you've eaten?"

"Long time. I don't know."

"As soon as you're not shaking so badly, I'll get you some juice and crackers." Dr. Wolfe always pushed juice and water at the clinic to rehydrate the patients when they'd been on a heavy drinking binge.

We waited a few minutes and I brought the crackers, V8 juice and a cup of tomato soup into the living room. I set the tray on the footstool and gave him a cracker. He could manage them by then. We didn't rush and he ate four crackers, drank all of the juice and some of the hot soup.

"Will you go to the farm with me?"

"Yes, I will. Do you want me to call Dr. Wolfe for some Delvinol?"

"No, I don't want anyone but you to know I'm home."

"Okay, I'll go take care of you, only if you are ready to stop drinking." I'd paved the way to be in control, knowing I had to let him know I was in charge. He'd seen me on duty and undoubtedly he knew I meant business.

"I'm ready."

"I'll be right back." I had put a few things in an overnight case, but needed to change into my uniform. He didn't notice the white uniform when I came down. I put the coffee I'd made in a thermos, put milk, bread, ham, eggs and juice in a sack, got Jitter's bed and food and we all three got in Jake's car and headed for the farm. I turned into the circle drive a little after 1:00 a.m. on Easter Sunday morning.

"It's Easter," I said as we made our way up the stairs. Jake's clothes smelled like whiskey. They were very dirty and wrinkled. I hung up his coat and suggested he just lie down. I helped him with his shoes. He got into bed fully dressed and I covered him up.

"When do I get my next drink?"

"Two-thirty."

"Man, I hope I can make it."

"You can, I'll see to it. Jake, I'm going down to put the food away. I'll be in your girls' room across the hall."

"Oh, could you come back and stay in here?"

"Yes, I can."

Lord, he's so lost and frightened. I'll need your help. I need to taper him off but don't want him to go into convulsions.

I put the food away, poured myself a cup of coffee and went back upstairs. Jake's room was small. There was a rope bed, dresser and small chest. I propped the pillow against the headboard and stepped out of my shoes, then sat on top of the covers. Jake was quiet. I drank my coffee and waited. His respiration sounded good. He hadn't been shaking much for a while. I decided to hold it to three hours before I'd give him another drink, unless he started shaking.

Grateful that Jake was asleep, I sat in the dark. I heard the train go by. Jake had shown me where the railroad went on the backside of the farm the day we had our picnic. The grandfather clock struck two. Shortly after, Jake got up and lit a cigarette. I sat there and said nothing.

"Mel."

"Yes."

"Is it time for my drink?"

"No."

"You'll have to hang in here with me."

"I will."

"I may drive you crazy."

"I can handle it."

He put his cigarette out, went to the bathroom and came back in. "Man, I need a drink." He sat back down on the bed, lit another cigarette, got up and said, "I can't stay here; I've got to have a drink."

"Let's go downstairs." I said as I slipped on my shoes.

"What did you do with the bottle?"

"It's in the trunk of your car."

"Where are the keys?"

"I put them away."

"Man, Mel, I need a drink."

"It won't be long."

"How long?"

"Thirty minutes."

"I'll never make it."

"You're a lot better. You're not shaking."

He walked back and forth from the kitchen to the living room.

"Can't we cheat just a little?"

"No."

"Man, I just can't wait."

He reached in his shirt pocket and got another cigarette. He started pacing again. After a little while, I heard the clock chime two-thirty.

"I'll get your drink, Jake, and then we'll try for four hours."

"Man, I appreciate that." He sat down at the table. I set the drink in front of him, then some juice, a few crackers and some chicken noodle soup. After he ate and drank, he sat in his recliner and napped a little. I tried curling up in one of the pink parlor chairs, but they were too small.

I wish he had a couch, I thought and got up to make a fresh pot of coffee. While it perked, I finished the last that was in the thermos.

"Mel, where did you go?"

"I'm right here," I said as I walked into the living room.

"Man, I'd hate to be alone."

"You're not going to be alone. Just try to get some sleep. I'll try to take a nap." I turned out the dining room light, but left the kitchen light on. I stretched out on the living room floor and pretended to be asleep. He got up from his chair, came over and stood there wondering if he should wake me. He went over and looked out the window and then went upstairs to the bathroom. Soon he was coming down the steps and back over to where I was lying.

"Mel."

I rolled over, rubbed my eyes and rose up. "What time is it?" I knew. I had heard the clock chime while he was upstairs.

"It's 4:30. Man, Mel, I've got to have a drink."

"You can, in two more hours. We've got to get you on a four-hour schedule, so we can go to six hours and then get you well."

"I'll get well, but man, I feel like my skin is crawling."

"You're much better, Jake. Your hand hasn't been shaking since we got out here. I'm afraid you haven't been drinking enough liquids. Let's go have some water and juice."

"Oh, I don't want that."

"I know you don't, but we both know you need liquids and you've got me here to help you so let's do some things that will help you. Come on." I took his hand and we went into the kitchen. He drank some water. I poured him a glass of juice and he drank some of it.

"Man, I need a drink."

"Hey, come over here," I said as I pulled back the curtains to the kitchen window. "It's going to be daylight real soon. See, it's just starting."

"I've got to have a drink."

There was a small closet off the kitchen. I found a jacket and handed it to him. "Jake, put this on. I'll get my jacket and we'll go for a walk."

"No, Mel. Oh, man, I've got to have a drink."

"Come on, we won't be long. Let's get some air." I took his hand. "Come on. It's Easter Sunday." I opened the door, gave a light pull on his hand and we went out on the back porch and into the yard. "Everything is so still out here. Plantin' time's just around the corner. What do the sharecroppers plant?"

"Beans and corn. Man, Mel, I don't think I can make it without a drink."

"Every time will be a little easier. I'm going to hang in there with you, remember?"

"I remember."

We walked around the barn, then stood and talked a little and walked some more until we were at the front of the barn again.

"Man, we've got to go back to the house. I've got to have a drink."

I looked inside the barn. "Let's go in, Jake, I've never seen the barn," I said as I walked in, trying to stall for time.

"I've got to have a drink."

I got in front of him and put my arms around him. "You will when your time is up. Just think how well you did on the walk." I started up the ladder and stopped on the third rung and looked at the loft. It was light enough to see by then. "This is not as big as our barn back home."

"Now, Mel, I just can't make it. We've got to go."

Lord, we have almost another hour. You've got to help me. I can't do it without you.

We left the barn and started to the house. "What kinds of fruit trees are these?"

"Several kinds."

"Let's go see."

"Now, Mel, you're stalling. I have to have a drink." Even though he was desperate, he never got angry with me because he was too much of a gentleman. He knew I was there to help him and he seemed truly grateful for my presence.

"Come on, let's go see. I want to know if there's a cherry tree." I took his hand and started to the orchard. That worked until we got about half way through it.

He turned around and said, "I've got to go inside. I've got to have a drink."

How am I going to manage, Lord? I've got another thirty minutes. We went through the kitchen door and I said, "I'll be right back." I hurried upstairs and started running water in the claw-foot bathtub. While the water was running I went in his room, found clean clothes and spread them out on the bed. I called down through the open-grate register and said, "Jake, come up here a minute."

"Oh, Melissa, don't do this. I'm waiting for my drink."

"Just come up," I said patiently.

I waited at the top of the steps and took him into the bathroom and said, "Your clothes are on your bed. Get cleaned up and call me and I'll bring your drink."

"I've got to have it now."

"Not time yet. I'll bring it to you as soon as you're cleaned up." I hurried out of the room and closed the door.

I waited until he had time to dress, then said, "Jake, do you want me to bring it or do you want to come down to the kitchen?"

"You can bring it now. I need to shave."

Good, he's better. He sees he needs to shave.

"Oh, thank you, Mel. Man, I'm crazy for letting myself get into this shape. I'm sorry you have to see me this way."

"You'll start looking better after you shave and eat."

"I don't want to eat."

"Now, Doctor, if I were taking care of one of your patients, you'd tell me to push liquids and give them something to eat. So that's what I'm going to do."

"Yes, ma'am," he said with the hint of a grin.

"I'll leave you to your job of shaving and go fix some oatmeal. You don't have to eat much, but I want you to try."

"I'll try. Man, I want to get off this stuff."

"Good. We'll try for six hours," I said as I started out the door.

"Oh, that's a long time."

"We'll try." I hurried down the steps.

"Well, you look much better," I said as he walked through the kitchen door.

"Thank you for hanging in there with me. What a dummy to let myself get in this shape! Man, Mel, I thought I wouldn't make it."

"You did, though. I knew you would," I said as I set two bowls of oatmeal on the table. I said a short prayer and handed him the sugar and milk. "Would you like some toast?"

"No, ma'am. Thank you."

"Sick," but always the gentleman.

"Man, I thought I wouldn't make it to your place last night."

"We won't worry about that; you did make it." He only ate a few bites and then put his spoon down. I picked it up and said, "Eat six more bites for me."

"I don't think I can."

"Sure you can. Just start. It will give you strength." Finally, he finished the sixth bite. I poured him a small glass of water.

"I'd rather have coffee." Jake was a heavy coffee drinker, but the caffeine would only keep him awake, not sober him, and I was desperate for even a thirty minute break to sleep.

"We'll have coffee next. Drink this water first." I washed the few dishes. He sat at the table smoking.

About 9:00 a.m., the phone started ringing. "That phone is why I went to the hotel. It rang all the time."

"Everyone worries about you, Jake—your mother and your kids. Why don't you call your brother and tell him you're here getting sober. He can tell your mother. Maybe your children are calling him."

Jake asked me to make the call, so I phoned Zach and let him know about Jake's progress.

He put out his cigarette and started talking about his kids. He named each one of them and cried. I saw he wasn't going to take a rest, so I made a fresh pot of coffee. He spent the morning drinking coffee, talking and crying. When four hours went by, he became very restless. "I've got to get off this stuff, but I'm not sure I can last six hours."

He'd had coffee, juice and some water. At noon, I poured another glass of water and made chicken noodle soup. "Oh, I don't want that."

"You need to eat."

We each had a small bowl of soup. We took a walk in the pasture, hand in hand, down to the little spring. When we started back to the house, I looked at my watch. He'd gone five hours. He had wanted a drink for an hour or more. At five and a half hours, I gave in. He became willing to eat a little at a time and drink liquids. We split a sandwich and drank juice.

Jake stopped crying and apologized, explaining that he wasn't a crier.

"Maybe that would be a good thing."

"Oh, no," he said, "I don't like to see men cry."

"I hope you don't mind seeing women cry. I cry sometimes."

Mid-afternoon he was looking and acting like the old Jake. We pushed the pink parlor chairs together and held hands and visited. It was hard to believe that he'd been in such bad shape the night before.

He bounces back quicker than any patient I've ever seen. One minute he's a patient, the next minute just Jake, but always the man I love so much. Lord, it may not be right to have fallen in love with Jake, but I don't love him because it's right or wrong. I just love him.

He was much more comfortable in the afternoon. We talked about when we first met at the clinic. He smiled and said, "I knew you wouldn't date me. I thought if I went to your church, you wouldn't think I was just a no-good drunk." We laughed about my not understanding that he was interested in me.

Jake suggested we take a ride, but as we neared the car, he stopped and said, "Why don't we take another walk?"

I'm about to drop from no sleep and he's wanting to walk? I was surprised he wasn't wishing it was dinnertime so he could have his 5:00 p.m. drink. His last drink would be at 11:00 p.m., after which I was hoping he would sleep. I was exhausted.

"Okay," I said. "It's a nice, sunny day. Can we see the chicken house?" We went inside and looked at the nests. I was surprised everything was in such good shape.

"Jake, are you going to get some chickens?"

"Oh, I don't know. I've got to clean all these buildings out."

Over in a corner was an old drop leaf table that was covered over with a bunch of feed sacks. Walking over and lifting off the sacks I said, "Look at this, Jake. You should clean this up and put it on the back porch so you can eat out there."

"Maybe we'll do that."

He said "we."

I was ready to sit down when we got back to the house. Jake got us each a cup of coffee from the pot I'd made before our walk. We sat down in the pink chairs and he talked about helping his Grandfather Bell clean out the chicken house.

"I think that was the last time they were cleaned out," he said.

"The straw looked real old."

"I think I've got me a farm gal," he said, as he put his coffee cup on a table by his chair then reached for mine, putting it on the table next to his.

He scooted to the edge of his chair and took both of my hands.

We were both silent for a long minute. He was smiling like the old Jake. "Mel, I love you. I've never known anyone like you. I'm just coming off the bottle. I don't have a practice or much money. I have a big responsibility supporting my children and making alimony payments. I can't give you all the best, but I'm going to ask you a question anyway."

I caught my breath as he got out of his chair and down on his knees and said, "Melissa Ann, will you marry me?"

"Oh! Yes, I will!" He got up and pulled me to him. I was well aware of the great risk I was about to take, but I had to have that man. We stayed wrapped in one another's arms until the grandfather clock started to chime. The six hours were up and he hadn't asked for a drink.

We sat back down in our chairs to finish our coffee.

He looked over and smiled at me. "Do you think you can hang in there with me tonight?"

"Yes, but I need to call Mrs. Stone," I said getting up to go to the phone. "There won't be a problem about my being off because I spent so many extra hours while they were in Florida."

After the phone call I said, "Jake, let's have some ham and eggs for supper. How does that sound?"

"I think I can handle that. First, I want you to bring me my bottle."

"It's time for a drink, but don't you think I should just give you Dr. Wolfe's size drink instead of the whole bottle?"

"I'm done with the bottle," he said standing. "I'm going to pour it down the sink."

I went in the pantry and got the bottle and handed it to him.

"Man, I want to get rid of this stuff," he said turning it upside down and watching as it went down the sink. He then turned on the faucet and washed out the sink.

"Jake," I said as I got the ham and eggs from the refrigerator, "should we call Dr. Wolfe and go by his place or the clinic and get some of the 'brown medicine' to get you through the night?"

"No. I'm going to try it on my own without anything. Man, I'm crazy for letting myself get in this shape."

He wants to be done with the bottle but he'll never make it without the proper support. He needs to be in a Bible study with Christian men.

"The ham smells good, Jake," I said, going over and sitting down at the table. "I didn't realize I was so hungry."

"Grandmother Bell used to serve ham and eggs for Sunday night supper." He paused and said, "You must be awfully tired, Honey."

"Maybe we can take a nap after we eat," I said, going over to turn the ham.

"I'll try but I don't know if I can."

After dinner, we stretched out on the girls' beds and it didn't take long for me to drop off. Then I heard Jake say, "I can't lie here any longer. Let's go for another walk."

When we got downstairs, I suggested we watch TV a while. He turned on the TV and there was a beautiful Easter program on with lots of singing.

"Oh, Jake, this is wonderful," I said, hoping we could watch it and rest before walking again.

After two programs he could stay in the house no more. It was about 10:00 p.m. when we got the flashlight and went outside.

We walked all around the farm, to the pond and back, to the back field and back to the house. He tried to lie down to sleep but was soon up again. "Honey, my skin is crawling."

He lit one cigarette after another. All night we walked and he tried to lie down. I'd give him water or juice and try to get him to eat. I was totally exhausted.

We were coming down the steps when I saw through the window that it was almost light outside. "Come to the door. I want to show you something." I opened the door and we looked out. "The night is over, Jake. We have a whole new day."

"Oh, man, I'm glad."

"Dr. Wolfe will be up real soon. We can call him for the 'brown medicine'. You could eat better and get some rest."

"Man, I'm glad you stayed with me, Mel."

"I'm glad I did, too."

We were standing in the middle of the living room. He put his arm around me and said, "When do we go meet your folks?"

"I can go anytime because Dicky is walking and I still have extra time off."

"How about a week from today?"

"I'll write and tell them we're coming."

"Man, I'm glad that night is over. Is it time to call Dr. Wolfe?"

I looked at the grandfather clock at the foot of the steps. "Yes, he's talked to the clinic by now."

"I'll call him," he said. I went to the phone and dialed the number and handed it to Jake. "Hello, Dr. Wolfe, this is Jake. I'm home... Yes, sir. I had my last drink yesterday around noon... Awfully shaky... Yes, I've had liquids... Yes, I ate some... No, I didn't sleep a wink... I'd appreciate that... She'll come right away... Thank you, sir."

He hung up the phone and said, "Dr. Wolfe said, 'Send Melissa after the medicine.' How'd he know you were here?"

The cat's out of the bag. He knows I've called Dr. Wolfe.

"Doctor, you don't think I'd spend the weekend out here taking care of you without Dr. Wolfe sending me, do you?"

"No. No, I guess you wouldn't."

"I'll go now to get your medication. I'll get breakfast when I get back, then go home."

I put on my jacket, picked up the car keys and said, "See you in about forty-five minutes."

I turned on the interstate going to Dr. Wolfe's. *I'm so exhausted; I hope I can drive over there and back, then home. My, what a weekend! Dr. Wolfe would just faint if I told him Jake asked me to marry him and I said yes. What have I done? Could I be choosing to spend the rest of my life with weekends like I just had? Lord, I can't do without that man. I've never been in love before and I love him so much.*

I tapped lightly on the front door of Dr. Wolfe's home so I wouldn't disturb Mrs. Wolfe. He met me at the door with a big smile.

"Come in, Melissa, and tell me about your weekend."

"I'm grateful we got through it. He almost didn't make it to my house. I worried last night that he'd stopped drinking too soon. He had the shakes some and is still shaky. He hasn't slept more than an hour all weekend."

Dr. Wolfe knew that meant I hadn't slept either. "Are you sure you can drive? I'll send someone to drive you home."

"I don't think that will be necessary, Doctor. I'll leave as soon as I get breakfast."

"Give him a teaspoon of this as soon as you get there," he said handing me a bottle of the liquid Delvinol. "He'll be able to eat after he's had some medication. Then just before you leave, give him another teaspoon. He should sleep after he's eaten."

"Yes, sir."

"Can you go back tonight and see that he eats and give him his medication?"

"Yes, sir."

"After that, he can handle it alone."

"I thought I was going to have to come for this in the middle of the night, but he made it. He tells me he's through with the bottle."

We were standing in front of a large medicine cabinet just outside his office door. "Come in and visit a minute, Melissa." He motioned for me to sit down. He sat down, looked over at me, put his hands together and leaned forward with his elbows on his knees. "Melissa, Mrs. Wolfe and I love you very much. You are a smart girl and can be anything you want to be," he said. "As for Jake being through with the bottle, I've heard that before. He has a long history of drinking. He started as a teenager and drank heavily through college and medical school. He's admitted to the disease of alcoholism for at least ten years. His system craves alcohol. For someone with this pattern, never to drink again isn't likely. I know you need to deliver the medication and get home to bed."

He stood and I stood. He put his hand on my shoulder and walked me to the door. I turned and said, "Thank you, Doctor."

"Tell Jake he can call me any time, night or day."

"Yes, sir, I'll do that."

Jake was waiting at the door for me when I got back to his place. He was all cleaned up and looked very good. I fixed oatmeal and was pleased to see that he ate better. I cleaned up the few dishes, got Jitter in the car and said I'd be back to fix dinner. He thanked me for the weekend and reminded me to write to my folks as soon as I got some sleep.

I arrived back at the farm about 5:00 p.m. that night. Jake was pacing the floor when I arrived. I gave him his medication and he soon began to settle down. He read the paper while I cooked pork chops, mashed potatoes and gravy, green beans and a salad. He took a small portion of everything. I hoped he'd be able to eat it all.

He was pale, but very much himself. "Did you get a chance to write your folks?"

"Yes, I told them we'd be down a week from today. I'm anxious to take you to meet them. Jake, is your pork chop tender?"

"Yes, very. Is yours?"

"It's not easy to cut."

"Here, Honey, let me show you the proper way to hold your fork." He took my left hand and placed the fork in it. "Now, take your knife and just saw your meat and see if it's easier." I thanked him and he said, "It doesn't matter to me if you have all the social graces, but that's the way to hold your fork and cut your meat."

"I want to learn. It will never hurt my feelings for you to teach me all you know."

He looked at me for a moment then said, "I'm really going to try to make you happy."

I left the medicine with him and went home with the promise to be back with Dicky to see him the next day.

As I drove home, I felt encouraged. *He looks so good. He's such a gentleman. I'm so anxious to learn so many things that he's known all his life. I'm so anxious for him to find the Lord.*

Dicky and I went to see Jake each morning. As soon as I got to work, Dicky would ask if we were going to go see Dr. Jake.

At the end of that week, Dicky's doctor took all restrictions from his walking and playing. He'd always have a limp, but he was on his own. When we got back to his home, I told his mother she didn't need me any more and about Jake's proposal.

"Oh, Melissa, you'll be getting married soon. Stay with us until you do." I gladly agreed to that. I would really miss not caring for Dicky each day.

❧

As Jake and I neared my hometown, I pointed out all the familiar places and I took him by my high school. He'd never been to the Ozarks and he loved the spring, hills and the streams.

"Just around the curve is the country store," I said. As we rounded the curve, I saw a familiar truck. "There's my dad's pickup. Pull over." Daddy had seen us go by and turned around. He got out to meet us. He was wearing his blue striped overalls and Jake had on a dark gray suit and tie. I hugged Daddy and introduced him to Jake. *I can't remember a moment as wonderful as this,* I thought as I saw them shaking hands.

We visited a while and then Daddy said, "Your mama is waiting for you. I'll be home shortly."

I showed Jake where I stood waiting for the bus in high school, and we slowly drove down the country lane to the house. I felt such pride as we walked up on the porch of the small country home and I introduced Jake to my mother.

As I watched Jake putting away Mama's roast beef, mashed potatoes, and gravy, I thought about how this day seemed as if it would never come.

"Did you can these beans, Mrs. Jenkins?"

"Yes, I can about everything."

"My Grandmother and Grandfather Bell had a large garden. She canned everything," he said.

"I just can in quart jars now, but when the children were all small, I always canned in half gallons." Jake looked at me. I could tell he was thinking about us canning someday.

I can hardly wait. I know how to do that. He showed me how to hold my fork; I'll show him how to can beans.

Mama washed the dishes and I dried them just like we use to do.

"How do you like him, Mama?"

"He's very nice, Honey."

"I think so."

She asked about Dicky then said, "What do your Aunt Roxena and Uncle Jesse think of Jake?"

"Everyone likes Jake, Mama." I wasn't about to tell her more than that.

We left mid-afternoon to go back to the city. I was to work the next day.

As we drove home, Jake told me about all Daddy had shown him on our farm. He had never seen a hydraulic ram before. From the spring down under the hill, the ram pumped the water that we used until plumbing was put in the house.

"I would love to see it work. Your dad still has everything he needs if he ever wanted to use it. It's amazing how they raised you six kids on that rock pile."

When we went home a few weeks later, Mama had another good dinner. As soon as dinner was over, the men went outside. While Mama and I were doing dishes, I told her we wanted to get married in three weeks.

"Will you be coming home?"

"Mama, Pastor Dean doesn't have a license for this state and our pastor down here would never marry anyone who has been divorced."

"You know, Honey, your daddy and I can't come up there."

"I know, Mama. That's why I've told Jake I just want to go to the church and get married. We've asked his brother and his wife to stand up with us. You never put importance on a wedding; you just always talked about a good marriage. I've been to very few weddings because of my work schedule. A wedding isn't important to me. I've already told my patient's mother I'd work until two days before."

"I'll give you the E bonds you bought to buy your dress and all you need."

"No, Mama," I said as I hung up the dishtowel. "You sent me money to buy the Plymouth and I told you to keep the bonds. I have enough saved to pay for a wedding, but I'm not going to spend a lot of money; it's not my style. Jake agrees."

She patted me on the head and said, "I'm very proud of you."

I put my arms around her and said, "I love you, Mama. Thank you for teaching me what is important."

Jake looked a little nervous when he asked for my hand. The folks gave their approval and we left shortly for the city. All the way home, I thought how sick my parents would be if they knew about the drinking.

So far as I was concerned, our wedding day, May 21, couldn't come soon enough.

I had no time to shop because I was working full time. A friend met me at her dress shop on a Sunday afternoon. I found a white linen dress and three or four other summer dresses. The next week I went shopping for accessories in the evenings.

On our wedding morning, Jake called and said, "Honey, I'm working on it, but I may not have the new shower installed by the time I bring you home." The words "bring you home" kept coming to my mind all day.

I'm going home to stay, I thought happily.

We were married that evening at 7:00 p.m. On our way to our hotel, Jake said, "Honey, my friend who works for the hotel has reserved the suite where President Kennedy stayed when he came here campaigning in 1960."

"Oh, wow!" I laid my head on his shoulder. We were silent for a moment. "Jake, do you remember when you came home from Silver Hill and told me you weren't going to ask me to marry you?"

"Yes, I remember."

"I sat there and looked at you and thought, 'Just you wait, Doctor, in six months I'll have you.' That was November 21st, six months ago tonight."

A beautiful bouquet was waiting in the sitting room of our hotel suite. I noticed it as soon as Jake put me down from carrying me across the threshold.

"Oh, Jake," I said as I ran over to smell the flowers. When I turned around, he had an amused smile on his face. I went to him, put my arms around him and said, "I feel like Cinderella."

"Well, Cinderella, we have dinner reservations. Are you hungry?"

"No," I said gazing in his eyes. "I had a bowl of cereal this morning. I haven't thought of anything all day but being here with you."

The next morning Jake called room service and ordered brunch. The waiter wheeled in a table, covered it with a white tablecloth, set it with white linen napkins and silver, put the food on and left. It was a sight to behold!

"Look at this!" I exclaimed. Each plate was filled with smoked ham, scrambled eggs and grits, and we each had a large bowl of bright red strawberries. "Breakfast may not be this good ever again."

After brunch we drove out to the farm. We walked in on the back porch and Jake unlocked the kitchen door and turned around and said, "I carried you over the threshold at the hotel, but I want to make this official." The next thing I knew, I was standing in the middle of the kitchen. We stood there locked in each other's arms, looking at one another.

Jake said the most beautiful words I'd ever heard, "Welcome home, Mrs. Bell."

He grilled steaks that evening while I baked potatoes and made a salad. We took a long ride out in the country; he gave me the history of the farms and showed me where his aunt had taught school.

The rest of the week was spent making the place look like a country home. We bought a picnic table for the backyard and a swing for the front porch.

In the evenings of our first few weeks as husband and wife, Jake grilled outside or we went out to eat. Each evening we sat in the new porch swing and never lacked for something to talk about. On weekends we saw the kids, who seemed okay with their dad and me being married.

Soon after school was out, they came to spend a week. Jake had bought four gentle horses and a buckboard. The kids always wanted to go up the lane and see the train go by. When we'd hear it come into town, we'd jump in the car and hurry up the lane and be there waiting when the train got there. Early one morning, Wendy, Neil, Jake and I rode the horses up to the tracks and watched the early train go by. A little boy waved from the window. As I watched the train go out of sight, I thought, *I wonder if there is anyone on the train as happy as I?*

Jake looked healthy and relaxed. The children were there each Wednesday, Thursday and Friday evening and Sunday afternoon. Wendy and Neil were always awake early.

Jake was outside early one Thursday morning when I heard him yell, "Mel! Mel!"

I ran to the door, "What do you need?"

"Bring the kids to see the new colt."

"Oh, wow! Wendy! Neil! Come quickly!" Neil and Wendy, the two younger kids and the only ones awake, ran with me to the pasture.

Their horse Poco had a beautiful cream-colored colt with a white spot on its forehead, standing on wobbly legs, just born. They were so excited they ran back inside to tell the others. The kids named the colt North Star.

The kids and their dad spent the day outside with North Star and the horses. Bo was Candy's horse and she spent a long time that afternoon washing him. Jake and I stood watching, resting our arms on the white board at the top of the fence.

"He's beautiful, Candy," I said, "and his copper coat shines so beautifully in the sun."

Candy stepped back and stood a moment admiring a job well done. While we were all standing looking on, Bo made a short circle and, without warning, lay down and rolled over in the dirt. Everyone was disappointed for Candy, but the kids were getting used to farm life and Candy took it in stride.

"Jake, I'm going to clean up and get this partial plate out of my mouth. My gum feels sore. Maybe you could take a vote on pork chops or fried chicken for dinner," I said, starting for the house.

Fried chicken won the vote, so I started the chicken, potatoes and some Kentucky Wonder green beans. When I came to a point I could leave the kitchen, I headed upstairs, and as I got to the top of the steps, I met Wendy coming out of the bathroom with my partial plate.

I explained to her what it was and that I wasn't wearing it because my mouth was sore. She put it back and didn't say a word. *Now what was our little seven-year-old going to do with it?* I wondered, as I walked down the steps.

Back in the kitchen, I turned the chicken and was starting to set the table when the thought came to me, *What if Wendy goes back to get my partial? I'd better go hide it.*

When I got to the bathroom, the lid was lying beside the empty dish that held my partial. *Oh no!* Jake and I questioned Wendy but she just looked up at us and didn't say a word.

That evening Jake said, "Honey, you need to call your dentist as soon as your gums heal."

"Jake, that partial plate cost me $125."

"Honey, there's no way she's going to tell us where it is. You need to call your dentist."

I came to the edge of my chair and turned to look at him, "Just like that, call your dentist?" I asked, my voice rising. "And lose that hard earned money? You're nuts." He smiled and put his cigarette in his mouth.

"Okay, keep everyone out of the house for a few minutes," I said, standing.

"I'll see that you have privacy. You go and call Betty."

"How'd you know I was going to call Betty?"

"Because you think she's a good mother."

That night when the lights were out and all was quiet, Jake asked in a whisper, "What was Betty's advice?"

I whispered back, "Call the dentist and get a partial plate." We both laughed.

~

Workmen from Phillips Oil installed a new pipeline through our cornfield and cut down several rows of corn. So the next morning, Jake and I were picking up corn at daybreak. "You look like you're enjoying this," Jake said as he threw a handful of corn into his old truck.

"This is how I grew up. Mama and Daddy always worked side by side," I said as I started for another handful.

"Hey, wait. I've never kissed a girl in the cornfield." He came and put his arms around me.

We worked from early in the morning every day all summer getting the farm in tiptop shape. One morning, we dug up old bushes and planted new ones. About nine o'clock I went in and fixed a large breakfast of sausage gravy and biscuits while Jake got everything ready to start seeding the yard. As soon as we finished breakfast, he began seeding and I cleaned the kitchen. Then I went outside and painted the antique urns that I'd first seen the day Jake brought me to the farm for a picnic the summer before. I planted red geraniums and vinca vines in clay pots to put in them when they were dry. We worked until early evening that day and I went inside to fix another big meal. As soon as we finished, I cleaned the kitchen and went outside to help him finish putting everything away. That night, we fell into bed exhausted.

The next morning I opened my eyes to Jake saying, "Let's get up, Mel, and start building the fence around the barn."

I looked out the window and saw that it was dawn. "Oh, let's don't get up yet, Honey. We get up every morning at daybreak and go like lightnin' all day long."

He laughed and said, "How do we go all day?"

"Like lightnin'." By that time I was awake and laughing too. "You win. I'll get up."

That afternoon he dropped me off at the grocery store and picked up the kids. When we were getting ready to go to bed that night, Jake said, "Tomorrow is lightnin' makin' day."

Candy said, "What's lightnin' makin' day?"

"That's when we get up early to work and go like lightnin' all day long."

The next morning just as I was waking up, Jake got out of bed and said, "It's lightnin' makin' day."

Oh dear. He's trying to talk like me and I'm trying to talk like him. I smiled, loving him more for his teasing.

Our five-board-high fence was looking good. I held the boards and he'd level and nail. We took a break to eat lunch. The phone rang and I was pleasantly surprised to hear the voice of an old high school classmate, Joanne Hicks. She had seen our wedding picture in the paper and called to tell me she lived just half a mile from me.

I met Joanne for coffee the next day. She was still the same fun-loving gal. We started seeing one another a lot, but I had no idea we'd be there for one another for the next twenty-five years.

With the big country breakfasts we ate each morning after working two or three hours, Jake had begun to gain weight and seemed very contented. His children spent more and more time with us, as did his mother and stepfather. The kids helped us work when they were there. I was amused when Neil announced just before his sixth birthday, "Let's don't have lightning making day this time, Dad."

Another morning, Jake was going to get the kids up, and Karen heard him coming and said, "Here he comes. It's lightnin' makin' day."

Candy said, "Karen, the words are *lightning* and *making*."

"No, Candy, they're lightnin' and makin'." Karen had caught the spirit.

I was napping in the recliner one Saturday afternoon and Jake came in and said, "Hey there, lightnin'."

I stretched and said, "You sure are getting a lot of mileage out of that word lightnin'."

He smiled and said, "How would you like to go home to see your brother while he's in from Illinois? I'll take you home Monday."

"That was worth waking up for! You'll love Doug and Marilyn."

Monday evening we got to the folks just before dark. I could tell Doug and Jake liked one another right away. The next morning Doug, Marilyn, Jake and I went to Shepherd of the Hills near Branson. Fishing was scheduled for the day after that.

Doug knew I didn't drink, but as we were getting ready to go fishing, he said, "Jake, if I get some beer will you drink some of it?"

Jake shook his head and said, "No." It was never mentioned again.

We were getting settled on the "big rock" down at the river and I got the idea to act like I couldn't bait my own hook. *When Dicky doesn't want to do something for himself, he says, "I sure wish someone would do this for me." I wonder if I could get by with that.*

Jake was standing just a little ways from me, ready to cast his line in the water, when I said, "I sure wish I had someone to bait my hook."

He laid down his rod and reel and came over and sat down by me and said, "Here, Honey, let me help you." I didn't dare look at my brother.

Marilyn said, "Hey, Doug Jenkins, you need to take a lesson."

That evening Doug came in the kitchen when I was getting a drink of water and said, "What was that all about, you not baiting your own hook?"

I laughed and said, "Mama always told us girls when we got married not to tell our husbands we knew how to milk or we'd have it to do. It works the same way with baiting the hook, I just found out."

"Well, you ought to bait your own hook."

"Doug, you ought to bait Marilyn's hook." That shut him up.

Jake and Doug became very good friends while we were there.

September came and school started. Jake found an office to buy and we started working together. I was anxious to help him until we got the business going and we could hire a secretary and technician. His first patient was a lady he'd treated for cancer years before.

"How much do we charge for an office call?" I asked.

"Charge her three dollars. As of today, though, it has just gone up to five." I thought that was a little high, but didn't say anything.

We worked together well and the practice grew. It was wonderful seeing him in action.

I was in the examining room getting a two-year-old boy ready for a barium enema, while Jake was reading a film at the view box in an adjoining room. The boy's parents were standing back watching as I talked to him. *Jake will be so glad to see that the patient isn't crying*, I thought. I was relieved as well.

Then his dad stepped up beside me and said, "Now, don't you cry, Johnny. The doctor is going to give you an enema." The patient started howling at the top of his little lungs. I went out and closed the door. Jake looked over at me. He could tell I was distraught.

Through clenched teeth I said, "If those parents are going to be in there while you're examining that patient, I'm not staying."

He put the film back on the view box, looked at me with those brown eyes and simply said, "I wish you would." He walked over to the examining room door, opened it and stood back for me to go in first. I did.

We started to get more and more patients, and the paperwork, even with Jake's help, became too much for me. We heard that a lady who had worked at the University Medical Center for the chief of Radiology might be interested in working part-time. When she came for an interview one fall afternoon, we were far behind with the paperwork. I was on the phone scheduling a patient when she came to the window. I finished and turned to her. She smiled and said, "I'm Jewell Avery."

"Hi, Mrs. Avery. Come in. Doctor's busy just now, but maybe I can answer some of your questions."

"First of all, what is your name?" She asked politely.

"Oh, I'm sorry. I can answer that. I'm Melissa Bell."

She smiled, "Are you Mrs. Bell?"

"Yes, I am but just call me Melissa or Mel. Have you ever met Dr. Bell?" I asked with pride at the thought that he belonged to me.

"No, but I knew his late father."

"He'll be glad to hear that. Here he is," I said as he walked toward us.

I introduced them and told him she had known his father. They visited about people they both knew like they were old friends. She'd worked fifteen years for one of his radiology professors. She told him she was used to taking direct dictation. They decided she'd come from 1:00 to 5:00 p.m. each day. She said she could start immediately.

"Mel will show you the books. She's anxious to get free of all the book work."

Oh good. He called me Mel. I was glad for the informality. I turned to Jewell and said, "If the truth were known, he's just as anxious for me to be free of the book work as I am. I've been driving him crazy trying to do something I don't know beans about. From now on the only thing at this desk I want to be in charge of while you're here is stuffing the envelopes." We both laughed.

Time flew by as we worked and visited. By the end of the afternoon, she knew more about the job than I did. She had no problem taking charge and I had no problem letting go.

When Jake and I got in the car, we both were so grateful that we'd found her.

"Well, Honey," he said, "You won't have to struggle over that desk work anymore."

I laid my head back and said, "Jake, you were so patient with me, but you have no idea what this means to have her there. I can do anything I can figure in my head but getting it down on paper is such a problem."

"Honey, you need to let Betty find you a tutor."

"I'm afraid I'd never learn."

"Melissa, anyone who has a memory like you can master a learning problem."

He seems to think I can do it, Lord; I just wish I could believe it. One thing about Jake, he always encourages me.

There were so few free days with working, cleaning, helping Jake outside and being with the kids on Friday night and Sunday. One beautiful Sunday, the children had plans, so they hadn't come to visit us. It was the first Sunday they hadn't been with us in quite a while. On our way to church I said, "Since we went out with Lynne and Zach last night and the children aren't coming, I have no idea what we'll have for dinner."

He looked over at me. "Let's make a picnic lunch and hitch up the team to the buckboard and go west of the farm about a mile. Once when the cows were missing, I found them out there near a beautiful spot."

"I'll put the picnic lunch together as soon as we get home. I can hardly wait."

It was early afternoon when we headed west behind Dandy and Bo, their manes blowing in the wind. Jake had on his hat and casual trousers and I was ready for an afternoon outing in old pedal pushers. The spot was beautiful. It had been an old home place with beautiful, huge elm, oak and maple trees and blue grass. The leaves were beautiful colors. The only thing left of the house was part of an old stone fireplace.

Jake spread out the same quilt we'd used on our first picnic a little over a year before. We feasted on ham sandwiches and chips that we had stopped for on the way home from church. I brought along a pint jar of Mama's beet pickles and we ate nearly all of them.

When we were finished eating, we put the picnic basket back in the buckboard and we leaned up against a large tree. We visited about our different experiences when we were young just as we had done when we first met. After visiting for a while, we stretched out for a nap. It was so peaceful lying there with Jake's arm around me, listening to the rustling of the leaves and all the outdoor sounds. We napped about an hour then started back for home. When we got back on the country road, he let the horses go. I loved how they ran free down the road. Dandy was part Hackney and I loved to watch his feet and legs as he and Bo ran side by side.

When we got home, we cared for the team and I said, "Jake, I'd like to go to church tonight."

"I'll take you and we'll stop by that little hamburger place we used to eat at a lot."

That night when we were getting ready for bed I said, "Jake, it was a wonderful day but I know you missed your kids."

"Yes, I miss the kids when they aren't here." He paused and looked at me in silence then he put his arms around me and said, "I didn't fail to see the sparkle in your eyes when you saw your former youth group tonight."

"I do miss them. I'm so glad they have good leaders. We've needed a man to help with them for a long time. The couple working with them now is doing a better job than I. Two is always better than one, you know."

At the office things were moving along with much more ease with Jewell on board. With her taking direct dictation, the reports went out to the referring physicians the same day Jake saw the patient.

We became even busier and Jake's former tech, Dottie, came to work in the mornings for him. While Dottie was working, I took care of the front, answering the phone and scheduling patients. When she went home, I helped Jake with patients while Jewell sat at the desk. I was gone from home a lot and never got caught up with all I had to do there.

One afternoon, Jewell came to work and said she had found a wonderful cleaning lady who had been at her place that morning helping her with house cleaning.

"Does she have extra time?" Jake asked.

"I think so."

"Mel, you need to get her name and number."

"What for?"

"To help you out once a week. You're meeting yourself coming and going trying to keep up with everything."

I know that is true but my family will think I've become lazy if I end up with a maid. Before I had time to answer, Jewell had written down the lady's name and phone number.

On the way home, Jake said, "Honey, you didn't seem too excited about getting a cleaning lady."

I sighed, "Oh, I don't know what to think. I just always thought only the elite have help."

He laughed, "As far as I'm concerned, Mrs. Bell, you're the elite."

He's the most charming man I've ever met.

"Your heart's bigger than your back, Melissa. You cook a big meal for seven on Friday night. We take the kids home late, then you work until noon on Saturday, come home and bake for Sunday, clean house, cook another big meal on Sunday, start back to work on Monday, and help me outside on my day off on Thursday. You never have a few minutes on your own. You certainly don't need to feel guilty for needing help. I want you to do this."

"Okay. We can try it." *I apparently don't have to worry about him appreciating all I do!*

Ulma, the cleaning lady, was a beautiful African-American woman. She came each Monday and what a difference she made! She did the laundry that I did not have had time to finish and cleaned the whole house until it shined. I felt so thankful to have found her. The workload was still heavy but I slept well each night and loved working with Jake.

We had moved our cows away from the house to what we called the woods pasture. It consisted of about half field and half woods. The fences weren't very good, but Jake and I had spent Thursday afternoons mending them. In spite of all our work to keep them mended, we'd sometimes get a call from someone saying our cows were out.

Just after the Thanksgiving holiday, we were invited to several Christmas parties. The first was given by the Junior League; we were going as guests of

Zach and Lynne. I left the office early the afternoon of the party and went to the beauty shop.

My hair does look good, I thought, as I looked in the mirror when I got home.

Just as I was turning from the mirror, the phone rang. A very angry lady shouted, "You need to do something about these cows! They are in my yard!"

"Oh, I'm sorry! We'll be there to get them back in as soon as we can. I'm fixin' to go pick my husband up now and we'll be right there."

"Fixin'," she said with emphasis, "to pick your husband up won't do any good. Your fence needs fixin'!"

"Yes, ma'am. We'll be there as soon as possible."

I called Jake and told him our dilemma. When I arrived at the office, he was in the parking lot waiting for me. We hurried home and picked up some wire and hurried to the place where the cows had been. By the time we got them back through the gate, it was almost dark and starting to rain.

"Oh dear, my hair!" I touched my fresh hairdo with regret.

"You can sit in the car, Honey, while I fix the fence."

"I need to help you, Jake, or we'll never get done. It's almost dark."

"Here," he said, taking his hat off and lightly placing it on my head, "Jump in the car, we'll drive down there, shine the lights on the fence and try to make this quick."

It took about an hour to fix it but we thought it would hold. We hurried home and ran inside to get ready. My hair was damaged but we had to really hurry. Jake said it looked good after I had worked with it a little, but I couldn't stop thinking, *Jake looks so good in his tux. What if I don't look good enough?* I was very nervous as we drove toward the city. "Jake, I'm so worried. I'm not sure if I look okay."

He smiled. "You look great, Honey. With that green dress and all that red in your hair, you look just like Christmas."

I hope I don't embarrass him by not knowing what to do. "Jake, I'm going to be the only person there who doesn't know how to dance."

He kept looking at the road, but his voice was so strong and pleasant. "Just think," he sighed, "I'll have the only cow chaser in the crowd."

When we got to the door, a lady with red hair saw us and came hurrying toward us. Before Jake had a chance to introduce us, she took my hand in both of hers and introduced herself, then said, "Your husband is the best dancer in the crowd. I hope you don't mind my dancing with him."

"I don't mind a bit," I said.

"That's good. That's my husband right over there. You can dance with him while I am dancing with Jake." She put her arm around me while we walked toward her husband. "My husband can't dance very well."

"Well, that's good. I can't dance at all and I'm delighted Jake will have someone to dance with."

When Jake introduced me to her husband and several others who were standing with him, the woman piped up and said, "Mel doesn't dance, so I get to dance with Jake as much as I want."

Good, the news is out, I thought, as we started to our table. *I'll just smile and enjoy myself.*

The county medical society Christmas dinner was our next party. The first person I saw when we entered the door was Dr. Black, with whom I'd made rounds at Dr. Wolfe's before Jake went to Silver Hill and who referred patients to us now. Even though he knew I married a patient from Wolfe's, I was very pleased to be seen with Jake. Dr. Black and his wife Kay, whom I'd met at Dr. and Mrs. Wolfe's home, were very friendly, and she asked me to come to medical auxiliary.

When we went to get soft drinks, another couple came up and Jake introduced me to them as Dr. John Timmons and his wife Jane. They were about Jake's age and very friendly. He was in general practice—another one of our referring physicians. Jane had grown up in rural Oklahoma, so we had a lot in common. When it was time for dinner, the four of us found a table together. It was an enjoyable time. As other couples made their way to the dance floor, we continued to talk.

On the way home Jake said, "You sure were enjoying visiting with Jane Timmons."

"I like her a lot."

About midnight, I woke up and Jake wasn't by my side. I got up. He wasn't in the bathroom, either. I started down the steps and could see him by the moonlight through the windows, sitting in his chair, and smoking.

"I couldn't sleep and was afraid I'd wake you."

I sat down on his lap and said, "Don't ever worry about that, Honey. I don't want you to leave me even for seventeen minutes."

He laughed and said, "How did you come up with that number?"

"Sounded good as any," I said, putting a kiss on his forehead.

"You are a delight."

We sat there a long time before going back up. *These parties are bothering him; maybe I can talk him out of going.*

Two nights later, on Friday, was another party at one of the hospitals. "Jake," I said, "do we have to go to this party? Why don't we call and cancel?"

"No, Honey, I've cancelled out on too many things. I'm back in practice and I must show up."

When we got to the party, several doctors who knew his history of alcoholism came rushing up to see him. "Hello there, Jake! You're looking good."

I was afraid I'd never remember all the names. Everyone was friendly to me and while Jake was visiting a few feet away, one doctor came over to me and said, "How's Jake doing?"

"Really well. He's been very busy with the office and the farm."

"I've known him for years. I just want to give you a little advice. Be very careful what you say to him, you never know what might cause him to drink."

I couldn't believe my ears. *What I say or don't say isn't going to dictate whether or not he drinks. Surely this doctor knows that.*

～

Saturday at noon we left the office and stopped for a sandwich then Jake dropped me off at the shopping center. He was going home to take care of the stock and meet me at the department store to shop for the kids' Christmas presents. It was time for Jake to come. I was looking at a little yellow dump truck and someone walked up beside me. I looked up and there stood Jake... drunk.

The caregiver inside of me took over. Taking Jake's hand, I said, "Let's go to the car." Neither of us said a word as we rode the elevator to the parking level. I opened the passenger side door and he got in.

We were almost home when he said, "I'm sick." I pulled over to the side of the road. He opened the door and lost his lunch.

When we got in the house, he sat down in his chair and went to sleep.

I'm not going to say anything to him about this. Maybe this will be his only slip. I'm glad it made him sick. Maybe he'll remember. I'll not let him out of my sight until after Christmas.

I baked for Sunday and did laundry, all the while praying the phone wouldn't ring. But it did ring. It was Betty. We talked a long while. Jake woke up and went upstairs. When I went up about nine, he was on top of the covers fully dressed. To keep from waking him, I went to bed in the girl's room. It was early but I was exhausted. I lay there hoping by morning Jake would be okay. *He will be. I'll see to it*, I kept telling myself.

About midnight, Jake got up and went to the bathroom. When I heard him, I went downstairs and fixed him some juice, a light supper and a glass of water.

He was sitting on the side of the bed smoking when I came up. I went around with the tray and quietly sat down by him. He looked at me, then at the tray. "I really don't want that."

"I know, but try to at least drink the juice." He drank about half of it and took a drink of water. I walked over to the closet and got his pajamas.

"Are you going to stay in here?" he asked, as I was turning back the covers.

"Yes."

We slept very little. He napped a little then got up to smoke. About 4:00 a.m., we went downstairs and had oatmeal, orange juice and coffee.

"Man, Honey, when I saw that liquor store after I dropped you off, I went crazy. That was stupid for me to do that."

"Just eat and let's see if we can go back to sleep for a while."

We did go to sleep. I woke first and got ready for church. "Good morning," I said, as I took juice and coffee over to his side of the bed.

"Oh, thank you, Honey."

"You're welcome." *I hope he knows I'll hang in there with him.*
While he was drinking his juice and coffee, I laid out his clothes. "Look," I said, "I polished your shoes."

"You shouldn't have done that."

"I didn't mind." *I never mind doing things for him.*

I could see all the signs of his being desperate to drink. When his mother and brother both called that evening, he turned from the phone after talking to Zach and said, "They're checking on me to see if I'm drinking."

"No, Jake." I tried to reassure, "They aren't calling any more than they always do."

He lit another cigarette and walked around and said, "Man, Honey, I've got to get out of here. I need a drink."

I got our coats and said, "Let's go for a walk down in the south pasture. There's a full moon." We walked about an hour. I told him what an old lady down home said about the moon. "Look at that moon. It would make you willing to hug a fence post." It was so good to hear him laugh. *Thank you, Lord, that he can laugh. Someday I hope he can know real joy that's found only in You.*

I stayed by Jake's side, making sure he didn't drink before Christmas. We picked his children up on the twenty-third and had our Christmas with them on Christmas Eve.

Jake's mother and stepfather came for Christmas lunch. I made turkey pie and we ate at a small table by our Christmas tree. While we were eating I looked over at Jake. *He looks so relaxed. Thank you, Lord. I think we are over the hump.*

1964
WHERE'S MY BOTTLE?

During Easter break we were to have the children, picking them up on Sunday afternoon and keeping them the following week. On Thursday before, I got a call from my aunt saying Grandmother had died. The funeral was to be on Easter Sunday. There was no way we could go.

Jake heard me talking on the phone and after I hung up, he came to me and put his arms around me.

"I'm sorry, Honey. Your grandmother died, didn't she?"

"Yes. I need to call Stan and Anita."

He stepped back and looked at me. "Mel, you haven't seen Stan since you married against his judgment. Why don't you invite them by to spend the night on their way home?"

"Oh, Jake, you're wonderful. I hope he'll say yes."

"He will."

When I called, Stan said he would love to come by for the night.

"Oh, wow," I said as I hung up, "Stan and Anita are coming."

"Mel, come here," Jake said, and pulled me down in his lap. I started to cry. He waited sympathetically and then said, "Stan's little shadow has missed him more than he will ever know. We've got to find a way to get you to that funeral. I heard your mother ask you if you'd come when we were down home and you said you would."

"We can't, Jake. The kids are coming Easter to stay the week for Spring Break. There's no way we can do all that." He didn't say anymore but I got the feeling he was going to try to think of a way to get me home.

We had a nice visit with Stan and Anita. Jake and Stan visited like old friends. On Saturday morning, Stan and Anita left for Mama's as we were leaving for the office. Stan assured me Mama would understand why I wasn't coming.

We were finished with all the patients at the office just before noon. I was at the desk getting ready to lock the drawer when I heard Jake say, "I need to fly down to the Ozarks tomorrow and back here by 6:00 p.m." He hung up the phone and dialed another number. I got up and walked over to him. He held his hand up and signaled for me not to say anything. "Hello there, Karen, Honey. This is your ole daddy. Say, I was to pick you up tomorrow afternoon. We need to make that six-thirty. Mel's grandmother died and we're going to the funeral."

He is the most wonderful man in the whole world.

~

Shortly after Easter, Jake's mother started having a lot of back pain. He and Zach decided since Jake had trained at the Mayo Clinic and knew several of the doctors, she should go there for treatment. Jake would take her then Zach, Lynne and I would go later.

When Jake and his stepfather were boarding the plane with his mother, I got this sick feeling in the pit of my stomach. It was like a dark cloud of dread engulfed me. I remembered his saying when he slipped before Christmas, "If you had been with me, I wouldn't have stopped for a drink."

Somewhere I had heard the saying, "If it is to be, it's up to me." I thought about that as I drove down the interstate toward the farm. *I must get to him soon. His staying sober depends on my being with him.*

Later that evening while Lynne and I were visiting, I said, "Lynne, lately Jake has been having real bad headaches. I'm so worried about what this is doing to him that I can't concentrate. I just hate for him to be up there without me."

"Oh, dear," she sighed.

Now, I've got Lynne worried.

As the evening went by, I tried to get things done but my mind went wild. *Is Jake okay? Will he slip? What is he doing now? I should have gone.*

Finally at 10:00 p.m., the phone rang. It was Jake. His voice was strong as he said his usual "Hello, there!" after a second of silence.

Oh, praise the Lord. He's okay.

Each night he called and he always sounded fine. He was also calling Zach during the day to discuss their mother's care. When the doctors recommended exploratory surgery, Zach, Lynne and I went to Rochester.

By the time the report came back that she had cancer, no one was surprised. Her two doctor-sons were silently standing by her bed, and she said, "Now, we need to just say the word cancer. When you say it a time or two, it doesn't sound so bad."

She is handling this better than any of us.

The day we returned home was our first anniversary. Just before Jake had left with his mother, we had seen in an antique shop a beautiful hanging china oil lamp that had been wired.

"Honey," Jake said as we were nearing the city, "I didn't get you anything for our anniversary. Why don't we go see if that antique chandelier is still for sale?"

"Oh, that would be great, Jake. I haven't even gotten you a card. Let's just buy something for the house and let that be it."

"Maybe we'll start a tradition," he replied.

"That would be great."

That evening we hung our beautiful chandelier over the dining table. It looked just like it belonged in the farmhouse.

The next week Jake's mother was transferred to a hospital in our city. We went to see her on our lunch hour and every evening.

One day I got a call from Dr. Black's wife, Kay, asking me to come to the medical auxiliary meeting for guest day. It was a small group of about twenty women and we met in one of the members' homes. When I arrived, Kay was waiting for me at the door. Jane Timmons came to greet me also. All the ladies were very gracious and we had a lovely lunch.

Kay talked to me about joining the auxiliary. "We install our new president, Jane Timmons, today. She lives out near you."

"Yes, I visited with her at the Christmas party. I'd like very much to join."

I tried to pay attention as the new officers were installed but my mind kept wandering to Jake. He was fine when I got back to the office. *I've sure spent a lot of time worrying*, I thought.

Earlier that year, Stan had made plans to bring Daddy to our place for a visit, and then we'd take him home. Since the plans were made, however, the children's visitation had been changed to that same weekend I was to take Daddy home. The only solution was for Jake to stay home with the kids while I took Daddy home.

Late Sunday morning when Daddy and I left, Jake and the kids were standing in the drive. I could tell he knew I was worried. As I pulled out of the drive, I had a sick feeling. *He'll take the kids home in the truck, go to the hospital and go to get a bottle. Oh, I need to be with him so badly.*

Jewell and Dottie were both scheduled to work all day Monday while I was gone. I got home mid-afternoon and called the office. *I mustn't sound too anxious*, I thought, as I dialed.

Jewell's voice always had an up-beat to it. Her "Doctor Bell's office" was so professional and free of concern.

"Hi, Jewell, I'm back."

"You are? You made good time."

"The folks get up at the crack of dawn, and after all those biscuits and gravy, I didn't need to stop for lunch."

"The chief left about an hour ago."

"He did? Was he going to see his mother?"

"He didn't say. He dictated all the reports. We didn't have any more scheduled patients. He said since Dottie was here for the walk-ins, he'd see us in the morning."

Trying to sound casual, I said, "Maybe I'll have time for a nap before he comes home."

"You probably need one after that long trip."

When I hung up, I dialed the hospital. The private duty nurse that we had for Jake's mom said he hadn't been there. She'd have him call me if he came by.

I hung up the phone with a sinking feeling. *He's drinking, I just know it. I've got to think positively and do as I normally would. He mustn't think I've been worried when he comes home.* I did laundry and checked his clothes to make sure he'd look good for work the next day. Later in the afternoon, I made a meatloaf, just as I would have on any day.

I knew good and well it wasn't just any day. The frantic feeling I had inside was everything but normal. I walked to the kitchen window, pulled back the curtain and looked for the farm truck to come in the drive. Then I looked out the living room window. "Where is he?" I heard myself ask out loud. *Oh, Lord, watch after him and don't let him have a wreck and get killed or kill someone.*

Just before dark, I put dinner away, untouched. There was no way I could eat with the knot in the pit of my stomach. When it became dark, I turned out the light and sat on the steps by the phone at the top of the stairs and close enough to the hall window to see each car light that came down the road. The grandfather clock at the foot of the steps struck nine times just as the phone rang.

It was Lynne. Zach was on call and hadn't gotten home. She was checking to see if I was back from my short trip. I debated if I should tell her that Jake wasn't home, and I decided if something happened, they needed to know. "Oh, dear. Do you want Zach and me to come out and stay until he gets home?"

"No, I don't think that's necessary. He's somewhere in the truck asleep."

"He was doing so well. I'd better get off here in case he tries to call you."

Each time I saw a car light coming down the road toward the house, I prayed it would be Jake. The grandfather clock got louder with each chime and strike, 10:00 ... 10:15 ... 10:30. *Oh my, it's getting late. Where is he? Oh, Lord, let him be okay.*

The lonely moan of a freight train sounded from the back of the farm as the clock struck eleven times. *Will I have to spend the night sitting here waiting? No way can I sleep with him gone. I feel like I'm going to be sick. Is he in a ditch?* Then I saw another light. *It's slowing down.* I heard our dog bark. *That's him!* The truck turned into the drive.

Thank you, Lord, for bringing him home safely. I waited and watched as he finally got out of the truck and started walking unsteadily toward the door. I made it to the kitchen, turning the light on just as he came through the door from the back porch.

Trying his best to look sober, he stopped and looked at me. "Good evening, Honey."

"Good evening."

"I've been drinking," he slurred, without taking his hand from the doorknob.

"I see."

He laughed and closed the door. "Can't fool you now, can I?"

I wasn't laughing. "Would you like something to eat?"

"No, thank you. I'm going to bed."

Hand in hand we started through the dining room. When we got to the living room I guided him over to the recliner and said, "Sit down here for a while, Jake, and then we'll go up."

He staggered a little as he turned to look at me. "I can walk up the steps, don't you worry. I drove home and I can walk up the steps." I stood and listened, wondering how in the world he had gotten home.

He tugged at my hand. "Now you come on, Honey. We're going up those steps." He staggered a little at the bottom of the steps and grabbed the banister. He looked up the steps then looked over at me and said, "Now... I'll tell... you... how to get to the... top. It's one... step... at a... time." He stood there a few seconds. "Here goes." He put a foot on the bottom step and lurched forward. I put my arm around him with my hands holding to both his sides. He swayed some but we finally got to the top of the stairs.

I helped him with his shoes and clothes and sat with him while he smoked. He began to nod and I took his cigarette, put it in the ash tray and said "Here, put your head on the pillow and I'll cover you up." He did as I said. I covered him and turned out the light.

I went to the truck and found a fifth of Jim Beam with maybe two more drinks in it. I poured it out and searched the truck for more bottles but there were none. I went back to the house, turned out the lights and went to bed.

I lay there in the dark with the smell of whiskey coming from the other side of the bed. *How will we get through the day tomorrow? Oh yes, I know, the way we got up here: one step at a time.*

The next morning I got up early, got ready for work and made coffee and orange juice. Then I went upstairs and started getting Jake's clothes together. When he heard me, he sat up on the side of the bed. "It's getting late," he said as he looked at the clock, "I need to hurry."

"Good morning to you, too," I teased.

"Good morning, Honey." He put down his cigarette and looked at me.

"We have an hour. Take a quick shower and dress. I'll go down for your coffee," I said, as I sat down by his side and put my arm around him.

I fixed oatmeal and toast and when I heard the shower door close, I hurried and put it on a tray and set it on the bedside table.

"This room is so small you couldn't cuss a cat without getting hair in your mouth." My country expression put a smile on his face.

"That coffee smells good," he said. We sat down on the side of the bed. I silently drank my coffee while he ate.

"Where's your breakfast?"

"I've had my juice. I'll eat while you shave and finish getting ready. I polished your shoes."

"Oh, you shouldn't have done that again."

"I like doing it. I want you to look spiffy."

"I'm sure you do. How do I smell?"

"Better."

"Man, I couldn't pass up that liquor store."

Just keep quiet, Melissa Ann, and let him talk, I cautioned myself. *I have my job cut out for me to keep him sober. It's almost like I'm on duty. A wife one minute, a nurse the next.*

I inspected him as we drove to the office. *His face is a little flushed but he looks so stylish in that new suit. He has such a wonderful way with people. No one will ever dream the kind of night we've had.*

My twenty-nineth birthday was on a Saturday in late July. We worked until noon and went by the hospital to see Jake's mother. As we headed home, we were both quiet for a little while, and then Jake said, "Honey, I'm sorry we're not going to have time to celebrate your birthday, but I've just got to mow that pasture."

"I'm sorry, too," I teased, "because this is the last year I'm going to be in my twenties. Next year I'll be an old lady." He looked at me, and I knew he believed I really was sorry that we weren't going to celebrate.

When we got back to the farm, Jake changed into his bib overalls while I fixed a quick lunch. We were eating on the back porch when Lynne came to bring my birthday gift. I noticed Jake looked troubled while we visited around the table. *He's really upset about his mother. I'm just glad I can be with him all the time, but at the same time, I'm worried about my father; he is getting worse from emphysema. I wish I could go see him but I don't dare leave Jake. I have to be here to keep him sober.*

"Ladies, if you will excuse me," Jake said, standing, "I need to go mow that pasture."

Lynne and I visited another hour, during which I became more and more anxious. *I need to go check on Jake. Could he be drinking, I wonder? No, I've been with him every minute. He hasn't had a chance to get a bottle.*

I walked Lynne to her car, then fixed Jake some ice water and got in the car to drive to the woods pasture. I saw him in the distance—he was going full speed.

Oh dear, he's drinking. When did he get a bottle? I've got to get the keys and get him off the tractor. I stopped the car and watched. He didn't slow down at the ditch but hurried across it with the mower bouncing. I jumped out of the car and hurried to meet him as he turned the corner of the pasture and started my way.

When we met, he stopped. I climbed up on the tractor with him. He held on to the key.

"Jake, come to the house and take a nap so you can go see your mother tonight."

"I'm... not... going," he slurred while holding onto the key.

He's sober enough to know if he takes his hand off the key I'll grab it. I've got to think of a way to get that key.

"I'll go to the house and clean the kitchen and be back."

"You... don't worry, Honey. I've got... to get this mowed."

"Here, have a drink of ice water before I go."

"No... thank... you," he said, holding onto the key.

I went home and started to clean up from lunch. Then I thought of a way to get the key. It made me feel sick. *I'll do whatever it takes. If I don't get that key he'll have a wreck for sure. I must get down there and make sure that doesn't happen.*

He had definitely been drinking more! He was leaning to one side and going very fast. I was more convinced than ever that I had to get him off the tractor. *The very thought of what I'm about to do makes me ill but I've got to go to any length to get him off that tractor.* I got out of the car and started running toward Jake as fast as I could. He saw me running and stopped the tractor.

Maybe he's drunk enough to forget to hold on to the key. Oh, I hope I can grab it and not have to tell this awful lie. When I got up to the tractor, I was acting frantic. I put my head on his shoulder. *Oh dear, he's holding on to the key.* "Jake, Uncle Harold called. Daddy died about noon."

"Oh no, Honey," he said as his hand came off the key. He put both arms around me. "I'm so... sorry," he slurred.

Just as the words left his mouth, I reached with my right hand that I had in position and grabbed the key. I kept behind him long enough to put the key down the front of my dress, and then off the tractor I climbed.

When he realized what I'd done he said, "Give me back the key, Honey." As he started to get off the tractor, I put my hand to my mouth and took a big gulp, acting as though I had swallowed the key. He looked horrified. "Oh, my, oh! You shouldn't... have done... that, Honey," he said as he got off the tractor.

I ran around to the other side of the tractor, opened up the toolbox and found a half-pint of Jim Beam about three-fourths gone and another full bottle.

He was slightly staggering. "Give me the whiskey, Honey, I mean it," he said as he staggered sideways.

I started walking quickly toward the car. "Come on, let's go home. We'll take Jim Beam with us, Jake."

"You got my booze, Honey? I've got to have it," he slurred.

"You'll get it, Honey. Get in the car. We've got to get you sober so you can see your mother tomorrow."

"I don't like... this, Melissa... Ann."

He must be mad at me. He calls me that only when he wants to make a point; but at least he's getting in the car.

Jake slept in his chair. It was getting late so I called Lynne and said, "Lynne, Jake wants to get the mowing done. Would you tell Mom we'll be there tomorrow early?"

"Sure. We're going tonight."

"We'll go in the morning. Lynne, you and Zach take the boys to church and spend some time together as a family. We'll stay through the lunch hour and visit a long time since the children are out of town." *I did such a good job making that all sound so natural*, I thought, as I hung up the phone.

I walked in the living room. Jake lay back in his recliner in a deep sleep. *The smell of Jim Beam is stifling and his face is so red. He is as drunk as Woody Tom was the night they put him under the store building over twenty years ago. I'm glad I got him off that tractor. He would have wrecked it, for sure. But what I had to do to get him off of it! I need to tell Betty what I just did.*

Betty answered on the second ring. She listened as I told what I had done to get Jake off the tractor. When I finished, I began crying. It seemed almost real. We'd been expecting Dad to die and I knew Jake would believe me. I could tell by Betty's silence that even she was shocked.

"Melissa, the bottle rules Jake's life and you're beginning to let it rule yours."

"Lately, I feel so sinful I can't even pray."

"Now, Melissa, you know prayer is not a part of my life. But it is yours and don't you stop it now."

When we hung up, I knew she was right. I sat down on the window seat by the phone and thought, *I need to go and get down on my knees and give this to the Lord.*

Lord, I feel guilty and burdened down and I just don't feel like I'm worthy of your help. The things such as lying and pouring drinks and avoiding people who mean so much to me have become such a part of my life. I'm so worried about Daddy and Jake's mother. I'm so grateful the kids are out of town and don't have to know that their dad is drinking.

My thoughts were interrupted by the phone. I grabbed it on the first ring. To my relief it was Betty calling back. "Melissa, I just remembered today is your birthday. You're going to make it, Melissa, and I'm going to help you. You said you couldn't pray because you felt sinful. Isn't that the kind of business your God is in? You pray and you'll have a happy birthday."

Wow. She claims she doesn't believe in God.

When we finished talking, I took the phone off the hook and went to bed. In the middle of the night, I heard Jake coming up the steps. He came into the room and turned on the light. I sat up on the side of the bed and said, "Hi."

"Hi, Honey." He sat down by me, put his arm around me and said, "Man, I feel like my skin is crawling, but, Honey, I'm really sorry about your dad."

"Jake, I was desperate to get you off the tractor. I knew if I told you that, you'd take your hand off the key and I could grab it."

"I sure need a drink. I had a full bottle, didn't I?"

"Yes, I saved enough for one drink."

"What did you do with the rest of it?"

"I poured it out."

Somehow we got through the weekend. *Maybe we'll make it*, I thought as I sat at the desk Monday morning.

Dottie was leaving and Jewell was coming in. Jake came in and said, "Cancel all patients for the rest of the week. I'm going to be out of town."

"Yes, sir," replied Jewell.

Oh no, he's planning on drinking. We'll see about that.

On the way to visit Jake's mother at the hospital, I said, "Jake, we need to stay here and take care of the office," knowing good and well he wasn't planning on going out of town.

"We'll do that, but right now I need some time off."

"Where are we going?" Silence. *Oh boy, how am I going to handle this? I know he's going to drink.*

"We'll stay home for a few days."

"And do what?"

He sighed, looked at me, and then looked straight ahead. "I'm not through drinking."

"Honey, tonight's AA. Why don't you go? You haven't been in awhile."

"I'm not going to AA anymore."

"We can't just give up, Jake. Too much is at stake. You'll lose your practice again. Your mother needs you. The kids will be back in town Saturday and will be coming out on Sunday."

"I'll be ready to see them."

"We're almost to the hospital. Why don't you call Dr. Wolfe, and I'll go over to the clinic and get some Delvinol while you visit with Mom? That will get you over the hump."

"No. We're not calling Dr. Wolfe. I'm going to handle this my way. It won't do any good if you call Dr. Wolfe, Mel, and I'll resent it if you do."

The memory of a lady from up north who had brought her husband in the clinic two years earlier flashed in my mind. He was the administrator of a large hospital. As I took their information, she kept saying, "He's going to really resent me for this." I had walked her downstairs about 1:00 a.m. and unlocked the door for her to leave with the people who'd helped her bring her husband to the clinic. "I'm glad he's here for help, but I dread to see him the day he comes back home. He's going to really resent me," she repeated.

I sure don't want Jake to resent me. I'll just ask him not to drink and plan to go to work tomorrow. Maybe he'll listen.

We stayed about an hour with Jake's mother. When we left, Jake said we wouldn't be back for a couple of days.

Instead of going toward the interstate when we got in the car, we went in the direction of town.

"Jake, please don't do this. Let's be here for Mom. You'll always regret it if you're drinking when something happens to her." He kept driving.

I thought about praying, but it seemed out of place. *I'm not sorry I married Jake, but when I've gone against what I think the scripture says and what my pastor advised, I just hate to ask the Lord to get me out of cracks.*

"Jake, please don't do this," I said as he pulled up by a package store. He got out and went in and came back with a paper bag that looked full. *My, he's planning on drinking a lot. He isn't going to stop short of a binge.* He got in the car and started toward home. "I need to stop for groceries, Jake."

"We don't need groceries."

"Oh, but we do. The kids will be back from their trip in a few days and we don't have much in the house to cook." He kept driving.

Nothing matters to these patients but the bottle when they get ready to drink.

When we got home, he went to the basement to work on refinishing some chairs we'd bought at a farm sale. And he got loaded. He had hidden all the liquor and folded the empty paper bag and placed it neatly on the basement steps.

He'll never get up these steps without a banister to hold on to as drunk as he is. I wonder if I could make him a bed in that old bathtub. I could fill it with quilts and pillows and let him sleep there.

Jake had sandpaper in his hand, but could hardly stand, as he slurred, "What... are you doing... with those... pillows?"

"I'm going to make you a bed."

"Don't bother, I'll go... upstairs."

This, I want to see.

After another trip for bedding, I got everything piled high in the claw-foot tub. It looked comfortable enough for anyone. Jake staggered over to the tub and put his arm upon my shoulder.

"I hope you're comfortable in that tub," he said, swaying. Then he started laughing. Up to this point, nothing he did had been funny, but to see him laughing and looking at that tub full of bedding was really funny to me, so I laughed with him.

"Melissa Ann, you sleep in the tub if you want. I'm going to bed." He threw his cigarette on the concrete floor and stepped on it and started staggering toward the steps. Each time he'd raise his foot off the floor to put it on the step he'd almost fall. Finally he sat down on the steps. I sat down by him.

"I can't go, yet. I didn't get my bottle."

"By all means, you must get that."

He staggered across the room. Close to the bathtub on the workbench in a three-pound coffee can that had a few nails in it was a half-pint of Jim Beam. He put it in his overall pocket and started toward the stairs, but staggered, sitting down in the chair he'd been sanding. He reached up to his pocket, got a cigarette from his overalls and lit it. I stood watching and wondering how I could get him in that tub. Soon he was nodding, the cigarette about to burn his fingers.

I got an old ashtray from the workbench and put the cigarette in it. I took his arm and said, "Jake, you're awfully uncomfortable there. Come with me and we'll sit over here where it's softer." I helped him up. He lurched forward and we made it to the bathtub. I sat down on the end and he in the middle. Our feet were dangling in the air but he didn't know the difference. He started nodding again. I got out of the tub and pushed on his shoulders a little and his head rested on the pillows.

"He's out!" I said, triumphantly. "This was easier than I thought it would be." I lifted his feet up and placed his legs on the tub edge and took off his shoes.

I slowly made my way up the steps to bed. All the lights were off so no one would know we were home if they drove by. I'd used the flashlight to go through the house with all that bedding, so I shined it down on the floor just as I had when I had checked the patients in the clinic.

I got ready for bed by flashlight. I lay there a long time and thought of my late Aunt Vergie. *If she were alive, she'd pray for Jake. No, I'd never tell her. Dean and Vonda will pray. I just wish the two couples that we had out for dinner a year ago would have called and invited us to do something with them. They would be a good influence on Jake. He liked them a lot. I don't know what to do next. Oh well, I can't worry about that now. I need to get some sleep. No telling what tomorrow will bring.*

The next day started early. I took my flashlight and went to check on Jake about 4:00 a.m. He had been awake. His bottle was beside him, but he was asleep.

Daylight came and I fed the chickens and the dog. *Now that's done, I won't need to go outside anymore today. I want to lay low and keep out of sight.*

The day went by slowly. I called Joanne. I had confided in her earlier about Jake's drinking problem. I asked if she was going to the store. She said she was, so I told her I needed some juice and bread. "Just knock on the back door three times and I'll know it's you. Jake's still in the basement and I'm not answering the door or the phone."

I went down to the basement to be with Jake. He had slept a long while and was up working on the chairs between drinks. I'd found a bottle in the coal bin and one in the fruit closet. I didn't pour them out because I knew he wasn't about to quit drinking yet. I heard three knocks on the back door and went upstairs. I opened the back door and there stood my beautiful friend with my grocery order.

"Take these. I have something else in the car," she said. I took the groceries into the pantry, set them down and went back to the door. Joanne was carrying a pan with something wrapped in foil on top of it. It sure smelled good. Cornbread! I lifted the lid and saw a big hunk of ham and beans.

"Oh, beans and cornbread," I said, and then just lost it.

Joanne wasn't one for a lot of affection but she was loving and cheerful. "Now, I had no idea you'd hate seeing me that much. You need to dry them tears up or you'll miss your supper. Can't have that." We both laughed.

"I can't stay sad around you, Joanne, but I'm so embarrassed about you seeing us living like this."

That night, I slept very little. The next day, Jake was still in the basement in the same clothes. The smell of Jim Beam was so stifling sometimes I almost gagged. The phone rang off and on all day, and each time, Jake would tell me to answer the phone. I'd go upstairs but wouldn't answer it. At about 4:00 p.m., I was in the kitchen making coffee, thinking how tremendous Jake was when he wasn't drinking. *He's real sweet, even if he is drinking, as long as he has his bottle. He's a tremendous guy.* Just then the phone rang. I didn't answer.

"Answer the phone," Jake hollered from the basement.

I was silent while the phone kept ringing.

"Answer the phone," Jake demanded with a slur. Then I heard him fall on the steps. "Answer... the... phone!"

I hadn't cursed in fourteen years, but I had this urge to call him the worst name I could think of—this guy who was tremendous one minute and such a problem when drinking. The phone seemed to get louder.

"Answer the phone!"

"You... you tremendous son of a bitch, you shut up!" I walked out of the kitchen with "son of a bitch" echoing in my ears. I started up the stairs and sat down on the steps. It was hard to breathe after that awful outburst. I turned around and went back and took the phone off the hook.

Jake made his way up the basement steps with his bottle.

Even though he's drunk, I think my outburst shocked him. Join the crowd, Doctor. It shocked me, too. What's going to happen to us?

I decided to take Jake out of town until he sobered up. I went down to the basement to get the bedding out of the old tub. As I moved the bedding, I heard something rattle. I reached down along the side of the tub and found two full half-pints. I took the bedding and whiskey to the car and put it in the trunk. *If I have to, I'll sleep in the car with him to keep his children from seeing him that way*, I thought as I slammed down the trunk lid hard.

I put the empty bottles in the trash, packed our suitcase and cleaned the kitchen. I looked at the clock. *Joanne will still be up. I'll tell her my plans. She'll feed the dog and chickens while we're gone.*

"Oh, thank you, Lord," I said, the next morning as I turned the car onto the interstate heading out of town with my patient. *If I can get him sober, we can go see about my folks. This is a good excuse to leave town. If I say I'm going to see my ill father, it's not a lie.*

"Don't hit that car," Jake slurred, as I turned at a light. His head was hanging down, but he was trying to look up. I didn't reply and just kept thinking.

Oh, I hope no one sees us before we get out of town. Why am I going down home with him in this shape? I sure don't want anyone seeing him from down there. This is the week that I always went to the family camp when I was a teenager. It will be going on. Oh, how I wish Jake was sober and we could go to that. What wonderful memories I have of being at camp when I was young.

When I looked over at Jake, he was asleep, his head hanging almost to his knees. I kept driving until about noon, then I pulled off on a country road and parked under the big oak tree where we had stopped before. I ate the lunch I had packed, then got a pillow from the trunk and put it in the back seat. I opened the car door on Jake's side and stood there just looking at him, with his head hanging down near the dashboard, the front of his shirt wet from drool. *How pathetic—someone as smart as he is letting himself get in that shape.*

"Jake," I said as I shook him. "Come get in the back seat." He had his bottle in his pocket and took a swig. Tugging lightly on his arm, I said, "Come on, your neck's going to break." He took another swig and put his bottle in his pocket. I put his feet out on the ground and he took hold of the car door, while I helped him to get on his feet. He staggered and almost fell onto the back seat. I put his feet in the car and closed the door.

In late afternoon we were approaching a good-sized town. Jake was awake and drinking in the back seat. I looked through the rearview mirror to check on him and behind us was a police car.

I snapped an order at Jake. "Put your bottle down on the seat. There's a policeman behind us."

"I'm not afraid of him," he slurred, leaning to one side. I turned on a side street to get out of traffic.

"Oh, thank the Lord he didn't turn this way. I'll go down here and take the highway going south. It's a little out of the way, but we won't be seen."

I drove out into the country, but I wasn't sure where I was going. I was just glad I was out of town. Just as the sun was setting in the west, I saw another country road, so I started to turn on it. Then I saw red lights. "Oh, no!"

"What is it?"

"Jake, I'm being stopped. The policeman must have been keeping watch of us."

"I'll take care of him."

I'm sure you will, I thought annoyed. "I'll be right back, Honey." I got my purse and met the officer half-way.

"You drinking out of that bottle, too?" the officer asked, as he approached me.

"No, sir."

"I guess you don't drink at all?"

"That's right, I don't," I said, handing him my driver's license.

"That's what they all say. I've been watching you for thirty minutes and you're not driving too well. I may have to put you both in jail."

Oh well, that would be one way of getting him sober, I thought. "You do what you have to, Officer. My husband is an alcoholic. His children were coming back in town from their grandmother's and I didn't want them to see him in this shape. I thought I'd be able to find a place to park the car and sleep until morning. By then maybe I could get him to eat something and into a motel and start tapering him off."

"Will he agree to that?"

"I think so. He's cooperative most of the time."

"I can lead you to a safe place to park. We watch it all night, but first I need to see how cooperative he is."

I led the way back to our car and opened the back door. I could tell Jake was feeling no pain. The caregiver kicked in and I handled Jake like I would when dealing with patients at Wolfe's.

"Jake, the officer will lead us to a park where we can sleep in the car for the night or he can put us both in jail. Shouldn't we choose going to the park?" I said as I sat down facing him and took his hand.

He tipped his head to one side, looked up at me and said very slowly with a thick tongue and half-closed eyes, "Whatever you say... Darling."

"Okay," I responded, as I got out of the car, "that's what we'll do." I stood and looked at the officer. He was grinning from ear to ear.

The roadside park had a few cars and a truck. Jake slept about six hours. When he woke up, I poured him a small drink in a paper cup and told him he could have another just before breakfast.

It was the usual "Man, I'm desperate" for the rest of the night.

At 6:00 a.m., we walked in the restaurant where several men were eating breakfast. We looked a mess. Our clothes were wrinkled, Jake's clothes were stained with Jim Beam and his face was red and puffy.

We got to the motel mid-morning. Jake was asleep in the back seat, so I unloaded the car, took a quick shower and cleaned up.

When he woke up, he came in with his bottle and got in to bed. I explained that I was going to drive out in the country to see my folks. As I drove by the street that led to the family campgrounds, I saw the sign about family camp with the current week's date on it. *Oh, wow, this is the week of the camp. I thought so. Oh, how I wish I could go and talk to Reverend Good. I know he'd pray with me. I wouldn't want him to know I married an alcoholic, though.*

Mama and Daddy, to my great joy, were sitting under the oak tree in the front yard. I drove up and got out. As I walked around the car, I warned myself, *Be cheerful and say as little about Jake as possible.*

"Where's your old man?"

"Well, he has these terrible headaches and he just isn't feeling well. I left him in a motel in town. He needed out of the heat and into the air-conditioning," I said as we hugged. "We hadn't heard from you, and Jake took a couple of days off, but we're going back early in the morning. We don't expect his mother to live very much longer."

The conversation went to his mother and all the time I was thinking, *He doesn't have a headache. I didn't say he had one right now, I said, "He has these awful headaches," and that's the truth. He does.* I couldn't enjoy visiting with the folks because I felt so guilty.

Daddy was very weak and tired, but he was up and about the yard and could drive to the store. They seemed happy to see me but Mama worried about Jake. She said, "If he was down here, I'd take good care of him."

You'd faint to see him like he is!

I stayed with the folks two hours, so I'd be gone no more than a total of three. I went directly to the motel. When I started to open the door, this terrible feeling of dread came over me. *What would I find after being gone three hours?* Jake was lying on the bed sound asleep.

I hadn't eaten, so I went across the road to the Coney Island restaurant for a foot-long hotdog and milkshake. I remembered going there as a teenager, after camp meeting and youth convention services.

As I backed the car out of Coney Island's parking lot, I felt compelled to turn toward the campground. It wasn't time for evening services but I just had to drive by. I saw the Reverend Good, wearing a hat like always.

Oh, how I wish I could go for the evening service. I wonder if Tom is still leading the singing. If so, he'll sing "Got any Rivers." How I used to love it when we sang that. Now I've got rivers that are uncrossable and mountains I can't tunnel through.

My next stop was to a phone booth to call Zach. I found him at the hospital. His mother was weaker and he didn't think she'd be with us long.

"Is Jake drinking?"

"Yes, but Zach, I can crack down on him and get him home to see your mother."

"I'll leave it to you. Call if you need to."

"Thanks, Zach."

I got into the car, closed my eyes and laid my head back. *I'm so tired. It's going to be a battle getting him sober, but I've got to do it. Zach is so wonderful. He never makes me feel like we are a burden.*

Lord, I need help to get Jake off the bottle. Please help us to get home while Mom still knows us. If I could only go over to camp and ask them to pray, but I wouldn't be able to stand the looks on their faces when I told them I'd married an alcoholic. Well, I can't think of that now. I've got my work cut out for me. I'll start tapering him off tonight. As soon as we get to the city, I'll call Dr. Wolfe for some of the brown medicine.

I went back to the room and lay down on the bed exhausted, but unable to sleep.

It was late when Jake woke up. He lit a cigarette and said, "Mel."

"Yes."

"Where's my bottle?"

"I took it."

"I want it."

I rose up and scooted over to his side of the bed and put my arms around him.

"Jake."

"Where's my bottle?"

"I called Zach to see about your mother. She's still with us, but much weaker. We need to go home and be there for her."

"We'll do that, but where's my bottle?"

"Jake, listen to me just a minute. I'll give you a drink. We need to go on a four-hour schedule and leave for home in the morning. I'll call Dr. Wolfe when we get to the city limits and get some brown medicine so we can go see your mother soon."

He got up and started to the bathroom. "I've got to have a drink now."

"I'll get it and then go get you something to eat."

After a restless night walking the floor and hearing "Man, I'm desperate," we went to eat after showers and Jake's last drink. We started out of town, Jake in the back seat, smoking. I looked back at him through the rearview mirror. He looked so lost. We were so close to help. Reverend Good and all the ministers would have loved to pray with us. After the shock, they would have loved us and helped. I know they would have. I felt so lonely to see those people that were so dear to me during my teenage years.

"Mel, Honey, I need a drink."

"Jake, I've got to get you home sober so you can see your mother. You'll never forgive yourself if you're drinking and can't see her."

"Man, I don't know if I can make it." This went on for two hours.

With agitation in my voice, finally I said, "I'll stop at the next package store and get you one can of beer. Will you agree to shut up if I do that?"

"Oh, thank you, Honey," Jake said, as I came back and handed him the beer.

"Jake, we're going to get help from Dr. Wolfe and you are going to be there for your mother. I don't care what I have to do, I'll go in the store and tell them not to sell it to you or whatever, but you are going to be there and sober for your mother." He looked at me and took his second gulp of beer, but didn't answer.

No one would believe it if I told them how he tolerates my bossing. I think for the moment he knows who's in charge. I looked back at my patient. He was nodding with the beer can in his hand. *How much he needs Christian men to give him some attention and win him to the Lord! Our life would be so wonderful if Jake would give his heart to the Lord!*

We reached the city when traffic was bumper to bumper. I had called Dr. Wolfe and asked that his nurse give the first dose of medication. The trip from the clinic to the farm was a forty-five minute drive, and I wanted him to get to sleep so we could go see his mother.

We got the medication. He was calm while I drove through the traffic. When we got home, he was lying in the back seat asleep. I parked behind the barn in the shade and rolled down the windows. *No one will be stopping to see us. He'll be okay in time to go see his mom.* I went into the house to the sound of the phone. *That may be the kids. I won't answer it. When Jake wakes up he'll be okay to call them and tell them we're back in town.* I got cleaned up and laid clothes out for Jake, including a sports shirt his mother had given him. *I hope she's able to notice. It will make her happy to see him in this shirt.*

It was late when Jake woke up. He called the hospital on my insistence. The nurse said his mother was still awake.

His mother recognized us and asked about my dad. I could tell we didn't have her fooled. We stayed about thirty minutes and told her we'd be back at noon tomorrow. On our way out of the hospital, Jake called the children telling them we'd been to my folks and that we were at the hospital.

We got back to work and visited Jake's mother in the hospital twice each day. About ten days after we returned, Jake's mother died. I had just known her for two years but I missed her a lot. Jake, however, was my main concern. I concentrated on staying close to him.

1965
JAKE'S BEEN HURT

We began to see more of Jane and John Timmons. Jane and I loved to cook, but she was much better than I. She did lots of entertaining.

One day I stayed home from work to get caught up on some extra cleaning. She called and said she was in a bind. Her cleaning lady was supposed to help her get ready for a luncheon, but she caught the flu. She asked if I knew of a housekeeper who could help. "I'm desperate," she said.

"I don't know anyone who can come today, Jane, but I'll come."

"Are you serious?"

"Yes. I'll be right there." *She knows so much about entertaining. I may learn a lot from her today.*

When she came to the door, I could tell she was overloaded and worried that she wouldn't be ready.

I blurted out, "Never fear for Mel is here!"

So many things had gone wrong before her three children had left for school and she was far behind. She had rolls rising and the table set.

"You're doing good, Jane. Your table is beautiful."

"Oh, but Mel, look at this mess."

"As Jake would say, 'That's no hill for a climber!' We'll have this place in shape in no time. Now show me where everything is and you take care of the food." We laughed and talked as we worked, and we had everything done when the first of the twelve ladies rang the doorbell. I ran out the back door as I heard Jane say in her cheerful voice, "Come in."

When the luncheon was over, she called to tell me how it went and said, "The first day you have free to do whatever you'd planned to do instead of helping me, I'll be there to help."

"Jane, will you teach me to make those rolls? I've invited my former supervisor and Dr. Wolfe's secretary this Saturday evening. I always make rolls the way Mama did, but yours looked so good the way you rolled them up. I'd like to learn. Do you call them rolls?"

"No. I call them butter horns. I'll do even better. I'll come and help you fix the entire dinner."

"Oh, wow!"

Friday afternoon after I came home from the office, Jane came over and mixed up the rolls while I watched. I felt comfortable enough to tell her I'd learned most of what I knew about cooking from watching others. I shared about my reading problem and how hard it was to understand directions.

Saturday morning, as Jake and I were getting ready for work, the phone rang. It was Alta, my former supervisor, calling to tell me she and Georgia couldn't come that evening for dinner. Dr. Wolfe had died during the night from a heart attack.

Oh, no! What will we do if things get bad again? was my first thought.

Jake and I were both stunned.

When we got to the office, I called Lynne and invited her and Zach to the dinner meant for my friends from the clinic.

"I'm worried," I told Lynne, as she and I put the finishing touches on dinner. "With Dr. Wolfe gone, what will happen if Jake gets really bad?"

"Melissa, I'm not so sure he helped Jake that much. He'd go over there for treatment and Dr. Wolfe would do anything Jake wanted. Zach went over one day and Jake was sitting at Dr. Wolfe's desk talking on the phone with his feet propped up. Then he'd come out of the clinic and start drinking again."

Monday afternoon we went to Dr. Wolfe's funeral. I saw lots of patients that I'd taken care of at the clinic, some from other states. Dr. Wolfe was their friend. *They are all wondering, as I am, what will we do? Patients could go to his place day or night and get their "brown medicine." Jake can get his own but someone besides me should supervise it.*

⁓

One afternoon in March, I was at home waiting for Jake and the kids to arrive when the phone rang.

"Hello, there!" came his usual enthusiastic greeting.

"Hi, Honey." I sensed something was wrong. The silence was a little longer than usual.

"Mel, I won't be home for dinner. I've stopped at a bar."

"Jake, where are the kids?"

"I called to tell them I'd see them next weekend."

"Jake, listen, come on home."

"Not for a while, Honey. You go ahead and eat. I'm going to be drinking."

"What am I supposed to do with this big casserole I've baked for seven people?"

"Freeze it. We'll eat it next weekend."

"Please, Honey don't do this!" I started to cry. Then I remembered that Dr. Wolfe had told me, "Okay, I can't talk you out of marrying him, but when he starts drinking, don't you cry."

So I stifled my tears and said, "When do I expect you home?"

"I won't be long but I'll be drinking."

"You can't do this, Honey. What about the office tomorrow morning?"

"I'll be there. I've got to go now. Bye, Honey."

"Jake, please don't do this," I said as I heard the phone placed on the hook.

Now what do I do? Then I remembered Reverend Good saying at the family camp when I was a teenager, "The Lord always does us a favor when he brings us to our knees." *How can this be a favor?* I slowly got up from the window seat in the dining room and went in and knelt down by Jake's chair.

"Bring him home safely, Lord, and soon. Make him change his mind and not drink this weekend." As I heard myself asking all these things I wanted the Lord to do, I thought of the verse of scripture I'd heard many times and that Dean quoted when I told him I was going to marry Jake.

He had said, "There's a price to pay, Melissa, when we go against the Lord's will. His will is for all of us, 'not to be unequally yoked together with unbelievers.' The Lord doesn't want his children to be miserable and when his child, Melissa, finds herself yoked up with an alcoholic, she will be miserable."

I had thought I could never be miserable with Jake. Now I understood what Dean was saying. I was miserable wondering if he would wreck, get killed or kill someone else.

"Lord, could you please place Jake on the hearts of the men at the church that they will pray for him and seek him out as a friend?"

I got up, put the casserole in the freezer, ate a sandwich and took a walk out in the pasture.

I hate to talk to Dean after his warnings. Aunt Roxena doesn't have a phone down in the country. I put my arm up on the white board fence and my chin down on my hand. *It's always peaceful out here but not tonight. I feel like something awful is going to happen.* "Lord, take care of him." I turned around and went back inside and called Betty. When I told her that I thought Jake would do a lot better if men who didn't drink (like the men at church) would become his friends, she said, "Oh, Melissa, you don't believe that."

"Yes, Betty, I think that's something he really needs."

"Melissa, you married him regardless of what those people at your church may or may not have thought. Now you're hoping they'll give him enough attention that he won't need to drink; but we all have to live with the choices we make."

"I know. Oh, Betty, he just drove up. Thank the Lord he's off the road."

"Thank you, Lord," I said out loud, as I ran to the steps and looked out the window from the landing. It was dark and all I could see was him sitting in the car. I turned on the back porch light, turned all the others off and got ready for bed. Then I sat in the dark by the window until time for the news. About 3:00 a.m. he came in and went to bed. He had slept in the car all that time.

The next morning I went outside and checked under the seat. I found one half-pint partly gone and a full pint. I poured them out and threw the empty bottles in the trash.

At 8:00 a.m., I had everything laid out for him to wear and took his breakfast tray up for him. "Jake, you need to get up."

"I need to feed the chickens."

"I've done that."

"Oh, aren't you the one."

While he ate, I sat on the bed and looked out the window, thinking about what Betty had said the night before.

We left for the office on time. Jewell didn't come in on Saturday, but Dottie was there and had everything turned on. I walked over to the desk and sat down. That dark cloud of dread completely engulfed me. For a moment it was hard to breathe. *Oh Lord, help me to help him not go get a bottle.*

We had a busy morning and left the office at 12:45 p.m. As we were walking out to the car, I said, "Jake, let's stop for lunch."

"Not now, Honey, you know I'm not going to do that." We got in the car. He reached under the seat. "You found my whiskey."

"Honey, I know you can keep from doing this. Let's do something for the two of us tonight."

"We'll do that another time. Man, I'm desperate; I've got to have a drink."

"No, you don't. You don't have to let that stuff rule you," I said, louder than I intended.

He turned out of the parking lot and instead of going home, he headed for the nearest liquor store.

"I'll lick it someday, Honey, but now I've got to have a drink."

"Let this be the day you start."

"Now, Melissa, you're not going to talk me out of this."

When he went into the liquor store, I thought about just driving off and letting him get home on his own, but I'd be beside myself until he did.

When we got home, we went inside, and he changed into his bib overalls and chore jacket and went to feed the cows. When he was gone about an hour, I went to see about him. He was working on some harnesses in the saddle shed and getting more loaded by the minute. It was almost dark when Jake came through the back door—drunk.

One of his pockets was wet. He looked at me, stuck his hands in his pockets and said, "Look, Darling, I gathered your eggs." Some of the eggs were broken and dripping in his hand.

If it wasn't so pathetic, I'd think it was funny.

I got the good eggs from his jacket and overall pockets. "Stay in the kitchen, Jake, until I go get you some clean clothes."

"I'll go with you."

"No," I said, and led him to the sink and turned the water on his hands. "You stay right here or we'll get egg on the carpet."

"Now we wouldn't want to do that, would we, Darling?" he slurred.

"No, we wouldn't want to do that."

I hurried upstairs and when I came back to the kitchen, he was trying to get broken eggs out of his pocket. Egg was on the sink, the floor, and all over the front of his jacket. He looked up and saw me and staggered backward. "I... just... about... have it... cleaned up."

"I see."

After cleaning up the mess, I decided to go see Betty instead of fighting with Jake all night over the bottle. Betty and Leo seemed glad to see me. They had eaten, but when I came through the door, they started heating up some food for me. As we visited, Leo laughed at the story about the eggs but Betty wasn't amused. "I'm glad you left him on his own. We'll just forget about him and enjoy life."

"Oh, I can't do that, Betty. I worry that he'll burn himself up out there."

"I know you do, Melissa, but we'll all stand by you. Let's don't think of that just now."

We visited until about eleven then she and I made up her son Johnny's bed for me to sleep in. "He's going to be shocked when he sees his bed occupied," I said as we were finishing.

"He'll see your car and he knows when we have company, he sleeps in the other twin bed in Jimmy's room."

The next morning Betty made pancakes. "You know, Melissa, I wish I'd kept you from marrying that man," she said as she brought both of us a plate full.

"Oh, Betty, no one could have kept me from marrying that man."

"Well, I don't know. I kept you from going on a trip."

"Yes, you did."

Betty said, "Melissa, you are loved over here."

Leo added, "Those two rooms were built when you agreed to stay and care for Betty's mother. You'll always have a room here."

"I don't doubt that one minute."

After lunch I called Lynne and told her Jake was drinking and I was at Betty's. "I wonder about just leaving him for the entire weekend. I'm afraid he'll burn himself up."

"Well, he hasn't yet. Zach just talked to him."

"How did he seem?"

"Zach said he could tell he was drinking but he didn't think he was in bad shape. Are you going back home today?"

"I thought it might be good for him to wonder where I am."

"Why don't you come out here for the rest of the day and stay the night if you want? Zach can check on him and see how he is."

"That's good. Thanks, Lynne. I'll come out."

That evening, I went to bed early but slept very little. The darkness reminded me of my circumstances.

Zach and Lynne are so sweet to me and the boys are great, but I don't belong here. I didn't belong at Betty's last night. Wherever I go, I'm out of place. My place is at home. It's hard to put my thoughts into words, but I'll be out of place anywhere from now on except at home with Jake.

Will there ever be a way out of this hole? How will I get Jake sober? What do we tell his kids? Each time he goes on a binge, the practice suffers for a little while. Will he be able to keep his help? Will he be ready to go to the office when I get home, or will he be passed out like on skid row?

I heard sounds in the other rooms. Morning had come. I hurried and got ready for the office, not knowing if I'd go or not.

"Good morning, Melissa," Zach said enthusiastically, as I entered the kitchen. "Have some coffee. Sit down here with us and let's talk things over."

"Lynne, you have him trained really well."

"His mother did that."

"Yes, she did a good job."

"Now, Melissa Ann," Zach said, trying to sound like Jake, "How do we go about getting your husband shaped up?"

"I don't know if he is willing to stop drinking. I can help him get back on his feet, but I don't want to give him the liquid Delvinol on my own. That's not wise. I need a doctor's instructions and to follow them to the letter. I think he'd follow your directions, but I'm not sure. He's driven me crazy before, wanting it early."

Zach went to the phone and dialed our number. "Hello there, Jacob. How are you? Your wife is having coffee with us. When are you going to go to work? Well, why don't I order you some liquid Delvinol? Melissa will help you, if you'll follow directions. Okay, if you're ready for that, then that's what we'll do."

I was at the door with my overnight bag in hand talking with Lynne, when Zach came to the door. "Your husband said to tell you he'll be ready for work when you get there. I'll call the drug store this morning for the Delvinol and you can pick it up at noon."

"Thanks for everything. You two are wonderful." I had my hand on the doorknob and said, "Zach, call him back and scare him. Say, 'Now I'm just not sure how long she's going to put up with not being able to stay at home.'"

"I'll do it."

As I drove away, I thought, *I shouldn't have done that. I just gave him a silly order. I didn't ask either one what they thought. Now that I think about it, it sounds silly.*

Jake was standing at the door waiting when I drove in. He got in the car and said, "Hi, Honey. Boy, I'm glad to see you."

I didn't say anything.

"I know, I know," he said. "You shouldn't have to leave your home. I'll try to lick it."

"You can do it, Jake, if you give your heart to the Lord."

"I know you want that really badly, Honey."

That's the problem. That's what I want, but until he wants it, life will be rough.

When we got home that evening, more than an hour had passed since he could have had his second dose of medication. He was restless. I poured it into the teaspoon that he was holding over the sink.

"Put a little more in that spoon."

"I can't, Jake. It's full now."

"Try."

I tried. "See," I said, "It spilled over."

We're both crazy.

He was resting in his chair when I went to get him for dinner. He got up and came in and said, "Thank you for the 'spill over', Honey." Then he laughed and said, "I'm embarrassed about that." Before we went to bed he said, "Get the brown medicine and I'll have another spill over." By then, since we had had a good evening, I was ready to laugh with him.

Just before school was out, Jake mentioned that he wanted to get a new station wagon so that all seven of us could drive to California and visit his Auntie May and Uncle Bill in Escondido, as well as go to Disneyland.

I was a little worried about making the trip. We would be leaving a lot of garden produce for someone else to harvest and I thought it unwise to spend the money. We wouldn't have much left in savings after the trip and if he started drinking again and missed work, what would we do?

"I want you to be happy about this trip, Mel," Jake said. "Part of the reason I want to go is so you can go somewhere you've never been. There's a meeting in Denver the weekend after the trip. The four younger kids and I will fly back and I'll work a few days. I'll ask Karen to help you drive back to Denver. Then I'll fly to Denver Saturday morning."

Jake had headaches and seemed tense at times. The feeling of dread loomed over our heads and there was so much to do before we left.

We arrived in California in Escondido on Sunday afternoon. We ate a wonderful steak dinner at the Lawrence Welk Restaurant and went swimming in the pool. Since I couldn't swim, I got on the air raft. Jake had gotten out of the water to visit with his aunt and uncle. Karen was encouraging me to learn to swim but I was afraid to try.

Candy said, in fun, "Mel, if we tipped you over, you'd have to swim." No sooner had the words left her mouth, than Jacob tipped the raft and off I went in the water. The next thing I knew, Jake had dived in the pool and was bringing me to safety. The kids were a little frightened, but Jacob had done it without meaning any harm. Jake made sure they knew the seriousness of it. Nonetheless, I stayed out of the pool.

Our visit coincided with the Watts Riot in Los Angeles. We had heard about it on the radio and Auntie Mae and Uncle Bill talked a lot about it.

When we went to our rooms that evening, I said, "Jake, is it safe for us to go to Disneyland? What if we get in the middle of the riot?"

"I talked to Uncle Bill about that. He said if we stay at the Disneyland hotel and then go to the beach, we'll be away from the trouble."

The closer we got to Disneyland, the more we heard on the radio about the riot.

At one point, Jake looked over at me, and I said, "Do you think we should go home?"

The kids in the back said, "Home?"

"No, we'll stay out of the thick of it. Now don't you worry."

Disneyland was fun and eventful. One morning we stopped and were standing together talking about what we would do next.

All of a sudden, Karen said, "Where are Wendy and Neil?"

Jake took charge. "You stay here, Mel, in case they come back."

I watched as they started back the way we came. "Oh, Lord, take care of the kids, that no harm will come to them," I prayed, as I sat down on a bench under a small tree.

Soon I saw them all coming. Jake was in front with Wendy on one side and Neil on the other, both holding on to his belt.

"Oh, thank you, Lord, for that beautiful sight," I said.

That Sunday as we were driving through Los Angeles, the radio announcer said, "Well, folks, except for an occasional sniping, it's just a normal Sunday afternoon."

Jake laughed so hard I thought he should pull over for fear he'd have a wreck. The five kids had the happiest look on their faces seeing their dad laugh so much. That was my best memory of the California trip.

On another day, I dropped Jake and the kids at the beach and then went to the laundromat. I thought I knew where I was to meet them but I went to the wrong place. They had to wait in the sun for over an hour before I found them. Jacob had a very fair complexion and got a bad sunburn. We went on to dinner but Jacob was sick. I couldn't sleep that night for worrying about him. I thought it was my fault that he'd been sunburned. Also, Jake was more uptight and that dark cloud of dread became even stormier.

We left two days later. We were grateful we'd planned for Jake and the four younger kids to fly home, but I worried about Jacob, convinced that Jake would drink while he was home without me.

Oh, I wish I could fly back with him, I thought, as they boarded the plane.

Karen and I watched the plane take off and then headed out of Los Angeles toward Las Vegas to spend the night. I couldn't think of anything or anyone except Jacob and Jake. Will Jacob be okay? Will Jake drink? I prayed he wouldn't but I knew he would.

We got to Provo, Utah, about 8:00 p.m. the next evening. I called Jake and knew by his voice that he was drinking. It was almost impossible to sleep that night, but the next morning when Karen got up, we started toward Denver. We checked into the Brown Hotel a little after dark. When I got a few minutes alone, I called home. Jake had started drinking again after work.

"Jake," I said, "If you're going to drink this weekend, don't bother coming out here. I will not have you coming out here drinking around Karen."

"Oh, I'll be okay, Honey. I'll see you in Denver at 8:00 a.m. and go to the afternoon meeting."

"Okay. You be sober when Karen and I meet you."

It was another night of almost no sleep. I lay awake making a plan for how I'd keep him from Karen if he was drinking. I got up early the next morning, went down to the desk and rented another room just down the hall from the one Karen and I had. I left her a note and told her I'd pick up her dad and we'd be in room 312. Then I went in a cab to the airport to meet Jake. I felt I could manage him better in a cab. When I met him, I could tell he'd been drinking until late the night before. I hugged him as though nothing was wrong.

"Where's Karen?"

"I let her sleep."

"Man, Honey, I've got to have a drink."

"No, Jake! Karen will be waiting and the important thing is that she doesn't know you have been drinking," I said as we got near the outside doors. There was a bar next door.

"I've got to go in here, Honey."

"You do, Jake, and I'll go tell the bartender he's not to sell you one drink," I said, knowing it might not work, but that I'd do it. Through the outside doors I saw a cab leave and another pull up. I took Jake's arm and said, "Here's our cab now."

When we got to our room, Jake said, "Where's Karen?"

"She'll be here soon. Take your shower before she gets here," I said as I started getting clean clothes for him. I could tell he had slept in his clothes the night before.

"I don't want to worry with a bath now, Honey. I really need a drink."

"Jake, you can't let Karen see you like this. Your clothes smell. I can hardly be near you." I started helping him with the buttons on his shirt.

"Okay, Honey, you win, but man I need a drink."

While he showered, I ordered breakfast to be brought to the room and then ran down to Karen's room. She was still asleep. I wrote her another note and told her to order her breakfast. We were going to eat and take a nap. After Jake cleaned up and ate, he felt much better and was able to sleep for a while. When Karen knocked at our door, he was in good shape and ready to go to the afternoon meeting, where his friend Dr. George, from the Mayo Clinic, would be speaking.

Thank the Lord I've kept the drinking from his family once again.

At home Monday morning when Jake woke up, I greeted him with, "Happy Birthday."

"Thank you, Honey."

You'll thank me more in the morning, Doctor, because the only time you're going to be out of my sight is while you're at the office.

I took him to the office and picked some tomatoes when I got home. Then I checked the orchard. We had a bumper crop of apples. *Oh, I mustn't let them ruin. They'll be ready soon. Wouldn't Mama have a hay day in this orchard?*

I took so much pride in getting Jake's birthday dinner. All the time in the back of my mind was, *He'll want to celebrate by drinking. I'll be under the wheel and won't stop. I'll keep him from it.* My elderly friend used to say, *"You can do anything in balance of reason if you want to do it badly enough."* I want to do it badly enough, so I'll keep him off the bottle on his forty-fourth birthday.

I picked him up after work and we started home. He didn't mention stopping for a bottle.

"I baked you a cake and have your favorite meal of smothered steak, mashed potatoes and gravy," I said, looking over at him as we entered rush hour traffic.

He shifted his feet nervously and said, "I'm not hungry, Honey, and I want to work on the mower a while to get ready to mow the north pasture."

"Honey, I can have it ready real soon. I left the potatoes on low. I'll have them mashed while you're changing your clothes."

"No, Honey, I don't want to eat yet."

When we got home, I went in and mashed the potatoes. I had just dished up our food when Jake came downstairs.

"It won't take long to eat dinner, Jake. I have it ready," I said as he came past the table on the back porch. He put his hand on the back door. "What do you think of your cake?"

"Oh, look at that. I'll have some later. I've got to work a little on the mower then hook it up to the tractor and mow a while. Thank you, Honey. You've worked hard, I can tell," he said as he walked out the door to the barn.

I ate my dinner, put the food away, did some laundry and went out to see him. I hadn't taken time to change and still had on a dress. Jake was lying on his back under the tractor. I got down near him and could see that his face was red and could smell his breath. It looked like he was almost finished attaching the mower. I looked to see if the keys were in the tractor; they weren't, so I got up on the seat. When Jake got out from under the tractor, he saw that it was occupied. I could tell he'd drunk a lot during the time he'd been at the barn alone. I saw he had a bottle in his pocket and he was a little unsteady on his feet.

"Jump down, Honey, I've got to get the pasture mowed."

"No, Jake, you're not getting on this tractor drinking."

"Now, Honey," he said, trying to look under control, "get down. I'm going to mow the pasture."

"No, Jake."

He reached up and grabbed my arm and pulled so hard I had to step down, but I held on to the wheel as long as I could. When I got to the ground, I tried to reach in his pocket to get the key. He took a hold of my right arm while I held on to the tractor with the left.

"Now get out of my way, Mel."

"No, Jake, I'm not letting you get on that tractor."

"Melissa Ann, I'm warning you, get out of my way."

He gave a jerk and I turned loose of the tractor. When he released my arm, I landed in the middle of a fresh cow pile. By the time I got up he was on the tractor.

"Well, you go right on and drive the tractor and if you fall off and kill yourself I won't be here to watch it," I yelled, as I stomped toward the back yard. I heard the tractor going toward the north pasture as I turned on the hose and had a bath with my clothes on. I took my clothes off in the kitchen, went upstairs to shower and called Betty.

"Betty," I said, crying on the phone, "I need to come over."

"Melissa, what's wrong?"

I told her everything through my sobs.

"You come on. We'll figure something out."

"Betty, I don't want to take one of your boys' rooms. May I just sleep on the couch?"

"Yes, Melissa, the main thing is you just get here."

I called Jewell and told her I doubted he'd be at the office the next day. I explained that I'd tried to get the tractor keys and to keep him off the tractor. I told her I was going to Betty's and I'd come home the next morning and bring him to the office if he was okay, which I doubted he would be.

In the middle of the night, I heard the phone ring. Jimmy answered it upstairs, and then I heard him come down to his mother's room. Betty came in and sat down by me. A fear gripped me. I knew something was wrong. I thought I couldn't breathe. "Melissa, Jewell called. Jake's been hurt. He fell off the tractor."

I sat up. "How does she know?"

"The police called her when they couldn't find you. The tractor ran into the fence by the road. Someone saw the lights and found Jake under it. He's at the hospital. We'll drive you over."

I went through the motions of getting dressed and hurried to the car while all the time the words "If you fall off and kill yourself, I won't be here to watch it" kept ringing in my ears.

I got in the back seat of Betty and Leo's car. Betty turned around and said, "Melissa, whatever happens, you are not to blame yourself." She knew me so well.

We got to the hospital at 3:00 a.m. Jake was pale and his breathing was labored. I went over and took his hand and said, "Jake, I'm here."

I heard a weak, "I'm glad."

Betty and Leo stayed with me until we met with the doctor, a senior surgery resident. The x-rays showed that almost all of his ribs were broken. Dr. Gentry said he should go to surgery soon; he needed a tracheotomy. He'd be in the hospital at least a month, maybe two.

When we finished talking to the doctor, I wrote down some numbers for Betty to call and suggested that they go on home. They left about 4:00 a.m.

I was able to stay with Jake a little while, and then I went down to the surgery waiting room at 6:00 a.m. Dr. Gentry came in about 7:00. He said the chief of surgery, Dr. Lambeth, would operate soon.

When he left, I put my head in my hands. *What will I do if something happens to him? I can't face being without him. What if they come in and say he died and I'm here by myself?* I heard a footstep at the door. I looked up. It was Dean. I couldn't speak or move. I just looked at him. He sat down across from me and waited silently for me to say something.

"If he doesn't live, Dean, I don't know what I'll do. I know you and Vonda didn't want me to marry him, but even though he has drunk some, I never knew life could be so complete before. Dean, he is the kindest man I've ever known. He is so loving and such a perfect gentleman whether anyone else is around or not."

"Vonda and I both see how happy you are. When Margaret was here on furlough, I told her you were very content being Jake's wife. I think you've been good for him, but I think he's also been good for you. You're not the same. You're much more contented than when you were single. When you and Jake are together, I can tell you're very comfortable with one another."

I was glad Dean could see that.

"I don't know what I'll do if something happens to him."

We were silent and just sat there for a while. Then he opened his Bible to Isaiah 40:10 and started to read. "They that wait upon the Lord shall renew their strength, they shall mount up with wings as eagles, they shall run, and not be weary, and they shall walk and not faint." Then Dean prayed.

I tried to pray too but I couldn't get peace. *How can I ask you for help, Lord? I've strayed so far away from you.*

It seemed like an eternity but finally the surgeon came to the door. Jake had survived the surgery but would need private duty nurses around the clock for a few days.

As he left, I told Dean, "If Zach and Lynne were here, I know things would be taken care of properly. My friend is trying to find them; they are at the lake. They'll be here this afternoon if they get word."

A friend from church, Naomi, worked at the hospital. Dean said he'd go by and tell her that I was there. He'd be back that evening. Naomi came at noon and asked me to go to lunch at the cafeteria. Jake was in the room with his nurse. He looked so bad. I didn't know if I should go but I hadn't eaten anything since the night before. We got on the elevator and went down one floor and stopped. The door opened and standing in front of the door waiting to go up stood Zach and Lynne. "Oh, Zach," I said, and just walked off the elevator. Then I remembered Naomi. I turned around as the door was closing and said, "Tomorrow, Naomi."

Zach and Lynne had cut short their family vacation. I filled them in as we went to Jake's room. I still wasn't sure he'd make it but I knew everything would be done right with Zach there.

I spent most of my time at the hospital. When I did go home, I was trying to take care of the fruit in the orchard. Jake was pleased that we had so many apples and was looking forward to lots of apple pies.

Earlier in the year, Jake had started to go twice a week to a hospital about forty-five minutes away that needed him as a part-time radiologist. Now Jewell had to find someone to cover these shifts, as well as keep things running at the office. Zach helped out a lot. Several nights a week, he would go to Jake's office and read films then go by the hospital and see Jake. Lynne never complained. She was always there when needed in any way. Karen could drive and she and Candy went often.

Jake recovered slowly. I spent many hours by his bedside. I ate at the hospital each day with Naomi. Pastor Dean came often, always when I seemed to need him most. After Jake had been in the hospital about a month, he suggested that I skip seeing him Sunday morning and go to church. I got there in time for the Sunday School class. Everyone seemed glad to see me and asked about Jake. As far as I knew, only Dean and Vonda knew that he was drinking during the accident.

The class was discussing how to give the good news to a lost world. There was a big emphasis on missions since Margaret from our church was in Africa.

Dean had been quiet. He shifted in his chair and said, "Wherever there are people, there's a mission. During the last minister's meeting that was in town, I brought a friend out to see the church. As we were going back to the meeting the friend said, 'Dean, how can you stand this traffic?' I looked at him and it dawned on me that people who need the Lord are in those cars." He looked over at Vonda and seemed to struggle to know what to say next. Then he said, "One of the churches on the east side had a drunk from off the street walk into an adult Sunday School class. They weren't prepared for that. They didn't know what to do to help him." His chin began to quiver as he looked down at the quarterly. Then he looked up and around the circle and with genuine emotions said, "I don't know what to do."

After six weeks, Jake was released from the hospital. That Sunday afternoon, we were in the living room watching TV when the kids drove up. I got up to meet them. As I was going through the dining room, I saw an unopened half-pint Jim Beam bottle hidden under a chair.

He hid that in the buffet when he came back from California. How am I going to keep the kids from seeing that? I grabbed a dishtowel on the way to the door. As soon as everyone was in the living room and out of sight, I reached under the chair with the towel and lifted the bottle out from under the chair and covered it with the dish towel in case someone came in before I could get it out of sight.

I left the kids and their dad in the living room and went to the basement. I started looking in the fruit closet at the foot of the stairs. I pulled out empty jars from the top shelf. There was nothing hidden there. I looked behind the beans and tomatoes. Finally I started looking behind some things I had stored on the bottom shelf. I moved a coffee canister and something rattled. Inside were two half-pints.

I combed the basement, but found no more. I poured all the liquor out and then went to search the bedrooms. The younger kids hadn't seen their daddy since the accident and they were having a good time, so no one wondered what I was doing. I didn't find any more upstairs, but I had this sinking feeling that I hadn't found them all.

It was uncomfortable for Jake to get in and out of the rope bed, so he slept in the recliner. Zach and I had moved a cot down to the living room for me, so our bed was empty. One day Jake went upstairs to shower. I'd laid his clothes on the bed, and when I went up, he was dressed, but he had his hands on the cover up by the pillow.

"Jake, you'd better just rest in the recliner until you heal more."

"Okay. I guess you're right."

Just as we got downstairs, the phone rang. It was Anita. Stan had broken his arm. He'd fallen off a ladder while helping paint their church. He wanted to take advantage of his time off to stop by to see Jake. He'd be in town at 7:00 p.m. I told Jake and then went upstairs to change our sheets so Stan could sleep in our bed. On the bed frame behind the headboard was a half-pint of unopened Jim Beam.

He was planning to lie down here and drink and hope I'd think he was sleeping. Wow, I'm glad Stan didn't see this.

We'd had a man taking care of the stock, but Jake said one Saturday afternoon that he wanted to go out and check on things at the barn. I was doing the dishes and thought, *I'll let him go and then follow him.* I'd searched all the buildings out there, but had a strong feeling he was going to drink.

I waited until he got in the barn lot, then I went around the chicken house just as he was going behind the shed with a shovel. *He's buried it! Oh dear, I didn't out guess him!* I walked up close behind him. He didn't hear me. I knew he'd bend over slowly, so when I saw the Jim Beam bottle come out with a shovel of dirt, I grabbed it.

"Oh, Honey, you've found all my bottles!"

"I doubt that. Now Jake, you're in this shape because you wouldn't listen to me." I opened the bottle and turned it upside down and poured it out.

"Oh, Melissa, I really needed that drink."

"You need to be sober a lot worse."

We went in the house. He sat down in his recliner and was smoking. He was very quiet. I walked through the living room and said, "How are you doing?" He looked straight ahead and said nothing. "Are you mad at me?"

"Yes."

"Well, Jake," I said, standing in front of him, "When I was a kid, my Mama used to say something to me when I got mad that I'm going to say to you. 'You can just scratch your mad place and get glad.'"

As I went up the steps, I remembered again the lady who brought her husband to the clinic and told me, "He'll resent me for doing this."

It took a long time before Jake felt himself again. We slept in the living room for six weeks.

The practice started picking up as soon as Jake started back to the office and the workload at the hospital became heavier as winter progressed. We went to fewer Christmas parties that year and spent a lot of time at home and with John and Jane Timmons. Jane was a great party giver. It was good to be at parties where no one was drinking. Jake and I were at different tables. I could see him talking and laughing with a surgeon whose office was in Jake's building.

How wonderful to see him really enjoying himself among friends who aren't drinking. Maybe he'll desire more times like these.

1966
AND BABY MAKES EIGHT

We were home more in January, February and the first week in March than we'd been for a while. We had lots of snow and cold weather and taking care of the stock was a challenge.

We took advantage of the time to redecorate the downstairs of the farmhouse. We papered the living and dining rooms. I had some of the chairs reupholstered and had new curtain panels made for the windows. I was very pleased with the outcome. The colors were light and everything looked like it belonged in my country home.

When I was called to see if I could have the Medical Auxiliary meeting at my house the coming spring, I chose to have it in May. "I'm ready for the auxiliary gals to come," I told Jake one morning at breakfast. He put his hand on his coffee cup and looked at me.

"It pleases me the way you tie into things."

I looked at him and said, "I'm glad," then I noticed this troubled look on his face. *Oh boy. I need to watch him like a hawk; he's got drinking on the brain.* As I poured him another cup of coffee, I remembered Dr. Wolfe saying that having an alcoholic as a patient and being married to one is altogether different. *Oh well, right now I've got to try to be the faster thinker.*

I stayed home on Saturday mornings to bake and cook for the kids. They always arrived on Sunday anticipating what we would eat. On the third Saturday morning in March, Jake and I parted at the back door, and when I turned around to go back in the kitchen, I had a tight feeling in the pit of my stomach. *Oh, I wish I'd gone to the office with him. I sure hope he's not drinking when he comes home.*

That day I chose to bake the kids' favorite, maple nut cake, and had just finished icing it when I heard the car drive up. Jake was about an hour late and all morning I had worried that he'd be drinking when he came home. I ran to the window and looked as he opened the car door. When he got out, I could see his face was red. He seemed to be making an effort to look sober. I went back into the pantry as though I suspected nothing, playing the games that were becoming more and more a part of my life. *Why don't I get him in this pantry and lock the door and leave him in here to sober up on his own? I'll find his bottle and by dinnertime I can let him out.*

When I heard him walk through the kitchen door, I said "Hi, Honey. Come see the cake I just iced for the kids."

"Well, look at that," he said, trying to sound normal. I didn't look at him; I just picked up a dishcloth and acted like I was going to go to the sink. I walked out of the pantry, closed the door and turned the skeleton key just as the phone rang. It was Joanne.

"What are you doing?"

"I've just locked my husband in the pantry."

"Mel, you let me out of here!" Jake yelled.

"I can hear him," Joanne laughed. "Mel, are you just going to leave him in there?"

"Better than turning him outside with the bottle and letting him get on the tractor."

All of a sudden I heard a noise, then a tearing sound.

"Oh, I think he's going through the window! I thought it was too small." We hung up and I ran outside just as his feet hit the ground. The window wasn't high, but his new brown suit coat was torn beyond repair.

He got in the car and drove out to the barn.

There's no telling how many bottles he has and where he will hide them. It's amazing how he never gets mad at me for doing things like locking him in the pantry.

Later I heard him in the kitchen. When I walked in, he was standing by the refrigerator. When he saw me he said, with his eyes half-closed and his head turned to the side, "Hello, Darling."

"Hello. Would you like to have something to eat?"

He came over and put his arm on my shoulder and said, "No, thank you. Say, Mel, did I ever tell you how wonderful you are?"

"Yes, you've told me."

"Just one thing I need to tell you."

"What's that?"

"You need a bigger pantry window. Oh, excuse me, I mean 'winder.'"

He took his arm off my shoulder and walked into the living room and stretched out in his chair. I called Betty, then called Jane and told them what was going on. I asked Jane if I could come over on Monday morning for prayer.

"You just come on. Would you also like for me to pray right now?"

"I'd love it, Jane."

Finally, I went upstairs and lay on the bed, listening to the grandfather clock chime every fifteen minutes and to the lonely sound of the train as it passed the backside of our property.

It was a long time before I heard a stir downstairs. I went over to the register in the bedroom floor and I heard Jake go into the kitchen. I heard him go over to the far side of the refrigerator. After a while, he turned on the light and I heard him go over to the new cabinet we'd built by the stove and get out a pan. *He's going to fix something to eat. If I go down and help him, I'll set the table and at the same time, try to find his bottle. I think I can go right to it.*

"Need some help?" I asked as I walked through the kitchen door.

"No, thank you. I'm fixing bacon and eggs," he slurred, as he tried to stand while putting a slice of bacon in the iron skillet.

"Well, I can at least set the table," I said as I got the silverware from the drawer.

"Now, that... my Dear... I think you... can handle."

Oh, I can handle that and Jim Beam, too, if I can just get my hands on it.

I walked over and put silverware at the side where I always ate. I looked to the corner of the refrigerator, but didn't see anything. Then I moved to the end of the table where Jake always sat. I looked in the spot where I thought it might be and sure enough the neck of a fifth of Jim Beam bottle was just barely visible. I reached it just as Jake turned around. I headed for the stairs and started taking the cap off of the bottle. Jake was right behind me and he grabbed the tail of my shirt just before I got to the steps. I pulled loose but I didn't think of turning the bottle upside down and pouring it out. Instead, all of a sudden, I turned it up to my lips and drank all the way up the steps. That slowed me down considerably, and he caught me and got the bottle just as I went into the bathroom to vomit.

That was my first and last drink, I thought, as I came out of the bathroom.

I got ready and went to bed. I could hear Jake in the kitchen and I smelled bacon. I hadn't eaten but I couldn't handle anything in my stomach. Jake was passed out in the chair with the bottle by his side when I went down at 2:00 a.m. I walked over by him. I could see from the dining room light that not much would disturb him. I reached down between him and the chair arm, took Jim Beam to the sink and watched as what was left went down the drain.

I had slept so little that night that I decided not to go to church the next morning.

I would never have missed before unless I was working. Now when I miss, I think very little about it. If my former youth group could see me, they'd be disappointed. Oh well, there will be a youth group of five, ages eight to seventeen coming through that back door shortly after noon, I thought as I started fixing chicken for dinner.

Jake got up around 11:00 a.m. "You look a mess, Doctor," I said as he came up the steps.

"Yes, I'm sure I do. You took my bottle."

"Yes, and I'm sure you have more; but if you want to see your kids, you'd better stay off that stuff. If you're going to drink, you call them now and tell them you won't be seeing them. I'm not sitting in this house all afternoon with the phone off the hook."

"I'll clean up and pick them up at the usual time," he said.

"I'll go get you some coffee. What do you want to eat?"

"Nothing. I don't think I could eat just yet. Honey, are you okay? You turned that bottle up and drank all the way up the steps."

"It didn't stay down. I'm fine."

"I'm sorry, Honey, that you got that desperate."

"Stop drinking and I won't get that desperate."

He is the most tender, kind man. He knew I was beside myself.

We had a good time with the kids. Jake was very tired, but he kept up with them.

Monday morning I took Jake to the office, picked up Ulma, dropped her off at my house, then headed to Jane's. *If ever I need to pray, it's after that wild weekend. I can't believe I drank that rotten stuff*, I thought, as I walked in Jane's back door.

We sat down on her couch in the upstairs den. I told her all the happenings of the weekend. I really was expecting her to laugh about my drinking all the way up the steps. To most people it would be funny. To me, it still made me feel sick.

We prayed, and then she looked directly at me and said, "Mel, you have lowered your standards more and more. I see you becoming less and less conscientious."

"I know that Jane, but I don't know how to keep above it all."

Karen graduated in May; she had been an excellent student. That summer Karen worked for Jake and he enjoyed picking her up and taking her home each day.

She'd been working with him about two weeks when I got a call from him one morning. We exchanged a few words then Jake said, "Honey, when Karen got in the car this morning she said, 'Daddy I'd like to move to the farm and live with you and Mel if it's okay with her.' I told her I knew it would be okay with you."

"What time will she come?"

"Her clothes are packed. We'll swing by and get them."

"Tell her I'll be waiting. Oh, Honey, this is wonderful. I can tell in your voice that you're thrilled."

"Yes, Mel, this makes me very happy."

Jake and I loved having Karen with us. She was fun and so sweet and seemed content. We were delighted to have her go with us most everywhere. When Jewell went on vacation, Karen took her job and Candy also helped at the office. Six weeks after Karen moved in with us, Candy said she wanted to come and live with us during her senior year in school. We were equally pleased to have Candy. She moved in mid-July.

It was very lively with two girls around. One morning I needed the car, so I rode with them to the office. As we drove, we discussed the latest styles.

Jake said, "Some of those new styles are ridiculous."

I chimed in. "Most of the new styles aren't so bad, but I wouldn't wear those big sunglasses to a dog fight."

Karen said, "Mel, turn around." I turned to see that both girls had on "those big sunglasses" and were grinning from ear to ear. We all had a great laugh about that.

After dinner one night, Jake and I went out to see our new calves. As we stood with our arms on the white board at the top of the fence we'd put up, I thought, *We've come a long way. This post is about where he buried Jim Beam a year ago.*

Jake interrupted my thoughts: "Honey, I talked to the attorney today about having the support check stopped for Candy now that she's living with us. I told him that you and I talked about asking for Jacob since he was here often last year working on math. I said I'd talk to you tonight to see if you still thought you could do that."

"Yes, we can still do that. I wish we had room to ask for Wendy and Neil."

"I do too, but we'll never get them."

We had all the kids for Karen's last week at the farm before going to college. That Sunday, we had a party for the office staff and families and those who worked in the Radiology department at the hospital. Everyone seemed to have a great time riding horses and riding in our horse-drawn buggy. The kids did a great job helping their Dad with the horses. After the party, a couple of friends dropped by to visit Karen and Candy. While they were visiting, I looked over at Jake who was sitting on the window seat drinking a cup of coffee. He had the most relaxed look on his face as he listened to the teenagers talk.

Could it be possible that he will continue to be this healthy and happy? Oh, I hope so. The past few months, he's been the real Jake.

When school started again, it was just Jake, Candy and me during the week and on Friday night and Sunday, the other kids came.

Candy had to change schools to live with us. I was a little concerned about that, but the worry was short-lived. The second day after school started I was on the phone at the kitchen window when she drove up with a friend. They came in and Candy introduced me to Sandy Bell. Sandy was a very sweet girl and I figured we'd see a lot of her. They sat together in one of their classes. They made a cute pair: Candy and Sandy Bell.

One evening, Jake, Candy and I were in the living room. He was reading the paper. Candy put down the magazine she was reading and stood. "I'm going to go up and study now." At the bottom of the stairs, with her hand on the newel post, she paused and said, "Good night, Daddy; good night, Mel."

She looks so sweet. She's so polite and kind, a real special girl.

Jake said, "Good night, Candy, Honey."

"Good night, Candy. You are very special." She took her hand off the newel post, started up the steps and rolled her eyes. *Maybe she didn't like my saying that. Is that why she rolled her eyes? She had a sweet look on her face. I'm not sure but I think maybe she likes being called special.*

The next night when Candy started up the steps, we went through the usual "Good night, Daddy; good night, Mel" ritual.

I said, "Good night, Candy. We love you. You're special." She looked over at me, her long brown hair in place. Her dark eyes seemed to sparkle. She took her hand slowly off the newel post and turned her head toward the top of the steps, sighed and rolled her eyeballs. She walked a little slower than usual up the steps.

Jake had seen the rolling of the eyes. He looked over and smiled. We both could see Candy was okay with life at the farm.

One beautiful September day, I looked out the upstairs window and saw the calves had gotten out of their pen.

I hurried out to the barn and was trying to herd them back into the pen when the phone rang. I reached inside the barn and picked up the phone just inside the door.

After my "Hello," there was that familiar silence. It was Jake, calling from the hospital where he worked in another town. *Oh dear, what's happening?*

"Honey?"

"Yes, Jake, is something wrong?"

"No, nothing's wrong."

"Why are you calling long distance? The calves are out and I was trying to get them back in," I said as three ran past the barn.

"Mel, there is a baby girl here in the hospital that was left for adoption. She's three days old. She has sandy hair and blue eyes. She looks just like you and I want to bring her home to you. Mel, what do you think?"

"I don't know, Honey, come by on your way back to the office. We'll talk at lunch."

Jake came home at lunchtime, smiling from ear to ear. "Honey, wait 'til you see her. You'll love her. She's a beautiful baby and very healthy. My, she's a dandy! I can't wait for you to see her."

"Jake, I'm not sure we should do this." I said as we were eating lunch.

"Why, Honey? She's a perfect baby." He reached across the corner of the table and took my hand in both of his and said, "Mel, I want us to adopt this baby. I want this baby for you."

"Jake, when the doctor told me I'd never get pregnant, you were more disappointed than I. I married you a little over a month after you'd been drinking for some time. I remembered thinking before we were married that I was going into this with my eyes wide open and I shouldn't bring a baby into our home not knowing if there would be drinking problems. When I learned we couldn't have children, I thought it was probably for the best."

"Mel, I want you to have the privilege of being a mother. Once you see her, Honey, you'll want her as much as I do."

"Number one, we can't bring a new life in our home, Jake, and you all of a sudden start drinking. It isn't right for us to do that to a baby."

"I know you're apprehensive, but I haven't been drinking lately."

It has been five months and he wants this baby so badly. I've never seen a man who loves children like he does.

"Number two, where would we put her?"

"Oh, you'll think of something; you always do. Honey, we've just got to have her."

"Jake, you don't even know you can get her. You don't just go to the hospital and pick out a baby."

"Oh, Honey, I've already seen about that."

"How?"

"When I saw her and found out that Ted delivered her, I called him. I said, 'Ted, what's the circumstance of the baby in the nursery?' He told me a sixteen-year-old had come from school on Friday. She got to the hospital eighteen minutes before she delivered. She said, 'Doctor, I want you to find the best home you can for my baby.' He told me that if I knew someone who wants her, he would see to it that person gets her. I said, 'Ted, I want her myself. I need to talk to Mel about it and I'll get back to you.'"

There's no way of talking him out of this. It sounds like love at first sight.

"Let's think about it, Honey."

"I'll call the attorney as soon as I get caught up at the office."

"Shouldn't we take more time to think about this?"

"I won't have him do anything yet. We'll just find out the steps we need to take."

He stood to go but I couldn't move. He reached down and kissed me and said, "Thank you for that good lunch, Little Mother."

That's the first time anyone has ever called me "Mother." I just never thought of it before. Oh, he always knows how to get me going his way. I would like to see her. Aunt Roxena will be so pleased if we adopt this baby and name her Roxena. What should the middle name be? Roxena Lynne will be perfect. We'll call her Roxie; that will be perfect... But, what if Jake drinks?

I always called Betty when something new came into our lives, but I dialed Jake's sister-in-law, Lynne, first and told her about Jake finding the "perfect" baby girl.

"Oh, that's just wonderful!" She was so excited.

"I'm not sure we should do this, Lynne, but if we do, I've picked out a name. If it's okay with Jake, I want to name her after Aunt Roxena and you."

Shortly after dinner that evening, Jake and I took a walk down to the pond. He had talked to the attorney. It had been decided that we should wait to bring the baby home until after the court hearing about the custody and support of Candy. There wasn't a problem; it just had to be done through the court.

I felt myself getting anxious. "How long will that take?"

"He's going to try to hurry things along. When do you want to see her?"

"Maybe Lynne and I could go while you and Zach are at the meeting tomorrow night."

All I could think of the rest of the evening was the baby. *When will we be able to bring her home? Where will we put her? When do we tell the kids?*

Jake arranged with the hospital for Lynne and me to go see the baby the next evening. The nurse led us into the nursery and picked the tiny bundle up so we could see her.

Oh wow, her daddy was right! She is the perfect baby. Oh, I just thought of him as her daddy. I can't wait to get that baby in my arms.

"May we hold her?" I asked.

"No."

Oh well, I'll hold her soon enough. I've got to have that baby as my very own.

Not knowing how things would turn out, we told only Candy about the baby. The attorney couldn't give us a court date and we were getting very impatient.

One afternoon Jake stopped for lunch on his way back to the office. "We've got to get your baby. She's too long for the basket in the nursery and Pediatrics isn't the place for a healthy baby. She'll catch something. We're not waiting for court any longer. We are going to get her."

"When?"

"As soon as I leave the office. Take me to work then you can stop and get some clothes and things. I'll go get her right after work."

"Oh, I want to go, Jake!"

"Honey, you get things set up for the baby, and when I drive up, I'll present you with your gift of a lifetime."

Sounds like this is very important to him, I thought as we got in the car. *When he first told me about her, I had no idea she'd be so important to me, too.*

We had a quick supper and Jake told Candy that he'd be going to bring the baby home that night. She was very quiet and I wasn't sure how she felt about it.

Jake left and just before I went out the door to my meeting, I heard Candy talking to her friend Sandy. "Daddy's gone to get our new baby!"

Candy and I were both ready for Jake and Roxena Lynne to get home. She'd done her homework and told me, "My friend Sandy is excited about the baby, too." I didn't miss the "too." It was very important to me that all the children would be glad about the baby.

Just then the car horn sounded. I ran out the back door just as Jake stopped. He got out of the car and took me in his arms. "I brought your baby home, Little Mother." He opened the back door, reached in and got the handles of the car bed that I'd bought that afternoon and carried her inside. We all three gathered around. I took her out of the car bed and sat down on the settee to hold her. She was beautiful in her little pink dress and booties. There were no words to describe the moment.

It was so much fun giving her the bottle that evening. I hardly slept before the 2:00 a.m. feeding. I wanted to look at her. We had her in the car bed in our room at the foot of our bed. I'd taken care of babies in the nursery, but nothing compared to this. The next few days were busy and happy, with people coming and going to see the baby. On Friday, the other three children came for dinner and to get acquainted. Everyone seemed pleased.

Sandy came to spend the night with Candy that Friday night after the game. At 2:00 a.m. when Roxie cried, Candy knocked on our door. "Mel," she said, "May Sandy and I feed the baby?"

"Sure, just as soon as I get her changed. Come on in."

"We'd like to do that, too."

"Okay, Roxie, go to your big sister," I said as I handed her to Candy.

We could hear the girls in Candy's room laughing and talking. Jake said, "It's good to hear that. I think Candy is happy with us." That was the first of many Friday nights with Candy and her friend or friends taking over the 2:00 a.m. feeding.

We had the baby home a little over two weeks when Jake heard from Bob, our attorney, that the court date was set for Thursday. Bob had also spoken to the Jake's ex-wife's lawyer about Jacob coming to live with us. He replied, saying maybe we should ask for all of them.

"Do you think that would be a possibility?"

"No, there's no way that's going to happen. I think they may later ask for more child support, but I doubt that even Jacob comes. I'll bring him out evenings to work on math like we did last year."

The day came for Candy's custody hearing. It was to begin at 9:00 a.m. At 9:45, I got a call from Jake.

"Jake is there a delay in court?"

"No, it's over."

"Over? What did they say about Jacob living with us during the school year?"

"We got all the children!"

I was silent, and then said, "The lawyer was serious. When do they move in?"

"This weekend."

"This weekend?" I repeated, with panic in my voice.

"I'll tell you about it when I get home. I'm leaving the courthouse now."

I stared at the phone. *What will I do? How can I make a place for everyone and their clothes? We don't have enough closet and drawer space.* I heard the baby cry and went to get her. We were sitting in the rocker when Jake came home.

He walked into the room and we just looked at one another. He broke the silence by saying, "I got your bread. I told the lawyer you wanted me to stop and get a loaf of bread and he said, 'You'd better get two.'"

We laughed and I said, "What happened?"

"When we got there, the attorneys met with the judge. Bob came to the table and said 'All the kids can come to live with you.'"

"Was this the same judge that you had from the beginning?"

"Yes, same one."

"Were you surprised that he let you have them?"

"No, he didn't care as long as everyone was in agreement. The children's mother had written a letter saying she needed to go back to school. When the alimony runs out in 1973, she'd need to work. The children were needing more help with their homework than she could handle alone."

"Was she there by herself?"

"No, she had a lady friend with her."

"Was she all broken up?"

"Oh, yes, she was very upset. The friend had her arms around her when we left the courtroom."

"I feel sorry for her," I said.

"Yes, I do too," Jake said, "And I worry that this is going to be hard on the kids. I doubt if she told them before she knew for sure. They aren't going to understand. They are not going to want to leave their home and friends at this age."

"How are we going to manage in this house? I've never run a household with that many people."

"It will take some doing. I want you to call Ulma to see if she has any extra days."

"She has Friday free. I'll call her today. Surely a cleaning lady Mondays and Fridays will be enough."

"Get as much help as you need. I'm going to call Sears right now and order you a portable dishwasher."

We also needed to add on to the house. Jake called a contractor and an architect.

On Sunday afternoon, we picked up Jacob, Wendy and Neil. Jake took the farm truck to get their things. We were wall-to-wall. Ulma and I had moved my chest out in the upstairs hall for Wendy's things on Friday. I had put my things in a box.

When we got home, there was room for the boys' clothes in their closet, but we needed to find a place for Wendy's dresses. I had an ironing caddy, so we put it in the hall at the top of the steps and hung her dresses on it.

Candy came home from her friend Sandy's house. She was quiet but pleasant.

When it had been just the three of us, I always washed the dishes after dinner if Candy had homework or needed to do something. When we got up from the table that evening, she was still quiet, but went over to the sink and started filling it with water.

"We have a new portable dishwasher coming tomorrow, Candy," I said as I was cleaning the table. "It's going to be crowded in here but we'll be glad to see it."

Living in a house under construction was an exhausting experience. I was filled with stress from so much to do and the kids having such a hard time adjusting. Practically the only time I ever sat down was when I was holding Roxie. I'd talk to the baby and she'd smile.

The Monday after Thanksgiving, a caseworker came to interview us for Roxena Lynne's adoption. I worried that she might ask if either of us has an alcohol problem.

If she does, they'll take my baby, I thought. I couldn't imagine life without her. *I can't do without her, Lord! Please let us adopt her!"* Then it dawned on me: *The only time I pray is when I need help. It's been such a long time since I've really taken time out to pray.*

Roxena Lynne was crying at the top of her lungs when the caseworker knocked on the front door. I got her seated and ran upstairs to bring Roxie down. Jake came home shortly after the caseworker arrived. He answered most of the questions. She said she'd write up her report and all would be in order when we went to court for the adoption on the 13th of December. As I closed the door after she left, I gave a sigh of relief. She hadn't asked about an alcohol problem.

The attorney picked us up at the house on the morning of the adoption hearing. I had gotten ready before everyone else got up. As I held the baby in my arms and admired how beautiful she was, I prayed, *"Oh Lord, work it out that we can bring her home."*

We started up the courthouse steps. They were a little steep. Jake had one hand on my back and as I looked down at the bundle in my arms, and then beyond her to my feet, I said, "Oh, no!" I was wearing my house shoes. Both men looked at me. "I didn't change my shoes!"

"The judge won't care," the lawyer, said laughing. Then Jake and I laughed.

It was good to come back home that day with a baby who belonged to us. Lynne had met us at court and came home with the baby and me. She sat on the kitchen stool holding her little namesake while I fixed lunch.

"You need a pink sweater and if you don't get one at the shower tomorrow, your Aunt Lynne will buy you one." *I'm sure you will,* I thought, as I put our chicken salads on the dining table. *What a wonderful aunt my little girl has.*

Neil was sick with the flu and was home in bed all day Saturday. He was still feeling bad on Sunday morning. Jake and the other children went to church while Roxie and I stayed with Neil. I knew his fever was going down some, but when I checked on him, he had tears in his eyes.

I sat down on his bed and said, "Neil, would you like to see your mama?" He nodded his head.

"I'll go call her."

"Deborah, this is Mel."

"Oh, Mel, I was just going to call to see how Neil is."

"He's better, but I saw some tears in his eyes and asked if he'd like to see you and he said yes. You're welcome to come."

"Oh, thank you, Mel. When would be a good time?"

"Anytime this afternoon. We'll be through with lunch by 1:00. Candy is coming home after church and if Neil is okay, the nurses wanted us to bring the baby down to the hospital between 2:00 and 3:00. Come when you can, and stay as long as you like."

"I sure appreciate your calling, Mel, thank you."

"You're welcome."

I took some juice up to Neil and told him his mother was coming. He sat up to drink his juice and smiled.

I had always left those kinds of things to Jake, but I felt it necessary to call Neil's mother when I did.

The kids reported a good visit and Neil was still up and feeling better when we returned.

That night I said, "Jake, it did all the kids good to have their mother come."

"Yes, I'm glad you called her."

—

The evening before Karen was to come home for Christmas, the builder came and put rods in our closets to hang our clothes on. We moved our furniture in the bedroom on the sub flooring just after the sheet rock went up. The downstairs bathroom fixtures had been installed the day before. "This is like living in a hotel," I said as we fell into bed exhausted that night.

Jake and the kids met Karen at the train station early the next morning. It was good to have her home. She was able to spend extra time with the kids, which they needed a lot.

We had our usual Christmas Eve dinner with Zach and Lynne and Christmas dinner at Jake's cousins with our large, extended family.

The day after Christmas, Wendy, the baby and I went to my folks to take their Christmas gifts and to pick up ours, which was a side of beef. The folks enjoyed the girls. As it got dark on the second evening of our visit, I wondered if Jake was okay. *Oh, I hope he isn't drinking.* All of a sudden I got the familiar sick feeling in my stomach.

"I think we'll go home in the morning," I announced. Wendy didn't want to go so soon and the folks hated that we had such little time, but they knew with a big family I probably needed to get home.

We got home with a station wagon loaded with beef just before Jake usually came home. He and Candy were sharing the other car and she had gone to pick him up. Karen and the boys were home.

Karen came down to the basement to help me put the meat away. As she handed me a large roast she said, "Mel, Daddy drank while you were gone."

I stood straight and said, "Oh, no."

"Candy got his bottle and said, 'Now Daddy, if Mel were here you wouldn't do this and don't you do this with us.'"

"I'm so sorry. I shouldn't have gone."

"The boys were watching TV, and they didn't know it. He didn't have more than two drinks," she said.

—

When Jake came home with Candy, he seemed happy to see me.

Just two more days until Karen goes back to school, I thought as we gathered around the table in our new family room, *then it's a New Year. I hope it's free of drinking.*

1967
DR. SEARCHBRAINS

On Friday evening in mid-March, Wendy and I were invited to go to a school function with Jane and John Timmons and their daughter, who was Wendy's age.

We came home to find the boys watching TV and Jake asleep in the chair. I went over when no one was watching and got close enough to smell his breath. Sure enough, he had been drinking. I found his bottle and poured it down the drain.

Saturday morning when Jake was ready to go to the office, I was under the wheel to drive him. He got in on the passenger's side and said, "I figured I'd have my police woman on duty this morning."

When I got home, I told Jacob, "I don't want you to worry about your dad drinking last night. I'll see to it that it doesn't continue."

"I didn't know he was drinking."

Oh boy, I blew it that time. "He had one drink, but that's all. He'll be okay." *Who am I trying to convince?*

Jake was restless for a few nights, then he became his old self again.

A few days later, Jake made his coffee as usual and unloaded the dishwasher. Then he went to wake the kids with the "Good Morning" song. I heard him go to Jacob's room the second time and say, "Jacob, I'll not call you again. If you don't get up in time, you'll have to walk."

Oh he won't stick to that; he always calls him over and over.

Jake was pouring a glass of juice when Candy came into the kitchen and announced, "Jacob is still asleep, Daddy."

"That's okay. He's going to get a big part of his life's education this morning."

He'll be gone when Jacob gets up. I'll be the one who has to tell him he's walking.

We ate breakfast and the three kids left for school. Just before Jake left he went to the phone. I heard him talking to the junior high school principal. "Jacob will be late this morning. He's still asleep. He's going to be walking this morning. It's five miles. Expect him about noon. He's to call me when he gets there."

"Now, Honey, don't you fix an extra breakfast. He can eat cereal. You just tell him to call me when he gets up."

It was ten o'clock when Jacob came down ready for school. I was sitting in the family room feeding the baby. "Where is everyone?"

"They are all gone. You're to call your dad."

He made the call, ate some cereal, put on his jacket, smiled and said, "Five miles."

"I don't think your big brother will oversleep again, Roxie." I said after he left.

Every waking minute was busy taking one to music lessons, someone else to ball practice, and the list of things to do was growing by the week. And we still had a lot to do to the house.

Anytime Jake and I sat down for a conversation, someone would call "Dad." One night he answered a call upstairs while we were visiting in the family room. I could hear the laughing and talking and finally after a half-hour of waiting, I just went to bed.

Am I jealous? I don't believe so. I know the kids are starved for his attention and he loves having them call for him to come. I don't know what it is, but with a house full of people, I feel so lonely. Maybe my loneliness is for what I used to have with the Lord.

Before I knew the kids were moving in with us, I had signed up for the auxiliary meeting again for May. Jane and I spent some extra time getting ready for the auxiliary meeting at my house and I decorated the addition, except for our room. Jake took the afternoon off and took the ladies for a horse and buggy ride. They had a great time. It was the largest meeting we'd had since I had started attending.

One morning I woke up and thought, *It's May 21, 1967. Four years ago today, I became Mrs. Jacob Bell. I don't even have a card for Jake. Oh well, I'll take his coffee to him this morning. I've missed doing that,* I thought, as I put two cups of coffee on the tray.

Jake had gotten up while I was in the kitchen and was sitting on the side of the bed smoking. "Happy anniversary, Doctor." I said as I entered the door.

"Well, look here! Thank you, Honey."

It never ceases to amaze me how charming and polite he is.

"You're welcome. Jake, I don't have a card or anything for you," I said as I sat down beside him.

"You're still here, Honey, hanging in there with me."

"I won't be leaving, that's for sure. I don't have time to pack."

We laughed and he put his arm around me and said, "Happy anniversary to you, Little Mother. You've made me the happiest daddy in the country. I don't have a card for you, either. Dinner can be our gift to each another. We've both been a little busy. Do you have a sitter lined up to take care of the children?"

"Yes, you pick her up at 5:30."

He paused, "Oh, okay."

Now why did he hesitate? He and the boys usually do that for me.

"If you can pick up the sitter, Honey, I'm going to have the boys help me outside," he said. "We need to work in the saddle shed and mend the fence behind the barn, and then I'll need to clean up. I've got a big morning at the office. I may not be home before two o'clock."

"I'll pick her up. It's not far," I replied.

"Remember, I don't have a card for you, so don't be giving yourself an extra job by running out to buy one."

Jake got home a little after two p.m. As soon as we ate lunch out under the trees, he went in, changed into his bib overalls and said, "Come on, boys, let's go make lightnin'."

"Oh, do we have to?" was the reply.

Jake came in before five and said, "Shouldn't you pick up your sitter, Honey?"

"I will at 5:30. It just takes five minutes to get there."

"Oh, you need to give yourself more time than that."

"Okay, I'll give myself ten minutes."

"I'll go take my shower now," he said as he started through the family room.

"Mel," Candy said as she came through the kitchen, "Will you go by Macy's and pick me up some of this cologne?" She handed me the paper with it written down. I heard the shower going. "Okay, if I leave now, I can do that. Go get me your daddy's billfold, Honey, I may need more money," I said as I got my purse. "Wendy, you and the baby can go with me and Candy can have time to get ready for her date."

"I'll watch her, Mel, I'd like to stay here," Wendy said.

"Okay." I reached in the billfold Candy handed me, grabbed some money and hurried out the door just as I heard the shower stop. *That was quick,* I thought, as I went around the circle drive.

I was a little late picking up the sitter, but our reservations for dinner weren't until 6:30 p.m. I was ready except for changing my shoes, so I knew we would make it.

When we walked in through the family room door, no one was in there. "Where is everyone?"

"In the living room, Honey."

"Well you're awfully quiet," I said as the sitter and I walked through the French doors into the dining room. When I got to the living room door, I looked toward the staircase where Jake was standing by a marble top table that we'd seen in an antique store nearly two months before.

"Oh!" I yelled, running to him and throwing my arms around him. "That's why you wanted me out of here." I ran my hand over the smooth marble. "I can't believe I have a table this beautiful."

&

On Memorial Day Zach and Lynne and their family came for a Sunday cookout. When we got up to take pictures, I was so tired I could hardly walk. That night I fell into bed. About midnight, I heard something and tried to figure out what it was. Finally, I was awake enough to figure out it was a Beatles song coming from upstairs. I tried to ignore it for about two hours, but finally went upstairs and found Karen sound asleep with the radio filling the farmhouse with Beatles music. *I remember when I was a teenager Mamma saying, "You'll never pay for your raising until you raise your children." I still like Hank Williams better than the Beatles, and for sure, I'm working off my debt.*

The next day, I asked Jake what he thought about us giving everyone a time for the house to be quiet. He said, "I think I can handle that."

Just after dinner he said, "Everyone, try to hold down the noise tonight. Mel's having a hard time sleeping."

After midnight the upstairs was quiet, but about 2:00 a.m. Jake was restless and he got up and sat in the family room. I went in and sat with him. We went back to bed a little after 3:00. At 4:00 the guineas that Jake had gotten a year before started making their early morning noise. As all thirty of them came out of the tree close to our bedroom window, I saw there was no chance of sleep. There was so much to do in the garden. I went out to pick the last of the strawberries just after it was daylight. I loved going to the garden early, but lack of sleep was becoming too frequent.

A few mornings later with the radio going upstairs and very little sleep, I said, "Jake, I'm very tired. I've not slept four hours at night for a long time. You need to give a time for everyone to be quiet at night. That doesn't mean they can't read in their rooms, but when I mention turning off the radio, I'm thought of as the bad guy."

The next morning after Jake left for work, I held Roxena Lynne and wished I could go back to bed. *Everyone will be down soon and I couldn't sleep anyway. I'll call Betty.*

"You come over here, Melissa. You can go upstairs in your old room and I'll take care of the baby."

So I wrote Jake a note saying I had gone to Betty's to rest because I was exhausted. I got some things for Roxie's and left.

When I got to Betty's, she took the baby and played with her. I lay on her couch and worried that I didn't know how to raise a family. In the back of my mind ran the memory of something Grandpa Fred had said when the children first moved to the farm: "Those kids were sent out there to break up your home, and don't you let that happen."

"All my wedding presents are being ruined," I said to Betty. "My nice white tea towels that an elderly friend hand embroidered for me are all dingy. I wouldn't dare hang them on the line for someone to see."

"Melissa, that just happens in a large family. It has nothing to do with anyone."

"What am I going to do? Just let everything go to pot?"

"You need to find a counselor to help you sort it all out so both you and the kids will know how to communicate."

"Betty, everyone will think something's wrong with me if I do that."

"Oh, heavens, Melissa, we'd all get a counselor if we could afford it."

After resting, I was sitting alone in the living room. The drapes were open and I saw Jake drive up. He looked so healthy and good. I met him at the door. He kissed me and said, "Hi, Baby."

"Hi," I said, just looking at him. We went over and sat down on the couch.

"Honey, I'm sorry you got so tired. I think you're letting things worry you too much."

"Jake, we don't have a time for the house to be quiet. We don't have a time for breakfast to be over. If I make a suggestion, it's ignored. I had to get away."

"Now, Mel, you're taking everything personal."

I just looked at him. "Well, at least I had a day off."

"Let's go in and visit with Betty and Leo for a while then get our baby and go home."

"Did you think I wasn't coming?"

"No, I knew you'd be home. I just didn't know when and I don't want you to leave me for seventeen minutes."

After a few more days with very little sleep, I was going from the laundry room with four of Jake's freshly ironed white shirts on hangers, when all of a sudden my stomach started churning and I got sick. I tried to protect the shirts, but I vomited on them, the floor, all over the toilet and myself. When I took the shirts back in the laundry room to re-wash and iron, I sat down on the floor so exhausted I could hardly move. *I haven't felt sick until a few minutes ago; I don't know what's happening. I try to tell Jake I can't sleep with so much noise. Maybe if I had something to help me sleep. I'll call Zach and see what he says.*

"Zach," I said, "I hate to bother you, but Jake isn't hearing me when I tell him how I'm feeling. I'm exhausted; I vomited just a few minutes ago. I don't think I can go on like this much longer."

"Do you think you can drive to my office?"

"Yes, I think so."

"If you don't feel like it, ask one of the girls to drive you over."

"Okay, I'll see you soon."

I got Roxie from her playpen and asked Karen if she'd take care of her while I was gone.

"Sure," she said, and reached out her arms and said, "Come here, Teebs," her pet name for her little sister.

The office manager asked me to wait in Zach's office. In about ten minutes he came in, sat down in his chair, took off his glasses, rolled his chair closer and said, "Well, now Melodious," his nickname for me, "tell me your problem."

I started crying and told him, "There is no place to sleep in that house with all the noise, and I'm so worried that I'm not doing a good job with the kids. I feel like they wish I wasn't there and sometimes I wish I wasn't." I stopped to wipe my eyes then continued, "Zach, for about two weeks I've been so tired, it's an effort to do anything. Then this morning, I got sick to my stomach." Zach listened and said, "Why don't I put you in the hospital for a few days and see if something is wrong? In the meantime, you can get some rest."

It sounded like a life line to me. The only thing I could think of was putting my head on a pillow in a quiet room.

When I agreed, Zach picked up the phone and dialed Jake.

"Hello there, Jakey," he said, in his upbeat voice. "Jake, your wife is here. She's exhausted and has been vomiting. I think we need to put her in the hospital." Before hanging up, he handed the phone to me.

"Honey, I'm sorry you're feeling badly. I'll call Karen and ask her to take you over to the hospital. She'll take care of everyone for you. I'll be over to see you at noon."

While in the hospital, I was so distraught. I worried about my mistakes with the children and wondered if I could raise them. I worried Jake would drink while I was gone. I felt so guilty for leaving my baby.

The medication didn't put me to sleep.

Jake came each day at noon and in the evening.

When he and Karen came to see me on his day off, he was restless and I could tell he'd been drinking the night before.

I was a basket case when Betty came to see me the next day.

"Betty, I'm so worried about everything. I'm afraid I'm losing my mind."

"Melissa, we all wonder that sometimes, but there's help for you."

"How am I going to get it?"

"Well, Melissa, I know you worry about getting a counselor, but you don't need to. A lot of people have them. I wish I could go. Your brother-in-law would get you the best if you'd ask him to. Just think, Melissa, you could talk to someone every week and the first thing you know, things will clear up. You'd start believing in yourself. And I want to see you get help with your reading problem. Seeing someone and sorting things out will open up a whole new world for you."

I started crying and said, "What will people think of me if I go to a head shrinker?"

She reached for my hand and said, "Oh, Melissa, people are so caught up in their own problems, they don't worry what you or I are doing. Who knows, you may get so much help you'd go to college. I'm going back in the fall to get a master's in psychology."

"I'll just wait until you're finished and come to you."

When time came for Jake and Zach to come see me, I heard them talking softly outside my door.

I wish they'd come on in and tell me I need a psychiatrist and get it over with.

Finally Jake and Zach came in. They both had a look of dread on their faces as they came near my bed. Zach got to the point, but I could tell he was dreading what he had to say. "It's time to call in another doctor. There's a doctor out near you. His name is Ira Smith; he's a psychiatrist."

In spite of how uncomfortable we all were, the sense of humor I inherited from my dad surfaced and I said, "Zach, do you think I'm nuts?"

"Oh no, no, no, I don't think that."

Jake chimed in as he took my hand and said, "You'll really like him, Honey. He's down to earth and real practical."

"When do I see him?" I was relieved.

"I'll call him today," Zach said.

No time was wasted. Dr. Smith could come that evening. I was standing at the window and saw him get out of his car. My room was at the far end of the hall. I waited until I heard footsteps, then I sat in a chair pretending to read a magazine. He stopped at the opened door. I looked up and Dr. Smith was looking at the room number, so I stood.

"Mrs. Bell?"

"Hi Dr. Smith," I said, walking toward him to shake his hand. "I'm Melissa Bell. I know your wife, Jean."

"Oh, do you now?" he said, in his British accent. "I know your husband Jake."

We sat down and talked casually about when I'd met Jean. Her first auxiliary meeting, when they moved to the city, was at my house and I'd heard him speak at one of our meetings. He'd been in the medical society with Jake since starting his practice. He took a pad out of his pocket and reached for a pen. He asked me when I married Jake and if I had children and wrote down their names. "Where did you and Jake meet?"

Oh wow, it's now or never. "At the former Wolfe's clinic here in the city. I was working there. It was a private hospital for alcoholism. Jake is an alcoholic."

"Oh, I didn't know that." *I thought everyone knew.*

He made a short note on his pad.

"Are you afraid he'll drink while you're not there with him?"

"He hasn't been on a binge since a year ago last March. He drank a little two days after Christmas and had about two drinks in March of this year. He's been doing well." *I should have just said, "Yes, Doctor, I'm scared to death that he'll drink. When he was here today, I thought he had been drinking during the night." My, how hard I have to work not to lie.*

"Tell me about yourself. Your brother-in-law tells me you are exhausted and have been vomiting."

"Yes, I can't sleep and medication doesn't help."

"Yes, I understand that."

"Doctor, I seldom feel very sick, but I just vomit."

"Well, you know, we vomit sometimes when we have more than we can stomach."

He asked about my schedule. I told him I had a cleaning lady twice a week. She had been on a month's vacation. He asked if Karen was working. I told him she hadn't found a job yet. He suggested we pay her to run the house for the summer instead of getting a job and for me to take the summer off and not have any regular responsibility. We'd start with my getting rest, time alone and time with the baby. He wanted to see me at 9:00 a.m. each Tuesday.

Jake and Jacob picked me up at the hospital on Saturday morning. We drove to the car dealer where Jake had picked out a new Delta Eighty-Eight for me. The Oldsmobile was beautiful, but I didn't think we should spend the money. It was so soon after adding on to the house. Jake won and I drove the two-tone gold car home. The kids knew we'd be bringing home my new car and ran out to meet us. Karen had dressed Roxie up in a little yellow dress that one of the ladies from the auxiliary had given her. Her little bare feet looked so cute as her sister stood there holding her.

＊

Karen agreed to continue taking care of the family. She was good with the kids and it was beautiful how she accepted the baby. The following Monday, we were in the kitchen and had been talking about the young man, Phillip, she'd written us about while she was away at school. There was a lull in the conversation, and then she looked at me and said, "Mel, Daddy drank while you were gone. It happened Wednesday night before his day off on Thursday. We kids were all asleep when a storm came. We heard a crash. The branches of the big oak tree out front had blown down and the hit the porch roof. The cows were out in the yard because another tree had fallen on the yard fence."

"Who got them in?"

"We did. Jacob went to get Daddy, but he was gone. It took two hours to get the cows back in. We had to put them in the barn lot because the fence was down."

"When did your dad get home?"

"Shortly after we went back to bed, I didn't look at the clock. Then he came up about 7:00 a.m., saying 'This is lightnin' makin' day.' The kids didn't move so he got a little stern. Daddy went back downstairs and Jacob came into my room and asked if Daddy had been drinking last night. I told him yes and to go back to bed, I'd handle it.

"Mel, the kids were worn out after being up for so long chasing those cows."

"I shouldn't have been gone."

"You had to, Mel. You were exhausted. I came downstairs and told Daddy that I sent Jacob back to bed. I told him we were chasing cows while he was gone and that the cows could stay in the barnyard a while longer so the kids could get some rest. Daddy said, 'Okay, Karen, Honey, you know best.'"

"Your dad has a problem and messes up, but is always kind about things like that. He saw you were right and accepted it. I'm so glad you're home, Karen."

As I was driving to my Tuesday morning appointment with Dr. Smith, I practiced telling him Jake had slipped while I was in the hospital. *Oh, I hope I don't make Jake look bad. I also hope I don't run in to anyone I know. Oh well, if I do, they'll probably wish they hadn't run in to me in the psychiatrist's office either!*

Dr. Smith came to the waiting room himself to get me and chatted all the way down the hall. He motioned for me to be seated in a very comfortable chair and pulled up a chair in front of me. He was Jake's age, but said, "Well, young lady, how are you doing?"

I forgot the speech I'd practiced on the way to his office and blurted out, "Jake drank on Wednesday night while I was gone. The kids were up chasing cows half the night. I worry that I put pressure on him by going to the hospital. He knows the kids don't want to respond to me. Karen will take care of them and the house this summer. I'll need to help her some, but she'll do most of the running and dealing with them. She's very good with them, and she and Candy don't resent me or at least if they do, I can't tell it. I'm sorry; I'll stop talking so you can say something."

"That's all right; these are things I needed to know."

At the end of the session Dr. Smith said, "Melissa, I know a retired social worker. I think she would be willing to work with you. She'd spend time with you and the children to help you know how to deal with their emotions and understand what they are going through. You have a big job with a family that large. She's a very nice lady. She knows about stepfamilies and children of all ages in a situation like you have."

I could hardly wait to tell Jake.

That evening after dinner we were in the back yard with Roxena Lynne. He laid his paper down and said, "Well how did you and Ira get along this morning?"

"Oh, Jake, he has a lady who will come here and work with me in learning what's going on with the kids and how to make it easier to manage a large household. She's a retired social worker, but he thinks she'd be willing to do it."

"Honey, we are not having any social worker coming in here to show you how to do anything. I want you to raise my kids. You're doing just fine."

"I really need some help, Jake."

"You can get more help in the house anytime you need it, but we'll have no social worker helping us."

When I told Dr. Smith, he suggested that instead, we try a family meeting with him.

We went, but I got the impression that the three younger kids thought I was responsible for all their problems.

When we got home, Jake said, "You go right ahead and see Ira each week, but we don't need to all go in there for you to go through that. It's going to take some time, but the kids will accept you as their stepmother."

I continued to see Dr. Smith alone.

The noise upstairs lasted late into the night, and yet I was always awake before 5:00 a.m. When I went to see Dr. Smith, I was exhausted and feeling like I never got any time with Jake. I was tired and discouraged.

"Well, my friend," he said as he pulled his chair up and sat down, "Tell me why you look so tired."

"I didn't know it was that obvious, but there is no sleep in that house. One of the problems is my waking so early. I've gotten up early all my life. The morning is my best time of the day. If I slept until eight o'clock each morning, I'd get enough rest, but that's not me."

"Are you able to get to bed early like we talked about?"

"Yes, I go on to bed, but I can't sleep until it's quiet and so many nights, Jake gets up with a headache or gets up because he's restless and can't sleep. I always get up with him. Sometimes we go outside and sit in the lawn chairs. It's very important that I do those things with Jake. Has been since we first married."

"Tell me what happened that you couldn't sleep last night."

"I went to bed. Jake was upstairs joking and playing around with the kids. I could hear them. They were really having a good time, but I thought it was a little late."

"Did you wish he was down playing with you instead?"

"Doctor, there's never time in that house for privacy or rest. Last night for the longest time, I heard the Beatles singing, if you want to call it that."

"Does that happen a lot?"

"Every night."

"How would you like it to be?"

"I'd like the noise to stop at 10:30 and all to be quiet. The main thing, I just want us all to have the proper amount of rest and eat breakfast together and have everything run smoothly. Jake needs a lot of rest also. Doctor, I'm not sorry we have the kids. I'd fight to keep them if I had to. I just want everyone to do what they should so we can keep their dad sober."

It was time to go, but I wasn't finished talking. I needed to talk to Betty.

"Betty," I yelled at her back door.

She came running. "Oh, Melissa, I bet you've been to your head shrinker, haven't you?"

"My head isn't shrunk, Betty, it's about to explode. That man searches my brain each time I go in there. Maybe I ought to call him Dr. Searchbrains."

I told Betty about what I'd said about wanting the kids just to do everything they should to keep their dad sober.

"Melissa, they've got to be kids. You've got it backwards. Jake needs to stay sober so the two of you can guide them to do what they should."

"Oh wow, Betty. How am I ever going to get through this?"

"I don't know, but we'll think of something."

When I left, she walked me to the door and said, "Come back, Melissa. I miss you popping in like you used to."

"I will sometimes when I go to see Dr. Smith, I mean, Dr. Searchbrains."

We laughed, and she said, "You'll make it, Melissa."

⁓

Karen and Candy went off to college, the kids started back to school, and Roxena Lynne turned one year old. With Karen gone I couldn't go with Jake everywhere and instead started sending the kids with him more and more.

One Sunday afternoon, Dean and his four children came home with us from church. His younger children stayed with us while he took the older boys somewhere. Later Candy arrived with a boyfriend, Greg.

"Daddy, Greg needs to go back to his college, so I need a ride back to mine."

"Well, let's go," Jake said, closing the door to the saddle shed.

"Jacob, you go with him," I hurried to say.

"Why?" he asked.

"Because I said so."

Everyone looked at Jake and me, and then Jake said, "Honey, that won't be necessary." He paused then said, "Come on, Jacob, it's not far, and we'll be back soon."

An hour later, all the other kids and I were walking back from the pond when we saw a car driving slowly. It was the daughter of a patient I'd had before working at the clinic. I was so glad to see her. She followed us to the house and her three boys fit right in with the other kids. While everyone was getting acquainted, my thoughts were with Jake. *Oh I'm glad I sent Jacob. I had to do that. What if Jake came in here loaded while these kids are here?*

We heard the horn in the drive. I was relieved to introduce a healthy and handsome Jake to my old friends.

On my next visit to Dr. Smith, I told him about my trip to Betty's and his new name.

He looked pleased, leaned forward and said, "Tell Dr. Searchbrains more of what you and Betty talked about and why you have that worried look on your face."

So I told him what Betty said about me having it backwards, and about it being mine and Jake's responsibility to guide the kids. I told him I knew I was unfair to order Jacob to go with his dad, but I had to have the kids' help to keep their dad sober. I talked the whole fifty minutes. I told him of how when I crossed one child the other two got quiet. I was trying to figure out how not to cross them, but the only way to do that would be to leave the TV on all the time and never say anything to them. As he opened the door for me to go, I said, "Doctor, I wish I could get the social worker."

He replied, "I do, too, Mel, but you and I will work together."

Jane and I planned to bake for Christmas. Jane had taught me how to make the perfect pie crust and each time we were together we would always pray before we parted.

We were going to meet at my house one day to make pecan pies. We counted how many we needed for her parties, family dinners for the holiday and for mine.

The evening before she was to come, I had all the work I needed to do the next day on my mind and couldn't get to sleep. So, about midnight, I got up and went in to start my work. I loaded the washer and had intended to make pie crust, unload the dishwasher, put the second load of wash in and go back to bed. But after making pie crust, cleaning the kitchen and loading the washer, I still wasn't sleepy. So I got out my Christmas cards and wrote notes while the clothes were drying, then I reloaded the machine and folded the clothes. I went back to bed, but kept thinking how much I had to do before the girls came home for Christmas. I got back up and finished the laundry and worked on more Christmas cards.

When the family got up the next morning, the laundry was all done, the Christmas cards completed, after a lot of mistakes, and breakfast was ready.

Jane is to come at 8:30. We'll bake the pies and I'll go to bed when the baby goes to sleep at 1:00 p.m.

Jane called at 8:30 and said she'd be late. She needed to make a stop. I said, "Take your time." I was thinking she'd be thirty minutes to an hour, so I rolled out pie crust for her pies and mine, made some of the filling and put some pies in the oven and the rest of the pans with crust in them out on the table on the back porch and covered them with a towel. I looked at the clock. It was after 10:00. I bathed the baby and started looking out the window like I often did if Jake was late. Noon came. I was very worried. I tried to get Jane at home. I called John's office and he said when he talked to her, she was going to come to my place. He didn't seem concerned, so I waited a while longer. I put the baby down for a nap, baked all the pies I had filling for and became more and more worried. I just knew she'd had a wreck. Finally, at 2:00 p.m., she drove up. I met her at the door and burst into tears and told her how worried I was and how I hadn't slept.

"You said for me to take my time and I found more and more things I needed to go do, but I have a suggestion."

"Well, don't suggest prayer, for I'm not in the mood!"

"No," she said in her soft tone, "I was going to suggest you go upstairs and sleep and I'll finish and take care of the baby and the kids when they get here. My cleaning lady will be at my house for my children."

Jane was a friend indeed.

—

When the girls came home for Christmas, the house was busy almost around the clock. Between their going to bed late and my getting up early, the lights were out what seemed like a very short while each night.

Karen talked a lot about her friend Phillip. When she mentioned his name, I saw an extra sparkle in her eye. She was doing really well in school and we hoped she would not get too serious about Phillip.

Our usual family dinner at Zach and Lynne's on Christmas Eve was always a joy. Lynne knew how to make everything so festive. Before we left home, I made homemade cookies in case we wanted a snack before going to bed. Lynne had ordered her desserts from a bakery. They were beautiful and very tasty, but as we were riding home, I thought, *I liked Lynne's dessert, but I bet the kids will like the homemade cookies the best.*

The thought had just crossed my mind when Jacob said, "Why can't we have dessert like Aunt Lynne serves once in a while. Why do we always have homemade stuff?" The next time I talked to Lynne we had a good laugh about that.

Karen left on the train to go back to school on New Year's Eve. We had gone the whole year without a drinking binge.

1968
I WILL NOT LIVE WITH DRUGS

Zach, Lynne, Jake and I started going to dinner or doing something special once a month. It was always so good to be with them. One night we'd been in the city. As we were nearing home, Jake suggested we stop to get a cup of coffee and a piece of pie. We stopped at a place we hadn't been to before and sat down in a booth. We were all in a fun mood as we decided what we wanted. Jake and Lynne got pie, Zach ordered a sandwich and I ordered a salad.

When the waitress brought our food, we picked up our forks as she was refilling the coffee cups. I started to eat my salad when I noticed a white worm curled up on top. I handed the salad to the waitress and said, "The salad has a worm on it."

She took the salad from my hand, and looking from it to me, said very calmly, "Do you want me to take the worm off, or do you want me to get you another salad?" Across the table, Zach's eyes were about to pop out of his head.

"I'll just have coffee," I said with real effort. As soon as she left we could hold our laughter no longer. We were more careful where we stopped to eat after that.

In late March, Karen called.

"Hi, Mel. May I please speak to Daddy?"

"Hi, Karen. I'll get him."

That was different. She always talks to me a little when she calls. What is going on between her and Phillip? I thought, as Jake took the call.

I heard him say, "Well, Honey, this is not the end of the world. We'll stand by you. Where are you? How about school? Karen, I'll talk it over with Mel, but your 'Ole Daddy' wants to come to see you."

When he hung up he said, "Karen was calling from Phillip's parents. They've both left school. She's pregnant. We need to go see about her."

"When do you want to go?"

"Since I take Thursday off anyway, I'll call the travel agency to see if we can leave late Wednesday afternoon and come back early Friday morning."

I called my cousin and arranged for her to come and stay with the kids. On Wednesday, Jake picked me up after work and we hurried to the airport through heavy traffic.

We were in the air and the flight attendants started coming toward us with the cart loaded with drinks. Jake said, "Honey, I really need a drink."

I lay my hand on his and looked at him. "Jake, you have to be strong. We must forget about ourselves. You've got to be rested when we meet Phillip and his parents."

"You're right, but man I'm desperate."

What's it going to be like getting him home Friday morning? Lord I can't do this alone. Oh, I hate that I just call on the Lord in a crack anymore.

"Would you like a drink, ma'am?"

"I'll have a Coke, please." *Why didn't I say we'd both have coke?*

"You, sir?"

"Coke, please," he said, very softly as though he was afraid to say anything.

We arrived in Tucson that night late, rented a car, and went to our hotel. We were up early drinking coffee in the dining room. When we got into the little town where Phillip's folks lived, we stopped and called for directions to their place. The mother sounded very friendly and said they'd be waiting. As we approached the house, we saw Karen and a good-looking guy, with auburn hair, waiting for us by the street. They were holding hands and both had smiles on their faces. Phillip's mother was very gracious and we could tell she liked Karen very much.

Karen and Phillip let us know they wanted to be married. Phillip would work a while and go back to school in the fall. As we discussed their plans, Jake offered our help. They just wanted a simple wedding, but Karen wanted us to bring the family.

We invited them to go to lunch, but Phillip's mother declined the invitation so she could prepare dinner for us. Jake and Phillip walked around after lunch while Karen and I shopped. I felt that I needed to tell her that her dad and I would stand by her if she changed her mind about getting married.

The afternoon went well. The dinner hour was very pleasant. We liked Phillip's dad as well. The six of us worked out a few details about the date Karen and Phillip would be married and when we'd be back.

Shortly after dinner, we took Karen to Phillip's grandmother's house, where she was staying, and drove to the hotel. As we were boarding the plane Friday morning, Jake said, "Honey, it will never last."

"Well, it may not, but Karen is determined to keep her baby. She'll get an education and will be able to raise it if her marriage doesn't work out."

Two weeks later we all, except Roxie who stayed with Zach and Lynne, went to see Karen get married.

Soon after the wedding, we drove to Flagstaff and took the train home. Jake said he didn't think it would be long before the passenger train would be a thing of the past and he wanted the family to have a train ride together. It was a pleasant trip.

Late afternoon on Sunday, Candy got off in the town where she was attending college. We were all tired when we got home. Jake was up most of the night with a headache. He pressed against his temple while tears ran from his right eye. The two of us had almost no sleep.

The next morning everyone was tired and I found myself short-tempered with the kids.

That evening we went to pick up Roxie. She had enjoyed all the attention from her cousin and she could say Zach and Lynne's names. I bundled her up with her pink kitty tightly in her arms and we went back to the farm. It was so good to hold her and know we were home.

We'd been home from Arizona about two weeks when Jake came home late from work loaded. That night at the dinner table, he lay his head down on the table to sleep. I got up and went to the other end of the table while all the kids looked on. I took his arm and said, "Come on, Jake, you can sleep in bed."

He raised his head up, turned it sideways and tried to focus on my face. "I'm fine."

"I know you're fine, but you'll be better in the bed." I helped him up and we staggered to our room.

I came back to the table and said, "Your dad will be fine. I'll see to it." No one said a word.

"How was school today?" No response.

"I asked a question," I said, anger rising in my voice.

"Okay."

"Fine."

"Okay, I guess."

Oh dear. What's going to become of us?

I got the household settled down and went to bed. *I wonder where the bottle is. He had another drink before dinner. The only place he went was the bathroom, so it's got to be in there.* I went in and looked under the sinks, but there was no bottle. I checked the trash and it wasn't there. Just as I was putting the wastebasket down, I spied the toilet tank. I took a candle off the tank lid and lifted the lid. There it was a partly empty half-pint of Jim Beam. I poured it out, put the bottle in the trash and went to bed. I had out-guessed him one more time.

Sleep wouldn't come. I remembered again what Dr. Wolfe said before I was married: Taking care of an alcoholic on the job and being married to him is altogether different.

I understand more clearly now, but I still love being Jake's wife. He treats me better when he's drunk than some men treat their wives when they're sober.

There was a stir on the other side of the bed. I turned over facing that direction. He put his feet on the floor and lit a cigarette. Soon he got up and went to the bathroom.

Oh boy, the truth is about to be revealed.

I listened and heard the top come off the tank. Then he came back to the bedroom and went to his closet.

"What do you need, Jake?"

"I'm going after another bottle."

"Honey," I said, getting up and going over to him, "Come back to bed. We'll beat this together." I put my arms around him and said, "You have a heavy schedule in the morning."

"Man, Honey, I've got to have a drink."

"Come lie back down and let's try."

"It won't do any good, I'm desperate."

"Try, Honey."

"Okay, but, Mel, I need a drink."

It's amazing that he never gets mad at me when I pour out his booze.

We were up and down all night. He would go to get dressed. I'd put my arms around him and tell him how much he was needed at the office. Finally just before daylight, he went to sleep. I lay still for a long time then got up to start the day.

I'll let him sleep as long as he can and I'll get the kids up, I thought, as I went toward the stairs. *Oh, I hope he'll be okay.*

I got all the keys to both cars, got breakfast for everyone, and got Roxie dressed. Just before the kids came down, I took juice and coffee in to Jake and said, "Good morning," as I set it on his bedside table.

"Hi, Daddy," Roxie said as she climbed up on the bed and sat by him.

He put his arm around her, "Hi, you sweet thing, you."

I laid out his clothes and went back to the kitchen. No one was down yet, so I yelled for them to hurry. I found myself becoming more agitated as time slipped by. Finally I got the kids out the door and Jake was ready to go.

"Where are my keys?"

"I'm going to take you," I said as I put Roxie's arm in her jacket.

"Honey, there's no need for that."

"There might be, Jake. You know how hard it is for you to pass up a liquor store."

"Well, I don't like being policed."

"Well," I said, lifting my voice, "I don't like you going to sleep at the table in front of the children."

He said nothing more. We all three went to my car and I gave him the keys. He was silent as he drove down the highway.

That evening after school, Neil, the baby and I dropped Wendy off at Girl Scouts and picked Jacob up after his cross-country running practice. We swung by the office and picked up Jake. He looked great and was glad to see us.

Maybe things will settle down now. I sure hope we don't have another crisis, I thought, as I was holding my baby in the back seat. *When will we ever live normal lives?*

That thought kept coming all evening. Each time I'd think, *If he could find peace with the Lord, things would turn around.*

When all was quiet that evening, I sat down on the side of the bed by Jake. He looked from his newspaper.

"Jake, school will soon be out. Candy will be home. The kids do well with her and, I was wondering, instead of our buying another piece of antique furniture, like we have the last four years, I'd like to go somewhere for a few days for our anniversary."

"Where do you want to go?"

"Indiana, to the church convention."

"Find out when it is and I'll take you for a few days."

I threw my arms around him and said, "Oh, Honey, you will never know what this means to me."

⌐

I was sleeping soundly and the phone rang. As I lifted the receiver I saw the time: 2:00 a.m. The first thing I thought of was my dad.

"Mel," Candy said, "I just had to call. I heard from Karen. She's afraid they've made a mistake by getting married. I'm so worried about her." We talked a little while. I assured her we'd stand by Karen and maybe when they started back to school for the summer, things would get better.

When she hung up Jake said, "Things aren't good with Karen, are they?"

We talked a while and decided we'd see if Phillip wanted to continue in school. If so, we'd still help them some, but if he didn't and it didn't work out for him and Karen, we'd help her finish school. We both wanted Karen to finish her education.

The morning of our fifth anniversary, Jake told me that he had made arrangements to take off a few days in June and we'd fly to Indiana for the church convention. "Oh, Jake," I said, wrapping him in a bear hug, "You could have bought me anything and I wouldn't have been as happy." He looked down at me and grinned like he was puzzled at my actions. *I don't think he has any idea what this trip means to me.*

I ran out that day and found a wonderful card to give to him. After everyone was settled for the night and we had some time alone, which was seldom, I could hardly wait to give it to him. He took hold of my right hand and said, "Mrs. Bell, I'd like to pray." Then he bowed his head and said, "Lord, thank you for this wonderful woman," and all of a sudden I felt a ring being slipped on my finger. I forgot that we were praying and looked on my right hand and saw his late Mother's ring that her husband, Fred, had given her before they were married. I had always admired it. There it was on my hand.

"When did you get this?"

"Last week."

"Oh Jake, you must have given a fortune for that."

"No, Fred sold it to me for one-fourth of its appraised value."

I kept looking at it. I couldn't believe I had a ring that beautiful.

Long after Jake had gone to sleep, I lay in the bed and by the moonlight watched the ring sparkle. I'd shake my hand and watch the sparkles on the ceiling.

On Thursday of that week, Jake was to pick Candy up at college. Early that morning she called and said, "Mel, are you coming with Daddy to pick me up?"

"No, I hadn't planned on it. Neil gets out early today."

"Would you please have Daddy bring the baby?"

"I think he'd do that. She'll probably sleep all the way there."

He didn't mind taking Roxie. I dressed her up in the little blue dress and bloomers that my parents had bought her and she was ready to go.

That night Jake said Candy took the baby and all the girls crowded around. "She was seen by them all," he beamed, as he recalled Candy and her little sister going down the hall to see everyone.

June finally came and I was getting ready to pack our things to leave the next day for the church convention. The phone rang; it was my sister Shirley.

"Melissa, have you heard from the folks?"

"No."

"Well, one of their neighbors wrote to their daughter who lives close to me and said Dad is sick. I want you to get some things that I think they'll need and take them down home and see about them."

"When did you want me to go?"

"Today or tomorrow."

"We're leaving on vacation tomorrow."

"Where were you going?"

"A church convention."

"Oh well, you can go there another time; they need these things. The neighbor said it's real hard for Dad to get his breath."

I called Jake.

"I know you're disappointed, Honey, but we'll go another time."

Candy said she'd handle everything and I left for my parents' home. When I got there, Daddy was feeling much better. He had been having trouble breathing, but had improved.

Jake came down the next evening and on Thursday we went into town and talked to Daddy's doctor. Jake looked at his chest film. We went to the nearest city and found a tank of oxygen. We had a good time being with the folks and knew they were pleased to have us there. I hated missing the convention but was glad to take care of my parents.

The rest of the summer was very busy. We had a big garden and lots of fruit. I canned and froze produce all summer.

On my birthday, Jake was going to take me to dinner and we asked Grandpa Fred to go with us. When we picked him up, Jake suggested we swing back by the house so Grandpa Fred could see the kids. We stopped in the drive and Jake told Fred to come in and see the kids. We all got out and went in. *Wonder where everyone is, it's so quiet in here.* As I walked into the kitchen everyone started singing "Happy Birthday."

Several of my special friends were at the surprise party. Candy had gone to her high school friend, Sandy's, home to do all the dinner preparation and make the phone calls. She had done an elegant job. It was a lovely time. The kids had decorated the house and were very pleased with themselves. It was my first surprise party.

After the guests left and the kids had gone upstairs, I looked over to the back door, which Jake was locking, and said, "Jake, didn't Candy do a super job on the dinner?"

He turned around and walked toward me and said, "Yes, she sure did."
Oh no, he's been drinking. He has that look like he's trying to focus.

We started down the hall together, but I didn't smell anything. He went to sleep quickly and soundly. I lay awake a long time thinking about the day. Wendy was supposed to have gone somewhere. When I commented that she had not been able to go with her friends, she said with the sweetest look on her face, "I wanted to stay for the party." *What a special party it was.* I let my concern fade about the look on Jake's face.

Jake and I thought we should check on the folks again before school started. He was busy moving into a larger office, so I suggested Wendy, Roxie and I go down.

The folks were happy to see us, but my dad seemed very weak.

When we arrived home two days later, Jake and Zach were there with two men who were interested in buying the wooded pasture where I had gotten the tractor key from Jake when he was mowing while drunk. They were in the yard and Jake asked me to join them. Before he told me what they were talking about, he asked how my dad was.

"Not good. He's much weaker than before."

"I'm so sorry, Honey."

I stayed and listened to the realtor's proposal. When there was a break in conversation, Jake said, "Honey, I'm really sorry about your dad."

When the realtors were getting ready to go, Jake said for the third time, "Honey, I'm really sorry about your dad."

Then I took notice. *He doesn't look right, he has that look.*

The thought lingered long into the night. *He's not drinking, yet he has that look. They've been moving all day since it was his day off, maybe he's just tired.* Each time during the night when he got up, I got up with him. I had to know he was okay.

The end of the summer was busy with everyone getting ready to go back to school. Jake would take a nap after dinner each night. *He's tired,* I'd think. He was up a lot during the night and I always was up with him. I felt sick at my stomach often and sometimes vomited, but I didn't tell anyone, for fear I wouldn't be believed. When it was time for Jake to get home, I started looking out the window and saying out loud, "Where is he?" or "Where is that man?"

Karen and Phillip had moved back to school for the summer with plans to stay. Jake and I were planning to take Roxie and go see them when the baby was born. The last day of August, Phillip called and said we had a granddaughter. They named her Melonie. We planned to leave on Friday afternoon to visit them.

That night Jake said, "Honey, let's take Candy with us to see the baby."

"Jake you know how hard it is to get someone to stay with the kids."

"Well, I've got a problem. She looked at me with those big brown eyes and said, 'Please Daddy, may I go see the baby?' I couldn't turn her down."

"She can have my plane ticket and Roxie and I will stay here."

"Are you sure?"

"Yes, the girls are very close and Candy has worked hard helping me all summer."

All weekend while they were gone, I wondered if Jake was drinking. I kept telling myself he wouldn't drink while on a trip with Candy, knowing full well no one or anything makes a difference when an alcoholic is desperate for a drink.

Sunday night around midnight, Jake came in and said, "Honey, wake up and see the pictures." I looked up. He was sitting on the side of the bed with his hand on my shoulder. I rose up to kiss him. *Oh no, he's drinking.*

"Jake, when did you start drinking?"

"As soon as we got on the plane Friday afternoon."

I got up and hurried out to the kitchen and said, "Candy, if you'd called me when you changed planes in Denver, I'd have come on Saturday and your dad would have stopped drinking."

She put her milk glass in the sink and said in a disgusted tone as she left the kitchen, "I wish I hadn't gone."

"I do too." I was angry that I hadn't been there to control the one that I thought was my responsibility.

"You were too hard on her, Mel, it wasn't her fault," he told me. "She tried. She said, 'Daddy, if Mel were here you wouldn't drink; now don't you do this.'"

We were both awake most of the night.

The next night Jake went to bed early. When I went in, I could smell Jim Beam. I looked in all the usual places and finally found it under his pillow just as he was waking up. He grabbed my arm and got the bottle. I hauled off and slapped him. He didn't say anything, just took a drink. I tried to get the bottle, but he was stronger than I. I was so short tempered—I started yelling. He just stayed calm and let me rant.

"I can't raise these kids if you're going to drink."

The next evening when he came home, there was no smell of liquor, but he was acting like it was an effort to listen. He went to sleep in the chair for a little while then got up and went to the basement to work on a piece of furniture. I went down too; there was no smell of Jim Beam.

Two or three more weeks went by with Jake spending more time in the evenings in the basement. One night he hadn't worked down there, but went down after getting ready for bed. *That's not right,* I kept thinking.

I was getting my gown from the closet when he walked through the bedroom door. I saw a guilty look on his face. The next moment was the worst of my life. I saw blood on his pajamas.

"Jake, you went downstairs and gave yourself a shot!"

"Oh, Honey, I've been so afraid you'd find out."

"What is it?"

"Demerol."

Dr. Wolfe had said no patient ever got off Demerol.

"Jake, I will not live with drugs."

"Oh, Honey, I know. I've got to beat this," he said, sitting down on the bed.

"Where is the Demerol?"

"Downstairs in a coffee can in the fruit closet."

"Do you have any more?"

"Yes."

"Where?"

"At the office." I gasped, and he said, "I always give myself a shot before I start home, but not before."

"Be dressed when I get back from the basement. We are going to the office." I ran down to the basement and got the vial of Demerol and took it over by the washing machine where there was a drain in the floor and smashed it with the hammer. Then I hurried upstairs and wrapped a blanket around Roxena Lynne and carried her to the car with Jake behind me.

When we got to the office, I put her on a settee in the waiting room and went back, got the Demerol and emptied it with a syringe.

When I finished, I repeated, "I will not live with drugs."

"I'll beat it, Honey. I'll go see Ira. I'll do anything. Man, I was crazy. I went to see a patient at home and the Demerol was in my bag. That night I was desperate and I knew if I drank, you'd smell it and if I just took one shot to get me over the hump you wouldn't know."

Oh, Lord what should I do? What's going to happen to us? I thought, as I picked up my sleeping daughter and went with Jake to the car.

Jake dozed off and on all the way home. I kept telling myself to be calm and try to hold things together. He slept through the night, but there was no sleep for me.

How will I hold this family together? What will happen to Jacob, Wendy and Neil? Will we lose custody of them? How will I take care of everyone? All night my thoughts raced with troubling questions. The main one was why hadn't I seen what was as plain as the nose on my face. I had to admit that I had not wanted to know that Jake was taking drugs.

Just before it was time for Jake to leave for the office he said, "I'll call Ira and see when I can see him."

"I'll take you to work and come and get you."

"That won't be necessary, Honey. I'll beat this. Man, I've got to."

I picked Jake up at noon. We got a sandwich and then headed to Dr. Smith's office. Roxie and I waited in the waiting room. I tried to read to her, but was very sleepy.

Jake looked worried when he came out. I knew he doubted that he would be able to get off the drug.

"I'm going to start seeing Ira. Man, I was crazy for giving myself that first shot," he said again, as we got in the car.

During September I spent all my spare time watching Jake. If he went to the barn, I'd look to see if he stopped by the chicken house, then I'd go look for Demerol. I found one vial over the door in the shed where we kept the garden tools and another in the garage. I wanted to make sure none were at the office. One morning I got up to search his office at 5:00 a.m. with a friend. If a tile in the ceiling wasn't just right, I got on a step-stool and lifted the tile and looked with a flashlight. I came home relieved that I'd found none.

I tried to make everything look normal. However, it didn't take long to see that regardless of how hard I tried, we were not beating the drug problem. Nonetheless, I gave it my best, thinking it was up to me to keep the family together. We got through the days, but at night I knew he'd had a shot.

It was a beautiful Monday in October. Roxena Lynne and I dropped Jake off at the office and picked Ulma up. We'd been home a few minutes when the phone rang. I answered it in the kitchen.

"Hello."

"Melissa, this is your Uncle Harold."

I got this sinking feeling. "Uncle Harold, are the folks okay?"

"That's why I called. When I was going to work this morning, I saw your mother at the mailbox. I stopped and she said she'd come to mail you a letter. Your dad was sick and he's out of oxygen. I went down to see him and he's awful sick and can hardly get his breath. Your mother has been up with him two nights. We sure do need Jake down here. Your dad doesn't want to go to the hospital."

"Uncle Harold, Jake has a big morning at the office, but I'm sure we'll come as soon as we can and we'll bring oxygen."

I made arrangements for my cousin to stay with the kids that night, packed our things, and was ready when Jake called a little before 2:00 p.m. We took medication and a tank of oxygen and were at the folks' by 8:00 p.m. Uncle Harold and several other aunts and uncles were there.

Daddy was awake and glad to see us and especially Roxena Lynne. Jake got the oxygen going and spent a lot of time with him after all the company left.

I could tell Jake was restless, but he had really come through for us.

My mother hadn't slept for two nights and Jake sent her to bed. I stayed by my daddy's bed all night. Jake came in often.

Thank you, Lord, that he's okay and taking such good care of Daddy.

Daddy died at 6:30 a.m. Mama, Jake and I were there. I wrapped my arms around my heartbroken mother and told her she had no regrets and what a wonderful job she did taking care of Daddy. Shortly after, Roxie came in. I took her in my arms.

"Your Uncle Harold just drove up," Jake said. "You two go meet him. I'll stay with your mother."

"He just died, Uncle Harold," I said, when he stepped inside. He put his arm around me and we hugged. I could tell he was surprised I wasn't crying. I seldom cried in a crisis and I couldn't start now; too much depended on my holding things together.

Uncle Harold was Mama's youngest brother. He was just three years older than Stan and he was so sweet and good to my mother. He soon left to call the funeral home. I took Roxie and we went to a cousin's house to call my sisters. Both brothers were on their way.

When I got home, Jake helped me get breakfast. He was restless. I knew he was desperate, but would be okay. *Oh, I hope he doesn't slip when we get home. Oh, Lord, I can't leave home and come spend time with Mama. How am I going to manage?* I felt so desperate to make sure Jake was okay.

Everyone who came in was crying and I could tell they were wondering what was wrong with me. *One thing I can't do is lose it.*

My brother Doug came about 10:00 a.m. We went into town that afternoon to make arrangements. I asked that we have the funeral on Thursday. *We've got to do it fast, or Jake will be out of shape for sure.*

That afternoon we left for home.

Jane offered to care for Roxie until after the funeral. That evening, with Roxie at Jane's, I took a nap after dinner. I was so exhausted from almost no sleep for two nights. Jacob came in to wake me and said, "Mel, I can't get Dad in here to bed." I was still dressed lying on top of the covers. I jumped up and saw by the clock that it was 1:00 a.m.

"Oh my, Jacob, I'm sorry."

We went in to the family room and the two of us got Jake to bed. While I was napping, he had gotten loaded. Jacob had stayed up with him so I could sleep. *In a crisis, my kids are always so understanding,* I thought.

I spent the night making sure he didn't make another trip to the basement. I was still awake and ready for the trip to the funeral when Jacob came down to go to cross country practice. It was dawn when I left Jacob at the high school. My mind heavy with worry, I started to cry as I turned to go out of the parking lot. I stopped the car and started to lay my head on the steering wheel and thought, *I can't let myself fall apart. If I lose it, I don't know what will happen to us.* I raised my head and wiped my eyes.

My mother is expecting me today. Jake may be in no shape to go. Lord, I just need your help right now. A verse I'd heard from the Old Testament ten years earlier came to my mind. *"Go and thy way will be opened up before thee step by step." Thank you, Lord, that's my answer.*

Jake was asleep when I got home. I got the kids up and made oatmeal. I laid out Jake's clothes and went in with coffee and juice just in time for him to get ready.

"Jake, we need to leave soon." He rose up and sat on the side of the bed. He looked a mess.

I sat down in front of him and looked into his eyes. "Jake, I've got to go to my dad's funeral for my mother's sake. If you plan on staying well, you can go with me, but if you aren't, you tell me and I'll go alone."

He looked at me and said, "Honey, you won't need to worry one bit. I will not misbehave when I take you to your daddy's funeral."

"Okay. Jump in the shower and get dressed. If we leave at 8:00, we'll get to the funeral home at 1:00. They are going out to the church at 1:30 p.m."

"Who will be here for the kids tonight?"

"Zach or Lynne will take them to dinner. Zach stayed with them the other time, but if Lynne's not busy, she'll probably stay. One or the other will."

I got the kids out the door, the cinnamon rolls and coffee in the car and we pulled out of the drive on time. We parked our car behind Stan's in line to go out to the church. Stan had been watching for us and met us at the door. The next person I saw was Aunt Roxena. I was so glad she was there. Two of my sisters were standing together. One said, "You're late." The other said, "You overslept, didn't you?"

"No, no, I didn't oversleep."

What would it be like to oversleep? Oh, get us through this day, Lord.

I could hear the brothers telling Jake how much they appreciated his being there when Daddy died. I sat down on the couch by Mama and held her hand. Words weren't necessary between Mama and me.

When it was time to leave I asked Aunt Roxena to drive behind us. "Aunt Roxena just always brings that sweet spirit with her wherever she goes," I told Jake as we got in the car.

"It's wonderful the way you two love each other."

"She's one of my blessings in life."

"I'm your burden, Honey, I know that," Jake said, taking my hand. I didn't comment.

The drinking and now drugs are a problem, but he's not always a burden. Just now he looks so strong and handsome. I'm so proud to be walking in the church on his arm.

It was 11:00 p.m. when we got home. Our night was restless and with morning came a lonely feeling, knowing Daddy was gone.

The week went by without Jake drinking or taking a shot, but he didn't seem to want to talk about Daddy yet. I found myself so lonely and needing to talk. A week after we came home, I heard a knock at the door.

Roxie led the way to the family room. *Oh wow!* I thought, as I threw myself in the arms of my brother Stan. *He just always knows when to be there for me. Thank you, Lord, for sending him by.*

We went upstairs and Jake saw him and said, "Well, hello there," as they shook hands. Then Jake gave me a knowing look.

He knew I needed Stan to come by.

The next morning after I got everyone off to school and work, Stan and I had time to talk about Daddy. We both longed to talk about him. After a couple of hours, he stood up and said, "I need to be going," and started walking toward the door. I followed him to the door. He put his hand on the doorknob and then turned around and said, "Melissa, you're my sister." Then he just walked out the door.

Wow, I love him so much. The Lord knew I needed a visit from Stan that day.

At about 3:00 p.m., I called the office to talk to Jake. Jewell said he had checked out for the day two hours earlier. He hadn't said where he was going, so I knew he would come home loaded. I hated that he was driving.

I was hanging up the phone and a knock came on the door. The knock came again. I opened the door and there stood Pastor Dean.

He came in and sat down. "How are you, Melissa?"

"I'm fine. Stan was here overnight, so that helped."

"How's your mother?"

"Stan thought she was doing okay."

"Dean, Jake left the office two hours ago and we don't know where he is," I blurted out.

"Melissa," Dean said, as he put his elbows on his knees and put his hands together, "Let's tell the Lord about this." When he finished praying, I had peace. I felt I didn't need to worry.

When Wendy and Neil came in from school, they went upstairs. In a little while Neil came down and said, "What is the station wagon doing up in the field?" He'd seen it through the upstairs window.

"I don't know." I remembered Joanne saying the kids could deal with the truth. That's the way it is with skid row, the families have to be a part of the whole painful mess. Then I said, "Your dad left the office about 1:00. Jewell didn't know where he was going. He's been restless lately, so he may be drinking. He must be up there in the car. I'll pick Jacob up from running and we'll eat. I'll go up and bring him home if he doesn't come by the time we're finished."

It was a windy, fall evening when I walked through the south pasture down by the little spring and climbed the fence. He was under the wheel asleep; head bent over, with tie and suit wet from drool.

I opened the door, got his Demerol from his coat pocket and said, "Jake." He opened his eyes and tried to focus. "Jake, move over and I'll drive you home." He didn't seem to understand so I went over to the other side, got in and said, "Scoot over here to me, Jake." I put my knees in the seat and my arms around him from the back and started pulling. I got him over some. Then I went back to the driver's side and pushed. I moved his feet and got under the wheel.

Everyone was at the door waiting when I went inside. "Your dad's asleep in the car. It's not too cold. When he wakes up he'll come in."

I worried about the kids. They looked sad, but resigned to this way of life. The more I thought about our situation, the more desperate I became.

I got up about midnight, went in the family room and got down by Jake's brown chair and said, "I don't know what I'm going to do, Lord. No one that I know of has ever gotten off of this drug. I have no one to turn to. I'm not so sure that I even believe You're real." There in the dark of the night, I sobbed.

A scripture I'd heard first as a teenager and several times since came clearly to my mind. "I know in Whom I have believed and am persuaded that He is able to keep that which I've committed unto Him against that day."

"Thank you, Lord. I know You're real," I said as I started down the hall to the bedroom.

Jake came in at dawn and slept in bed for three hours. He showered, but ate very little breakfast. He went to the office at the regular time, but left at noon. I went upstairs and looked out the back window. The station wagon was parked in the west field, where corn had grown during the summer.

Finally, Dr. Smith insisted that he be hospitalized. Jake didn't want to do it, but Dr. Smith wouldn't take "no" for an answer.

He remained in the hospital for a month. Zach helped with the office and Jewell got someone else to come in part-time and cover for him at the hospital. The practice suffered because Jake wasn't there.

I couldn't talk to Jake until he'd been at the hospital for a week. I could hardly stand not talking to him. On Saturday night after Jake was hospitalized, I said to Betty, "I'm dreading going to church tomorrow. I don't think I can face it."

"Melissa, you can face tomorrow. I'm coming out to get your breakfast. Don't try to go to church. Let the kids get up when they want and I'll be there to make pancakes for them. You know you can face the day with my pancakes."

"I'll see. I'll call you in the morning."

Betty came with bacon, pancake fixin's, butter and syrup. When each one of the kids came down, she fixed their breakfast.

That afternoon I remembered Psalms 121 again. It was like an old childhood friend. "I will lift mine eyes unto the hills from whence cometh my help. My help cometh from the Lord who made heaven and earth." *And,* I added, *who sent Betty, who doesn't claim to know you, Lord, to make my kids that wonderful breakfast.*

⁓

Finally the week was up and I jumped each time the phone rang. It was Ulma's day to clean house and I talked to her about Jake. I'd talk and cry. Ulma's love for the Lord was so genuine and we had developed a wonderful friendship. I was still talking and crying at the table where I'd been trying to work on some bills. She stopped sweeping and leaned on her broom and said, "Hmm." It dawned on me that there is really nothing anyone can say. She'd listened all day saying very little, just leaning on the broom and looking at me was about all anyone could do, except pray, and we'd done that earlier. She let me talk all day and I knew it would never go outside our home.

The phone rang just before the children came home. It was Jake. His voice sounded so healthy. I was so glad to hear from him. He was talking about going back to work. His physician thought he should stay a month then go back to the hospital for an indefinite period each day after work. The best news was that the kids and I could call and I could go see him.

I could hardly wait to have his arms around me. I called him before I left home, just after dinner that night. He knew about how long it would take me to get there and was waiting at the elevator. I didn't care who was watching; I stepped off the elevator and into his arms.

It was very hard taking care of things with Jake gone. There was so much running to do with three children in activities and a two-year-old. To make matters worse, all was not well with the two girls living away from home either. We got word from Karen that she and Phillip were separated, so she and the baby would be home for Christmas. We encouraged her to start school in January. A letter came from Candy saying she'd left school and was going to California. She planned to find a job. Jake was upset. I knew she'd have no problem finding a job, but California seemed like a long way from us.

The weeks went slowly by. Jake was now going to the office during the day and back to the hospital at night. I'd get up early, fix the kids' breakfast, dress Roxie, and as soon as the kids were off to school, I'd go pick Jake up and take him to work. When Wendy and Neil got home, I would go to the office, pick Jake up, take him back to the hospital, swing by the high school and pick Jacob up on the evenings he ran, as well as whoever else had something going on. Then we would race home to get dinner off the stove or out of the oven. With my reading problem, I wasn't any help in the homework department, and the two younger kids really needed help. I felt overwhelmed and sometimes helpless.

We had Thanksgiving at Zach and Lynne's that year. I looked at Jake, and for the first time, saw just how bad he really looked. He was so thin and looked totally exhausted.

A couple of weeks before Christmas, Karen came home with the baby. Everyone was happy to have them. To me it was like a breath of fresh air.

One morning I took Jake to work. He was so restless. His practice had suffered because the office hadn't been covered like it needed to be. We were strapped for money and we were still paying on the loan for the addition to the house. As I drove out of the medical building parking lot I thought, *How are we going to manage with so many expenses?* I felt numb as I drove up the street and stopped at a red light behind another car.

What if he doesn't get well? He's so depressed. What would I do and how would I raise my kids if something happened to him?

All of a sudden I felt a bump and realized I'd taken my foot off the brake and hit the car in front of me.

We both got out of our cars to look at the damage. We recognized one another. He smiled and said, "Don't worry, Mrs. Bell, your car's not hurt and your insurance will take care of mine. Just call my office today," he said, and hurried to his car so we wouldn't hold up traffic.

"Thank you, Doctor."

"You bet."

"I can't trust myself under the wheel any more, Karen," I said as we were cleaning up the kitchen. "I'm forever in that car taking the kids places and picking up their dad. I seldom keep my mind on my driving."

"Well," she said as she picked up the iron skillet and put it in the sink, "you've just lost your job. I'll take Daddy to work and pick him up. I'll take the kids wherever they need to go. You take time for yourself and the little girls."

Oh how wonderful it will be to have time to hold my little girl without having to say, "We've got to go now."

"Karen you're a lifesaver." I wiped my eyes and picked my two-year-old up as she came in the kitchen.

Jake was finally dismissed, but continued seeing Dr. Fox, a psychiatry resident, and he went to the hospital each day for his medication. Dr. Smith had arranged that because I didn't want to be responsible for giving it to him.

We had Christmas Eve with Zach and Lynne. It was special for the kids, because they always loved going to Aunt Lynne's. Christmas morning I awoke with the flu and we didn't start opening gifts until 9:00 a.m. Jake and Karen took care of everyone. I just sat in the chair and went back to bed soon after.

In the middle of the afternoon Jake came into the bedroom and said, "Honey, I didn't go to the hospital for my medication at 11:00 a.m."

"Oh dear, we all forgot about that. You'd better go now." Karen drove him over and I thought no more about it.

The next day I went to see Dr. Fox. I waited in his office, wishing I didn't have to be there, but thinking, *I've got to see that Jake gets well and can be on his own.*

Dr. Fox opened the door and walked in with Jake's chart, looking at it as he went behind the desk and sat down. He looked at me and said, "Mrs. Bell, why didn't he come in for his medication on time yesterday?"

Believing I was responsible for everything pertaining to Jake's health, I said, "Doctor, we forgot about that yesterday morning."

"I do not believe a man who wants to get well just forgets to come to the hospital at the appropriate time to get his medication."

Still I thought it was up to me to explain. "I was sick with the flu and we didn't start opening gifts until 9:00 a.m. Then I went back to bed. He came to our room in the middle of the afternoon to tell me he'd forgotten to come for his medication."

"Well, he needs to be responsible when it comes to his medication."

Oh dear, I must not let Jake forget again. I hate having this man lift his voice to me. I went home feeling so discouraged.

When I told Karen about my visit she said, "Mel, that wasn't your place to remember that. That's Daddy's place."

—

With Candy in California and Karen in college and a single mom, neither of the girls will be coming home for a long while, I thought on New Year's Eve as we saw Karen to the train. *I'll miss them. I hope '69 is a better year than the nightmares we've endured this past year.*

1969
A Back-Breaking Job

By early January, Jake was no longer seeing the doctors at the hospital. He made everyone believe he'd start seeing Dr. Smith.

"Jake," I said, one night when we were in the family room alone, "when are you going to make an appointment with Dr. Smith?"

"Melissa Ann, he's your doctor. He's the best in the country and that's why I'm glad you're seeing him. You need someone to talk to and I want you to see the best." He reached for a cigarette. I got up to take the coffee cups to the kitchen.

That means all that talk about seeing Dr. Smith was just so he could stop seeing the other doctor. That con artist doesn't plan on seeing anyone. Is this what they call game playing, or is it downright dishonesty? The main thing is hopefully there'll be no more drugs, but if he got help, it would mean he'd stop drinking. Now he'll probably be drinking before the month is up.

It was the second Sunday in January and the sun was shining. On the way home from church, Jake said, "Let's go to my old military school and see the parade after we go to lunch." Jake's high school roommate, who was teaching there, was the first to see us. We sat with the colonel and his wife, who'd been to our house for dinner two years before. It was a pleasant afternoon. Roxena Lynne batted her eyes real fast when the band stopped in front of us. We all saw it and smiled.

When the parade was over, we visited with several of the people that Jake knew.

"There's one more place we need to go, kids. I want to take you over where your grandparents took your Uncle Zach and me to supper on Sunday nights," he said.

"Did they come every Sunday?" Jacob asked.

"They came real often. It's not far. Coming on Sunday was a nice outing for them."

Wonder when he's going to suggest to Jacob that he should go to school here next year?

The place where we ate had changed hands since the days Jake was in school, but we enjoyed visiting with the couple that ran the place now.

"It's a friendly place," I said on the way home. "The lady at the restaurant said she has an antique store in her home."

In the back seat Jacob said, "Why don't we buy something new once in a while?" Neil and Wendy agreed.

Jake smiled and looked back in the rear view mirror. "Are you getting tired of antiques?"

"No," Jacob replied. "It'd just be good to have something new."

That night when we were in our room getting ready to retire, Jake said, "Each time we've been down to see a parade, I can tell you liked it."

"I loved it, and I'd like to have seen it when you were there—except when you first started marching, I was a baby." We both laughed.

"I know what you're thinking, Jake. You've always wanted the boys to go there when they got old enough. Now that Jacob is in high school, you hope he'll want to go there next year."

He took off his last sock and looked up. "You know me like a book. It's a wonderful school, Honey. Jacob is a smart boy, and he'd do real well down there. I want to give all of my kids the very best education. Maybe in the fall, he will want to go."

One Sunday morning we were halfway to church and I asked Jake if I could borrow his fingernail clipper. He got it out and started to hand it to me. Then he said, "I'm not sure you'll give it back to me."

In fun, I replied, "Well, I may not, but give it to me anyway."

He put it back in his pocket. I waited and said, "Jake, I need to clip this hangnail."

"Where's yours?"

"I guess it's at home. It's not in my purse."

"Well, you can't have mine."

I started to become angry. *This is crazy. I've been up since five o'clock, made breakfast, saw that everything was done and he's playing games in front of the kids, acting like it might be a risk to let me use his nail clipper for one hangnail.* The car became very quiet. The tension inside of me was mounting.

"Jake, I just want to ask you a question. Why is it a big deal that I clip a hangnail with your clipper?"

"I'm not sure you'll give it back."

I turned my head toward the window trying not to cry, but feeling very sorry for myself. *I've already done a half-day's work. He was restless all night; I didn't sleep more than four hours; and he treats me like a kid. Why is he doing this?*

Dean's message was good, as always, but on our way home Jake said, "That preacher of yours just doesn't get it, Melissa Ann. He gets on that social gospel kick nearly every Sunday."

I was still angry about the nail clipper. *Is he trying to get my goat so I'll get upset and he'll have an excuse to drink?* He continued finding fault with the message, and then out of the blue said, "Do you want to go to the usual place for lunch?"

"We've already had lunch," I snapped.

"What do you mean?"

"We've been eating 'roast preacher' ever since we left the church."

That one was new to him and he thought it was so funny. The first thing I knew, I was laughing, but the kids didn't laugh. The tone had been set on the way to church. They were quiet during lunch and on the way home. I sensed trouble to come.

Jake started going by the bar each night after work. I figured it wouldn't be long until he'd bring a bottle home with him and eventually he'd go on a binge. Each evening, at the time when he should have been arriving, I'd go to the window and look for the car. That went on a few nights. He came home later each night and it was becoming plain to all the children that something was wrong. One night when he should have been home, Roxena Lynne went to the window and put her nose to the glass, hands on each side of her face and said, "Where's that Daddy?"

For the next few weeks, he came home in time for dinner, but would always go to sleep in his chair. I didn't think it was Demerol, but suspected him of coming home with sleeping medication and hiding it throughout the house.

The kids had gone to bed and he was asleep in his recliner. I was walking over to wake him and my eyes fell on the gold chair nearby. I thought how the patients used to hide pills at the clinic and I lifted up the cushion. Three white Doriden pills were under it. *There's no telling where they all are, but if they are in this house, I'll find them.* I went throughout the downstairs looking for pills, but I didn't find any more. I flushed the three down the stool and went to bed. Jake slept the rest of the night in the chair.

It wasn't long until he was leaving the office early. He'd drive his car to the field and be asleep when I'd go to get him. I'd take all the pills I could find and drive him home.

One afternoon, I was gone when Jake parked in the field. I got home just before Wendy and Neil came home from school.

As they came in the kitchen, Neil said, "I see Dad's up in the field again."

"Yes, I'm going to leave him there until after we eat and you get your homework done. When Roxie goes to sleep, I'll walk up and drive him home. I'll try to find all of his pills so he'll be able to work tomorrow." The kids were quiet and I knew they were worried.

I never know what's best—drag him in front of them or leave him out there and worry what I'll find when I do go.

When I got there, he was asleep. I went to the passenger side, pulled Jake over and drove him home. I parked with the side of the station wagon as close to the back door as I could get it.

I've got to get him inside or he'll freeze to death. I'm almost frozen just walking to the field.

I opened the door and shook my patient. "Jake, wake up. We've got to get you in the house. You've got to help me." I put his feet out on the ground. He couldn't hold his head up, let alone stand. I got my arms around him and got him down on the back porch. I left him lying down and propped the storm door back open, opened the back door, put my arm around him under his arms and dragged him through the door. A pain shot through my back.

I got him a pillow, covered him and left him on the floor. There was this brilliant doctor all dressed up in suit, white shirt and tie, lying helpless on the floor. White collar skid row.

I went to bed, but couldn't get comfortable. I got up, took some aspirin and tried to get to sleep. My whole back and shoulder ached. Morning came and I took two more aspirin and made it through the morning. Jake took a shower and ate a little. *He'll leave the office by noon today*, I thought, as I poured him a second cup of coffee.

The kids were quiet, but they got out the door on time.

When Jake was ready to go, I said, "Jake, I'm going to take you to work."

"No, you're not. I'm driving myself."

"I'm not fighting with you, Jake, you go on."

While Roxie was still eating breakfast, the phone rang.

"Mel, it's Jewell. Doctor called. He's not coming in. I asked him if he'd be home if I had to reach him. He said, 'No, Jewell, I'm not being a good guy today.' So, I thought you should know. I'm canceling the patients. Call me tomorrow so I'll know what to do Friday."

"Okay, Jewell. I'll try to get him well on his day off."

Now what do I do? I thought as I hung up. *He's missed some of his days down at the hospital. I may not be able to get him well before Friday. If I don't, he'll skip going to the hospital again. I don't expect them to hang in there with him too much longer.*

About 10:00 a.m., I saw his car in the field. I took Roxie to Joanne's and walked up there to see about him.

I opened the door and said, "Jake, scoot over. We're going to the house."

"I'm busy. I'm not going."

"Jake, listen to me. I hurt my back getting you in the house last night. I won't be able to get you in again tonight and you'll freeze to death."

"I'm not going."

"Come on, Jake. You can take your pills and I'll get you in bed. It will be better. The kids worry about you out here in this weather. Scoot over and let's turn on some heat." He scooted over.

He was able to walk inside when we got home. He went to bed with the bottle of pills under his pillow. I covered him over, took the phone off the hook and went to get Roxie. I had dinner ready when the kids came home. They were quiet as we ate an early supper.

I know it's hard for them to study. I can't think what I'm doing half the time. Just seeing that we survive is all I get done.

We had him in good shape by Monday morning and he was fine on Monday night, but restless. On Tuesday morning after he got his work finished at the hospital, the administrator handed him a letter of dismissal. We knew the doctors were pleased with Jake's work, but we also knew he had to show up when patients were scheduled. Zach and Lynne visited us often trying to help him get on his feet. It seemed to be a losing battle.

The next Tuesday when I went to see Dr. Smith, he said he thought Jake needed to be hospitalized for six months. I said, "Doctor, he can't keep the office open if he's hospitalized for that long. I'll start taking him wherever he goes. He no longer has the hospital job and the office practice has fallen off."

"All the doctors will refer their patients to him, Mel, if he'll just stay well."

"I know that. When I helped him at the office, I've seen him find things wrong with patients that the local hospitals didn't find. Somehow, I have to keep him well."

Things did improve somewhat. If he came home staggering, I'd spend the night trying to get him ready for work. Sometimes I'd get loud and spend the rest of the night worrying that the kids heard me yelling. In the mornings I often was short-tempered with the kids and hated myself for it.

I continued having problems with my back and Roxie spent a lot of time with Jane. If Jane was busy, she stayed with Joanne or Betty. Betty was driving back and forth to the university to get her second master's and she could only keep her on weekends, but she often came by.

We were talking to Candy on the phone one day shortly after Roxie had come home from spending the night at Jane's. When it was Roxie's turn to talk, she said, "Am I coming to your house?" I went into the other room and cried. I longed for a normal life with my baby.

Summer came and Jake started talking to Jacob about going to the private boarding school where he'd gone. Jacob asked about the football program. Other than that, he didn't say much.

On July 20, 1969, the night U.S. astronauts were to land on the moon, Jake came home loaded. I got Roxie in bed early.

Jacob, Wendy, Neil and I were watching TV and I said, "Kids, I need to stretch out."

Jacob said, "I'll come and get you when we're ready to land on the moon."

I went in and lay down. Jake was out like a light. *Isn't this sad? As interested as he is in world events and here he is passed out when we land on the moon.*

I was sleeping soundly and awoke with Jacob standing on my side of the bed saying as quietly as he could, "Mel, we land in about ten minutes."

"I'll be right there."

When I went in, all three kids were sitting on the floor in front of the TV that was turned down low. Jacob was explaining everything quietly so he wouldn't wake his dad. I sat down in the closest chair. I was so proud of the kids. They were going on with life and enjoying this wonderful time in history, even though they watched without their dad.

Candy had written, telling us that she was in love with a young man named Kevin. In August, Candy called and announced that she and Kevin were to be married in a civil ceremony in one week. She asked if we could come. We told her we'd be there.

Jake worked until noon on Friday. We were to fly out mid-afternoon. When he came home, we ate a quick lunch. I looked at him when he sat down in his chair. I could tell he'd taken a sleeping pill and probably more.

I sat down in the chair across from him and said, "Jake, you're taking Doriden, aren't you?"

"Yes."

"Well, I'm not going."

"Oh, Honey, we have to go. We are the only ones going."

"You should have thought of that before you got the pills. I'm not going."

"Honey, I got six. I've taken one. I have only five left. I'm going to get off them, but I just need to take a nap now and sleep at night while we're gone."

He raised his chair back and his foot rest came up. He crossed his legs at the ankles and one of his pant legs came up. I saw a bump in his sock.

Oh, no. He has them in his socks and no telling where else. I waited until he was asleep and lifted his pant legs. I found three pills.

He had hung his suit coat in the guest closet. I checked his pockets and remembered checking the coat lining at the clinic. I found two pills taped to the lining inside one of the sleeves. *That's the five,* I thought, as the sitter came to the door.

We were on the plane and he said, "Honey, what did you do with my pills?"

"I flushed them down the stool."

"Oh, no, Honey, you shouldn't have done that."

"If I hadn't found them, Jake, I wouldn't have come."

"I know I'm a trial."

We didn't mention the pills again. It was like if we didn't mention problems, they would go away. But it wasn't that easy.

Nonetheless, after the California trip, we settled back into our routine. We enrolled Roxena Lynne in preschool three days a week. Ulma was still with us Monday and Fridays. Without her I couldn't have made it. Jacob enrolled in the military school for his junior year of high school, which pleased Jake. We were invited to join a parents' club for Jacob's school. It met each month at a different restaurant in the city. A representative from the school always spoke. Jake loved our first meeting. The colonel, who'd been to our house for dinner and who was at the school when Jake was there, spoke the first night. His wife and I had a good visit also. Jacob went out for football and we went to all his games the first part of the season.

I had begun seeing Dr. White about my back pain. I got the impression that family and friends didn't believe anything was wrong with my back. One Tuesday morning during my appointment with Dr. Smith, I said, "Doctor, I have the feeling that no one except you, Dr. White, my sister-in-law and a few close friends believe I have back pain."

He wheeled his chair over where I was and looked me in the eyes. "Mel, that's not what anyone thinks. You have a back-breaking job."

It was a beautiful fall day and the yard was full of leaves. The kids and I were raking. Dinner was in the oven and Jake drove up. I went around the house and he was still in the car with his head down. *Oh no, he's drinking or taking pills.* The kids and I ate dinner. I gave orders: Turn off the TV, get homework, etc.

When Roxie was asleep and Wendy and Neil were upstairs, I went out to wake Jake. He got out of the car, staggered and fell down. I moved his legs and arms and saw he felt no pain, so I just left him in the yard. When I got in the house, the phone was ringing. *Oh, I wish I'd taken it off the hook. I'll tell them I'm expecting him in late. I am; it will be very late.*

"Oh, hello, Dean. I'm glad to hear your voice. The groom you married to your former youth director six years ago is drunk and has just fallen in the yard. I plan to just leave him there."

"I'll come and get him in."

Dean's face was so red when he lifted Jake onto the bed that I really got concerned. *He can't do this anymore. It's too hard on him.*

The next day was Thursday, Jake's day off and Halloween. Wendy and Neil were going to each have a friend go trick-or-treating around the neighborhood with them. I told them we'd go ahead with plans. We'd close the doors between the dining room, family room and the kitchen. They could have hot chocolate and popcorn in the living room.

While the four kids were sitting on the living room floor sorting their candy, we heard a crash. I got up as calmly as possible and went through the family room and down the hall to our room. Jake had fallen on the floor. I just left him and went back to the kids. No one seemed to care but I knew it was an uncomfortable moment for Neil and Wendy.

Jake was okay until the weekend before Thanksgiving. Each evening that week he came in loaded. We didn't make our usual family plans, having Zach's family over. Lynne understood and invited Grandpa Fred to her place.

Jacob's school didn't have classes on Thanksgiving and the boys who lived close enough or had an invitation to go home with someone could be free for the day. The parent's club chartered a bus to pick up the boys from our city and bring them to one of the malls. The parents picked them up and took them back to the bus at 7:00 p.m.

Neil and Wendy were going to the state youth convention with the church group, the same convention that I took my youth group to eight and nine years earlier.

We all went to pick Jacob up at the mall. The turkey was in the oven and most everything was done. It was just the six of us and we kept it simple. Wendy helped me. I could tell as we worked that she was anxious to get going to the youth convention.

We ate at noon and Jacob took Wendy and Neil out to the church to catch the bus. By the time he got home, Jake had started drinking. He fell asleep in his chair. Jacob watched football until time to go. I kept him supplied with food while he watched. When he was ready to go, Jake was still sleeping. I bundled Roxena Lynne up and we got in the car, with Jacob driving.

"Jacob, I don't know what to do. I'm glad the kids are at youth convention. This is what our life is like, and sometimes worse. It's almost impossible for the kids to have company. I don't know what to do." Jacob continued driving. I continued talking.

We got to the bus on time and I waited for it to leave. Several people asked about Jake. "Where's the Doctor? Couldn't he leave the game?"

"Oh, he's stretched out in front of the TV." *Well, his chair is in front of the TV and he's stretched out.*

Friday, Jake went to the office but came home early. Saturday he left at noon as usual, but didn't come home until mid-afternoon. He parked the car at the backyard gate far enough from the road so he wouldn't be seen. I wanted to get him in the house and to bed before the kids came home, so about dark I went out and told him it was too cold out there and to come in the house. He had switched back to pills. I was thankful that at least he didn't mix them with alcohol.

He got out of the car and started staggering to the back porch. I was staying close to him and just as he got even with the concrete porch, he started to fall headfirst. I immediately grabbed him and we both went down but his head missed the concrete. The pain shot through my back just as it did each time I lifted him, except it felt worse now.

I got up, opened the door and said, "Jake, crawl inside." It was so pathetic seeing him crawling on his hands and knees.

I called Dr. Smith. I told him what happened and that I couldn't take care of Jake while I was in so much pain. I told him that Zach and Lynne had left that morning for a medical meeting. "Mel, you call Dr. White about your back pain and I'll get Jake admitted soon. You have to do something, if nothing more than getting rest from all that lifting."

I called Dr. White at home and told him what had happened, but I didn't know how I could leave until Dr. Smith could get Jake hospitalized. He said, "I'll call the hospital and tell them you'll be there sometime this weekend. Go as quickly as you can, Mel. I'll leave instructions for them to call me at home when you arrive, and I'll come to see you."

"I need to get things taken care of for the kids but I should be there some-time tomorrow. Dr. Smith is hoping to have Jake admitted soon."

When I finished talking to Dr. White, I called Dean and told him what the plans were. "I worry that Jake won't go to the hospital. I can't go and leave him here alone."

Dean said, "Mel, Vonda and I have been so worried. When I lifted Jake the other day, I realized what you were up against. You've got a daughter to raise, and I'm afraid if you continue as you are, you won't live to raise her."

"Dean, even if I wanted to, I couldn't leave Jake. I've got more than just a daughter to raise. I've got three others that aren't through high school."

"I know Mel, but I just want you to know I'm concerned about you. When Dr. Smith gets the arrangements made, I'll help to get Jake in the hospital."

When we hung up I thought, *What would the kids do if they got home tonight and I wasn't here? Some of my siblings always refer to them as Jake's kids, but I couldn't do this if I didn't think of them as my children.* All of a sudden, I knew how very important they were to me.

Wendy and Neil got home about 9:00 p.m. Roxie was already asleep.

Sunday morning, Dr. Smith called. Everything would be ready for Jake to be admitted at 5:00 p.m. Kathy, a friend from church, came and got all three of the kids. She had a daughter and son that were Wendy and Neil's ages. I arranged for a sitter who'd be there when the kids got home. I packed Jake's bag for a week-long stay. It was all I could do to pack his things; I was in so much pain in my back and shoulders.

I called Dean and told him that Jake could go into the hospital at 5:00 p.m. "I'm going to call an ambulance to come for him, and then I can go on to the hospital. Dr. White has things arranged, and all I have to do is check in."

"You go on. I'll come and call an ambulance."

"I'll take you up on that."

"You're not doing well, are you?"

"No."

"Do you have someone to take you?"

"I'll call Betty."

After I hung up, I called Betty and told her what was going on.

"Melissa, should you leave before he does? You need to be there."

"You go on and worry about him, Betty, but I'm leaving," I said and then just hung up. *How childish. Oh well, Betty understands me.*

I felt sick all over as I was getting my things together. The pain wasn't in my back so much as my shoulders. I heard someone at the door. I thought it was a little early for Dean.

The door opened and Betty said, "Melissa." She came around the corner all smiles. "Man, Melissa, when you hung up on me, I told the boys, 'She's in bad shape boys; she hung up on me' and man, Melissa, I fairly flew."

I'd been in the hospital two hours when Dean called and said he had followed the ambulance. Jake was admitted to the hospital. He had awakened, but hadn't given them any argument. I thanked him and hung up. The minute I put the phone on the hook I felt sick. I grabbed a basin from the drawer. I was so sick I couldn't sit up. I rang for the nurse and lay there with the basin.

"Mrs. Bell, what made you so sick?" she asked, as she got a clean basin. I didn't answer for a little while. Finally, I stopped vomiting. She handed me a glass of water and said, "Rinse your mouth out and take a drink." I didn't think that was a good idea, but I did it. As I expected, I got sick again.

"Mrs. Bell, Dr. White's on the floor. I told him you're here. He'll be here to see you soon."

When he came in, I was still vomiting. He sat down on the bed. As soon as I could talk I said, "Doctor, maybe this is all emotional. My pastor called and told me they just admitted Jake. When we hung up, I got sick. You may want to talk with Dr. Smith." Then I got sick again. There was nothing much left on my stomach, but I couldn't stop vomiting.

Oh, I wish I didn't have to let people know about Jake.

That night, I slept soundly. I never even knew when the nurses had come in. Dr. White stopped by on his way to surgery. I was weak but didn't feel sick. He explained that they were going to start traction and therapy.

I felt worse after traction but the therapy seemed to help my shoulders. I was so worried about the children and Jake during my hospital stay.

Dr. White came to see me each day.

Dr. Smith spent some time with me one day, as well. While he was there he said, "Have you had much company?"

"No. My pastor comes by and his wife Vonda has come."

"Mel, you've got lots of friends. Why do you think they haven't been to see you?"

"Three of them are helping take care of things at my house. There's not time. I'm really fine."

"Do your friends from the medical auxiliary know you're here?"

"No."

"Mel, you're active in the auxiliary. You have them at the farm each spring. They'd like to know when you're sick."

I started to cry and said, "I don't want them to know about Jake." All of a sudden, I felt so exhausted and defeated. I took some Kleenex from the box, wiped my eyes and just lay there.

He patted my hand and said, "Mel, when a radiologist as good as he is isn't in his office for the other doctors to send their patients to, they are going to learn why. They are Jake's and your friends. You know, young lady, the disease of alcoholism is no respecter of persons, and you're not the only wife and mother in the auxiliary whose husband has this disease."

"You know, Doctor," I said, with a stronger voice, "I think it's sin. I don't think he'll get help until he sees that."

"You may be right. We also have to consider the fact that for at least three generations there was alcoholism in his family. Not doing something about it, I would agree, is sin."

"Thank you. I'm glad you agree with me." We both laughed.

On Friday afternoon as I lay under the therapy machine in my room, it occurred to me that all the attention goes to Jake. *Everyone worries more about the alcoholic than they do his family. Very few people seem to believe that I have anything wrong.* Finally, I got sick of feeling sorry for myself. I wiped my eyes and said, "Lord, I'm tired of my self-pity. If I have to stay here another week or longer, I'm going to be pleasant. If I don't hear from Jake and don't see anyone, I'm not going to fret."

Just then a young nurse said from the doorway, "Mrs. Bell, you have a visitor." I looked up and in walked Jake. He'd been to the office. He was dressed in a dark suit. He looked so healthy and more handsome than I'd ever seen him. I threw that machine back and rose up just as he got to my side. We put our arms around one another and forgot all about the nurse.

Jake had arranged to go to the office each day and back to the hospital after work for another week.

"I'll be home in plenty of time for Christmas," he said in a reassuring tone. "I haven't done any shopping."

"You don't worry about that," he said as he put me back under my machine and pulled up a chair. We'll get that done. I'll be home about two weeks before Christmas."

Oh wow, it's good to hear him talking like himself.

I was dismissed on the following Monday. It was good to be back home. Both Dr. Smith and Dr. White said I needed full-time help for a while. The lady who stayed with the kids could come in the daytime and take care of the meals and laundry.

Finally, Jake came home and Jacob arrived the next day. Candy and her new husband had moved close to Karen. The girls would have Christmas together instead of coming home.

Jake and Jacob went to pick up my mother and brought her up for Christmas. What a gift that was. Stan and Anita came to dinner and spent Christmas night. My cousin, Ike, and his wife visited with us in the afternoon on Christmas day.

Jake, Jacob, Wendy and Neil took Mama back home the day after Christmas. It snowed all the time they were gone. I was glad to see them come back on Saturday afternoon.

We had snow all the rest of the year. On New Year's Eve the kids were with the youth group. Jake put Roxie to bed then sat by the fire. He got up to put a stick of wood in the stove. When he finished, he turned around and said, "Melissa Ann, I have an announcement to make. This summer I'm going to take you to Indiana to your church convention."

"Oh, Jake, that will please me very much."

The thought was a good one to bring in the New Year.

1970
Jake Agrees to be Admitted

It was a cold day in February and Jake was late getting home. He hadn't called and my heart sank. We waited dinner, and sure enough he'd been drinking. As soon as Roxie heard him come in the door, she ran to him. He picked her up and she knew the smell. She followed me in the kitchen and said, "Mama, Daddy's drinking."

"I know, Honey. He'll be okay when he goes to sleep."

He was okay through dinner. His face was red and the smell of Jim Beam was strong, but we had our meal without a disaster. He went outside after dinner. I knew he'd hidden a bottle, but I hadn't found it when I searched earlier.

I went into the bathroom, left the light off and looked out the window. He'd hidden a bottle behind a flower bush at the edge of the garage. He took a drink and put it back.

Just before going to bed, I went out and poured out the rest. In the middle of the night, our three-year-old got up. I went into the bathroom where she was. She whispered, "Please, don't flush the toilet." *Bless her heart. At three years old, she wants to make sure we don't wake her daddy when he's been drinking.*

Things at the office had picked up. Jake had three full-time techs and two secretaries.

"I sure hope he doesn't blow it," I told Dr. Smith, whom by then I was referring to as Dr. Searchbrains to family and close friends.

"You know, Mel, you're pouring your money, as well as Jake's, down the drain when you pour out his booze."

"Doctor, I've got to get him to the office as much as I can. That's why I go with him so much."

"Jake Bell has got to want to leave the bottle alone and get himself to the office."

"What do I do in the meantime? I've spent seven years off and on trying to keep him out of the car when he's drinking. I can't convince him that he shouldn't drive for fear he'll kill someone on the road. Once he's drinking, he thinks he can do anything. That's why I follow him around after he starts drinking." My voice began to get loud, "What am I suppose to do?"

"Mel, you are very strong. One of these days you'll make up your mind to give the responsibility of the bottle to Jake Bell."

⁓

The choir from Anderson University in Indiana was to be at the church the next night.

Jake came home early from the office just before the kids came home from school. He came in with a brown paper bag in his hands. He had a very red face and I thought about what Dr. Smith had said the day before.

Okay, this is your test, Melissa Ann. Don't pour out Jim Beam and don't stay home to make sure he doesn't burn down the house.

When Wendy and Neil came home, I told them we'd go on. Their dad would sleep while we were gone. I felt a mixture of freedom and dread: freedom to be away from it, but dread to have to come back to it.

Dean met us at the church door. He knew Jake had started drinking again, so after the kids went in the kitchen, he asked how he was.

"He came home early so I just left him in bed. I told the kids he'd be okay. He'll sleep the whole time we're gone."

Dean listened and said, "I'm so glad you brought your children and came on. You've started, now keep doing it."

When it was time for the choir to sing, they marched in and made a circle around the church. They started singing "Kumbaya." "Come by here, my Lord, come by here. Someone's praying, Lord, come by here."

At first it didn't mean much to me. Then my own words came to mind. *Someone's drinking Lord, go by there. That's the answer.* Then I thought, *Go by there, Lord, go by there.*

When we got home, Jake was still in his suit, white shirt and tie, and was on the floor where he had fallen. *White collar skid row,* I thought and just stepped over him.

The next day was his day off and he drank all day. I worked all that night to keep him off the bottle. Saturday morning Jake went to the office. Dr. Smith knew he had been drinking the night before. He called him and asked that we come to his office mid-afternoon. Jake agreed to do that. On our way, I drove and he wrung his hands. He hadn't had a drink since the night before and was fit to be tied.

Dr. Smith usually took off at noon on Saturday but he was waiting for us. We sat down and he got right to the point.

"Jake Bell, you've built up a very healthy practice in spite of your misbehaving. You can't go on like this. I want you to go into the hospital for the weekend and spend nights over there next week so you can get on your feet."

"Ira, that's not necessary."

"Yes, Jake, it is."

Finally Jake agreed, so Dr. Smith called and made the arrangements. I was to take him directly to the hospital from the office.

We got in the car and Jake said, "Honey, take me on home. I'm not going to the hospital." I didn't answer but just kept driving. We got to the street that went to the hospital. I turned onto the street ignoring that Jake had said he wasn't going.

"Oh no, Honey, I'm not going to the hospital."

"Jake, you agreed to it in Dr. Smith's office."

He took off his seat belt and opened his door. "I've got to get out of here."

"Okay," I said as I pulled over, "If you want to get out, more power to you."
Oh dear, what did I just do? I thought, as he got out and closed the door.

He turned toward the main street and started walking. I drove home and called Dr. Smith at his house.

"Mel, you've got to call the police and tell them where you left him and ask them to pick him up."

"Doctor, I just can't do that."

"He needs to be protected against himself."

"Oh dear, I don't think I can do that."

"Mel, it will be tough. Right now he needs tough love and you have got to give it to him."

I sighed and was silent for a second. "Okay, Doctor, I'll call the police."

I called the police and told them that my husband was an alcoholic and he'd gotten out of the car on the way to the hospital. I described him, told them where I'd left him, what liquor store I thought he'd stop at, and what motel I thought he might go to.

The police called back in about an hour and said Jake was there visiting with them. They found him with an unopened fifth of Jim Beam just before he got to the motel. They would talk to him about going to the hospital and call me back.

The three kids and I ate an early dinner. The policeman called back and said, "Mrs. Bell, the doctor asked that you come for him. He says he wants to come home and to tell you he'll behave himself."

"Could you keep him?"

"No. He hasn't broken the law. We've been sitting here visiting and drinking coffee, but he hasn't had anything to eat. This would be a good time to come and get him."

"I'll be there shortly."

I drove up and parked my car behind the police car. *It's amazing I never worry that Jake will be mad at me,* I thought, as I got out and started to the door. I walked inside and heard voices in a room down the hall to the right. I walked to the door. Jake stood and smiled, "Oh, there you are," he said. I glanced at the officer, who was slightly smiling.

He must think we're different, I thought as he reached in his desk drawer and brought out a brown bag that was obviously a fifth of booze.

"I have something here for you, Mrs. Bell."

"Would you please just keep it?"

"We aren't allowed to do that, Mrs. Bell, but Doctor tells me you're the best pourer-outer in seventeen counties."

"I've had lots of practice."

We got to the car and Jake said, "Man, Honey, I need a drink."

"Jake, you give me trouble and I'll let you walk." We got in the car and I started through the parking lot.

"I'm desperate, Honey."

I stopped the car and started yelling, "You're desperate? You are... desperate? Well, I'm desperate! I'm desperate to get you to shut up telling me every day that you're desperate." I took the bottle I had between me and the car door, got out, slammed the door, opened the bottle and poured all of it out except one drink and handed it to him. "Now, Mr. Desperate, this is to SHUT YOU UP! I'm SICK of your drinking! I'm sick that my kids are left at home without me while I'm hauling you around. I'm sick that they can't have friends over like normal kids. So don't you say the word desperate to me again tonight!"

"I know I'm a trial but I really appreciate you giving me this drink."

When we got home, I drove my car up behind Jake's station wagon. *He'll not get out to go for a bottle tonight*, I thought as I unhooked my seat belt.

Roxie met us at the back door. I could never tell if she was excited to see her daddy, or if she wanted to smell if he had been drinking.

Neil and Wendy were quiet the rest of the evening as we watched TV.

All night Jake was awake saying, "I've got to go get a drink." I had both sets of keys to my car and since it was behind his, he couldn't go anywhere.

Sunday morning the kids didn't want to get up but I was determined we were going to church. I made two or three trips to the front part of the house calling through the registers.

They know their dad is not going to want to go either and they're going to try to out-wait us.

Finally, after a lot of yelling and two trips upstairs, they came down just in time to get in the car. A heavy silence hung over us as we were going to church. I could feel the kids' resentment that I'd insisted they go to church. I resented having so much to do on so little sleep. It seemed the only time I slept was during the evenings if Jake was asleep in the chair. So much of the time when he drank, I was up most of the night keeping him from the bottle.

When we got home after church, I asked the kids to straighten their rooms. Wendy wanted to go to her friend's house mid-afternoon. I took her and hurried home to make sure I watched after Jake. Neil was watching TV. Jake was back and forth getting a cup of coffee, then sitting down for just a little while, lighting a cigarette, and putting it out. It went on like that for a long while. I cleaned the kitchen and started dinner. Roxie asked me to come up to her room, and as I got to the hall at the top of the steps, I saw that both Neil and Wendy had ignored my asking them to straighten their rooms. I turned around and stormed downstairs. "Neil, you go to your room this minute and do what I told you to do. What were you doing all that time you were supposed to be up there doing that?"

No answer.

"You just forget your TV program, young man."

When I picked up Wendy, I started in on her for leading me to believe she'd cleaned her room. She knew she wasn't to go until it was done. She looked straight ahead and said nothing.

That night when the kids went upstairs, Jake said, "Honey, you were a little hard on the kids."

"Listen, Buster," I yelled, "You take your rightful place in our home and I won't have to be hard on them! Why didn't you get them up for church this morning? Why didn't you see they did their rooms? Why didn't you do something with Neil instead of sitting in front of the TV all afternoon?" I kept getting louder, hating myself for it, but unable to stop. "Jake, the first three years of our married life I took care of just you and the kids when they came to visit. I can't give them what they need from you. I can take care of them in the proper way, or I can take care of a drunk night and day, but I can't do both."

I went into our room and sat down in the chair by the window. *The kids, all three of them, have heard my yelling. They are up there now feeling unloved and unwanted.* Just then Roxie came through our door. She came over to where I was and said, "Mama, are you going to yell at Daddy again?"

I took her on my lap and said, "No, Honey, I don't think so." We sat there a little while and I took her to bed.

Both Jake and I were restless all night. It was very cold and the weatherman said we were to get snow. I got up early and looked out the window. Sure enough, it had snowed.

I picked out Jake's clothes and got the kids off to school. When he was ready to go, I had Roxie ready to leave for preschool. I handed Jake his overcoat from the closet and said, "I'll take you to work."

"No, I'll drive myself and I'll drop our little girl off at preschool."

"Jake, I want to take you. We can't have what we had this weekend."

"No, I'm taking myself."

"Okay, Honey," I said to Roxie, "You go with Daddy. I'll pick you up at noon."

When I picked up Ulma, I was quiet from being so tired. She sat silently for a while, and then she said, "How are things at the farm?" I told her about Jake getting out of the car and my calling the police and how he and the policeman had a good visit.

"I can just see Doctor sitting there visiting like he had nothing else to do." She cocked her head to one side and said, "Mrs. Bell, I'd turn him loose. You need to let him be completely on his own."

"And what do I do with my kids in the meantime? How many wrecks can we count on while he's driving under the influence? What do the kids do when they have company and he's drinking?"

"I don't have the answers, but you need to give him responsibility for his own actions."

I'm not going to pay attention to that. As we say down home, she doesn't know her head in a bean sack when it comes to this—even if she has been with us six years, I thought. However, she was right.

～

The kids were going to be out of school a week for spring break. Jake had been taking pills again and kept promising he'd go into the hospital. Jewell lined up a doctor to take his place, but instead of the hospital, Jake spent his days in the station wagon in the field. I told the kids if we got him in the hospital, we'd go see friends in Denver while they were out of school for spring break. I had it all arranged and really wanted to go. We hoped to leave on Saturday, but were unable to get Jake to go to the hospital.

Each night it was a struggle to get him in the house. On Tuesday he was up in the field. I decided I would just leave him in the car. My friend from church said to bring the kids to her place. So I did, and when I got home, I walked up to the field to bring him home. It was very cold and I knew he'd freeze to death if he stayed in the car. I pulled him over to the passenger side and drove him home. He never woke up. I got out of the car and started toward the house and thought, *I'll call Zach. I can't let him freeze to death.*

"Zach, your brother is passed out in the car. I went up in the field and drove him home. I've been dragging him in the house, but I don't think I can get him in."

"I'll come get him and take him to the hospital."

The next morning I met Zach and Jake at the hospital. Jake was awake and to everyone's amazement, agreed to be admitted.

I went home, called the friends in Denver to tell them we could come after all, and then made arrangements for us to fly out that afternoon.

We had a great time. The Harrises had three children and it was so good to see my kids having fun. They went to see the Denver Mint, among other new experiences.

The ride back on the train was a fun time as well. The kids were joking back and forth with one another, playing with their little sister and everyone around seemed to enjoy it. It was a joy for me to see them happy and a relief not to dread what we might find at home.

Candy came home for the three remaining days of the break. She went to visit her dad in the hospital, and when she came home, she said, "Mel, Daddy wants you to call him."

I've got to have tough love, I thought, as I walked over to the phone in my room later that evening. *Dr. Searchbrains has taught me that when a drug or alcohol patient messes up, he wants his enabler by his side to see how badly he is hurting. While he's safe in the hospital, I need to let him have time to work through his problems without me. I want to take care of my kids.*

He sounded so good when he answered the phone.

"Oh, Honey, I'm so glad to hear from you." He asked about the trip and then said, "Are you coming tonight?"

"Jake, we leave the kids too much. I want you to work through your problems and come home determined to leave drugs and alcohol behind. I can't just run to the hospital when you're there for that reason. I believe that you're strong and don't need to keep depending on drugs and alcohol. The kids and I will be here waiting when you get home."

"Okay, Honey. Thank you for calling. I'll sure be glad to get out of here and go home."

Finally, Jake was dismissed. Things got very busy at the office and Jake started going to Scouts with Neil as well. We were also enjoying the parents' club at Jacob's school. Each time we went to Jacob's parade, we saw other parents we knew from the monthly meeting.

The good time lasted just a little while until the old pattern started again. I was standing at the window watching the rain from our bedroom. The chickens had all gone inside away from the downpour. *Even the chickens can hide from unpleasant things. I wish I could just go hide.* Part of a scripture verse I remembered hearing through the years came to my mind. "Thou art my hiding place." *I think David said that. I wish I knew how to hide. It's so hard to face people. I hate being involved with the medical auxiliary because all the other doctors know Jake has a problem, and if I don't show up at the auxiliary meeting this Friday, the wives will suspect he's drinking or taking drugs again.*

All of a sudden, I remembered telling Dr. Smith that I thought I'd start going with him everywhere. He hadn't been too enthusiastic about my doing that, but leaving Jake on his own wasn't keeping him sober, so I decided to give going everywhere with him another try.

I called the office. Jake was still there and answered like he was glad to hear from me. I got right to the point. "Jake, I've got an idea. You've started your old pattern of slowly getting back on pills. Soon you'll be bringing a bottle home. Then you'll be missing work. I've decided to go to the office with you each day and take you wherever you go until you get totally on your feet."

"Oh, no, Honey, you can't do that. I can lick it on my own."

"Sure you can, but if you don't choose to, then just remember I'm going to take over."

"You don't worry, Honey, everything's going to be all right." *I've heard that before. We'll see how he is when he comes home tonight,* I thought after I hung up.

Jake was home on time that evening but the next evening he came home slurring his words. Friday and Saturday he didn't go to work. Saturday morning Jewell called and said, "Mel, I've scheduled all of Friday and this morning's patients for Monday and we have a full day. Two of the patients are doctors' wives. He's got to be here."

"I'll have him there if at all possible."

I found all the pills and put his station wagon between the garage and my car and made sure I had all the keys.

Saturday evening he was desperate. Dean had called just after dinner and I told him Jake was walking the floor.

"I don't know how we are going to get through the night."

"Leave a light on at your back door and when our family time is over, I'll drop by and see how things are."

Jake kept getting up, coming to the family room to ask for the keys. I'd try to kid with him, and then I'd hug him. He'd respond to me, "But I've got to have a bottle." Dean slipped in the back door as one of our hugging times was going on. He was standing in the hall at the back door where he could see us.

Jake said, "Come on, Honey, let's go for a bottle."

"I'd rather hug."

"We'll do that again when we get back, come on."

Soon Jake started to the door where Dean was standing.

"Oh, hello, Dean."

Dean stuck out his hand and said, "Hello, Jake."

Jake was polite but said, "Excuse me, Dean. I need to go out this door."

"Oh, I'm disappointed, Jake. I came over to visit with you."

"Yes, sir, I want to do that sometime. Now, Dean," he said, putting his hand on the doorknob, "I know you're a man of the cloth and I respect that, but I've got to get past you."

Dean didn't move and I put both my arms around Jake. He tenderly put his hands on my shoulders. I reached up and kissed him and said, "I want you to stay here with me."

He looked down at me and said, "You're... a good... woman."

Dean could hardly hold his laughter.

We kept on trying to entertain him until sometime after 1:00 a.m., when he went to bed. Dean stayed until 2:00 then went home to get a few hours of sleep before church.

Jake was up at 6:00 a.m. He went in the kitchen and made coffee. I fixed his breakfast while he showered and dressed. *He's going to church. I can't believe how he bounces back.*

Dean acted like he had slept all night as he stood before his congregation that morning.

As we were going out the door, Dean said, "Good to see you, Jake." Jake took Dean's outstretched hand.

"Yes, sir!"

The next morning, I said very nonchalantly, "This is the morning I start going everywhere with you. I told Dr. Smith if I went with you a year, you'd get on your feet."

"Honey, how are you going to do that?"

"It will be hard but I'm going to do it. Nothing is as important as your staying well."

"Now, Melissa, this is going a little too far, taking me around everywhere."

"You can drive and I'll sit in the car and wait for you at some places. I'll do errands while you're at the office, or Roxena and I will stay in the room where you keep supplies. There's a desk and she can color and I can write letters. I'll stay out of sight. I've been planning this a long time, Jake. Your office manager called me. If you continue this pattern, she and her girls are all going to quit. You will never be able to replace them. I've talked to Dr. Smith. He said if you don't lick this problem on your own, you're going to have to be hospitalized for six months."

Jake got up off the side of the bed and put out his cigarette. "Melissa Ann, I can't have you driving me around."

"Jacob Bell, I can't have you falling over at the table and sleeping in front of the children. I can't pull on you anymore. If you're hospitalized for six months, how do I take care of the children?"

He picked up his red and blue striped tie, put it under his white collar and stood before the mirror. He tied it and then turned to face me.

He's so handsome and intelligent. Whatever it takes, he's worth rescuing.

"Let's give it another week."

"No, I'm starting today."

He became very quiet. I wondered what he was going to try next. I suspected that some time when I turned my back, he'd take off. *Oh well, I'll not turn my back.*

I dropped Jake off at the office that morning, took Roxie to preschool and went to pick up Ulma. I ran upstairs to make sure the kids' clothes were all brought to the laundry room before picking up Roxie at eleven o'clock. We went back to the office and waited until Jake was ready to go to lunch. That day it wasn't until 1:00 p.m. When Jake got the morning work done, we went home for lunch. He and Roxie took a short nap while I got the evening meal started. I left a sleeping Roxie with Ulma, took Jake back to the office, went back out to the farm, got Roxie and we took Ulma home. And then we went to the office for Jake. This was a short version of the schedule we had for the next ten months.

Betty, Jane and Joanne all said it was impossible with so many children and so much running around. "But," I said to Betty, "if he's going to get well, it's up to me."

"Melissa, it should be up to him."

Jake told me I needed to be home with the kids, even if they were capable of staying alone, but I insisted I take him everywhere. To make sure Jake didn't leave while I was in the shower, I'd get up much earlier than he. I was always close by to see that he stayed "well."

I'd give the kids jobs to do and come home to find them still undone. I was becoming a broken record, telling Neil and Wendy I needed their help, and I criticized them sharply when I was ignored. They'd look at me and say nothing.

Neil played ball that summer. One day, I had put his uniform in the washer before taking Jake back to the office. Roxie and I went to the store, then back to the office. I called home to tell Wendy that we'd be late and to put the uniform in the dryer for me.

When we got home, knowing we needed to leave soon, I expected Neil to have on his uniform. Both kids were in front of the TV. We carried in the groceries and I said, "We'll have to eat after the game. Neil, you should be dressed." Neither of the kids looked up. I went to get the uniform from the dryer and it wasn't there. "Wendy, what did you do with Neil's uniform?"

"Oh, it's still in the washer."

I came unglued. "What do you mean!" I yelled, as I lifted the lid of the washer, grabbed the wet uniform and threw it in the dryer. "How do you expect us to get to the game on time with the uniform still wet? Neil, you also knew that your uniform needed to be dried," I said as I turned off the TV. "No more TV tonight." Jake just silently watched and both kids left the room.

I sat down so angry and exhausted. When I talked to Betty about it, she pointed out that giving orders as I went out the door and explaining a need for the kids to help was a big difference. "Melissa, you've taken on the job of keeping Jake sober but the kids haven't taken on that job. They have no idea that they should do that."

Each time I talked to Betty, I knew I got an honest evaluation from someone with a lot of wisdom. Plus, Betty was never critical and I never doubted her real love and concern for me. Her time was limited between family and graduate school but she was always willing to talk when I called.

Over the Fourth of July holiday, Jacob went to visit his mother and Jake and I took the three younger kids on a camping trip at the river near my mother's. The kids had fun swimming and playing in the water on a large inner tube. Roxena Lynne found a turtle that she named Barbara. Mama gave her a box to bring it home in.

We'd been home for a few days when Jake announced, "Roxie, Honey, we need to turn Barbara loose and let her find a friend and more to eat than we're feeding her." With great reluctance and a promise from her dad that when he was in the garden or the barn lot, he'd always look for Barbara, she put the turtle down on the ground in the barn lot and we watched her go under the fence to the cornfield.

Every time we were in the barnyard, she would say, "Come on, Daddy, let's find Barbara." We would help her search for a short time and she was satisfied.

One Saturday, we were preparing to host the annual picnic for the parents' club and faculty from the Jacob's school, with Jake and me presiding as co-presidents. Though the event was to be catered, there was much to do. Jake was teasing me about getting the house immaculately clean. He'd run his hand over everything like he was checking for dust. I knew there was no worry about that because Ulma had been there the day before. Walking over to the refrigerator, he ran his finger across the top and said in jest, "The colonel will give ten demerits for this."

Jacob walked in and said, "Dad, I'll finish mowing the south pasture, then I'll mow around the barn."

As Jacob went out the back door, I said, "Go with him, Jake, so I can get something done. Take your little girl and give me two hours alone. Don't call me unless there is an emergency."

"Come on, Roxie, Honey," he said, taking her hand, "Let's get out of here. I'm driving your mama crazy."

They had been gone about ten minutes, and I was cleaning off the top of the refrigerator, when I heard Jake calling, "Mama! Mama! Come now!" I hurried off the stepstool and ran out the door. He continued to yell. I couldn't see him because the chicken house was in the way. I got to the back of the chicken house and answered to another, "Mama!"

"I'm coming!" Then I went around the building and saw him standing there.

"What happened?"

He held up his hand and gave a gesture of victory, as he said loudly, "We... found... Barbara!"

When I could get my breath, I said, "Jake Bell, I'd like to ring your neck."

Just then our little girl came around the barn with a turtle and all smiles. "Look, Mama, we found Barbara."

"Yes, Honey, I see you did."

With an impish grin on his face, Jake said, "Okay, Darlin,' you can go back to your work now."

When I told Betty, she laughed and said, "When he's not drinking, he is a real fun guy."

"Yes, Betty, and he's a loving daddy."

The colonel didn't give me any demerits the next day. We had a wonderful time. Everyone was so gracious and was looking forward to a good year in the parents' club. We got our meeting places lined up for the year and the speakers scheduled.

The day of our first meeting, while Roxie and I were in the office, Jake came back to our room and I gave him the list of things he was to do and say. I kept it simple, but everything he needed to do was listed.

Everything went well. I was so glad to see Jake at the head table, because he dearly loved the military school and was so glad Jacob was there. On our way home, Jake looked over at me and said, "I was terrific. I knew just what to do."

Each month after that he'd say, "Do you have my agenda ready?"

"Yes, sir!" I'd reply.

One weekend we went to Jacob's school to attend a football game and Dads' Day. In our free time, we went over to look at the antiques in the home of the lady who ran the restaurant. She had a very large carved oak table with carved chairs and sideboard. "Oh, Jake, look at this."

"My, that's the real thing."

"It's beautiful but what we have is just fine," I said.

On December twenty-third, Jacob went to the office to pick up his dad. I was in the kitchen rolling out pie dough when a knock came at the back door. I grabbed a towel to wipe the flour off my hands and went to the door.

"Mrs. Bell," the man said, "I'm from the furniture store up town. I've come to get your dining room furniture."

"I'm not selling my dining room furniture. There must be a mistake."

"Oh, boy, I've blown it," he said. Just then I saw another truck come in the drive that I recognized as belonging to Jake's cousin's moving company.

Jake had bought that antique dining furniture that we looked at when we were at Jacob's school.

I had to hurry and unload drawers and get everything ready for the new furniture. The older kids all knew it was coming. It was a lovely surprise.

I was down on my knees unloading the lower part of the buffet when I looked up and saw Jake standing in the kitchen doorway. I got up and put my arms around him and said, "Oh, thank you, Jake."

He patted me on the back, gave me a tender kiss and said, "Merry Christmas, Baby."

1971
NOW THE KIDS?

Ulma ran her hand over the round oak dining table. "Just look at all this. That doctor went all out for you this time. We'll have to do a lot of dustin' to keep this stuff clean. I sure can see, Mrs. Bell, that you had a great Christmas," she said, as she went from one piece of dining room furniture to the other.

It was our first day back to work after the Christmas break. The kids were back in school and I was back to driving Jake around.

That evening Zach called. "Well, hello there, Melissa. How in the world are you?"

"I'm fine, Zach, driving your brother crazy taking him around everywhere."

"Not many men would want their wives doing that, but if that's what works, hang in there." We visited awhile then I gave the phone to Jake.

I went to get my purse off the washstand to get some money to put in a birthday card for my nephew. I went back in the family room just as Jake got off the phone. "Jake, did you get some money from my billfold?"

"No, Honey, you know I would have told you. Why?"

"I thought I had more money than I have." We had suspected stealing before and I remembered seeing Wendy pick up my purse when I came in the door one day. We were both concerned about the kids spending so much time in their rooms. It was all starting to add up to me. "I wonder if Wendy is buying drugs."

"Oh, I don't think so, Honey."

"The neighbors across the street told us Steve Green was selling them."

Just then Wendy came through the family room and said, "I'm going out to play with the dogs."

After she walked out, I said, "Jake, I wonder if she's going out to meet someone to buy drugs." I went to the laundry room window and left the light off. I could see a young man coming across the road. "Jump up, Jake, and come to the door." I hurried to the door and stepped outside where the boy could see me and said, "Come on back in the house, Wendy."

The young man who I suspected to be Steve Green turned around and went back across the road. When we talked to Wendy, she admitted everything. Our suspicions were correct.

Wendy went upstairs and Jake said, "Check and see if your little girl is asleep and tell the kids we'll be back soon. I'm going to see that young man."

Roxie was asleep. When I came downstairs, Jake was standing at the door.

"Jake, we need to call his parents and see if they are home."

"Okay. I'll start the car."

The young man's mother was a teacher we had met before. When she answered, I told her that her son had been to our house, and we'd like to come and talk to the three of them if we could.

"Yes, Mrs. Bell. Come on down."

When I hung up I thought, *She's probably used to dealing with this. Her voice was so matter of fact. I think I understand. She's probably wondering when it will end!*

"Jake," I said as we drove to their place, "These parents are probably burdened down with this kid and don't know what to do next."

We talked about how to handle it. I knew I didn't have anything to worry about; Jake was going to talk as kindly as possible.

Both parents met us at the door. Jake and the dad shook hands and Jake said, "We need to talk to Steve. He came over tonight to meet Wendy outside and when we went to the door, he turned around."

His mother said, "I'll go get him."

His dad, Jake and I waited silently. His mother went to the stairs and said, "Steve, would you come down please? Dr. and Mrs. Bell are here to see you."

The dad asked us to sit down. Steve sat in a chair across from us and started bouncing up and down.

Jake put his hands together, his elbows on his knees and leaned forward. "Young man, you came to our house tonight to sell our daughter drugs."

The bouncing became faster.

"I don't do drugs. I help people get off drugs," he said, looking to the ceiling.

"Steve, just listen until Dr. Bell finishes what he needs to tell us," his mother said.

Steve continued to bounce.

"When Wendy went outside tonight, we saw from the window someone come from this direction. He was tall and we thought it was you. When we stepped outside, the young man turned around and came back this direction. When we questioned Wendy, she told us it was you and that she'd bought drugs from you before. Young man, if you come on our place again, sell or give one of our kids drugs, I'll call the police. Do you understand?"

"Yes," Steve said, looking to the ceiling and still bouncing.

"Thank you very much for letting us come," Jake said to the parents as he stood.

"Thank you for coming, Dr. Bell," the father said, sticking out his hand.

"You're most welcome."

"We're sorry," the mother said.

"We understand," and as I said it, I thought, *I really do.* Those parents didn't know what to do. They knew, as most everyone in our neighborhood did, that Jake had a drinking problem, but they seemed to be glad the problem with their son had come to a head.

How am I going to watch Wendy and her dad both? I thought as we drove home.

Jake said, looking over at me, "What do we do now?"

"She needs to start seeing Dr. Searchbrains. She's going to need someone to talk to."

"Well, she doesn't want to talk to us, and with you seeing him, she might resent him also. Ask Jane about the psychiatrist in their Christian medical group."

"That's a good idea."

Roxie was asleep and both kids were in their rooms when we got home. I called Jane. She gave me Dr. Mark Fox's number and said she thought we'd like him.

I went upstairs and sat down beside Wendy on her bed. I told her there was a doctor that saw a lot of young people and his name was Dr. Mark Fox. She would have someone of her own to talk to.

"What do you think?"

"We need to do something," she replied with a sad look on her face.

I put my arm around her, "I'll call the doctor in the morning."

"Okay."

After saying good night to both of the kids, I went downstairs and told Jake she agreed.

"I'm worried about her," I said as we were turning out the family room lights.

"When you go see your Dr. Searchbrains tomorrow, ask him about this doctor before you call him."

"Now you're calling him Dr. Searchbrains."

I lay awake wondering if Wendy was okay. I tried to pray but I felt guilty because I only talked to the Lord when I had an emergency.

Jake still isn't comfortable at church. Wendy and Neil seem to be doing okay with the youth group, but not really excited about going. I had such hopes that the church would really take my family to their heart, but it isn't working out that way. I'm free around Dean and Vonda but I feel like a stranger at church.

The next day, when I got Jake to the office and Roxie to preschool, I went to my regular appointment. I was trying to be cheerful when Dr. Smith motioned for me to sit down.

"Doctor," I said, "Even Jake is calling you Dr. Searchbrains."

He laughed and we chatted on for a while. He took a drink of coffee, put his cup on his desk and said, "Now, young lady, why don't you tell Dr. Searchbrains what's really going on?"

I lost it. I took a Kleenex from the box on the table beside my chair. Dr. Smith waited patiently. I told him about the night before.

He said, "Children steal because they feel deprived."

Dr. Smith knew and had a lot of respect for Dr. Fox and he thought that would be a good choice for Wendy and Neil also. He said, "Anytime there is an alcohol problem, the whole family needs counseling. It's better if everyone goes to the same person, but Jake doesn't want that, and we'll discuss the reason. The main thing is that the kids get help."

On the way back to the office, I continued to think of what Dr. Smith said about children stealing when they felt deprived. The more I thought of it, the more I saw what he was saying.

With Jake's drinking history, they've been deprived of what matters—parental involvement. The kids really don't feel they are cared for. I don't know how to show it to them. To keep them fed, clothed and taken all the places they want to go is about all I can do. Other than that, they don't respond to me.

I scheduled an appointment with Dr. Fox for Wendy before going to pick up Roxie from preschool. He could see Wendy the next afternoon at 4:00 p.m.

The next day it was raining. Roxie and I picked Wendy up from school and went directly to Dr. Fox's office. Afterwards, Wendy was quiet.

We went to pick up Jake. He met us at the back door of the medical building. When he got in, he turned around and said, "How'd it go, Wendy?"

"Okay."

"That's good. I've heard Dr. Fox sees a lot of teenagers."

Wendy didn't comment.

—

March came in like a lion. The last Sunday in the month, Neil and Wendy went to see friends after church. After we dropped them off, we went home. Jake turned on the TV and soon was asleep.

"Come on, Roxie, Mama will read to you before your nap." The last I knew we were on page five. All of a sudden I sat up in bed. I'd gone to sleep. I ran in the family room. Jake's chair was empty. I went to the door and looked out and the station wagon was gone.

About five minutes later he drove up. I met him at the back door. He walked in and said, "I know what I did. I know you don't like it but today I'm going to get relief from tension."

"Well, Buster, you go right ahead. But before you get too much relief with that bottle of pills you're carrying in your hand for me to see, I need to say something."

"I'm sure you do," he said as he went to the kitchen for a glass.

"Yes, I do," I said, getting in front of him. "I've followed you nearly ten months. Your practice is doing so well that it's almost more than you can keep up with. But now, you are on your own. I'll never follow you another place to make sure you stay well. If you enjoy getting sick, help yourself."

As I turned around, I realized I had spoken the truth. I would follow him no more.

I went in the bedroom and thought, *What have I just done? Tomorrow night is the parents' club meeting. We have to be there. Well, he knows that if he isn't in shape to go, I'll leave him at home. I'll get the sitter to come stay with the kids and get there when it's time to start so they won't ask questions. Then I'll do it myself.*

I sat down at the kitchen desk and wrote out everything that needed to be discussed at the meeting the next night and then put the notes in my purse. I called the sitter and told her what was going on. She could come if I needed her. Wendy could take care of everything unless Jake was home drinking or taking pills.

As I walked through the family room, I looked at Jake. He wasn't in bad shape yet, just asleep.

"Mama," Roxena Lynne said as she came through the door.

"Hi. You had a long nap."

"Mama, Daddy doesn't look right."

I looked in the family room. He had awakened and did look sleepy, but he was okay. I tried to reassure her. I hated having Jake slip back into the old pattern, but it had to be his decision to quit, even though it meant the kids seeing him in bad shape. He slept in the chair until after bedtime and then was restless until very late.

The next morning I jumped out of bed and hurried to the shower before Jake was awake. I reached for a towel from the linen closet and it dawned on me I didn't have to hurry. I would pick Ulma up and come home. We'd get caught up on a few things. I needed to check Jake's summer suits and clean out some closets.

I like the idea of staying home, I thought, as I went to the kitchen to plug in the coffeemaker.

Bacon was sizzling when Jake came in the kitchen.

"Good morning, Mrs. Bell," he said sheepishly.

"Good morning, Doctor," I returned. "Are we going to be formal this morning?"

"No, no, I just like knowing you're Mrs. Bell," he said as he poured himself a cup of coffee.

"I have everything written out for the parents' club meeting tonight."

"Oh, aren't you the one! I'd forgotten all about that. Has everyone been called?"

"Yes, Jake, last week. Will you drop your little girl off at preschool?"

He looked at me like he was hearing things. *He was expecting me to continue following him.*

"Oh, sure."

"Good. Call your kids to breakfast."

I can't believe that I'm not rushing through breakfast and shouting orders. Oh, I hope he doesn't come home sleepy from the Doriden and insist on going to that meeting. You've got to let go, Melissa Ann. I wonder what Dr. Searchbrains will say about this. My thoughts raced while we were eating.

We had a good meeting that night. Jake acted as though the list I'd made out on Sunday and read to him on the way to the parents' club were things he'd been thinking about all along.

When he said mothers were to meet the next week at one of the ladies' homes to address invitations, I thought, *I couldn't leave Jake to go do that.* Then it dawned on me. *I'm not following him anymore.*

The rest of that week, Jake was on edge. He was trying to stay off Doriden on his own. He might for a while, but I knew it could be a few weeks or even months, but he would probably go back to them, or to whiskey.

The next Monday evening after we got through with dinner, I said, "Jake, I'm going to go and help address invitations for the mixer."

He looked up from the paper and said, "Okay, I'll hold down the fort."

He looks and sounds so good; I think he'll be okay. I told everyone where I was going and left the phone number on the kitchen desk.

Three other ladies were there. We all sat down at the table and everyone had their list of names. I picked up an envelope and thought, *What if he leaves and gets a bottle? Or what if he has one in his car? I should have checked.* I started to write the name and address of a young lady and I made a mistake. Each time I addressed an envelope, I'd look at the address, but without fail, I'd made a mistake. I was so embarrassed. The hostess was very gracious when I said, "I really don't want to waste any more envelopes." My hands were shaking a little and I saw one of the ladies looking at them. *I wonder if they think I'm the one with the drinking problem.* I was acting like someone having withdrawal symptoms.

"Mel, I was going to stuff the envelopes tomorrow. Don't worry about addressing any more unless you want to." The hostess got the notes she had ready and placed them in front of me to stuff. We worked until we finished and I left soon afterward.

They are bound to be talking about me, I thought, as I backed onto the street. I was in a hurry to get home, but dreaded to get there all at the same time.

When I parked the car after arriving home I jumped out and hurried to the door.

This won't do. I can't let him think I expect him to be bent out of shape. I had that tight feeling of dread in my stomach. *Maybe that's the way the kids feel each night they get off the bus, wondering what it's going to be like the rest of the evening.*

Jake's back was to me when I walked in. I went around his chair and he looked up from his radiology journal and smiled at me, knowing I was wondering if he was okay.

"I read your little girl a story," he said, still looking at me and smiling.

"I bet she enjoyed that."

"How was your meeting?"

"Oh, Jake, I ruined every envelope I tried to address. I'd get the letters backward or write ahead of myself."

"You were away from your husband and didn't know what to do. Honey, don't you think it's time for us to get you a tutor? You'd be so much more comfortable when you need to do something like you did tonight."

"I'm not ready for a tutor, Jake."

"Okay, but you've struggled with this for years and it isn't necessary."

I really didn't think Jake understood just what a problem I had. I got up and went to clean my face, wishing there was a way out of all my problems. My main concern was Neil. He had become very quiet and wasn't doing well in school. The military academy was now taking younger boys, and Neil had expressed some interest, but I didn't think he was old enough.

After I checked on Roxena Lynne, I paused at Neil's door. I heard him in there and said, "Goodnight, Neil." He didn't answer.

I went by Wendy's room and said, "Goodnight, Wendy."

"Goodnight."

Neil had grown much too quiet lately. When we talked to him, although he was looking at us, I sensed he wasn't really seeing or hearing us. I went into the family room. Jake was still reading his journal. I sat down and waited. He looked at me, laid his journal on the table by his chair, and got a cigarette from his pocket.

"Jake, did you talk to Neil tonight about going to see Dr. Fox?"

"Yes. He told me the same thing he told you, that he didn't want to go. I hate to make him."

"I do too. I was hoping he'd want to go. It's getting more and more difficult to have a conversation with him. Sometimes he answers and sometimes he doesn't."

"What do you think we should do?" he asked.

"I don't know."

The next day, when I went for my appointment, I told Dr. Smith I was wondering about Neil. I explained some of my concerns. I shared with him that we were trying to get him to go see Dr. Fox but he didn't like that idea.

"Doctor," I said, "I think we should all come to you. I've been seeing you for four years and you know the whole family. Jake thinks the kids want their own doctor. He thinks they'll feel freer and won't resent going so much."

"Plus," Dr. Smith said with a twinkle in his eye, "You can't all gang up on Jake and figure him out if the kids and you are going to different places."

"Do you really think that?" I asked.

"It's something you may want to consider. If everyone saw his game playing and decided to stick together, it would make it a little harder for him to get by with his behavior, don't you think?"

I wasn't sure what to think. Dr. Smith was always bringing up something for me to think about.

That evening after the kids were in bed, Jake was looking at a catalog and said, "Melissa Ann, I want to get you some chickens for Mother's Day. If you had some baby chicks, I'd buy these caponizing instruments and we'd have capons to butcher."

"You sure I want chickens for Mother's Day?" I said amused, knowing this was his way to break the news.

"Oh, I think you'll like having capons. After the operation the cockerels can't crow and they get real large. The meat is wonderful. My dad did that one year."

"Sounds like we'll be having capons."

It was time for the state medical convention. On the way to the meeting we talked about Karen's graduation from college and Jacob's from high school. They were to be on the same day. We decided to go to Flagstaff for Karen's birthday, May sixth, and be home for Jacob's graduation the end of the month.

On the day we were to leave to fly to Flagstaff, I got a sore throat. By noon, I had a fever. I called Jake and told him I didn't think I should go.

"Oh, Honey, you'll be okay. I'll pick you up in two hours. You can rest on the plane."

He's afraid he'll drink if I don't go. Maybe I should try, even though I said I wouldn't follow him around.

Candy was home at the time and helped me pack and get Roxie ready. When Jake came home, I went to the car and lay down in the back seat.

When we arrived at the airport, I said, "Jake, I'm really feeling badly. I don't know if I can do this."

"I'll take good care of you, Honey."

We got in the air and I felt really sick. Jake was so kind and helpful, but I could tell he was not going to let himself believe that I was as sick as I was.

Finally, we got to Karen's and she put me to bed right away. The next morning, I said, "Jake, I think I have strep throat."

He looked at my throat and said, "You know, Dr. Mel, I think your diagnosis is right."

He and the girls took Karen to college and when they came back, Jake had a syringe and an antibiotic. Roxena Lynne and her little niece Melonie, two years younger, put their elbows on the bed with their chins in their hands and watched their daddy and grandpa give me a shot.

That afternoon I was much better but still felt best lying down. I suggested that Jake go to the bakery and get a cake for Karen's birthday. When she came home from college, she put on a roast for dinner. Jake went alone to get the cake.

Soon after he returned, Karen came in and said, "Mel, daddy brought in a bottle and put it in the kitchen. It's in the trashcan by the refrigerator."

I got out of bed and went directly to it. It was opened and looked like he had taken one drink. I grabbed it up, left it in the paper sack and when I went past Jake who was looking at me over his paper, I said, "Don't you dare follow me."

I went in, poured Jim Beam down the drain and then got my pillow and lay on the living room couch. Jake was sitting at one end. He took my feet and placed them in his lap and kept reading the paper.

Did he go get that bottle knowing I'd get up and come in here? This is crazy. Is this another way he's using the bottle? Well, it worked. I'm no longer in the bed, I'm out here with him and he looks very contented.

As I lay there, I began to understand that I used to feel a certain satisfaction when I poured out his liquor, like I was in control. Now, it didn't mean that much.

We flew back the day before Mother's Day. I was feeling much better.

On Friday night of that same week, I awoke about 1:00 a.m. and I could see the kitchen light. I went in to see which one of the kids was up and if they might be sick. I walked through the door and Neil was standing with the cabinet door open and the lid of the breadbox down. He had a very wild look on his face. "Don't come closer," he said holding his hand out to stop me.

"Why, Neil, is something wrong?"

"Yes," he said, with his hand blocking space between the cabinet and me. "They're going to electrocute us."

"What is going to electrocute us, Neil?"

"These bugs—they're everywhere."

"We can go on back to bed and take care of them in the morning."

"Oh no, I can't leave them."

"I'll tell you what, you watch them and I'll go get your dad." I ran down the hall to our room.

"Jake," I said, putting my hand on his shoulder urgently, "Wake up."

He rose up, looked at the clock, and said, "What's this all about? It's 2:00 a.m.?"

"Neil's on a trip, Jake. I need you to come help me to make sure he's okay."

"Are you sure he's on a trip?" he said as he started for the door.

"I'm afraid he is. He's seeing bugs and he thinks they are going to electrocute him."

Jake walked in the kitchen and said, "Hi, Neil. How are you doing?"

Putting out his hand again, he said, "Stand back, Dad, these bugs are everywhere."

Jake turned around to me and said, "We need to move that little cot into our room."

I hurried to do that. When I went back in the kitchen, Jake had him away from "the bugs" and steering him toward the door.

"We'll leave was everything until morning, Neil, and I'll take care of it," he said, as he led him to our room and got him on the cot. He got his black bag out of the closet, took Neil's blood pressure and checked him to make sure he was okay.

Neil went to sleep soon and so did his dad, but I was wide awake. Every thirty minutes I took his pulse to see if he was okay. In between times, I tried to pray. I felt guilty for losing patience with Neil, Wendy and Jacob and for being too critical.

The next morning, I was frying bacon when I heard Jake and Neil talking. As soon as I could, I went to listen. I got there in time to hear Jake say, "The school principal will be discreet. We need to let this be known, Neil, before other kids buy more from this young man than you did. I'm just glad we caught it when we did. This selling has to stop. You can trust me." He tied his tie and continued, "Now your 'Ole Dad' misbehaves himself, so I understand; but let's get you some help, Neil, before it's too late. You need someone to talk to that sees your side of things. Dr. Fox sees a lot of kids your age, or you can go to Dr. Smith. He knows all of us and understands what you're up against. What do you say?"

"I don't want to go to anyone."

"I wouldn't think you were normal if you did, but it's real necessary."

"If I have to go, I'll go to Dr. Fox."

"Okay, we'll get it arranged."

I stood there in the bedroom watching Jake get ready for work as he talked kindly to Neil, who had a hopeless look on his face. The sad thing, as I saw it, was that Neil's life was beginning to reflect how Jake lived—getting into trouble and getting bailed out.

It was hard not to go with Jake that morning. I was afraid he would be worried about Neil and want to drown it out by drinking. I'd been tempted several other times to go with him, as well.

I asked Betty why she thought it was so hard to not follow him. "Betty," I said, "It's like I'm addicted to following him and have to keep myself from it."

"Melissa, you are in the process of deprogramming your thinking. You've started and it's working. Someday you'll stop looking for his bottles and stop pacing the floor when he's late."

"I don't think that time will ever come."

"Oh, I think it will. You just keep going to Dr. Searchbrains and keep your faith."

Even though Betty doesn't believe in the Lord as I do, she has always encouraged me, I thought as I hung up.

Jake was late that Saturday afternoon and he hadn't called. I went and looked out the window and thought about what Betty had said. I decided I'd try not to look out the window anymore. Several times I started to look, but caught myself and turned away to something else.

It was about 2:30. He was always home by 1:00 p.m. on Saturday afternoon.

I sat down in the chair in the family room. *Oh, I don't know what we'll do. Tomorrow is Jacob's graduation and I'll be up half the night keeping him off the bottle so Jacob won't be disappointed.* Just then I heard his horn in the drive. *Well, now's a good time to stay where I am and not look anxious.*

I heard him talking to the kids in the yard. *He seems fine, but where has he been? He always calls when he's late.*

"Mama, come here," he called. Just then Roxena Lynne came through the door smiling from ear to ear.

"Mama, Daddy said your late Mother's Day present came." I had started to the door. She took my hand, "Hurry, Mama, we have one hundred baby chicks."

By that time, he'd taken the boxes out of the car and I could hear them. We walked out the door to see him grinning from ear to ear. "Your Mother's Day present was late, Mama," he said, "but here they are."

"I see and hear."

The next day was sunny and beautiful for Jacob's graduation. It was a wonderful ceremony. As the cadets were throwing their hats in the air, Jake said, "Half of the kids have graduated, Mama. It won't be long until it will be just you and me."

"We've got a while yet."

The next week we started making plans to go to the church convention. Jake said we could go Monday through Thursday or Thursday through Sunday. I called Dean to see when Dr. Dale Oldham would be speaking. He was scheduled to speak Tuesday evening, so we decided to go the first part of the week. I had grown up listening to Dr. Oldham speak on the Christian Brotherhood Hour each Sunday afternoon and was anxious for Jake to hear him.

We got to the convention tabernacle just as Doug Oldham started to sing. We sat down in the first two empty seats we saw. Jake sat there listening then turned to me and whispered, "Haven't we heard this fellow sing before?"

"Yes," I whispered back. "You bought me his record. It's Doug Oldham."

Soon we were asked to greet everyone around us.

The couple in front of us turned around and I couldn't believe my eyes. It was a couple who had been friends of mine from youth rallies and camp in high school. He was teaching at the college. "Oh, wow," I said to Jake as we sat down, "This is great."

We saw others that night that I'd known years before. I hated to leave the grounds.

Early in the morning I said, "Jake, are we going to early prayer meeting?"

"Melissa Ann, you brought me all the way up here to this 'meetin'" and we're taking everything in."

The minister whose home I had stayed in when I took some of my youth group to convention in 1961 was in charge of the early morning service. That afternoon while we were sitting at the pool, I told Jake about going to the altar and telling the Lord that I was in love with him. He sat silently for a while and looked over at me and said, "You know, I think my dad would have liked that early service this morning. As the people shared, they all sounded so happy." He paused then said, "Mel, I'm through taking the Doriden. I just wanted you to know."

I didn't comment.

Every time we went to the campgrounds, I saw people I'd known from years gone by. Reverend Good, whom I had seen on the campgrounds at the family camp down home when I had Jake in the motel, was there. Jake really liked visiting with him.

On Tuesday night, we heard Dr. Oldham speak. In his sermon he said, "What a wonderful day it is for the alcoholic when he finds peace in Christ." *Oh, thank you, Lord. That was worth the trip.*

After the morning service on Thursday, we drove back to Indianapolis and flew home. It had been a wonderful vacation.

Maybe, just maybe, better times are on the way.

⚬

Jacob got a summer job in a factory close to home working the evening shift and helping a farmer part-time early mornings and Saturdays. It was hard work loading and unloading the truck with hay bales. Jacob was a good worker and was getting ready to go to college. He'd chosen a school a couple of hours drive from home.

Our garden was wonderful that summer. Jane and I put the corn away together while our kids spent time outside. Wendy volunteered at a day camp for children with developmental disabilities until noon each day. Her dad took her and I picked her up. Neil went to Boy Scout camp. I was forever sewing patches on his shirt. He was quiet and not very cooperative about chores, but was doing well in Scouts. He and Wendy were still seeing Dr. Fox. We hoped it was helping but we weren't sure.

Jake went on a camping trip with Neil, so I called my friend in Denver and the girls and I spent our vacation there. We went to Estes Park and spent the day. It was a great vacation. I went to see a former pastor's widow that I always tried to visit when we went to Denver. It was such a joy to see her. Yet in my heart I knew I wasn't as close to the Lord as I had been when she knew me. When I hugged her and told her good-bye, she said, "Oh, Honey, it was so good to see you."

With no warning, tears started down my cheeks and I said, "Pray for us," and turned and left.

As I reflected on the visit that night, I felt far from the Lord.

⚬

Our little girl started kindergarten in the fall. It had been fun getting her ready. She was so proud to start, but as I walked down the school steps to the car, I cried—my little girl was growing up.

Jacob left for college. Wendy kept her summer job, but on Saturdays only. One Saturday we went to pick her up and were told that she and a friend had walked to K-Mart and we were to pick them up there. When they came out of K-Mart, they each had a sack. We asked them what they'd bought and they said records.

That's strange. I don't think Wendy had much money, I thought, with a little worry.

That night I mentioned it to her dad. He said her mother and grandmother might have sent her money. Surely it was easier to think that than to think she was stealing, but I kept recalling what Dr. Smith had said about kids stealing because they feel deprived.

Dr. Fox wanted to see Jake and me, so I made an appointment for Thursday, Jake's day off. The doctor asked us several questions, then looked at me and said, "Why is it so important to you that Wendy keeps her room clean? Why can't you just close the door and let it go at that?"

I answered him the best I could but I was surprised by his question.

When we were going home, rush hour traffic was at its peak.

Jake looked over at me and said, "What do you think about Dr. Fox?"

"Well, when he started talking about my closing the door on Wendy's room, I didn't think he knew his head in a bean sack."

Jake must not have heard me say that before. He started laughing so hard I thought we'd have a wreck.

"Jake, you need to get a hold of yourself or pull over. You're going to have a wreck." Finally he calmed down but he really enjoyed that.

A few days later, he was talking about someone making a ridiculous statement, and then he smiled and said, "He doesn't know his head in a bean sack."

When I told that to Betty, she laughed and said, "Oh heavens, he's going to use all those country sayings better than you do, Melissa."

Wendy's first year in high school wasn't going as well as we'd hoped. One morning about 9:00 a.m. her friend called to talk to her and I said, "She's in school."

"No, Mrs. Bell, we didn't have heat at school today so they let us out."

She had spent the day with friends. When it was time to come home, she called and asked us to pick her up at the school. When she got in the car, Jake turned and said, "Wendy, before school started, I wanted you to go to a private school because I heard the kids had too much freedom here. Now, I'm giving you one more chance. If there's another time that we don't know where you go or who you're with, we'll look for a private school." Wendy didn't say anything and we dropped the subject.

Neil's grades weren't good and Jake started talking about sending him to the academy.

Both the kids were seeing Dr. Fox regularly. He knew what they were up against.

Jake was drinking evenings and I was sleeping while he slept in the chair. Then I'd fight with him all night to keep him off the bottle. Often I'd get loud and when he did settle down, I'd worry that the kids had heard me. Jake went on a full-fledged binge, but by early November, he was getting back to himself.

One day while I was Christmas shopping, I ran into a lady I knew from one of the kids' schools. I casually asked how she was.

"Oh, okay," she said as we stood by a row of men's blazers. "At least my husband's not on the golf course in this weather. I guess I'm like the alcoholic's wife. She doesn't want her husband to be drunk, but when he gets sober, she doesn't know what to do with him."

Are there actually people who think that? I wondered. I didn't dare comment for fear I'd give her a clue that I was an alcoholic's wife. Yet, I wished I could correct common misconceptions about alcoholics and their families; they bothered me a great deal.

After Thanksgiving, Jake and I went to Chicago for the Radiological Society of North America's annual meeting. I always enjoyed going to those meetings. We had the evenings free and went to the theater and sometimes a hockey game.

One of Jake's old instructors from the Mayo Clinic was scheduled to speak at this meeting. Jake introduced me to him and his wife. She was a delight. She shared with me what it was like to be a doctor's wife in the 1930s and all she planned to do as soon as her husband retired in the spring.

The morning we were to leave, I went down to the lobby to check out and wait for Jake. Our plane was to leave shortly after noon.

I sat down where I could see him come out of the conference room. All of a sudden I just wondered if he might be across the hall in the bar. I went to the door and stood just inside. There he sat on the barstool. I walked over to him. His glass was almost empty. "Finish this so we can go," I said, touching the glass. "Our things are down here and we are checked out."

"Oh, aren't you the one."

I had the bellman take our luggage to the cab outside and we were off to the airport. We were early and the first ones to board. I stepped behind Jake before we got on the plane. He had the boarding passes. He was a little unsteady but could still function. He handed the flight attendant the passes and started to walk on. I said, "I'm with that patient. He's an alcoholic. I have to get him to St. Louis sober. If he asks for a drink, just ignore him, please."

"What if he argues with me?"

"I don't think he will, but if he does, pay it no mind."

"I'll see what I can do."

"Thank you."

Jake went to sleep as soon as we sat down. We got in the air and the flight attendant came down the aisle with her refreshment cart. The man across from us told her what he wanted to drink.

"I'm sorry, sir. The captain informed me we wouldn't be serving liquor on this flight."

I couldn't believe my ears.

Jake slept all the way to St. Louis. I felt very satisfied when we got home to the kids and their dad was sober.

It was tempting to start following Jake around during the weeks before Christmas but I held tight. He was trying very hard to stay sober. He was up and down all hours. I'd get up with him and we'd sit in the family room or walk around. He'd try to read. I'd fix a snack. We'd eat. One minute he'd say he was desperate, the next he'd say how stupid he was for visiting the bar in Chicago.

One morning when I went in to see Dr. Smith, I told him of one of our nights.

"He had you convinced that he was totally sorry for going to the bar and drinking, didn't he?"

"Yes, he did."

"When you see how Jake suffers, you don't want him to drink more. Then he shows you his great effort to stay off it, so that when he does slip, you'll understand."

"Do you think his getting up and down was staged?"

"No, I think he was hurting, but he didn't just quietly get up and go in the other room."

"No."

"Did he say, 'Mel, Honey, I'll be fine. I'm restless, but I'll read or fix myself something to eat, you go on back to bed,'?"

"No."

"Of course not. He wanted his enabler there with him. Alcoholics are con artists and Jake Bell is the best. Sure he hurts, but if he stops for a bottle, you'll know he's put forth an effort. He has that already taken care of."

"Makes sense."

My last day to see Dr. Smith before Christmas, I felt worn out just meeting needs, mainly Jake's.

I told him, "I feel like my job is too great. I'm exhausted and sharp with everyone."

"Mel, give the care of Jake Bell to Jake Bell. Refuse to be his keeper."

In the car on the way home I thought, *Now, how am I going to do that? If I mention it to Betty, she'll remind me of the word de-program. I know that's what I need. Makes me tired to think about it. What will life be like in 1972?*

1972
It's the Life I Chose

On January 2, the kids were watching a game show on TV. Wendy was hemming a new pair of blue jeans. *That's different. She always asks me to do that or at least help her.* I finished mixing up a banana cake and placed it in the oven. I glanced in the family room and Wendy wasn't there. *That was quick,* I thought. *Just why was she hemming her jeans?* I wondered, and then, *I bet she has plans that she hasn't mentioned.* I turned the timer on the oven and started for the stairs. As I put my hand on the banister, the thought came to me, *She's gone.* I hurried to her room at the top of the steps. Her door was open, her old jeans were on the floor and her closet door was wide open. I panicked. *She's gone. I knew it.* "Wendy!" I called. I looked everywhere upstairs. I went downstairs and checked the front door. It was unlocked and so was the screen.

"Boys," I said as I went back in the family room, "Do you know where Wendy is?" They each said, "No." I hurried to the phone and called Jake, but he was with a patient. I hung up and hurried to the barn.

Oh Lord, when do the problems stop? The phone rang and I picked it up at the barn.

"Hello there, Mrs. Bell."

"Jake, Wendy's gone."

"What makes you think she's gone?"

I proceeded to tell him.

"Oh now, Honey, you know you jump to conclusions. She's probably out at the barn."

"I'm at the barn now, Jake," my voice rising. "We've got to be serious about this. I know deep down that she's gone."

"Did she take her things?"

"No, but..."

"Honey, she'll be back," he interrupted.

"Jake, I need you to come home. She's gone! You can't put this problem off. You need to be here!"

"Okay, I have to call the doctors. The reports can be dictated in the morning."

I hung up and ran to the house. I thought of a young man, Tom Johnson, who had come to the house with some of Wendy's friends. I called one of the friends. "Val," I said after I told her who I was, "I need Tom Johnson's number. I need to talk to Wendy and I think she's with him."

"Oh, yes, Mrs. Bell," and she rattled it off.

I dialed the number and his mother answered.

"Mrs. Johnson?"

"Yes."

"I'm Melissa Bell. I need to get in touch with my daughter Wendy and wondered if I could speak to Tom?"

"Oh, Mrs. Bell, didn't you know they were going to Sikeston?"

"Sikeston? No, she didn't have permission to go."

"Oh dear, we didn't understand that. They were going to go with a friend who is dating a girl there. They are to be home Sunday night."

"Do you have the girl's number?"

"No, but I'll give you the number of the other boy's parents. They are a real nice family and, Mrs. Bell, if Tom calls home, I'll tell him to bring your daughter home immediately, and I'll call you." Her voice sounded strained.

She gave me the name and number of the other boy's parents, and just as we were saying our good-byes, I heard Jake's horn. *That was quick. He's worried too.*

Jake called the other boy's dad and got the telephone number of the Sikeston girl's home and called her mother. He explained that Wendy had gone without permission and we were leaving to come and get her. The mother ran a motel and told Jake the boys and Wendy had rented a room before they went to pick up her daughter at work. At that point we were beside ourselves.

Jake drove extra fast. He was determined to get there as quickly as possible.

Finally Sikeston came into view. We drove to the motel office. The woman said the kids had been in the room about fifteen minutes. She gave Jake the key. We parked in front of the door.

"Jake, are you going to just barge in?"

"That's what I'm going to do," he said as he opened his door.

"Honey," I said, holding his arm, "restrain yourself. You may feel like killing but just remember we are here only to get Wendy."

He looked at me with troubled eyes under his gray hat. I saw him put the key in the door. My heart was beating so fast; I wondered if I should have gone, but we'd talked about it and decided I'd be of more help to Wendy afterward if I just stayed in the car. Jake unlocked the door and went in. I looked at the clock in the car. It had been only five minutes when Wendy and Jake came out. He opened the back seat door and I could smell liquor; to our knowledge, she'd never had anything to drink before. We drove in silence for a while. Wendy soon went to sleep in the back. I wondered what took place in those five minutes, but I didn't ask for fear of waking Wendy.

Finally Jake said, "They'd all been drinking. They were sprawled across the two beds fully dressed. They never heard me enter. When Tom Johnson woke up, I had him up against the wall."

"Oh my, what did you do to him?"

"His eyes were as big as saucers, and I said, 'Young man, you brought my daughter here without my permission, and if this ever happens again, I'll skin you alive! Do you understand?' The young man said, 'Uh, uh, uh yes, sir.' I turned loose of him and shook Wendy and said, 'Come on, Wendy, you're going home with your daddy.' I got her coat off the chair, took her by the arm and we walked out the door."

"Didn't she have to put on her shoes?"

"She'd never taken them off."

We rode in silence for a long time. Then, with a cracked voice he said, "You know, Honey, I could have never gone to bed not knowing if she was okay."

We woke Wendy when we got home. She was a little dizzy. I made her a bed in the family room. We weren't sure just how much she'd had to drink, but she went to sleep right away. It was after 2:00 a.m. We hurried to bed because Jake had to work but sleep wouldn't come for me. I kept going in to check on Wendy; each time I checked she was sleeping soundly.

Jake had gone and the household was busy before Wendy woke up.

When her dad got home after work, we could tell she was dreading to talk with us.

After we'd eaten Jake said, "Wendy, we need to talk." He took off his glasses and looked over at her. "Now, Wendy, you gave us a scare. When we found out you were gone, nothing else but finding you mattered." Wendy was looking at him, but gave no response. Jake put his glasses back on and leaned forward toward her. "Wendy, your ole daddy could not have put his shoes under the bed and gone to sleep last night not knowing where you were."

We talked to Wendy about going to a private school, but we knew her problems wouldn't stop just by changing schools. Nonetheless, at our large public school the kids came and went without the parents knowing what went on, so Monday morning we went to a private girls' school and enrolled her. Wendy was very quiet and looked so lonely as we went into the office.

The girls' academy was about twenty miles away—more driving. Wendy talked very little about school but I would see her outside visiting with other girls when I went to pick her up. Soon she brought a friend home with her who lived with foster parents. She was a very sweet girl. We were glad that she seemed to be adjusting.

Dr. Fox asked to see us, so we went in with Wendy to talk to him. "Melissa," he said, "Wendy is going to have her sixteenth birthday in a few weeks. She needs a party. I don't hear her talk about fun things. She's a teenager and needs parties and that sort of thing."

I stammered a little. "Maybe we could have a party if we could do it closer to spring when her dad has a Boy Scout trip; that may be better." I looked to Jake. He was very still and knew I was uncertain because of not knowing whether he'd be drinking or not.

Dr. Fox looked over at me. "I really want her to have a party. Sixteen is a special birthday."

Yes it is, I thought, *that is why she shouldn't have to worry about her dad drinking. Why isn't he taking this up with Jake and getting him to make a commitment? This doctor knows Jake drinks. Why can't he guess the reason I'm hesitating? If we were seeing Dr. Smith, he'd know how to deal with it.*

"I think," the doctor continued, "that Dad should be there. A lot of times, a man on the scene is a good thing. What do you think? Could she have a party?"

It was obvious he was expecting his answer from me.

I looked at Jake. "What do you think, Jake? Do you see any problems in having a group of girls in for a night?" He moved his hand from his chin, put both hands on the chair arms and looked over at me.

"No, Honey, you're the one that handles those things."

I looked over at Wendy. "We have less than two weeks. Wendy, do you think we can get ready for your party?"

"Yes, I don't see why not."

I looked at Dr. Fox, and then I turned to Jake and said, "Jake, I'll have to have your help with this."

"Well, like Mark says, you're only sixteen once."

I felt so frustrated. He wasn't committing himself and the doctor probably thought I was holding back. I was always trying to do things for the kids' special days, while at the same time trying to make sure their dad wasn't drinking. They were all looking my direction and I was sure Jake saw my struggle and knew why I was having a hard time. Wendy looked like she thought I didn't want to have a party for her. Dr. Smith was helping me to see that everyone was feeling deprived and defeated because of Jake's alcoholism. That's what I saw in Wendy's sad expression that day. I felt if I tried to explain it, she'd still take it too personally, so, even though I was worried about the possibility of Jake drinking, I had to try to give her a birthday party.

We'd spent most of the evening with the doctor talking about fun things for the kids. When we left, I felt exhausted as more pressure piled up. That night, my shoulder and back ached, and sleep came very late.

At my regular appointment the next day with Dr. Smith, I started telling him everything as he was bringing in a tray of coffee. After I'd told him all the things the doctor thought I should do to make sure the kids had fun, I reached up and rubbed my neck and shoulder.

"You're tense aren't you, Mel?"

"Yes, Doctor," I said, starting to cry. "I feel a binge coming on, and my cleaning lady is off for six weeks because she has hurt her foot. Last night when I went to bed, my whole back ached from the neck down."

"Mel, I've explained to you that your stomach problems may have been from having a belly full. Also, I think, and I've said before, you have a back-breaking job. You're angry because the new doctor you wanted to help the kids seems to be loading you down with more things to do." He rolled his chair toward me. I took a tissue from the box by my chair and wiped my eyes.

"Mel," he said softly, "It all goes back to Jake Bell. He'll let you do the work. He'll hope Wendy will be happy, but he'll drink if he wants to and hope that you can keep coming up with things to make the kids happy. Then he can drink some more when he feels guilty for drinking in the first place. As long as you take his responsibility, you are enabling him to continue in his vicious cycle."

"What am I to do?" I said, louder than I'd intended. "I didn't know how to say 'no' to Dr. Fox with Jake and Wendy both there. I'll get ready for that party, Doctor, and I'll do my best to see that Wendy has a good time, but if Dr. Jake Bell goes on a binge, I'll put him in a motel and take all his money and maybe his clothes," I said, trying to control my emotions as my mind ran wild.

The party was planned for Friday night, February twenty-ninth. Thursday, Jake's day off, was spent with me trying to keep him from drinking. Even though I knew that reasoning with an alcoholic didn't work, I tried to explain we were having a party and he had to be sober. "I will," he said, but kept drinking.

I got nothing done on Thursday and was up all night trying to keep Jake sober, but Friday morning he was still drinking. Wendy didn't ask if we should cancel the party, so I decided to go ahead with it. I called Jewell and she canceled the patients for Friday and Saturday. I stopped trying to get Jake to stop drinking and went to work cleaning and doing the laundry. Joanne picked up the cake and brought popcorn, chips, drinks and a large hoagie that would serve all the girls. Roxena was to go to Jane's house after school and I'd pick her up as soon as I put Jake in a motel. I had tried to get him in the car earlier in the day, but couldn't. As soon as he got off work, Neil's Boy Scout master was going to help me get Jake to the motel. The girls were coming at 7:30. The plans were to pick up Wendy and she'd get the party room decorated. Neil would be home on the bus about the same time Wendy and I got home. The three of us would finish getting ready for the party, then we'd pick up Roxie and the four of us would eat at Wendy's favorite chicken place, the Red Barn.

Just as I felt like all was under control, I turned the corner at the school and saw Wendy standing with a friend. *Oh no. Surely she's not coming early.*

Wendy looked at me in a concerned way and opened the back door. "Mel, Susan's mom called. She had something come up and asked if Susan could come home with me." I watched as they got in the back seat. Wendy and I were looking at one another, both knowing that we were in a bind.

Lord, I need your help here.

"Hi, Susan."

"Hi, Mrs. Bell. I hope this is okay. If I'd gone home, I wouldn't have been able to come back."

"Well, we want you at the party." I saw Wendy relax but I knew she was wondering about her dad. "Wendy, I'm not done with everything yet, so I'll let you girls eat first then stop by and pick you up. You can do your room while I'm picking up Roxie. That should work."

"Sounds like it would," she said, knowing there was more.

We had lived this way for so long that we could communicate without mentioning our problem. I looked back in the rearview mirror and smiled at Wendy.

I gave Wendy money and dropped her and her friend off at the Red Barn.

When I got home, Jake was sitting on the bed trying to light a cigarette. I got all his Jim Beam from under his pillow and the extra bottle from under the bed and put them in the car. I opened the back door of the car. My only problem was getting him down the two steps. I went back in and took him by the arm. "Come with me, Jake."

"Where we going?"

"Your booze is in the car and we're going to go for a ride. Wendy's friend is on her way and I'm going to take you somewhere so you can drink."

He went with me like a little puppy. I got him down the steps and in the car, and then I went back inside and called the Scout master who had offered to help. I talked to his wife and told her that everything was under control, but I would call if I needed them tomorrow.

I went to the family room where Neil was watching TV and said, "Neil, I'm taking your dad to a motel so Wendy will have a good party. She and her friend are at the Red Barn. I'll take you as soon as I get back."

He looked at me with his dark brown eyes. *There is so much sadness in his eyes*, I thought, as I watched him turn back toward the TV without saying a word.

When we got to the motel, I drove up by the door and took Jim Beam in first.

Jake was asleep in the back seat. "Jake," I said shaking him roughly. "Your booze is in the room under your pillow. Come with me." He got out of the car with my help and leaned on me as he had before we left home. I took him to his bed and we both almost fell on it. I took off his coat. He laid his head on the pillow, I put his feet up and took off his shoes to take with me, and I took his money. He was asleep when I left.

Jacob was home when I got back. He, Neil and I went to the Red Barn; I gave them some money and asked them to send Wendy and her friend out. I took them home to do Wendy's room and I went to pick up Roxie.

The girls had the room ready and all the food in bowls and on trays when I got back home. "You're going to have a good birthday, Wendy. We have almost an hour before everyone comes and everything is done." I hurried to get dressed. I freshened up and put on a clean skirt and blouse. As the girls were being dropped off, the parents and I would smile and wave at each other.

About half an hour after all the girls came, a young man knocked on the door. He asked to see Pam. I was trying to figure out just how to handle that when the young lady came down.

"Mrs. Bell, we are going for a ride," she said, with coat in hand. "I'll be back in an hour."

"Honey, a ride sounds fun, but when I talked to your mother about you coming, she didn't say anything about that. I'll need to talk to her."

"She isn't home."

I turned to the young man and said, "As soon as I make connections with Pam's mother, she can call you. You two may visit here for a little while if you'd like."

He decided he'd go on and Pam turned to go back upstairs. "Pam, when you reach your mom, let me know and I'll talk to her."

I turned around and Jacob was standing in the living room shaking his head. When Pam went upstairs Jacob said, "Looks like you're going to have an interesting night."

"Jacob, I'm so glad you're here. I think he'll be back. If you'll sit in the living room and make sure no one goes out that front door, I'll be forever grateful. I know you'd much rather go do something, and I wish you could take Neil to a movie or something, but I really need you."

I fixed him and Neil up with snack food and moved a TV to the living room. Roxie spent a little time with the girls, then I put her to bed downstairs and started washing the dirty clothes Jacob had brought home from college. *I sure wish I didn't have to deal with this laundry. Ten teenage girls, a drunk and all this laundry in the same night. I'm thankful Jacob is here, though. He has really come through for us tonight.*

I looked out the living room window about 10:00 p.m. The young man's car was parked at the end of the drive. I went in the living room just as Pam was coming down the steps.

"Hi, Pam. Let's try to get your mother. I have her phone number."

"No, that's okay."

"Very well, but the only way that I can be sure you're safe and not in a wreck or something is for you to be here with me. When your friend sees you're not coming out, he'll understand I didn't talk to your mother."

She turned around and went back upstairs without saying anything.

I took no chances, and went upstairs to check on everyone after the house quieted down around 3:00 a.m. All the girls were asleep. We got through the party with all ten girls safe.

It was 4:00 a.m. when I turned out my light and fell into bed. Wendy had had a good time, despite the fact that her dad was passed out in a motel.

The next morning, the girls helped themselves to cereal, cinnamon rolls and juice that I had waiting for them. All the girls, including Pam, said they'd had a good time as they left.

All morning I worried that Jake would call while the girls were there, but the only calls we got were for the girls. I was relieved, yet at the same time, I wished he would call.

As soon as they were gone, I got this sick feeling in my stomach, wondering what I would find at the motel. I called Dr. Smith. He said he would arrange to have Jake admitted to the hospital and we could arrive around 1:00 p.m. I called Zach and asked him to meet us there. Then I called the Boy Scout master and another Scout dad to come help. I waited for them at my door with a large thermos of coffee and a pint jar of V8 Juice.

As we drove up the hill that led to the motel, I thought I was going to be sick. *What will we find?*

Jake was asleep on the bed. The Scout master was carrying Jake's shoes. I poured a drink out of the partial bottle he had left and took the rest to the trunk of the car. *There,* I thought as I closed the trunk lid. *If he doesn't go to the hospital, I'll have something to taper him off with.* I came back in, sat down on the bed and spoke his name. He opened his eyes.

"Hey, ready for some coffee?" I asked gently. He looked up at me and closed his eyes again. "Jake, Bill and Alan are here. We brought you some juice and coffee." He sat on the side of the bed and fumbled for a cigarette.

"Doctor," Scout Master Bill said as he poured coffee from the thermos, "We want to help you get off this stuff. Here, take a drink of this hot coffee." I took the coffee. Jake reached for it and I steadied his hand around the cup while he drank.

Dr. Smith would use the word "enabler" again if he could see me now.

"Oh, wow, Jake, that was good!" I said, when he finished the coffee with a little help from me.

He stood holding on to the bedside table. "Excuse me, gentlemen, I need to go to the bathroom." I took hold of his arm and accompanied him to the bathroom as he staggered. The men stepped outside the room.

When we all gathered again Bill said, "Dr. Jake, your office needs you Monday morning and Dr. Smith has arranged for you to go into treatment for the weekend and then go back and forth to the hospital for a few nights."

He leaned his head to one side, "Now, Bill, don't misunderstand me, but I'll be just fine at home. This woman is as tough as they come. She's hard to deal with," he slurred.

"She's been up all night with ten girls, Dr. Jake. We can't take you home and we don't want to leave you here."

He struggled with another cigarette. Tipping his head to one side and looking at me he said, "Where's my whiskey?"

"I took it to the car." I didn't tell him I had poured some in a glass and put it behind the lamp over on the other table.

"I need a drink."

I reached for his shoes and got down to put them on him. "Put your foot in this shoe, Jake."

"I need a drink."

I lifted his foot and started putting the shoe on. "I'll give you one before we start to the hospital. You need to go, Jake. Jim Beam is about gone and I'm not buying any more."

With head tilted, he laughed, and slurring his words, said, "Men, I need... to tell you something." Looking at me he continued, "This little... woman... doesn't care... for Jim Beam." Both men were silent.

Finally Jake agreed to go to the hospital. I worried he wouldn't stay, so I made another call to Dr. Smith.

"Doctor, you know, they've started asking patients if they agree to stay. If he says no, what do I do?"

"I'll take care of that, Mel. I'll call and tell them he's agreed to come. They'll admit him."

Zach was waiting for us. "Hello there, Jake," he said as he met us in the parking lot.

"Hello, 'ole Zach," he said, holding his head to one side. I'd given him a small drink just before we left the motel. He wasn't walking too straight but went in the hospital willingly. We gave all the necessary information to the lady at the desk. We waited a few minutes. A young psychiatry resident came in and asked Jake how long he'd been drinking this last period.

"Doctor, you'll have to ask my wife." Then he laughed, "She's got every drink recorded in her head."

Then the psychiatrist leaned back and said, "Dr. Bell, do you agree to be admitted for treatment?"

Oh no. Dr. Smith took care of that. Sure enough my thoughts were interrupted as I heard Jake say, "No, sir," he slurred, "I do not."

"Jake," I said, putting my hand on his arm, "You agreed to come. Dr. Smith arranged for you to come; because of that, you need to stay. I'm not taking you home."

"I'm sorry to disappoint you, Honey, but no, ma'am," he said, tilting his head to one side, "I'm not staying."

I looked at Zach.

Jake looked at the Scout men and said, "Thank you, gentlemen."

Getting up, I said, "Zach, I'll go call Dr. Smith." I hurried to a pay phone.

"Mel," Dr. Smith said, "Call Judge White at his home. I'll give you the number. Tell him I suggested that you call him, that the patient needs to be committed."

Zach and I both talked to the judge. He said he couldn't commit him for getting drunk. I explained it was a real problem for me to keep him from driving when he was drinking. I had all the keys, but if I was asleep, he could call a cab and go rent a car.

The judge understood that but couldn't commit him, by law.

Zach and I stood and looked at one another.

"We had it all taken care of and that young doctor blew it. How in the world did he ever get through medical school?" I said, half-mad.

Zach laughed. "You take your friends home and do what you have to, then come out to our house. I'll take Jake home with me."

"Oh, Zach, we can't do that to Lynne. Half of her life is given to our problems."

"Well, you leave that to me. You can watch him tonight. I'll take care of the booze. We'll have him ready for work Monday."

Zach walked over and said, "Jake, you can stay here and get on your feet, or you're going home with me. Take your choice."

"Well, sir," he said, trying to look straight, "Doesn't look like I have much of a choice."

"Okay, Jake," I said, "I'll take Bill and Alan home and be seeing you."

"When?"

"Oh, I'm not sure. I'll be out sometime."

"I don't like this."

Remembering the lady at the clinic ten years ago saying that her husband would resent her bringing him to the clinic, I thought, *If he thinks his resentment is going to control me from now on, he's got a lot to learn. It's getting less important each time he starts drinking.*

"I'm ready to go," I said to the Scout men.

They shook hands with Jake and said they'd see him at Scout meeting on Monday night.

When I got home, we fixed an early dinner and made arrangements for the kids. Jacob would be there with Neil. Wendy went to Lisa's and I took Roxie back to Jane's. She didn't want to go and cried that I was leaving her again. I did some crying myself on my way out to Zach and Lynne's. I felt so lonely for my family and so guilty for leaving them, especially the little one. I was so grateful that Jacob was home and that I'd done his laundry. The only problem was Jacob had to be taken the two and a half hour trip back to school the next day.

Jake was walking the floor when I got to Lynne and Zach's.

We went through the usual, "Honey, I've got to have a drink. Man, I'm desperate," until sometime after dark. Finally, he started for the door.

Zach went to the door. He knew Jake was scared of their German Shepherd.

"Jake, you give me trouble about going out this door and I'll call Biff in here and you won't go anywhere."

Hearing his name, the big German Shepherd came walking through the hall door. It worked like a charm. Jake walked back to his chair and every time he got up, he made sure he was away from the dog.

When it was time for bed, Zach said, "Now, Jake, I'm going to give you a drink and I'm leaving 'your friend' in the living room."

Our room was at the end of the living room, down a short hall. The only place Jake could go and not pass the dog was to the bathroom. He paced the floor, but I didn't have to worry about getting up to watch him. I was desperate from very little sleep the night before. About 2:00 a.m. Zach was up and could hear us talking. He gave him a drink and Jake settled down for a few hours.

The next morning I went in the kitchen to get coffee for Jake and me.

"Well, hello there, Melissa," Zach said, laying his paper down and getting up to pour me a cup of coffee. "You sit down here and talk to Lynne."

"I need to take your brother a cup of coffee," I replied.

"I'll do that. How is he?"

"He's showered already and is dressing. If you go back there, he'll want a drink."

"Well, now I can handle that," he said as he poured some coffee and started across their long living room.

"Jake, you can come out now," he called, his voice ringing through the house. "I put the dog in the yard."

Jake and Zach came into the kitchen; Lynne asked him if he was ready for bacon and eggs.

"Oh, you know me, Lynne, breakfast is my best meal."

"Here's your last drink, Jake, until this evening. When you get back from taking Jacob to school, come out and before you leave, I'll give you a drink so you'll be able to sleep tonight," Zach said.

He looked so good, you would never know it was the same man I had put in the motel on Friday evening.

We went home and took Jacob back to school. It was late when we got out to Zach's.

Jake was very calm as I drove us home and was beginning to nod off. The kids were all in bed and asleep when we got home. *The whole household is exhausted*, I thought as I fell into bed a little after 10:00 p.m.

I got everyone off Monday morning and called Betty. She asked me what I was going to do that day and I started crying.

"Melissa, what is the matter?"

"Oh, Betty, I've got thank-you notes to write, and when I start, I make a mess of them. I don't know if I'm spelling the words right, and just when I get one ready to mail, I see I've written a word backwards. The president of the state medical auxiliary wants me to take a job. I know it will involve reading and I'm so tired after this weekend. I'm a basket case."

"Melissa, you've got to do just the important things."

"But if I don't get these notes written, they'll know it's because Jake's been on a binge, or they may be able to figure out that I have a learning problem."

"Everyone has some kind of problem. You just told me the other day about your friend from the medical auxiliary not knowing potatoes grew under ground. So, don't worry about what you don't know. Everyone will already have figured out that Jake's been drinking. Don't worry about those notes and don't take extra jobs. Just spend your energy on daily living."

When I got through talking to her, I didn't feel so guilty about not being super woman. I got a roast out of the freezer to thaw for dinner and took a long nap.

Jake came home on time. He and Neil went to Boy Scouts. Neil was less and less interested in Scouts. His grades had fallen very low. His dad had wanted him to go to the military school the year before because he wasn't doing well in school, but I just couldn't see him marching to breakfast at such a young age. When Jake came home that night, he was worried about Neil because he had been very quiet while they were together.

How does he think the kids should be toward him after he has put them through weeks of uncertainty?

                                                          —

It had been about three weeks since Wendy's birthday party. Roxie, Wendy and I were in the car when Wendy blurted out, "Dr. Fox said if Dad keeps drinking, I can go to a foster home."

What do I do? If I consent to this, she'll think I don't want her. If I say I don't want her to go, she'll think I don't understand.

That evening I was so exhausted. Roxie came in while I was taking a nap. "Mama, will you take me to bed and read me a story and pray with me?"

"Oh, Honey, Mama is so tired," I said, not having the energy to move. "I'll be up to check and make sure you're okay when your daddy comes to bed." I heard her leave without a word. I couldn't sleep after that and yet I was too tired to move.

The next morning, I went upstairs to wake the kids and sat on Roxie's bed and we hugged. As she put her little arms around me, I felt so guilty for bringing her into such an upset environment.

When everyone was gone, I fell back in bed and fell asleep to the noise of the barnyard outside. The next thing I knew, the phone was ringing.

"Hello, this is Dr. Fox."

"Oh, hello, Doctor."

"You sound sleepy, were you napping?"

"Yes, sir, but I'm glad you called."

"Wendy has told me she wants to go to a foster home," he said. "She thinks she'd like to get away from things."

A strong, sick feeling swept over me. I took a deep breath and tried not to sound too anxious. "She mentioned it to me last night when we were driving to the mall."

"Now, that was an unhandy time to spring it on you, wasn't it?"

"I guess it was as good as any other time." Trying desperately to get my thoughts together, I sat up in bed. "I'm worried about this. Wendy belongs at home," I said. "Plus, I'm afraid this really may drive Jake to the bottle even more."

"You must take the full blame," the psychiatrist said. "Tell him it's your fault. Going to a foster home will be best for her." He paused as though rethinking what he had said. "You know, you and Wendy have been locking horns. She needs to be away for a time. I really don't have time to do all the calling," he continued, "I wonder if you could do that. We need to find a place for her soon."

When Dr. Fox hung up, I called Dr. Smith's office to see if he had a cancellation so I could see him. I explained to the secretary that it was very important.

"I bet he'd see you during lunch, Mel. I'll call you between patients."

I quickly got ready and when she called back, she said Dr. Smith could see me.

When I sat down in Dr. Smith's office, I felt drained and defeated.

I lost no time telling him about the phone call. "I guess it's my fault. Dr. Fox said I needed to tell Jake it is."

"The hell you will!" he exclaimed.

I perked up. I'd never heard him talk like that.

"No way are you going to take the blame. It's Jake Bell and his drinking that are making those kids' lives miserable. Mel, Mark Fox may not know the full truth. You know you are up all night sometimes and don't tell the kids. They probably don't know why you're sleeping when everyone else is up."

I asked Dr. Smith what he thought of my having Wendy stay at a friend's for a while. He thought that might be the answer. He agreed with me that going into foster care might make her feel unwanted.

On my way home, I stopped by my friend Kathy's house and blurted out my dilemma. She'd check with her husband Dennis and her daughter Heather who was a friend to Wendy, and see what they thought, but she didn't think there would be a problem for Wendy to stay a couple of weeks. We both thought we should stick with two weeks. Wendy would get a break and yet it wouldn't interfere with Kathy's family for a long time.

Early evening, Kathy called and said the family had agreed to have Wendy for two weeks. She could move in on Friday night.

Dr. Fox had asked that Jake and I come to his office the next evening. Jake didn't want to go, but he consented to do so. I didn't tell him about Dr. Fox wanting Wendy in foster care. Since Dr. Smith had explained it wasn't my fault, I wanted Jake to hear it from Dr. Fox.

When Dr. Fox announced that Wendy wanted to go to a foster home, Jake said, "Oh, no, we don't need to do that, Mark. She needs to stay at home."

"Jake, she's going to blow."

Jake shifted his feet, put his lower lip between his thumb and index finger and looked at the doctor. We were all silent a little while. Jake put his right hand down on the chair arm and without looking up said, "We don't want that to happen."

"I wonder if our friends, Kathy and Dennis, would take her for a couple of weeks to give her a break or until a place could be found for her. We could try that and see how she does. I bet Kathy would do that," I said.

I'm not sure he'd agree with me if he thought I'd worked that out instead of trying to get her in a foster home. I'm afraid to be honest anymore. Dr. Smith would call it game playing. Some have accused me of being against my step-children, but if it wasn't for them, I'd have been long gone by now.

"That would be great if she could go for just a little while. See if they could take her soon." Then he said, "Is that okay with you, Jake?"

"Yes." Turning to me, he said, "See if Kathy will take her," and looking back to Dr. Fox he said, "I think after that she should come back home."

"If they take her, we'll all need to meet on Thursday night and talk to them," the doctor said. "Then I need to talk with the two of you and Wendy together before she comes back home."

"I'll talk to Kathy tonight and call you in the morning. We've been close friends for fifteen years. I think she'll do it."

Jake and I were silent as we walked to the car. As he started the car he said, "That was a good idea that you had about Kathy taking her." Then with a poor attempt at a country accent, he added, "You done good there, Melissa Ann."

"Jake, Dr. Fox called me this morning and told me to find a place for Wendy. I went to see Dr. Smith and then stopped by Kathy's. Dr. Smith thinks, like we do, that she shouldn't be shifted around any more than necessary. Kathy and Dennis can take her. I just need to tell them we need to meet with Dr. Fox on Thursday night, and then I'll tell Wendy."

"Mel," he said, reaching for a cigarette, "when something like this comes up, I think, 'Well, Melissa will think of something to get us out of this crack.'"

I thought of the times even before we were married when he'd say, "I'm in a crack." *When will it ever end?*

I checked on Roxie and said goodnight to Neil. Wendy was propped up in bed with her homework. I went in her room, sat down on her bed and said, "Wendy, Dr. Fox hasn't had time to check on a foster home, but Kathy said Heather didn't have any weekend plans for two weeks and they'd like to have you come stay two weeks with them. Dr. Smith said the school has a bus that picks up girls in that area. His daughter used to go to your school." Wendy was holding her pencil, her hand resting on the notebook, while she looked directly at me. I couldn't tell if she was pleased or unhappy.

"Kathy's family likes you a lot and you and Heather always have a good time. Do you think that would help?"

She shrugged her shoulders, "I guess."

I sat there a moment; she was still looking at me. I really wanted to hug her but I was afraid of being rejected. *She needs a hug but she doesn't want it from me.*

"Dr. Fox said we'd all meet before you came back home." Wendy's expression never changed. I looked around the room and said, "Maybe we can get your room painted this spring. What color would you like to have?"

"Green."

"We'll start looking for paint and curtains and a spread when you come home. How will that be?"

Without moving or changing expression she said, "Okay, I guess." We said goodnight and I went downstairs.

"Well, how did it go?" Jake asked.

"I don't know, Jake. She agreed to go to Kathy's but didn't say how she felt about it. I suggested we redo her room when she comes back."

"Did she like that idea?" he said as he sat down in his chair and started untying his shoes.

"I don't know. When I asked her what color she wanted, she said green. I hate to put green on those walls, but I think I should start letting her have more say on things like that."

"Maybe that will give her something to look forward to." He went over and sat down on the side of the bed and lit a cigarette. "Man, I wish we could get the kids help."

"Jake, we all need help. I remember what my late pastor always said, 'We can't lift anyone higher than we go ourselves.'"

"You're right, Honey. Man, I hope you can hang in there with me."

That means he's desperate to drink and hopes someone else will help rescue Wendy.

I sat down by him. "Jake," I said, "I need you sober to help me with the kids. Wendy's mother is so far away and I'm not filling the gap. You're the one she needs."

He put his hand on his knee and started nervously rubbing his leg. "I know that, Honey, but man, I'm desperate."

I have my warning: A binge is on its way and I'm about to drop in my tracks already. When will it ever end?

The next morning after everyone was gone, I called Betty and told her all that was going on.

"I don't know how much longer I can go on like this," I said.

"I know that, but you're going to have to leave him or just accept it."

"Betty, how am I going to leave him? Wendy and Neil will not want to stay with me, then what will happen to them? They'll be sure in their hearts that no one wants them."

"Melissa, they are already sure of that."

"But I do want them. I'd like to just figure out what we each should do so we could cope day by day."

"Oh, Melissa, don't you see that would be controlling everything and everyone and that's just putting more pressure on all of you? Regardless of what you do or don't do, it's not going to keep Jake from drinking."

That evening, Kathy and Dennis met us at Dr. Fox's house. Wendy was very quiet. Jake slumped in the chair and was breathing extra hard. He put his hand up to his lower lip and held it between his thumb and index finger. *I've never seen him looking so undignified while sober. Oh, I'll be so glad when this is over.*

Kathy was very comfortable and was on top of the situation. She and I had agreed that Wendy needed Jake and me completely out of her life for these two weeks and we weren't to contact her. Kathy helped me to feel much better about our decision.

When Kathy suggested that to Dr. Fox, he looked at me and asked, "Can you abide by those wishes, Melissa?"

"Yes, sir, I can."

Friday night we took Wendy to Kathy's. Everyone helped to carry her things to Heather's room.

Oh, thank the Lord that we have her settled at Kathy's. Kathy really loves Wendy.

We rode home with no one except Roxie saying much. She was missing her big sister already. "Mama, when will we be able to see Wendy again? Can we go see her?" The questions went on and on. We went inside and I took Roxie to bed. We read a story and sang a song and prayed. Roxie prayed for Wendy.

She knows and feels the unrest even at the age of five, I thought, as I tucked her in and kissed her goodnight.

When I went downstairs, Neil was watching TV. Jake wasn't in the family room. I went to the door to see if both cars were in the drive. They were, so I went down the hall to our room. He wasn't back there. *He has a bottle hidden outside.* In a few minutes he came inside and sat down in his brown recliner and tipped it back. Soon he was asleep. I went into our room. *It would be easy to cry and never stop,* I thought as I sat down, *but to fall apart would accomplish nothing.*

I heard the family room door open and close about 1:00 a.m. I lay quietly until I heard Jake come back in. He fell asleep quickly but I lay there most of the night, wondering how Wendy would adjust. I was also worrying that Neil had watched TV alone and gone upstairs with both his dad and me asleep, knowing another binge was on its way. I was wide awake the rest of the night.

Jake continued drinking every night that week. The next week he became unable to go to work and Dr. Smith came out to see him.

"Jake Bell, you're not working and you need to go into the hospital and get off this stuff."

"Oh, no, Ira, I'm fine," he said, holding his head to one side and trying to focus.

"Wendy will be coming home Saturday morning. This is Tuesday and you need to be well."

"I will be."

Dr. Smith suggested he give me the bottle and let me taper him off.

Jake said, slurring his words and tipping his head, "Well, she knows how to do that."

Finally, Dr. Smith had to leave. He said he'd check with me the next morning to see if Jake was tapering off.

Jake didn't taper off. When Friday came, I got him in a motel while Roxie and Neil were in school.

After both kids were in bed on Friday night, I was sitting in the family room trying to pray, when a knock came on the door. It was Kathy and Dennis. I was glad to see them. We sat down and I asked how Wendy was and how they had gotten along. Kathy said she had heard Wendy tell Neil on the phone that if her dad was drinking, she wasn't coming home.

Dennis said, "I had a stepmother and lots of things I didn't like. I'm sure that's the same with Wendy, but her big problem, I think, is the drinking."

"I think so too, Mel," Kathy added. "When we talked to Dr. Fox the other day, we told him we thought that." She paused then said, "Heather is going to a friend's in the morning for the weekend. I'd really hate for her not to go."

"Oh, Kathy, she should go on. We said this would be two weeks and that's the way it is. I'll call Dr. Fox and tell him that Jake won't be bringing her to see him as planned and that I'll bring her alone. He'll know Jake is still drinking. I'll pick her up at 10:15 and go on to see Dr. Fox."

"What if she tells me she isn't going?" Kathy asked.

"Kathy, she won't do that. She'll just look defeated. Just suggest she get her things together in plenty of time. I think she'll do as you ask."

The next morning I called Dr. Fox at home and he told me he needed to reschedule to Monday evening at 7:00.

"Okay. I'll go pick her up and bring her on home. She will see you Monday evening."

Wendy had her things by the door and was ready for us to pick her up when Roxie and I got to Kathy's house. She didn't ask any questions. Kathy was so warm and loving, as always, and gave her a big hug. Roxie sat in the back seat with Wendy, who sat looking ahead, saying nothing.

"Wendy, Dr. Fox can't see you until Monday evening."

She just looked ahead, never changing expression.

She has such a defeated look on her face, Lord; I don't know how to help her. The doctor can't see her, her dad is drinking and her mother lives nine hundred miles away. All she has is her stepmother that she didn't choose. It must be terrible to feel so alone and unwanted.

For the first time I really saw how Wendy must have felt.

We drove in silence a little way and I said, "Have you talked to your friend Lisa?"

"Yes."

"Did you girls want to do something this weekend?"

"She wanted me to spend the night."

"That will be good. Ulma still has a bad leg, but I have everything done. There won't be anything pressuring us today. Your dad's in a motel. Hopefully he'll be sober at the end of the weekend." She was still silent all the way home unless I asked a question.

When we got home, the other car was gone. "Neil, where is the other car?" I asked, as I met him coming through the kitchen into the family room. "Is Jacob home?"

"Yes, he came just after you left. Dad called and said he was ready to come home and Jacob went to get him."

"He can't do that. I spent the day yesterday trying to get him in there." Looking at Wendy, I saw all my plans of keeping a tension free day for her had gone out the window.

We carried her things upstairs and I said, "Why don't you call Lisa and see what she's doing today? If she wants you to come early, it's okay. I'll see what we can do to have things settled down by tomorrow night. Lisa's mother and I have an understanding that anytime it's not convenient, we'll tell the other."

"I'll go call now," Wendy said.

Roxie and I waited while Wendy called. I saw a spark of excitement in her face.

"I can go anytime. She said come for lunch."

"Hurry and get what you'll need and I'll take you."

Oh, I hope I can get her out of here before her dad comes home. I just had the thought, when we heard the horn.

I went and met them at the back door. "Jacob, if you'd called and told me you were coming, I would have told you what problems we were having," I said as he and his dad came into the family room.

"I didn't know I was coming until the last minute when I was offered a ride."

Jake walked past me and sat down in his chair. He was in better shape than when I'd left him at the motel. I reached in his pocket and got his bottle. I took it to the laundry room and hid it to have to taper him off.

Jacob went in the kitchen; he was always starved. I followed him and leaned up against the cabinet as he opened the refrigerator.

"Jacob, what do we do now? I literally dragged your dad to the car yesterday and into the motel room. Wendy has been at Kathy's for two weeks because Dr. Fox thinks she's about to blow. The reason I took your dad up there was so Wendy could handle coming back home."

Jacob closed the refrigerator door and never said a word. Wendy came with her overnight case. She and Jacob greeted one another, and then I told the boys I'd fix lunch when Roxie and I got back. Jake was asleep in the chair already.

When I got in the car, I was having a hard time being cheerful with the girls. I felt so angry that all my efforts to have Jake in a safe place without access to a car so he wouldn't kill himself or others had in less than an hour been ruined.

Wendy and Lisa hadn't seen each another for more than two weeks, and I knew Wendy was glad to see her; but I also could see there was that cloud hanging over her that we all felt so keenly.

When we got home, I went in and fixed lunch. Jake slept the whole time. When he awoke, I started tapering him off. Jacob spent the evening with friends. Neil and Roxena Lynne spent the weekend with a drunken dad and an exhausted mom.

Saturday night I was up most of the night tapering Jake off. The next morning the entire bottle of Jim Beam was gone. Jake was restless but wasn't pressuring me to go get another bottle. I found the extra keys to the other car and the truck and left the boys asleep. I dressed Roxie up in her blue corduroy suit and we went to Sunday school and church.

Dean met me at the door. "How are things going?"

"Not good." Someone else was near so we walked on into the church and down the steps to our classes.

I took Roxie to her class and went on to mine. I sat down and wanted to sigh from fatigue, but didn't dare. No one asked about Jake. *Word gets around. Maybe they don't know that Wendy has been gone, since Dennis and Kathy go to another church. Hold your head high, Melissa Ann, and appear like everything is in control.*

After class, I went to the kitchen to get a cup of coffee. When I got to the door I heard, "I wonder if Dr. Bell is still drinking." I turned around so they wouldn't see me and went to wait for my daughter to come out of class.

I couldn't keep my composure through the whole service. Tears just seemed to come. *They'll know for sure he's drinking now*, I thought, as I struggled to listen to the sermon. Dean's sermon was on peace.

How do I have peace in my life? After all, it's the life I chose. I guess that's why the Lord has rules for us to follow, I thought. I just wish I had peace but most of all I wish Jake could have peace from the bottle. How can I ask the Lord for that when I got ahead of the Lord and married a man whose life was so messed up?

I tried to be cheerful on the way home. "Daddy will be okay when we get home, Honey," I said to Roxena Lynne, who was looking at her Sunday school papers.

She's sure a beautiful child. I love her so but I feel guilty bringing her into so much drinking and strife.

When we got home, Jake got up out of his chair to greet us. I could tell he'd been drinking. The boys were watching TV and didn't look up.

I went into the kitchen to check the roast and saw that the door to the basement was ajar. I opened it, and in the hall off the kitchen, behind the trash can, was a fifth of Jim Beam with just about two drinks gone. I poured it down the sink.

"Jacob, will you come here?" He came right away. "I just found this. I spent the night getting him off this stuff when I had hoped to get my first night's sleep for a week. Now it's started all over again," I said as I ran hot water in the sink to get rid of the smell of liquor. Jacob never answered; he just looked defeated and angry. He stood there a little while and went back to the family room.

"Roxie, Honey, you can come and help Mama set the table."

I went to the family room door and said, "Boys, which one of you will go to the freezer and get a pie you picked apples for last summer?" Jacob hopped up.

He tries to please. We are just all caught up in a web. It's choking us.

As soon as the gravy was done, I woke Jake. He came to the table looking red-faced. He put his hands together and said, "Teekers," his pet name for Roxena Lynne, "will you return thanks?"

Everyone took their plate to the dishwasher and helped me clean the table. The pie was done in time for Jacob to have a piece before I took him to catch his ride back to school.

We were eating pie when Wendy's friend called to see if she could stay until nine. That would give us more time for her dad to be in good shape.

Jake ate very little pie. I knew he was waiting for me to get out of the kitchen so he could make a visit to the fifth of Jim Beam. He had been asleep when I'd talked to Jacob about it.

I took Jacob to meet his ride. "Jacob," I said as he was driving down the interstate, "anytime your dad calls you to come get him when he's in a motel, wait and check with me. I'd taken care of him for nearly two weeks and he was there to get sober before Wendy came home. I didn't know he had a bottle hidden, but he started drinking when he got back, so I only slept about three hours last night. I just need to be rested when Wendy comes home." Jacob looked straight ahead and never said a word.

We are all defeated, I thought, as I drove out of the parking lot where Jacob met his ride. *Maybe I can take a nap before Wendy comes home so I won't shout orders. Thank you, Lord, that Ulma will be here tomorrow.* As I drove into the drive I felt that dread that maybe Jake had found another bottle he'd hidden or called a cab to go get one, but as I stopped in front of the back door, I saw he was looking through the window.

We walked in the pasture and did all the usual things when he was coming off a binge. At 9:00 p.m. we picked Wendy up. Jake was in good shape and Wendy had had a good time.

The next morning Jake took Wendy to school, Neil caught his bus, I took Roxie to her school then picked up Ulma. It was so good to see her. She seemed happy to be back with us. She always knew what to do and we always worked together until we were caught up with the work.

As I listened to the sweeper going upstairs, I thought that our house sounded almost like a normal household, but we didn't live normal lives; no one knew that better than I.

I decided to call Betty. I told her about the weekend and about Wendy when I picked her up. "Somehow, Betty, I've got to find a way to not be bossy. I don't mean to be, but I just need things done and I can't do everything for everyone. I need the kids to do chores. We are a big family. I wish I could just write down their chores but one of the older girls thought they wouldn't like that."

"Well, maybe she didn't like it when she was young. Sounds to me like it would take a lot of pressure off you and Wendy, Melissa."

"How do I tell her?"

"I'd just have it made out and say, 'Wendy, sometimes it sounds like I'm shouting orders and I don't want to do that. Let's try this. If you don't like to do it this way, we'll try something else.' Right now, Melissa, just be pleasant with Wendy and avoid a lot of talk."

"Ulma and I always put the clean towels and the kids' clothes on the steps for them to take upstairs. It is always Wendy's job to put the upstairs linens away and fold them, if needed. She doesn't fold them the way I need them folded so that they fit on the shelves."

"Melissa, it doesn't really matter. Let her have her way with things that don't make a difference. You know you care for her more than you do how the towels are folded. This she needs to see. Wherever she is right now, she's going to feel misplaced. Little things like this will help her to feel she belongs."

"Betty, I want the kids here but they don't believe that I do."

"Well, no, Melissa, they don't believe you."

"Sounds like you don't believe me."

"Yes, I do. You want them; but you don't want them to interfere with your mission of rescuing Jake from being an alcoholic." We were silent. I never resented Betty's honesty nor did I doubt her love. She broke the silence. "When you go see Dr. Searchbrains in the morning, spill your guts about how you feel your life has been taken over. Every one of you is feeling taken over by Jake's drinking. When you get your part worked out, it will be easier for your kids."

That evening I dropped Wendy by to see Dr. Fox, while I took Roxie to get a new pair of shoes. When we finished shopping, we got an Orange Julius. We sat on a bench and I asked her about school. We laughed when she talked about her friend Sarah. We got into the car to go get Wendy and she said, "I had fun, Mama."

"I did too, Honey."

When we got home, the evening went well. The kids had homework, I went to pray with Roxie, and then we sang while lying there in her bed. She seemed so happy. All of a sudden she stopped singing and said, "Mama, do you think Daddy will drink tonight?"

"No, Honey, he seems okay." We sang a little more and I went downstairs. I went to the kitchen desk and reached up above it in the cupboard for some thank-you notes. I had ruined three and had not finished any when Jake came in to see what I was doing.

"Isn't it a little late to start writing letters?"

"I'm a month late as it is. I've not thanked your Scout friends for taking us to dinner and the coin show."

"Honey, why don't you call and thank her and not worry about writing?"

"Okay," I said loudly. I lowered my voice and talked low through gritted teeth, while looking at him intently. "I'll just do that. I'll say, 'Oh, hello there, Ruth, this is Melissa Bell. I'm sorry I'm so long calling you, but my husband's been on a binge.' Now, SHIT," I whispered, shaking my head.

He put his hands together and shook his head like I had and looked at me so lovingly and said, "That's the second time I've heard you say that word, and I'll tell you, Mrs. Bell, each time, I've been able to smell it."

I started to our room and then stopped to go back and turn out the lights. I turned and saw Jake was doing it for me. *He's back. I wonder how long it will last.*

I slept well that night, knowing Jake was back to himself. The next morning he got up at the crack of dawn. I could hear him unloading the dishwasher and going outside for the paper. I lay there glad that he was sober. I needed to talk to him about so many things. The whole family had lost a month out of our lives, not just Jake. I needed to get up while I was fresh in mind and try to write that thank-you note, but it felt so good just to lie there, so that's where I stayed.

"Good morning, Mrs. Bell," Jake said, as he appeared in the doorway with the paper and coffee for both of us. I propped myself up as he sat down on the side of the bed. He handed me my coffee and opened his paper.

"Now, Missrus Bell," trying to say "missus" like we did in the Ozarks, "I'm going to read Missrus Ann Landers to you with feeling."

Later that morning when I was at my regular Tuesday morning appointment with Dr. Smith, I told him about that morning, how Jake talked to the kids in his fun, normal way and the way he helped with breakfast.

"Doctor, he'll be shocked when it dawns on him that they can't just step in the old routine, like we've been living normal lives."

"What do you think he may do when he sees the tension that was caused the last month?"

"Well, he may start drinking again, Doctor." Bursting into tears I said, "You have the wrong person in here. It should be Jake."

"I know I do, Mel, but I have you." He rolled his chair over in front of me. "I'll never have Jake Bell except when he's in one of his 'cracks,' but you, young lady, are making strides and you are holding your family together." I told him about the weekend and that I felt guilty that I'd been so hard on Jacob.

He smiled a little about my outburst the night before to Jake, then interrupted me, "Mel, it really bothers you when you say a bad word, doesn't it?"

"Well, yes, Doctor, there's all kinds of good words, why use the bad ones?"

"Mel, it's perfection that you want. Is that possible to achieve unless you get rid of all that anger and resentment?" He laid a hand on my arm as I looked down. "Work with me, Mel. Let's get rid of the anger."

I started crying again. I got a Kleenex and wiped my eyes and looked away.

"Maybe you do have the right person. Maybe it's a good thing I'm here. I was so highly thought of at church. Now the people just look at me." All of a sudden I thought, *I've got to go tell this to Dean.*

My time was up and my eyes were red. When I finished, I used the phone in the office to call Dean.

"I'm going to be out that way this afternoon, so I'll come by," he said.

I was always comfortable with Dean. When he came in, I didn't offer him coffee or anything to drink, I just started telling him how I felt we were neglected at the church.

I told him about hearing the ladies discussing us in the kitchen one Sunday morning. "You know, Dean, Kathy told me that was one reason they left the church—she was always being asked about us. I asked her if the people ever suggested prayer or said they were praying. She said they didn't."

Dean looked at me and I looked at him, but there wasn't an uncomfortable feeling between us. We'd always been honest about what we were thinking.

He slowly nodded his head. "I hear you. You need to be in a larger place where there are Christian doctors and lawyers that you and Jake can be friends with and where you won't be just a stepmother and an alcoholic's wife. You have a lot to offer and you need to be able to do that. I see you almost believing that you can't do anything anymore and we aren't helping you."

"I don't think I can bring myself to leave the church."

"You'll never leave the church; it's there deep within. When you're worshiping with other Christians, you're still in the church—you know that. If you don't move on, Vonda and I will be happy. If you do, we'll still be your friends. Jake's not responding to my messages..."

Soon after Dean left, the three kids came home.

Wendy didn't comment when I handed her the list of chores. Before we went to bed, I hadn't checked to see if her chores were done, but the clothes were gone from the steps. I could see where she'd been busy. The next evening

I had "fold towels" on her list and she folded them my way. When I saw that, I was touched. That night I told Jake about it and said, "Jake, when the kids ask me if they can do things, I'm quick to say no. I need to think first. I need to show them they matter."

Saturday morning after a good week, Lisa's mother dropped Lisa off until mid-afternoon. I had baked for the weekend on Friday, as usual, while Ulma got everything caught up in the house. Jake had called and was on his way home. Wendy and Lisa came through the kitchen door from upstairs. Wendy looked a little nervous.

"Mel, may I go with Lisa and her dad to a country music show in Farmington tonight?"

I remembered telling Jake I said no too fast. "I think that sounds like a lot of fun." The girls looked at one another and laughed. As they went back upstairs, I heard Lisa say, "See? I told you she may say yes and she couldn't do more than say no."

As we were all eating lunch, Jake said, "You got your things ready for the overnight campout, Neil?"

"I'm not going," he said, wiping his long hair from his eyes.

I followed Jake into our room and said, "Jake, you didn't tell me about the campout and something's going on with Neil that he doesn't want to go. Do you think you should stay home this time? After all, we've had no weekend with you for over a month."

"The boy doesn't want to do anything, Honey. His grades are all bad, you know that, but he's doing well in Scouts. If he keeps on, he'll be an Eagle. That will do so much for his self-esteem."

I sat down in the chair while Jake changed clothes. *Something's not right. I wonder if Jake's been drinking on the campsite. Maybe Neil doesn't want to go because he's afraid his dad will drink.*

"Jake, why don't you tell Neil you'll take him out there and he can stay by himself if he wants."

That worked. About 9:00 p.m., Jake came home by himself. *I wonder how many times he has been drinking when he was with the Boy Scouts,* I thought, as he came in all smiles. He paused at the back door, stood there a little while and said, "Neil seemed to be doing fine and wanted me to stay, but I thought I'd better come home to my strawberry blonde."

Roxie was already in bed but heard Jake and came down. When I heard her coming, I wondered if she was coming to greet him or to see if he was drinking. Most likely it was to check on him. It was, I saw, more and more on her mind—and she wasn't even six years old.

⁓

A couple of weeks later, as we drove home from church, Jake announced, "I don't know how much longer I can stand Dean's social gospel sermons."

Immediately, I knew it was time to make a change. I had a sinking feeling. *How will I ever be able to leave the church and go somewhere else?* "We'll talk about it this afternoon. I've been doing some thinking about it." He looked over at me. I could tell he was surprised that I wasn't upset. *Maybe he's trying to "get my goat" or playing games. Well, it's not working. I'm going to work with him and we'll find another church.*

Wendy and Neil were at a movie with their friends and Roxie was at a friend's house. We'd gone to our favorite place for lunch and I had a pot of soup on for supper. Jake was watching a documentary on TV. I went in our room to take a nap. When I lay down, I wondered what I should do to find a church. *No,* I thought, *I found my church when I gave my heart to the Lord. Jake never had that experience. I need to let him find the church that we attend. But what if he picks one that I can't accept? Hey, this is serious, but I haven't prayed, except in tight spots, in so long, I doubt if I know how to really have a conversation with the Lord.*

With that thought, I got down on my knees and poured my heart out to God in real conversation. I recalled when I first gave my heart to Him, how I had prayed about my love for the church, and how alone I felt now, not being involved. I stayed on my knees a long time. I told the Lord I wanted a church that taught salvation by the blood of Christ. I prayed for one Jake could accept and be content in and where we could find real friendship.

Then I got up and walked into the family room and stood in front of Jake. "Jake, I know you are very unhappy at our church. I'm willing to leave. I just ask one thing: that we go somewhere that teaches the message of salvation by the blood of Christ. You are the head of the house," I said. "I'm willing to turn the job of finding a church over to you. You pick it out and I'll go with you."

He sat there like he couldn't believe what he was hearing. When he realized I'd handed him the responsibility, he put his hands on his chair arms and said, "Okay." Then he nodded his head and said, "Okay, I can do that."

Monday morning I went by to see Jane and I told her we were going to change churches, but I had no idea where we'd end up.

"Mel, why don't you try River View Community? I think you'd like the minister. You're welcome to come to our church, but I don't think you and Jake would like it and I believe you'd like River View. They have a good youth program. It's a large church. You may want to try it."

I didn't mention it to Jake all that week. I'd told him he could pick the place. I'd leave it like that. Saturday night came; we hadn't mentioned it, except to tell the kids we were going to change churches. Neil asked why and I told him his dad wasn't comfortable there and wanted to see if we could find one we all liked.

As I was getting Roxie's things laid out for church I wondered, *How will it be to go to a new place, and where will it be? What time will it start? Is Jake even thinking about it?*

I tucked Roxie in and then went downstairs. I could hardly contain myself. I wanted to say, "You need to tell me where we are going to church." But I didn't say a word.

Sunday morning I was up early. I never turned on the TV in the early mornings but I turned it on that morning. A local Sunday morning talk show was just starting. The host said, "We have the Sr. Pastor Reverend Donn Hunter from River View Community Church and the youth singing group."

I was all eyes and ears. The pastor looked to be in his mid-forties and answered all of the questions with ease. He quoted scripture often and with such confidence, like he was quoting an old friend. I took down the times of services, just in case.

I hurried and got ready for church and took Jake juice, coffee and his paper on a tray.

"Oh, aren't you the one," he said, sitting up in bed. He took a drink of coffee, set the cup on his nightstand and said, "You're all ready for church."

"I'll start breakfast. Could you go wake the kids?"

"Yes, ma'am, I can do that."

I went to the kitchen and put on a wrap-around apron my aunt had made. I crumbled up the sausage in the skillet to brown for gravy and was cutting out the biscuits when Jake came downstairs.

He stopped and watched as I put the biscuits in the pan.

"I told the kids to get ready for church," he said.

I put the biscuits in the oven and started making the gravy. I was stirring in the flour and he said, "Melissa Ann, I've got me a problem. I don't know what church we should try. Do you have any suggestions?"

"Jane suggested we try River View Community, and this morning I turned on the TV, and the pastor was being interviewed. I really liked him. He used a lot of scripture and is close to your age, maybe a little younger."

"I need to go shave," he said, going through the kitchen door. He stopped and turned around. "What do you think, should we go hear that fellow?"

"It's up to you. I think we may be pleased."

As we were gathering around the table, Wendy said, "Do we know where we're going?"

"Well, there's this fellow over at River View Community that I think we should check out," Jake said.

I sure am glad he thinks we should check him out. I wanted to laugh but didn't.

"Many hands make light work," Jake said as he often did. "Everyone get the place in order and we'll leave here about 10:30."

We had passed by the beautiful red brick church many times but had never been there. The large parking lot was almost full when we arrived.

We didn't see anyone we knew, which was unusual for Jake. The ushers seated us in an empty pew, just as the choir started singing. It was beautiful. The pastor used a lot of scripture in his message and talked of God's strength. He held everyone's attention. There was a long line in front of us in the foyer to shake his hand, so we didn't wait.

"What did you think?" Jake asked after we got in the car.

"I liked it very much."

"We'll look some more," Jake announced.

The next Saturday rolled around and again I wondered where we were going to church. The kids didn't seem to care; one place was as good as the other for them. After the news, Jake said, "The paper shows that little church just east of us has an early service. Let's go to it and then eat breakfast on the way to watch the parade at the military academy."

"Sounds okay," I offered.

Sunday morning we had juice and coffee and I got cinnamon rolls out of the freezer to tide us over. Jake got the kids up and announced the plans. I worried that he waited until the last minute to tell them, but this was new territory for him, and he hadn't been sure himself until he looked in the paper on Saturday evening.

The people at the new church were friendly. The minister had some very good thoughts but didn't use much scripture. After hearing Donn Hunter the Sunday before, I wasn't too impressed with this guy.

We got in the station wagon and Jake said, "Well, he didn't do much for me, did he you?"

"No."

As Jake started out of the parking lot, he looked over at me and said, "Let's go back over to River View next Sunday morning and listen to that fellow again. What do you think?"

"I'd like that very much." I was silent for a while—something new for me. *So help me*, I thought, *this is going to be Jake's doing.*

Everyone at the parade seemed glad to see us. The colonel, who had been Jake's football coach in 1939, spent some time talking to Neil about coming to school in the fall. Neil had been interested in the school earlier, but now he didn't want to go. Jake's drinking had done a lot of damage to his motivation and he was doing poorly in school.

That evening, I decided to tackle some of the social mail that had stacked up. I struggled with one note for about thirty minutes. Jake came into the kitchen and set his coffee cup down to pour himself a cup of coffee. He knew if he disturbed me, I'd make a mistake, so he didn't say anything. I signed my name and said, "Hey, I'm finished with one note after thirty minutes. I have four more to go. Two and a half hours for five notes is a lot of time that I don't have, but I worry that if I don't get it done, I'll look like an ungrateful slob."

"Honey, I want you to call Betty and have her find you a tutor. You've struggled with this problem long enough."

I got up and walked over to pour a cup of coffee. He waited for my answer as I fought back tears.

"Honey, there is nothing the matter with your brain. Now, you go over there and call Betty and ask her to find you a tutor."

That opened the floodgates: "I'm thirty-seven years old and struggling with everything I do with a book or pencil and paper."

Jake stood there with me as I told him about my Business English teacher, Bonnie Clark, who asked me to explain the assignment one day. "I couldn't do it, so I said, 'Miss Clark, I read it, but I don't know.' I stood silent a minute and then started to speak again, but Miss Clark interrupted me: 'No, you didn't read it; that's plain to see. If you'd read it you'd be able to tell us what it's about.' I can still see the other six girls looking at me," I recalled, still feeling a little sorry for myself.

"Now, Honey, you can't stay mad at Miss Clark. She was worse off than you. She didn't know you had a problem but you know you do. Now go over there and call Betty."

"Hi, Betty," I said when she answered the phone, "I'm ready for you to find me a tutor for my learning problem."

"Oh, Melissa, that's wonderful. I'm not going to summer school and I'll tutor you. We'll have you reading better and knowing everything you read by the end of summer. I can hardly wait."

When I went in to tell Jake, I almost believed it would work.

The next Sunday we went to River View Community Church. When we left the parking lot Jake said, "I like that fellow's sermons. You can choose where we go next."

"Well, I think I'd like to come back here."

The next Sunday was Mother's Day. The organ began to play as we were being seated in the beautiful sanctuary. When the pastor, who by now was known at our place as "that fellow over at River View" got up to preach, I was ready to lay my anxious feeling aside and listen. That wasn't hard to do; he had a pleasant voice and read several scriptures about women of the Bible. All the women that he mentioned had struggles but they all were victorious. I walked out the door of the church holding Roxena Lynne's hand thinking, *There's victory for us. Oh, I hope we come here all the time.*

Jake got in the car and said, "What do you think? Should we just come here all the time?"

I looked at him and wanted to shout, "Yes!" but thought maybe I shouldn't act too anxious. "He uses lots of scripture, Jake. That's so important. Yes, I'd like it if we came here, but I'd like to go back to our old church next Sunday and tell Dean where we are going, so we can leave in a good spirit."

Jake looked at me. I could tell he knew if it were up to me, we would never leave the church that I'd been a part of for so long. Yet, as I thought about it, I really wasn't a part anymore. It was time to move on.

One night when we were eating out with Jane and John, John asked Jake about the new church.

"Well, John, I'll tell you, I like to hear that fellow preach, but I'm not sure my bride's all that happy in leaving her church."

John looked at me and asked, "How do you like Donn Hunter, Mel?"

"I like him very much."

"We've never heard him speak," Jane chimed in, "but we know some people who go there that think there is no other place."

I looked over at Jake. He looked so handsome and healthy. *I believe the new church is the right place for us.*

Summer came. Jacob came home from college and got a job putting up hay. Wendy worked again as a volunteer in a camp for children with disabilities. Neil continued in Scouts, and Roxie played a lot with her little friend down the road and went swimming often at the new pool that used to be our "woods" pasture. Zach and Jake had sold the "woods" pasture to a developer who built the pool.

Betty came out to the farm Tuesday, Wednesday and Thursday mornings to tutor me. I felt free with Betty. She started with simple books for me to read, and then had me tell her what I'd read. We also went over a list of words that were common for dyslexic people to see backwards.

We worked very hard for about two months. I was assigned to start reading a book one night and tell her some of what I had read the next day. It was *Swiss Family Robinson*; I struggled with it.

The next day, Betty and I sat together on the front porch swing while Roxie and her little girlfriend were playing with the puppies in the circle drive.

"Betty, I've had a hard time with this, but I may be able to tell you some of what I read."

"That's okay," then she went to a scene of the family in the outdoors and had me read it and tell her what it said. I read it without having to look twice at any of the words and then told her what it said. She threw her arms around me and said, "That was good!"

We were going camping, so my assignment was to slowly read *Swiss Family Robinson* and know everything it said before I went to the next page. It took me the whole week of our camping trip to finish. When Betty came on Tuesday morning after our trip, she had me give a book report.

"Melissa," she said when I finished, "You are on your way." Each week she picked up books about farm life or something she thought I'd identify with. She started with simple books like *The Little House* series and slowly increased the difficulty. Jake was so thrilled with my desire to read that he ordered every book he saw advertised that he thought I would like. Some of them were books he claimed Roxie would want to read someday, but I knew he was getting them because it would be easy reading for me. I read them all and was learning things I should have been reading about in grade school.

One evening a few weeks before school started, Jacob's friend Jim came by to pick him up. Not long after they left, the phone rang. I answered and Jim said, "Mrs. Bell, I'm at the emergency room with Jacob. He has glass in his eye."

"Oh, dear. Here's Doctor Bell, Jim, tell him what happened and we'll be right there," I said and handed the phone to Jake.

After ending the call with Jim, Jake immediately called an ophthalmologist. I heard Jake say, "Okay, Dick, I'll meet you there."

"We've got to leave," Jake said when he hung up. Everyone had come to the kitchen and both Wendy and Neil said, "What happened?" at the same time.

"Jim and Jacob walked in a bar and a couple of guys were fighting by the door and a fist meant for another guy hit Jacob. His glasses broke and glass is in his eye."

"I'll call you kids as soon as we know something," I said as we hurried out of the door.

"Jake, do you think he was in a fight?"

"No, I believe the story, Honey. They hadn't been gone from the house fifteen minutes."

"That's true."

Oh my, I thought, putting my head back on the car headrest. *When will the crisis end? And, what was Jacob doing in a bar?*

We got to the hospital quickly and met the eye doctor as we went in the door of the emergency room. I went to the waiting room with Jacob's friend, Jim. There was no liquor on his breath, so I too believed the story that the boys walked into a fight.

It was a long while before Jake came in the waiting room. The ophthalmologist had examined Jacob and affirmed he had glass in his eyeball. He had to have complete bed rest, couldn't sit up and needed to be very still. Jake said, "He'll have to have someone feed him."

Jim and I went in to see him, but he was almost asleep. I told him I'd be back to help with breakfast.

"Honey," Jake said as we walked to the car, "Jacob's in good hands. If the eye can be saved, Dick will be able to do it."

The kids were waiting up for our report. We agreed that I would leave early in the morning and ride in early with their dad. They could sleep late then Wendy could come and relieve me and we'd all take turns sitting with Jacob. *The kids will help; there's no doubt about that. When something like this happens, we stick together like flies and honey.*

Someone was there all the time the first few days. One day, we left Neil with Jacob after he'd eaten dinner and Jake and I went to eat. As we waited to be served, we were quiet. We were exhausted. Jake put out his cigarette and said, "Dick's the best we've got going for us."

Our food came. Neither of us had eaten lunch and we were very hungry. We ate mostly in silence. When we got back to the hospital parking lot, Jake turned off the car and said, "Honey, he's going to lose that eye."

"Jake, Honey, we aren't sure of that. Why don't we pray?"

"Okay, why don't you do that? My dad always said it wouldn't hurt." He reached up, took off his hat, held it over his chest and closed his eyes while I asked the Lord to give the doctor wisdom and take care of Jacob's eye so that he would be able to see.

By the end of the week, Dick told us he thought the eye would heal. They couldn't perform surgery and they'd have to leave the glass in the eye, but he still would be able to see from the injured eye.

Jacob remained in the hospital for a few more days. He couldn't do much when he came home.

~

There was one more weekend Boy Scout camping trip before school started. Neil was reluctantly getting ready to go to the military academy. When his dad reminded him of the camping trip, he said he didn't want to go.

One day, as Wendy and I were going to the mall, we passed the church that sponsored the Scout troop, and Wendy said, "Neil is dreading the campout this weekend. He's afraid Dad is going to get drunk. He said the Scout master and all the workers drink beer."

When we got home, I called the minister associated with the Scout troop and asked for an appointment. When we met, I got right to the point. "Reverend Henry, I just found out today that the leaders are drinking on the Scout trips, and also that my husband, who is an alcoholic, has gotten drunk. If the mothers find this out, they'll pull their boys out of your troop. I can't keep my husband from going, but I will tell my son he doesn't have to go."

"I can talk to the leaders that are members of the church," he said, "but I can't talk to the others, because they aren't members of this church."

That evening I approached Jake about the campout and told him I'd learned he'd been drinking on camping trips.

"Jake, you want me to treat Neil like he's mine, don't you?"

"Sure, Honey, you know that."

"Well, no mother in that group would want their boy to go if they knew the leaders were drinking, and I'm going to tell mine he doesn't have to go," I said as I started to Neil's room.

Neil was reading a letter with his door open. He looked up.

"Neil, I've learned about the drinking on the Scout trips. Your dad knows that I'm here telling you that you don't have to go. You've done well in Scouts, Neil, and you'll be an Eagle soon; but you no longer have to go when you're worried that your dad will be drinking."

He didn't say anything and I turned around and left.

"Jake, I've told him he doesn't have to go," I said when I got downstairs.

He looked up from his paper and said, "He needs to go, Honey."

"None of those boys need to be with grown men who are drinking. I paid a visit to Reverend Henry and told him all the mothers will be upset and take their boys out of the troop when they learn it."

"Oh, you shouldn't have done that."

"Jake, I remember when I worked in the clinic a lady who brought her husband in was so miserable because she was afraid her husband would resent her for taking him to the clinic. She never once thought about resenting him.

Jake Bell, I want you to know I resent you taking my boy on campouts and drinking while you're there."

"Yes, ma'am. I haven't done good, have I?"

That con artist doesn't have me convinced that he's sorry.

Neil's friend from Scouts came to visit and when he left, Neil said he had decided to go on the camping trip.

Saturday afternoon the troop and leaders were going to meet at a certain spot they'd agreed on and hike to the camp. Jake got dressed and put his duffel bag in the car. When I saw him put the trunk lid down I thought, *He has a bottle. I just know in my gut that he does.* I went out and opened the trunk of the car. I pulled everything out of his bag and put it on the trunk floor, but found no bottle. I put everything back, closed the trunk, and started to the back door; Jake stood watching me. He didn't smile, frown or comment.

That uneasy feeling hung over my head when I dropped Jake and Neil off. All through the night I woke up wondering if Jake was drinking. About 4:00 a.m. I got up. As I'd been trying to do early each morning, I took an hour to read history or other subjects, and my Bible. I usually read in the family room, but that morning I propped myself up in our brass bed and read my Bible. I always used the King James Version because I had memorized so much from hearing it through the years. I was reading in I Peter, chapter five. I got down to verse seven; I'd memorized it while in high school. A cousin had shared it with me and I'd taken it as my own. "Casting all your care on him for he careth for you." I read on and stopped at verse ten. "But the God of all grace, who hath called us unto his eternal glory by Christ Jesus, after that ye have suffered a while, make you perfect, stablish, strengthen, settle you." Could I ever be any of these? I asked the Lord what He wanted to do in my heart and life. Then I thought, *As unsettled as I feel, how wonderful it is to read and retain what I read.* I asked the Lord to give me a desire for His Word. If I were to ever let the Lord do anything in my life, it would be through reading His Word.

That day after church, I read verse ten to Jane. She said in her southern accent, "I like the word 'stablish.'"

"I like it, too. I just don't want to go through all these things in getting there," I said smiling.

At the end of the day, the girls and I went to pick up our Scouts. I had told Neil to always feel free to tell me if his dad had been drinking. As he was getting out of the van at the church, he saw me and put his fist up to his mouth as if he were drinking. *Oh no. Neil has had to go through that again. When will it ever end? How can I stay settled with all these upsets?*

When Jake and I were alone, I told him I knew he had been drinking while at camp. When I questioned him, he told me the truth, as he always did when he was sober.

He had gone to the campsite the day before and hidden the bottle.

On Monday night when Jake and Neil got home from Scouts, I asked Jake if Reverend Henry had said anything to them about drinking.

"Tonight at the meeting he came in just before we got started and read a statement that said, 'There is to be no drinking of alcoholic beverages while on Scouting trips.'"

"Was that all?"

"That was it."

I remembered what Dean had said about the man who visited a Sunday school class drunk: "I didn't know what to do." I thought it was more than that with Reverend Henry. I thought he was afraid to approach the men one on one. But why wait until after the campout to tell them?

After school started, I decided to join a ladies' Bible study that was just forming at our new church.

On the first day, at the stroke of 9:30 a.m., the pastor came in, paused, and looked at the room full of women and smiled. "Good morning, ladies."

He asked that we introduce ourselves and tell something about our lives. Everyone called the pastor "Donn," and he didn't seem to mind. He prayed and had us open our Bibles to I Peter. We read the first chapter and had a great discussion. I left feeling encouraged.

When I walked in the door at home, the phone was ringing. There was a silence on the phone when I said, "Hello," and I knew it was Jake.

"Is this the Bible student?"

"Oh, Jake, it was wonderful!"

"Well, that is great. How would you like to meet your husband for lunch?"

Jake had been restless since drinking on the campout, but he was trying. It never failed to amaze me that the same man who could get so bent out of shape from the terrible disease of alcoholism was the most charming and sweet person I'd ever known. I sat across the table from him at a little café a block from his office and was totally happy to be his wife, regardless of all the problems. I never doubted my love for him or his love for me.

When the waitress left after taking our order, he put his hands together on the table and leaned forward. "Now, Mrs. Bell, tell me about your Bible study."

I looked forward each week to Bible study and I was becoming better acquainted with the women. They all were interested in good books. Since I was reading for two hours each morning and getting through a lot of books, the ladies were beginning to ask me for recommendations of Christian books.

One morning after class, Pastor Donn said, "Mel, I want to come and visit you and Jake and get better acquainted with him."

Before I gave any thought to what I was saying, I calmly and in a low voice said, "Oh, Donn, that would be wonderful. He's an alcoholic."

"Oh, thank you for sharing that with me. I'll know how to pray," he said in a low, concerned tone. We set a tentative date for a Thursday afternoon three weeks later.

There's never a good time to tell something like that, I thought walking to the car. *Lord, I thank you for looking after us. I believe this is the church we can grow in. Maybe Jake will give his heart to you.*

I left with a good feeling. I couldn't decide just what it was but maybe it was hope.

Saturday afternoon of that week I was in the garden picking the last of the tomatoes and Jake sent Roxie to get me. Karen was on the phone. She had been working on a master's degree, but wanted to teach. She found a job in Australia but her visa had not come through in time. Now a school from a little town in Arizona had called to offer her a job teaching high school English. She had to be there on Tuesday. She had everything lined up, except that she couldn't rent a moving truck because she wasn't twenty-five years old.

Jake said, "Honey, Karen needs you to come and rent the truck and go down with her. She'll take you into Las Vegas Tuesday night. You can fly back Wednesday."

Of course, I wanted to help Karen. She was alone with a little girl, but what about my girls? I left them so much as it was. However, after considering it more, we saw no other way for Karen to move.

While I got ready to go, Jake and the girls packed my bag. We left for the airport and got there just in time. It was late when the taxi dropped me off at Karen's apartment. Melonie was asleep and Karen had boxes everywhere.

When I called home, Jake was fine, but I couldn't sleep for wondering if everything would be okay. I felt so guilty for leaving my girls and I longed to be home.

Karen and I had a good time getting her ready to move. Friends came and we had the truck loaded in no time. We got in the cab with Melonie and two gerbils and headed for Bull Head City, Arizona. The realtor met us shortly after we arrived and took us to a small place he had for her to rent until she had time to look. The place was clean and we moved enough stuff in to spend the night.

Karen was up at the crack of dawn the next day. She checked in with the school and made plans to start teaching on Wednesday. We got Melonie signed up for daycare, turned the truck in and rented a car for Karen until she could find one. Each time I'd call home, everything was going well.

Karen took me to Las Vegas on Tuesday night to leave for home at 7:00 a.m. the next morning.

All that night I worried about home. The next day on a stopover in Denver, I called Jane. Wendy had called her.

Roxie had gotten up and gone to get in bed with her daddy about midnight and he was gone. Then she awakened Wendy. Jake came home shortly after that; he'd been to a bar, but wasn't in bad shape. Wendy had taken Roxie to bed with her and the next morning called Jane.

"Oh, Jane, I wish I hadn't gone."

"You had no choice, Mel. You have a big family, and there's a lot going on."

When I hung up, I called the office. Jake was so cheerful when he said he'd be waiting at the airport. We'd eat and pick up the girls. "Now Honey, you're going to hear that I was drinking. I went to a bar and had some drinks when I couldn't sleep. The girls woke up and found me gone. I didn't bring home a bottle so you won't have to look for one."

"Okay, Jake, but I don't want to leave the girls again. When the older kids need help from now on, I can't do it."

"I understand, Honey. There needs to be two of you."

"If there were, we'd kill you."

He laughed and said, "I'll see you in a few hours."

He was waiting for me with a wonderful smile on his face like nothing had happened. When he put his arms around me, I forgot all about being mad at him.

I'd been home from helping Karen move just a few days when I answered the phone in the kitchen.

"Hi, Mel," came the voice on the other end of the line. "I got my visa for Australia. It came to Flagstaff the day after we moved and I got it today." Karen laughed so freely as she said, "I just had to tell you and Daddy."

Dr. Smith had an opening to see me Friday morning. I was doing fine until I told him I felt guilty for leaving Wendy and Roxie and for not wanting to help Karen. All of a sudden I felt like I was going to explode.

"To top it all off, Jake says if Jacob's grades aren't good at the end of the semester, he'll be coming home. Jacob has no patience with his little sister and I'm no better—I have no patience with him." I completely lost it and the floodgates opened.

"I've been married to Jake nine years, Doctor," I said wiping my eyes. "I feel if I'd had some real input in the lives of the kids, instead of just keeping them clothed, fed and watered, we'd be more of a family. My standards and Jake's standards are so different. I can't control what my little girl watches on TV because the grown kids ignore me when they are there. I hate not being able to have rules that are respected."

"Mel," he said after listening without comment, "Who are you really angry at?"

"I don't know," I said loudly, starting to cry again.

"Mel," he said leaning forward, "We need to see the real problem here."

I waited for him to say more, thinking he meant I was the problem.

"Doctor, how am I always going to take care of everyone's needs with so many interruptions and crises?"

"Mel, Jake Bell is the one who should see to it that your wishes are respected. He should back you up about the TV. He should let it be understood that your schedule is respected."

"But when the pressure gets too much, he starts drinking."

"That's right, so, Mel, it's Jake Bell you're angry with. You're mad that he drinks. You're mad that he lets you be ignored and then expects you to fix things that go wrong with the kids. Your anger is not so much how the kids regard you. Your anger is how Jake Bell seems to be regarding you. The reason he doesn't see to your wishes is because he doesn't want to cross his kids when he's sober. So he refuses to see that anything is wrong. Denial, Mel, is a big part of alcoholism. Jake Bell is in denial most of the time about all of the problems. You should be angry with him. You don't have to feel guilty about that. You're letting the bottle defeat you. You are not the alcoholic. You are not to blame yourself for the results of Jake Bell's drinking."

When I told that to Joanne at lunch that day, she said, "Good for Dr. Searchbrains."

All my friends knew him by that name. For me it seemed to take the edge off of seeing a psychiatrist. In the beginning, I was so embarrassed, but I was learning that getting help was something about which I should never be ashamed.

⁓

Jake and I invited Donn to lunch. Jane had given me a new recipe for hot chicken salad. I made rolls and baked an apple pie from the freezer.

We were at the table visiting. Jake and Donn shared freely about how hard divorce was on the kids, having both gone through divorce.

"Hey," he said as I placed his pie in front of him, "How did you two meet?"

Now I'm going to give this one to Jake. I always say I was working for an older physician who knew Jake. The truth, I always told myself. But Donn knows he's an alcoholic.

Then I heard Jake say after a short pause, "Donn, I've had an awful booze problem. I met this young lady in a clinic for alcoholics after a long binge. She was in charge of the eleven to seven shift and we became friends." He put down his fork and put his hand on his cup and looked over at me. "I had my eye on her, but it wasn't her style to date someone from a place for alcoholics."

"You're a nurse. I didn't know that."

"I'm not. I worked in a small hospital and nursing home. My love is private duty."

"She hasn't gone to school, Donn, but she's a natural with any kind of patient."

Jake and Donn became good friends. They would talk for hours about anything and everything.

The Lord answered prayer and gave Jake a Christian friend.

⁓

The air was crisp the last part of November. The Boy Scouts were going to take one last trip about two hours away in the country. Jake was to take all the gear in his station wagon and trailer. I didn't want him to go but he said they needed him.

On his way home, a police officer stopped him to tell him he had a flat tire on his trailer. When Jake got out to look at the flat, the officer smelled liquor on his breath. He had stopped in a bar on his way home. The police had him come to the station and call someone to come and drive the station wagon home.

When Jake called, I was angry. "Here it is, Saturday evening. Everyone is busy and you have to have someone drive you back home."

I called one of Jake's cousins and he took me to drive Jake back. When we got there, the men in the small police station in a little town two hours from us had taken him to get the flat fixed and were helping him put it back on.

Jake started asking to stop for a drink as soon as we got in the car. At every exit on the interstate he wanted to pull off and get a drink. When we entered the city, he said, "Now, Melissa Ann, you can stop at a package store or I'll get out of the car."

All of a sudden I turned and spit in his face and continued driving. He reached over to the tissue box between us and got a tissue and wiped his face.

We were silent for a few minutes and he said, "I'm sorry I've pushed you to this point."

"I'm sorry I spit in your face, Jake."

He reached over and patted my knee and I drove on home.

Donn's sermon the next day was about choices. Jake seemed to be listening. *We got though last evening. He didn't drink. I'm so sorry I spit in his face. He saw I'd come to my wits' end and he disciplined himself. He can do that.*

On Thanksgiving, Zach and Lynne had dinner with their daughter-in-law's family, so we invited Donn and his mother to have dinner with us. Jacob and Neil were also home for the day.

Donn and Jake got in one of their long discussions. Jake was trying to challenge Donn's views on tithing and other subjects. I listened for a while and went to clean the kitchen. Later Jake said, "Mel, that minister believes everything he's saying to be true."

Karen and Melonie came home for Christmas. Roxena Lynne and Melonie were just two years apart so we always bought them one big toy alike. That year it was large stuffed monkeys, which they liked a lot. They loved one another and always had a good time together.

Shortly after Christmas, we were invited to some friends' house with John and Jane and several others. We played games and had a wonderful time. For so long, I'd wanted to go to non-drinking parties and it was happening more. Also, my cousin Ike and his wife Ellen were coming to the farm more. He was a recovering alcoholic who'd been dry five years; and I prayed he could be of help to Jake and his wife Ellen would be a help to me.

We saw Karen and Melonie off to Australia on New Year's Eve.

1973
READING AND GROWING

In mid-January I awoke early to a very cold house and discovered we had no lights. We'd had an ice storm; trees were bent over and the ground was a solid sheet of ice. I looked at my watch; it was 4:00 a.m. I went to the back porch and got wood and kindling and built a fire in the wood stove.

The family room was warm when Jake got up. He looked out the window and said, "Well, it looks like we are going to be staying in today."

Thirty minutes later, I was pounding ice off the steps with a hammer and he was trying to clear the ice from around the steps. I stopped pounding and said, "When I was fourteen, we had an ice storm and I dug a path out to my grandparent's barn, which was a long way from the house. I remember thinking that I would go to the city and marry a doctor or lawyer and never have to work outside again."

Jake leaned on his shovel and looked at me with a grin on his face but said nothing.

"What are we going to do about our little girl?" I asked. "She'll freeze in this place."

"Now, she'll not freeze. She'll be right in there by that stove with her daddy."

"When you have to heat your water on that stove for a week, it won't be so pleasant."

"Now, Melissa Ann, you're just as happy as you let yourself be."

Wendy had spent the night at Lisa's. When she called, she informed us they still had power at Lisa's. Power was still on at the boys' schools as well. We heard on the radio that those out of power were to have it restored by the end of the day.

As I went past the family room door, I could tell Roxie was playing with her imaginary playmate.

Just then I heard her say, "Daddy, Katrina wants to sit by you."

I watched through the doorway as Jake scooted over and patted his chair and said, "Just climb right up here and sit with me, Katrina."

Oh my goodness, the man is nuts. Then I thought, *What a rare occasion this is and how much our kids have missed. Thank you, Lord, for the ice storm!*

The novel *Christy* by Catherine Marshall had become very popular. I read it while Jake studied his radiology journal and Roxie played, interrupting her daddy often.

I heard the furnace click on in the middle of the night. It had been fun making do without power and it gave me a new appreciation for modern conveniences.

A few weeks later we got a call from Jacob. I heard Jake talking and stopped to listen when I heard him say, "Well, Jacob, as long as you stay in school and study, I'll support you, but two classes won't cut it. Get ready to cancel them and we'll pick you up on Thursday."

Jacob's coming home. He's not going to like that one bit.

When Jake hung up he said, "Our college boy is partying and not studying and has canceled out on the classes he's failing."

"I heard you say we'd come get him. Jake, he's not going to stop partying just because you bring him home."

"No, but he'll need to find a job."

"He doesn't have a car."

"We'll have to take him back and forth until he can save enough to buy one."

I knew who the "we" would be and that Jacob would hate every minute of me hauling him around.

Jacob got a job in a factory not far from home. He had to be at work at 5:00 a.m. and got off at 3:00 p.m.

Taking him wasn't a big problem because I had been getting up early to read. As always, when I picked Jacob up at 3:00 p.m., he was quiet and had an unhappy look on his face. Dr. Smith said he was unhappy with himself, so not to take it personally. A lot of evenings he was out with friends, but when he was home, he was short-tempered.

Jake had gotten interested in old coins, and even though he spent a lot of time with a magnifying glass in our room at his desk, I was glad he wasn't drinking. Dr. Smith had said his constant interest in more and more coins was a substitute for the bottle, so I thought, *More power to him. At least he isn't drunk on the floor or in a motel.*

One evening after dinner, Jake was studying coins, Wendy was in her room and I thought Jacob was upstairs also. There was a child's program on TV and I had told Roxie she could watch it. I was on the phone and I heard her say, "Jacob, I was watching that." He paid no attention to her and she said, "Mama told me I could watch that."

"Shut up," he said.

I hung up the phone and went to the door of the family room. "Jacob, turn the TV back where it was."

"I've got just as much right to watch that TV as she does," he said, standing in the middle of the family room looking very angry.

I waited and he didn't turn the channel. I went over and turned the channel and said, "Jacob, you may be excused."

"You may be excused, you may be excused," he mocked, still standing frozen in his spot and very angry. "I don't have to leave. I'll stay down here as long as I please."

How am I going to handle this? Dr. Smith said that often when alcoholic families don't have a crisis, they create one. We've just created one. What should I do? I wondered, standing looking eyeball to eyeball at Jacob.

Without any warning I heard, "Young man, the lady of the house said you are excused and, Buster," he said with emphasis, "you are excused." Jake had walked in the room.

"She has no right to tell me what to do. I should not have to leave the room because I want to watch TV."

"Jacob, you refuse to fit in. You have no regard for anyone else. As of two weeks from now, no more free meals, no more free rides, no free laundry. You may sleep here; that's all," Jake said.

"Oh, you want to make it sound like you're not running me off," Jacob muttered as he stormed through the house to go upstairs.

I went in our room. I was shaking when Jake came in.

"How will we manage two more weeks? And if he stays longer than that, I can't eat in front of him and not ask him to eat," I said dropping into a chair. "What do I do about taking him back and forth to work the next two weeks with him as angry as he is?"

"I think he knows we've had enough of that kind of behavior. If he gives you trouble, he can find his own ride sooner than two weeks."

We had a lot of silence the next two weeks. The only fun time was Wendy's seventeenth birthday. I picked up Wendy's friend who moved away to a nearby town and brought her to our house. Jacob laughed and joked with the girls before going out with a friend.

The last day of the two weeks came. I worked all day on Jacob's clothes. I washed and ironed and mended and checked to make sure no buttons were missing. I'd see that he left in style, but after he left, I wouldn't do his laundry. No one had said any more about the outburst two weeks earlier. That day Jake called and said, "This is your boy's last day for a free ride."

"I'm so worried about that, Jake. What if he comes down in the morning and expects me to take him to his job at five o'clock?"

I think he'll move in with one of his friends tonight. If not, when he goes up to bed, I'll tell him to find a ride for tomorrow or plan on walking."

My thoughts were interrupted when Jake said, "Are all his clothes where he can find them if he plans to move?"

"Yes. Everything's ready, but I hate this. I think I'll make him a coconut cream pie, maybe he'll know I love him."

Jake laughed and said, "Well, if cooking can prove it, no one should have a doubt."

As I made the pie, I thought about how I loved cooking for the kids. *That's the one thing that I do that my stepchildren never seem to resent. Maybe that's why I enjoy it. Maybe it's a way of expressing my love.*

That night we had pork chops and rice, one of Jacob's favorites, and corn on the cob that we'd frozen. When we had our pie, I offered him a second piece. I was delighted when he accepted.

He went upstairs shortly after we ate and came down after a while into the kitchen and said, "Mel, are my shirts in the laundry room?"

"Yes, Jacob they are all washed and ironed and hanging in there." He went in and got them and draped them over a chair in the family room. I knew he was planning to leave. I went down in the basement and cried.

He brought the last of his stuff down just before his friend came. Jake asked him to write his phone number down and leave it on the kitchen desk, which he did. We all stood by the door and watched him go.

Wendy asked us if she could apply for a job at Kmart. Her dad had said she could work as long as she was doing well in school. The next day after school, she applied. When she told me she got the job, she had a smile on her face from ear to ear.

I hugged her and said, "Oh, Wendy, I'm so proud." She didn't respond, but she didn't resist. *Maybe I've made too many mistakes to really make a difference,* I thought as we went out the double doors of Kmart.

Wendy did a good job at Kmart. It was lots of running to take her back and forth but she seemed to like it.

One of our friends had been attacked in a parking lot by a man who stole her purse, so Jake got Wendy and me Mace spray, just in case. As I waited for Wendy, I kept my protector and so did Wendy as she walked to the car.

"I believe Wendy is going to be okay," I said to Jake one night after everything was quiet. "Maybe this part-time job is good for her."

One day on our way to Bible study I said to Joanne, "This is too good to be true."

We were halfway through the Bible class that day when the secretary came to the door and motioned for me to come. I walked out into the hall. She said, "Mel, Dr. Bell wants to talk to you."

Oh dear, I wonder what's happened now, I thought, as I walked into the office and picked up the phone.

"Hello," I said rather shakily.

"Hi, Honey. I just got a call from Wendy's principal. She's being sent home for the rest of the school year."

"Why?" I heard my voice rise.

"I don't know the details except that she had words with one of the girls and Wendy sprayed her with Mace."

"Oh, no. Is the girl okay?"

"Yes. She sprayed her in the face but the nurse said she's fine. Since you're close to the school, could you go get her?"

"Do I need to go now?"

"No, wait until you're finished. She's at the north door."

I went in and sat back down by Joanne. She looked at me and knew something was wrong. I sat there and tried to listen but my mind went wild. *When will it ever end? One crisis after another. What will she do during the day? Her dad said she couldn't keep her job if she messed up at school.*

As soon as we were dismissed, I said to Joanne very low, "Wendy has been kicked out of school."

"We'll go get her," she said patting my hand.

Joanne loved my kids and understood what they were up against. I knew Wendy wouldn't mind her being along.

We drove up the long school drive and there sat our beautiful girl with her long hair parted in the middle and wearing a suede jacket with fringes on it. She had bought it with money from her job. She looked a little worried as she walked toward to the car.

Joanne rolled down the window and said in her country way, "You git yourself in this car."

Wendy smiled and I could see she was relaxing. She put a large stack of books on the back seat and got in. I looked at her and said, "Hi, Wendy."

She smiled and said, "Hello there."

I wish Wendy knew that I care for her.

That evening Jake told her to call work and tell them she wouldn't be back. The agreement was she could work as long as she did well in school. Wendy didn't comment, she just turned and walked toward the stairs.

Thursday had always been my special day with Jake. If he was fixing the fence, I was with him. If he went somewhere in the truck, I went along. "What about our Thursdays, Jake? That has always been our day alone during the school term."

"We'll still have it. Wendy's not going to run around with me," he said, laying his journal down and looking across the room at me.

We tried to think of things to keep her busy. I suggested a sewing class and typing. She agreed to enroll in those.

The next Thursday was a little windy and Jake was going to work in the north pasture on the fence. He was having his last cup of coffee at the breakfast table when he looked at me and said, "I wish you could drive a stick shift. I need you to drive the tractor for me."

Wendy was very quiet and looked a little dejected.

I asked, "Hey, Wendy, would you rather do household chores or drive the tractor?"

"I'll drive the tractor."

Drive the tractor she did. They were stretching wire out near the yard and I could see that she was interested in what she was doing.

She's enjoying every minute with her dad, I thought as I watched them through the kitchen window. *Maybe I should rethink this. Wendy and all the kids, for that matter, haven't been able to spend a lot of time with their dad one on one.*

I talked to Dr. Smith about feeling neglected and wishing Jake would take me more places. He said I should make the plans when I wanted to do those kinds of things.

The next Thursday Wendy said, "What farming are we going to do today?"

That night after the girls had gone upstairs Jake said, "Wendy seems to be enjoying helping me outside."

"She's starved for time with you, Jake," I said sitting down on his lap. "We all are. How about meeting me for lunch tomorrow?"

"I think I can manage that," he said.

⁓

Spring brought the usual activities. We got baby chicks for capons and Jake planned the garden.

The medical auxiliary came to the farm again for our last meeting until fall.

The third week in May, just before school was out, Jake and I went to Rochester, Minnesota, to a radiology meeting and a retirement party for Dr. George, Jake's old professor who for years had been Chief of Radiology at the Mayo Clinic.

Joanne and I shopped for the perfect dress for the banquet. We found a long dress, black and white, with a rose colored flower. I couldn't wait to wear it to the dinner.

On the plane Jake seemed happy to be going back. He was looking forward to seeing everyone. I was always glad to go with him but the fear of alcohol was always in the back of my mind.

We got there mid-afternoon and Jake went to a meeting. Nothing was planned for the evening, so we were going to have time to go out to dinner alone. This was my favorite part of going on these trips.

I took a nap then finished the book I was reading.

When Jake walked in the hotel room about 5:00 p.m., I could tell he'd stopped at a bar.

We watched the news and he suggested we go to dinner.

"No, Jake. I won't go with you drinking." He went to the phone and ordered two steak dinners to be sent to the room along with beer for the evening.

Keep your cool, Melissa Ann, and don't blow it.

Jake stretched out on the bed and went sound to sleep. The dinner of steak, baked potato and asparagus with three cans of beer and coffee for me arrived. I ate dinner thinking, *The way you handle a drunk is: If he isn't giving you trouble, let him be.*

I poured the beer down the sink and ate my elegant and delicious dinner alone.

I put the cart with my dirty dishes and the beer cans in the hall and covered Jake's dinner with his napkin.

He slept until about midnight but was up and down the rest of the night.

We went down for an early breakfast. The waitress brought coffee and Jake got out our schedules. There were meetings for Jake to attend and we were to meet for a luncheon with one of Jake's good friends who visited us when he was speaking at a meeting in St. Louis. Then there was a party at the home of Dr. and Mrs. George that evening.

"You'll like his wife, Honey. She likes to garden and is a sweet lady."

"Jake, I've accepted the invitation already but I want to tell you one thing." I set my coffee cup down and felt power like I had never felt concerning the bottle. I looked him straight in the eye, "If you are going to drink today, tell me and I'll not show my face at that luncheon. If you're going to drink at that party tonight, you'll go alone and I'll tell the hostess myself why I'm not coming."

"I won't drink at either place."

"You may; and I will still cancel without blinking an eye."

He set his cup down and looked at me and said, "I bet you would." After a short pause he said, "Melissa Ann, has anyone ever told you that fire can be seen in those blue eyes when you're mad?"

I held his gaze but no way was I going to let him know that all I could think was, *This man is such a charmer.*

The luncheon went well. Afterward, I went back to the hotel and called Jane to see if everything was okay with the girls.

"Jane, I'm beginning to believe that someday I will be able to break free of the bottle. I've always tried to deal with whatever comes, but if Jake comes home before the dinner party drinking, I can call and give my regrets."

"Good for you."

After talking with Jane, I gave more thought to breaking free. *Somehow, sometime, I'm going to be free of the bottle. It may still rule him but it won't rule me. I don't know where I'll get help and when, but I'll stay with Dr. Searchbrains, attend the Bible study class and do whatever it takes to keep the bottle from ruling me. In two years, all my kids but Roxie will be out of high school. I don't want to do anything as long as the older ones are home. I can't leave them with their dad. They've got to know their home is intact. I promised the Lord if I could have Jake I'd never divorce him, but I know when Neil graduates in 1975, I'll break free of the bottle.*

We had a great time at the party that evening. Everyone was so friendly. Dr. George's wife was very sweet. I was very impressed with her flower garden. It reminded me of my sister's garden. We were standing near a beautiful flowerbed and I was telling the hostess how my sister planted vegetables among her flowers.

Jake walked up with a doctor who looked familiar. He stuck out his hand and said, "Mel, do you remember meeting me in the airport in Indianapolis when Jake was taking you to a church convention at Anderson a few years ago?"

"Yes, I do," then I lowered my voice and said as Jake walked closer to me, "He wasn't taking me to the church convention, I was taking him."

He slapped Jake on the back and had the most infectious laugh. Jake just looked at me and smiled.

After a lovely evening, we took a cab back to the hotel.

The next day, Jake was to go to lunch and golf with some of his classmates. I knew drinking would be heavy, but I knew if Jake drank, I wouldn't go to the retirement party. This was a new thing for me. I'd always gone regardless and tried to control things.

After lunch I had about an hour before Jake was due back. I went downtown and found dresses for Roxena Lynne and Melonie.

Later, when Jake came back to the hotel, I watched to see if he had been drinking. He was fine and was telling me that his doctor friend from Indiana had kidded him about my taking him to the church convention instead of his taking me.

"Let's go down to the coffee shop and get a snack," he suggested.

"That's good. I need to look for something in the gift shop."

In the gift shop, Jake said, "Honey, come and look at this book."

"How to Grow Spiritually," I read out loud. "Oh, wow, it's by Dr. Dale Oldham. Do you remember hearing him speak when we went to the convention?"

"Yes, I do, and I'm going to get this for you. I know he's one of your favorite speakers."

"Oh, thank you, Honey. He is one of my favorites." *Jake always does those things for me. He's so thoughtful.*

We dressed for the party and waited for one of the local doctors to come get us and two other radiologists who were staying at the same hotel on the same floor.

There were several in the receiving line when we arrived at the party. Radiology graduates from several years had been invited and the tables were marked accordingly. We sat with the doctor from Indiana and his wife.

The retiring couple was very cordial and grateful for all who came. The country club was beautiful and everyone looked elegant and happy.

I was talking with Dr. George's wife when Jake went to the bar. He came back with a coke for me, as always, but I could tell instead of his getting a non-alcoholic drink as he usually did, he had gotten "the real thing."

When we started circulating he said, "I'm drinking."

"I can see. Oh, Jake, please, discard it and get something else."

"I'll be okay, Honey."

I've heard that before.

It wasn't long until he went to the bar a second time. I tried to look like everything was just fine, all the time wondering what I should do.

"Jake," I said when he was making his way back to the bar, "it's your choice if you want to drink, but I don't choose to stay here and watch you get loaded. I want cab fare and I'll go back to the hotel."

"No, no, Honey, I don't want you to do that."

"Jake, I don't want to be here when you choose to drink."

"As soon as we go into dinner, I'll stop."

"Well, if you don't give me the money for a cab, I'll call one anyway and have him wait until I go up to the room and get money to pay him. I'm going to go call now," I said as I started to the door. I walked down the hall. I could hear him coming behind me. I turned to him; he looked at me as though he was wondering what I was going to say when I picked up the country club phone.

"Sir," I said to the man that answered. "I need to go back to my hotel. Would you please call a cab for me?"

"Ma'am, there's a pay phone near the front entrance."

I thanked him and turned to Jake as I hung up the phone. "Jake, I need a dime to call a cab."

"No, Honey, your place is here with me. Come on; let's get back with the others. We'll be going into dinner soon and I won't need any more to drink."

I've heard that before, I thought as I held up my head like I had everything under control. I knew in no uncertain terms that the evening was falling apart and crumbling down around me. *How will I ever survive it? Why didn't I bring some money so I could pay the cab?*

Jake was loaded by the time we sat down to eat. Dr. George came by on his way to the head table and laid his hand on my shoulder.

"Your friend is getting out of shape," I said.

"What can I do to help?"

"Come by the hotel in the morning to treat his black eye."

He laughed and said, "Call me and I'll come."

We got to our table and one of the doctors took it upon himself to tell us where to sit. Jake and I were separated with two people between us and the promise that he wouldn't drink at dinner was completely forgotten. I watched him getting drunker as the evening wore on.

What should I do? I thought, as I watched him trying to carry on a conversation, slurring his words and saying things that didn't make sense. I had watched my husband's wonderful personality gradually slip away, leaving a man in the same shape as Woody Tom on the night he was put under the country store all those years ago. The words "skid row" came to mind again.

Finally the evening ended. Holding to my hand, Jake staggered out to the car and fell asleep in the back seat. I sat silently beside him with his head against my shoulder, drooling on my new dress.

I'll be so glad to get out of this car. I know the other doctors are feeling sorry for this poor young thing married to this older drunk.

When we got back to the hotel, Jake sat down on the bed and struggled to light a cigarette. After several tries with his body swaying back and forth, he lit it and stretched out on the bed. I cleaned my face and got ready for bed. As I came out of the bathroom, I smelled scorched cloth. I hurried over to where Jake was sleeping—his cigarette had burned through the lapel of his new gray suit, almost to the skin. *I wish it had burned all the way through,* I thought as I got what remained of the cigarette and put out the sparks with a wet wash cloth.

Several times I've needed to stay home with my kids, but I wouldn't do it because I was afraid he would burn himself up. I've always made sure nothing happened to him. I go with him and see that he doesn't drink. I drive him places or I keep him out of the car. It's time I give him the responsibility of taking care of himself. How do I do that? I'd feel so guilty, I thought as I sat down on the bed and picked up the book Jake had purchased that afternoon.

It was hard for me to concentrate but I read with interest. On page twenty-two, Dr. Oldham told about a woman of perhaps forty (*I'm almost there*), a listener of Christian Brotherhood Hour (*so am I*), who wrote to pour out some of her problems with the hope that Dr. Oldham could help her. Her husband was an alcoholic. He went on to say later she made a trip to Anderson, Ind., for counseling. During their conversation, she said what I had asked myself so many times. "What can I do?"

Dr. Oldham wrote, "After our conversation, I outlined for her a program of spiritual disciplines and reading which I thought might help her rise above her problems."

Oh, I wish I knew what he had her read. Jake needs help so badly.

Then I read, "Months later I had a letter from her in which she said, 'Thank you for your help and guidance. The Lord is hearing and answering prayer, but not the way I had thought. Recently, I have found that peace can be mine, not through the removal of my problems, but in spite of them. My husband hasn't changed a bit, but I have. And I have found a closer walk with God and the ability to face the future without fear and without any sense of defeat.'"

Wow! I wonder if I could ever get to that place. I put my book aside and turned out the light. As I lay there on the bed by my drunken husband, I decided I would read my Bible every day and ask the Lord to speak to me through his Word. I also decided to let Jake be responsible for his own actions, starting with the flight home.

I decided that instead of leaving for home mid-afternoon and helping Jake feel less pain from his hangover, I'd leave on the plane that left at 9:00 a.m. He could go with me or wait and go later.

The last thing I thought before I went to sleep was, *If the lady who saw Dr. Oldham could get help, so can I.*

I was up early and got my things ready to go. *Oh, I hope there is room on the early flight,* I thought, just as Jake sat up on the side of the bed and reached for a cigarette.

"Good morning, Doctor."

"Did I sleep in my clothes all night?"

"Looks like it."

"What time is it?"

"Six-thirty."

He started to the bathroom and said, "You're all dressed."

"Yes. I'm going home on the 9:00 a.m. plane."

I picked up my book and soon I heard the shower going. *He must be planning to go with me.*

Jake came out dressed in a clean shirt and sports coat.

"Several of the gang is going to meet for lunch at twelve. I didn't know if you wanted to go or not but we are welcome."

"No, thank you. Call whomever you need to and tell them you can but I'm going home."

"No, if you go home, I go."

"Well, if you're going, call and see if they have two seats and cancel our three o'clock flight." He went to the phone and dialed it.

Keep quiet, Melissa Ann. As of today, you are starting a new life.

"Yes, sir," I heard Jake say, "We'll be there early."

We were silent for a while during breakfast. Jake was the first to speak.

"My new suit will need to go to the weaver."

"You can go that way in the morning and drop it off."

He looked at me. I'd always taken care of all his mistakes.

"Oh, okay."

"I like the book you bought."

"I'm glad."

We had finished eating and were still drinking coffee.

"I'm sorry, Honey. I'm an embarrassment to you."

Don't blow it; this is your chance to show a change. I leaned forward. "Jake, I will never get caught in a mess like last night again. Had I had money for a cab, I'd have left."

"I know, Honey. You wanted to go. I thought I'd stop but man, I can't stay away from that stuff when I'm around it."

"I have a request. Anytime you are going somewhere and are going to drink, just tell me and I won't be there. Jake, I don't want to lift my voice and say more, but I do not intend to be in public with you when you're drinking."

He looked at me for a long time.

"I know you were humiliated."

We rode to the airport without saying more. I read and he talked to the driver.

At the airport, as we waited to board, Jake was wringing his hands and walking around. As soon as we were seated on the plane, he dozed off and by the time we were in the air, he was sound asleep.

That's good. He won't want a drink, I thought as I opened my book to chapter seven: "Resentment Is Your Enemy." *Maybe I should skip this,* I thought. Dr. Smith had helped me to see I was full of resentment. Now, I was going to have to see what Dr. Oldham had to say about it.

I read: "Resentments are acquired so easily. Resentments against circumstances, against one's environment, against one's responsibilities; these are the things which, if you will permit them to do so, will frustrate the soul and sicken the body."

I closed my eyes and leaned my head back on the seat and thought about my resentments. *I resent that I have so much to do. I resent that I have to leave Roxie so much. I resent so much being humiliated last night. I resent always having to miss the important things I used to be able to do. If I plan to do something, Jake is drinking or I'm afraid to leave for fear he will start. I resent that he always wants me to go with him but he seldom wants to take me places that are important to me.*

I opened my eyes and continued reading and came to these words. "I remember the woman who poured out her heart in anguish about her alcoholic husband saying she was fed up, and couldn't take it any longer; that he'd have to get along without her the best he could from now on. As she talked, she shook her head and became red in the face. I told her I would pray for her husband, but that I would pray for her, also, because I detected in her attitude, that which needed maturing and refining by God's love and grace." He went on to say, "We can't just press a button and change. The change will come from within and must spring from a healthier, more mature relationship with Christ. If this is your need, be encouraged to ask the Lord for help. He has it for you."

I closed my book and thought, *I don't have much faith that I can change.* Then a scripture came to mind I'd heard a lot, "Faith comes by hearing and hearing by the Word of God."

That's my answer. Now that I can read, I have no excuse. I need to study the Bible daily.

Jake looked like a million bucks when we got home. We carried our things into our room. He hung the suits up in the closet. I started to take the burned one out of the garment bag and tell him not to forget to take it to the weaver. As I started to unzip the bag, I thought, *Hold on there, Melissa Ann, you don't need to start playing games. He knows his suit is ruined.*

By dinnertime on Sunday evening we had our girls home and it looked like all was well. Jake and I went out to the garden to pick strawberries. It was always fun going out to the garden with him. Roxie always followed us out there. We stooped down across from one another and commented about the size and quality of the berries being the best we'd ever had.

"I like to see things grow. It's our compost that has given us such healthy fruit," he said.

Wow! Maybe that's what the Bible did for the alcoholic's wife that Dr. Oldham was talking about in his book. I can't wait to get started.

Late that evening Donn called. "Hello there, Mel. How was your trip?"

"Oh, Donn, Jake bought me a wonderful book you'll want to read. It's *How to Grow Spiritually* by Dale Oldham."

"Hey, I'll look forward to that."

"You should be out here. We've just picked a large bucket of strawberries."

"Oh, I wish I had some of those. Say, I'm starting a Koinonia group for couples next Sunday night. I want you and Jake to be a part of it." (Koinonia is a Greek word that has come to represent intimate Christian fellowship or communion.)

"That would be wonderful." *Let this be Jake's decision and you go with him.* "Donn," I said, so Jake could hear me, "Why don't you talk to Jake? If he wants to come, I'll come with him." Donn laughed and I said, "Jake, come talk to Donn."

Jake came into the kitchen and took the phone. I went over to the sink and continued to stem strawberries.

Jake was telling Donn about some of the meetings he'd gone to, and then I heard him say, "Donn, I think my lady would really like that."

I love your charm, Jake. I enjoy you calling me "your lady," but your lady is going to find a way not to be defeated by the bottle. I'm going to see if I can become as healthy as these beautiful strawberries.

Jake hung up the telephone and poured himself a cup of coffee.

"Honey, I told Donn we'd come to his Koinonia meeting. I think I need to take you more places that you'd like to go."

"I appreciate that, Jake. If you want to join the group, I'll love going with you. You've done a good job choosing the church—and I think it's wise that we get involved—but I want you to choose the groups." I handed him a tray with several bags of strawberries on it and said, "Here, let's take these to the freezer."

He smiled and said, "Yes, ma'am."

On the next Sunday evening, we had our first Koinonia meeting.

"Well, what did you think?" Jake said as we drove home.

"I loved it, Jake. I'll go with you."

The next morning, I called Betty while I cleaned up the kitchen and told her about the group and about letting Jake choose so he'd go.

"Melissa, he should go with you anyway. Marriage is never one-sided."

That day in the mail, there was an invitation to a fiftieth wedding anniversary party for a couple I had known for years. I was well-acquainted with many of their friends too. I showed Jake the invitation and told him I wanted to go.

"Oh, Honey, you're not wanting me to go are you?"

I remembered what Betty said about marriage not being one-sided, and replied, "Sure. Just don't make plans for June fifteenth, Doctor, because you're going with me," and I handed him a piece of strawberry pie.

"Oh, aren't you the one." He handed back the invitation, took a drink of his coffee then gave me the cup for a refill. "Could I impose on you for another cup of coffee?"

"No problem."

Getting his coffee is never an imposition, I thought as I was pouring it. I want so much to go to that party, but now that I have told him, I must let it be.

The next two weeks were busy. On Friday before the anniversary party, Wendy went by plane to spend two weeks with her mother; Neil would go later.

On Sunday, we went to eat after church and dropped Roxie by Joanne's. Her daughter was five years older and had invited Roxie to go swimming. Neil was going to spend the afternoon with a friend from Scouts.

Good, I thought as we came through the back door, *everything has worked out; we can leave in an hour.*

"Honey, don't change your clothes," I said as Jake took off his coat and hung it in his closet. "Today is the Brown's anniversary party."

"Oh, Honey, I don't want to go to that," he said as he turned to go to the family room.

"Honey, I really want to go. Why don't you take a nap and I'll wake you in about an hour."

"You can go but I don't want to."

"I don't want to go by myself."

He didn't reply as he went and turned on the TV in the family room.

Well, at least he didn't change his clothes. No way do I want to go see the Browns without him. Everyone is going to wonder why he didn't come and I want so much to have him with me.

When the hour was up, I went in where he was watching a news panel.

"Honey, if we leave now, we have time to get there by 2:30."

"You go on, Honey, I don't want to go."

"Jake, I'm not going without you."

He looked up at me and said, "Now Mel, you know I don't know those people. They aren't important to me; they are important to you."

"Jake, why do you think I follow you around to all these places you choose to go? Do you think the people at all those meetings and social gatherings are important to me?" Then I started to cry. "No, Jake. I go to those places because YOU are important to ME."

Jake lit a cigarette and I saw he was not considering going. I went in the kitchen and got a glass of water then went to sit on the porch swing. As I sat there looking out on the orchard, I thought, *I need to just accept the fact that I chose this life.* I sat for what seemed a long time.

"Oh, here you are," Jake said as he came through the screen door. He came over and stood in front of me. "Honey, I thought about what you said about not wanting to go with me to all the social places. I know it's not your kind of life but you always fit in. I don't understand why you're so unhappy," he said, running his hand through his hair.

"Jake, I'm lonely. I'm lonely to go among the people I used to know. They knew me and loved me when I was up here without family. The Browns' doors were always opened to me. Now, I'm not alone. I have a husband and I don't want to run over there by myself like I did when I was single. I like the new church and the Koinonia group but I feel a longing for a reunion with the people that meant so much to me.

"I'm not around the life that I knew and loved. It's rare that I'm ever invited to participate anymore. I've turned them down too many times because you never wanted to go. I don't want you to hate going with me. You don't have to like it, but I need it to be important to you for me to have connections with the people who mean something to me. I don't think you really understand how deep friendships in a church family are. It comes with the new birth. Then you're in the family of God."

He stood silent, looking at me. "Well, I want you to know you'll never have any more problems with me. From now on, when you want to go to something like this taking place today, I'll take you. I'll go get my coat," he said turning around.

"No, Jake, the grandfather clock just struck 2:30. That's when it was to start. We're thirty minutes from there and I'm in no shape to go."

"Mel, I am very sorry I never really understood how much you've given up. I'll take you to that convention again back in Anderson. You saw lots of friends when we were there three years ago. When does it start?"

"Tomorrow night."

"Oh, that's a little too soon. We can't go to that. Well, we can have the Browns over here. I want them to come for dinner. You call and invite them. I want you to have your friends."

If I hadn't been so sad and emotionally distraught, it would have been funny watching him try to make everything right.

"Why don't you come and sit down in the swing and let's enjoy our front porch." He came over and sat down and just looked at me. We slowly swung back and forth.

He put his arm around me and said, "I am truly sorry, Honey."

"It's okay," I said. I felt so drained, but I thought maybe Jake hadn't seen just how fulfilling my life had been before I met him and how much I really missed it. Today Jake seemed to understand in a new way. He pulled me close to him. *I can be real mad at this man and when he puts his arms around me, I melt. I love him so much,* I thought as his lips tenderly met mine.

"I love you, Baby."

"I love you, Jake."

Wednesday morning, after I'd given Dr. Smith the report about Sunday afternoon, he looked at me for a little while and said, "Mel, you sound uncertain about confronting Jake about going with you."

"Doctor, I hate crying and begging people to do things for me. He knew I wanted to go. I feel a little silly crying about it."

"Mel," he said rolling his chair forward, looking at me in the eyes. "He needed to see what was important to you. I'm glad Jake Bell felt badly about not taking you. He should have. You have a right to expect him to go with you. See, Mel, in alcoholism, the enabler starts feeling unworthy. The things that are important to you have been put on the shelf long enough. When you want to go somewhere, you must expect Jake Bell to take you."

When I talked to Betty that day she said, "Melissa, you're going to win. You've already made up your mind to not go along on a trip if Jake plans to drink. Now, you can let him see you enjoying your own kind of life. It won't be forever before you're able to put the bottle behind you."

⌒

One summer morning, Jake was shaving and I was brushing my hair, when he said casually, "I just want to tell you I'm going to a weekend meeting on mammography the first of August. You are welcome to go along but I'll be drinking."

Stay cool. You've said he could go drink anytime, if he just tells you; so he's telling you.

"I have no desire to go but you go right on."

Just say no more to him about it. This may be his game playing. Maybe he wants to get my goat so I'll get upset, then he can have an excuse to drink.

Maybe this is what Dr. Smith means when he talks about alcoholics creating problems when there are none, I thought as I was frying bacon.

I could hear Roxie talking to her daddy in the other room. He was acting like everything was normal.

When we sat down at the table Jake said, "Let's ask our mama to return thanks."

Oh, he would do that, I thought. *I need to talk to the Lord but there are some things I want to say I don't want Jake to hear.*

I muddled through a short blessing. Jake was very upbeat during breakfast. I could hardly contain myself. *How could he spring that on me and then act as though nothing had happened between us.*

I was glad when it was time for him to go to the office. Roxie's little friend came up to see if Roxie could go home with her to play. I got my Bible and went down to the pond and sat on a big rock.

Dr. Smith had been working with me about facing my anger. So, that morning I looked across the pond and completely exploded into tears. "Damn him," I said slamming my fist down on my knee. I cried and beat my knees until I was all cried out. Then I said, "Lord, I'm not proud of this fit but I've said all these things in Your presence only. Somehow I feel that it's safe saying it to you. I'm so glad that my outburst wasn't in front of the kids or Jake. Forgive me, Lord, and help me to go to the house free of anger and self-pity. I don't want to continue to be locked into game playing. It would be so easy to call Jewell and ask her if a trip truly is scheduled for August, but with your help, I'll let go."

"Thou knowest the way I take," I read in Psalms. When I got up off the rock, I looked down at the water. A firefly lit on the water and I could see bubbles close to the rock where I'd sat. The fish were there eating the food we'd put in the water the night before. I walked up through the pasture feeling cleansed of all the anger I'd felt on the way down. After pouring out all my anger and reading the Psalms, I was hopeful that I could get through another day.

August came and went, but Jake made no more mention of the trip. When I talked to Dr. Smith about it, I admitted that I had wanted to call Jewell to see if a trip had ever actually been scheduled. But now I was more relaxed.

"Doctor," I said, "I think I can put the bottle behind me. I have no desire any more to make sure Jake is okay while drinking. Wendy will be a senior this year and Neil will be out of high school in two years. I don't plan to divorce Jake, but I think as soon as Wendy and Neil are gone, and if Jake is still drinking, I'll take my little girl and let him take care of himself. I see what you mean about enabling and I no longer want to be a part of it."

I stopped by Betty's on the way home and told her what I'd said to Dr. Smith.

"That's good, Melissa. Just make sure you don't tell Jake you're going to leave until you know for sure you can do it. That can be a way of game playing, too."

"Oh, Betty, you are so wise. Why haven't I listened to you more?"

"Well, you didn't go on that trip to Colorado before you were married," she said and we both laughed.

I got up from her table and said, "Betty, you are a rock. I thank the Lord for you."

Everyone was more relaxed at the end of the summer. Some months with no drinking had done wonders for all of us.

Roxena Lynne was in second grade. She rode with her daddy each morning to catch the bus.

Wendy was back in school and she was becoming a lot more fun. Instead of watching TV, Wendy and Roxie spent a lot of time outside. One evening while I was making dinner, they came in the back door and Roxie was blindfolded. Wendy had such a sweet smile on her face. They had been walking outside showing Roxie what it would be like to be blind.

My cousin Ike's wife Ellen and I made and froze apple and peach pies. Jake, Zach, Lynne and I started going to dinner or a play once a month. It was good to get back into a fall routine.

I was cooking dinner one Monday evening and Jacob walked in the back door.

"Hi, Jacob."

"Hi. When do you expect dad home?"

"Between five and six."

He leaned up against the cabinet and said, "I went down to school and enrolled today."

"Well, your dad will be glad to hear that. Stay for dinner and talk to him about it."

We got him settled back in college on Thursday of that week and took Neil to his school on Saturday.

I was still getting up early to read two hours every morning. In the Tuesday morning Bible study, Pastor Donn put a lot of emphasis on reading the Bible daily. I had read Dr. Oldham's book two or three times; I wanted the same help the alcoholic's wife got from her study of the Bible.

The first week in September, I began to see the old signs of restlessness and silence telling me something wasn't quite right. Wednesday morning I was reading in the family room. The grandfather clock struck five and Jake walked in.

"You're up early," I said as he went in the kitchen. He came in with two cups of coffee and handed mine to me with the handle so I could reach it. *His manners are still good, but something's not quite right.*

"Thank you."

"You're welcome," he said, as he was raising his steaming cup, taking a small drink, his eyes glued on me.

"What's on your mind?"

"You know me, don't you?" He took another drink of coffee and said, "There's a one-day meeting on mammography in Memphis on Saturday. I'm going to fly out of here at 4:30 p.m. Friday and be back at 7:00 on Sunday evening. This is the first time I've not invited you to go along, Honey, but I'm going to drink." He looked at me and I looked at him.

Keep your cool, Melissa Ann. Do not comment. Leave him to his own thoughts.

We continued looking at one another until finally he went back in the kitchen. In a short while I heard him refill his cup just as I heard the paper truck go by. I got up and went outside and as I was walking down the drive I thought, *Hey, I'm not going to get upset about this. It's still a warm fall. The girls and I can do something special.* I picked up the paper and started back up the driveway with plans for the weekend growing in my head. *I'll call my sister Crystal before I go see Dr. Searchbrains. She said when I talked to her last week that she'd love for me to see her flowers.*

It dawned on me that Jake and I had never gone to see my sisters together. We'd been to see my brothers, but not my sisters. I closed my eyes and could feel the anger rising. *This may just be the start of his going alone to meetings but that's okay. I have two more years and everyone will be out of high school except Roxie, then I can leave the bottle behind me.*

Breakfast was over and Wendy was coming through the kitchen while I was loading the dishwasher. "Wendy, how would you like to go to Oregon this weekend? I have two nephews a little older than you. We'd fly out Friday after school and come back Sunday night."

Wendy smiled and said, "I'll go."

"Okay. My sister's time is two hours behind ours, but I'll call and see if she can have us."

"I hope your nephews are good looking," she said as she started to the door.

"They are. Maybe we'll go to Mt. Hood."

As soon as Jake left, I dialed my sister. She was delighted to know we could come. She'd call our sister Shirley, who lived close, and their sons would show Wendy a good time.

I was out of breath when I breezed into Dr. Smith's office that morning at 10:00.

"Well, you look in a hurry and like you have a purpose," he said as he closed the door to his office.

I went directly to the green chair that seemed like my own and put my hands on the dark wooden arms. "Doctor Searchbrains," I said watching a smile come on his face as he sat down across from me.

"What has my good friend come up with today?"

When I got through explaining what had taken place that morning, he suggested I not give Jake my sister's phone number. He pointed out that I'd have a better time if I wasn't wondering if it was Jake each time the phone rang. Also, he said I shouldn't call to see if he was okay.

"You don't need to worry about that, Doctor. I'm so angry at him."

"You know, Melissa, when you first started coming to me, you'd never admit that you were angry. You'd say you were upset. Admitting that you are angry has helped you to deal with it constructively."

I left Dr. Smith's office a little more hopeful.

Friday morning Jake said, "I need to take my things with me this morning and leave from work for the airport in the afternoon." Since we had been married, I always packed Jake's bag, but not this day.

I picked up my novel and opened it and said, "This is a wonderful book. It's Catherine Marshall's novel Christy. I'll read another forty-five minutes and get breakfast."

"How long have you been up?"

"Since 4:00. I read one chapter of Proverbs and five Psalms. I've been on the novel about thirty minutes. Now that I can read, I don't want to do anything else."

"What's the novel about?"

"A young girl who taught in a mission school in the hills of North Carolina."

"Oh, that's right down your alley."

"You ought to read it, Jake. The missionary teacher is about to fall in love with a doctor. Right now she thinks she's in love with the preacher."

"Which one do you think will get her?"

"The crazy girl will marry the doctor," I said trying not to smile.

"I'm sure glad of that," Jake said with a smile.

I stayed out of sight while Jake was packing his things. When he came into the family room with his suitcase he said, "You do a better job at packing than I do."

As Wendy was leaving, I told her I'd pick her up at the school at 3:30. Roxie would ride home with Jane's children, and then we would pick her up and go to the airport. Our plane left one hour after Jake's. We would gain two hours so we'd get to Crystal's before bedtime.

The girls and I had a good flight. I was proud to take them both. It had been a while since my sisters had seen them. Wendy would soon be eighteen and was a very pretty girl.

Crystal liked to sew and had a skating dress made for Roxie. She told her about it on the way to her house. Roxie told her she and her daddy went ice-skating on Friday nights sometimes. Roxie loved her Uncle Al. She called him "Uncle Owl." Crystal and Shirley's sons took Wendy to the coast. She seemed to be having a good time.

The joy of my weekend was Crystal's yard. She had long stemmed roses all around the house and all kinds of flowers with vegetables in front or behind them. The yard was a thing of beauty. I sat down on a decorative bench and thought about Jake. It was so beautiful out there yet I couldn't help but think of Jake. I felt so restless with worry. I went over and inspected three cabbages in front of Crystal's dahlias. Behind the dahlias was asparagus fern. *I wonder if the Garden of Eden was like this.* I remembered my mama's favorite song, "In the Garden": "He walks with me and he talks with me and he tells me I am his own," came to mind. *I don't let the Lord talk to me much. I feel so far away from Him. Sometimes now when I'm reading the Bible I get thoughts that seem to help, but that closeness isn't there.*

Then I thought of a story about an old lady who said to her husband, "Look at that young couple in the other car. We used to sit close like that."

He had replied, "I never moved."

It's I who has moved, Lord, I know that.

When we returned on Sunday night, the dread that was always there just wouldn't go away. *Will he be home? Will he be okay? What if he's not there, whom do I call?*

The girls were worried too—and I knew it—but to talk about it made it more real. When we drove in the drive, Roxie said, "Daddy is home." We noticed that the TV was on when we went in the door. Jake was asleep in his chair but the smell of Jim Beam wasn't as strong as it usually was. He soon was awake. Roxie was telling him the news right away.

"Daddy, we went to Aunt Crystal's and Aunt Shirley's."

"Oh, you did?" he said.

"Yes, and we went to Mt. Hood."

Jake looked over at me.

You're in for a lot of surprises, Doctor, I thought, and then I suggested the girls hurry on to bed. I went up to tuck Roxie in and say goodnight to Wendy. When I came down, Jake was getting ready for bed.

"Your trip was a little sudden, wasn't it?"

"Yes. I decided to go when you told me you were going to Memphis. I don't think it's healthy for the girls and me to stay home and wonder what's happening with you when you are somewhere drinking. So the thing for us to do is make a life of our own."

He sat down on the bed to light a cigarette and said, "I know I'm a problem. Man, I shouldn't have gone."

I went to wash my face and when I came back in our room, he had gone to bed. I picked up my book and started to read. It wasn't long before he was up smoking again. *He must not have stopped for a bottle. He has whiskey on his breath but it's been a while. Maybe I should turn my light out so he'll settle down.* I put my book aside and turned out my light.

"Goodnight, Jake. I love you."

"I love you too, Baby," he said. There seemed to be a sad sound to his voice but I didn't feel sorry for him.

He was up and down all night as usual after drinking, but I never asked him about his trip, if he attended the meeting or what he did.

We started our usual routine on Monday morning. In the back of my mind, I was wondering, *Will he come home drinking? I hope he doesn't. I don't know how I'll react, but in two more years, Roxie and I can move away from the bottle. As soon as Wendy is in college, we'll be gone when he's drinking. I'll keep the home intact until Neil graduates, but I'm sick of the bottle ruling my life.*

As the weeks passed, Jake paced the floor at night. He was like a ticking time bomb. I knew he was desperate to drink.

Pastor Donn spent a lot of time with him and talked to him a lot about the Lord. Two Sunday nights a month we went to our Koinonia meeting. It was a wonderful time of Bible study. There was another doctor and his wife in the group. A couple that we liked a lot had a son in Neil's class at the military school. The whole group loved one another and took each other's burdens upon themselves.

Several were free about telling their problems. I thought Jake should share about his problem with alcohol, but he wouldn't, except with Donn. Several of the ladies in our group were also in the Tuesday morning Bible study. I knew they would pray without gossiping but I thought it should be Jake who told about his problem.

The second week in November, Jake came home from work saying he was going pheasant hunting with a doctor friend. I knew the doctor and his wife but didn't know if he was a heavy drinker. I did know Jake would probably drink. What had started in Memphis would eventually end in a binge. They left on Thursday and would be back on Sunday. I didn't have time to arrange a trip out of town, but Disney on Ice was going to be in town, and Ulma and I had already planned to take our girls to see that. It was a wonderful time and all three girls enjoyed it very much. The rest of the weekend, I tried to stay busy so the cloud of the bottle didn't completely engulf us. It was there nonetheless.

Jake came home with a lot of pheasants for the freezer. I knew he had spent time drinking when he came in with the cooler, put it down near the door and said, "Bag these pheasants and get them in the freezer."

"Oh no, Buster, you don't come in with a hangover and start ordering me around. I'll help you, but you're the one that decided to go on the hunting trip."

He went back out to his friend's car and got the rest of his things. He put his gun away and came back and carried the cooler in the kitchen.

"These birds may not be clean enough to freeze," Jake said.

"Put them in the sink. I'll wash them with your help."

I was washing them carefully and Jake became impatient.

"Let's get a move on it. It's getting late and I've got to work in the morning."

"Don't you get impatient with me, Jake Bell. I'll leave this mess with you so fast it will make your head swim."

Just then Roxie appeared in the kitchen—our angry voices had awakened her. Roxie dampened that argument but it was kept for another day.

The following Wednesday, I said, "You take your trips and start drinking and get all restless and start shouting orders." He just sat there looking at me and I couldn't shut up. "The girls need you to do things with them, Jake. When you're sober everyone needs your time and patience." He ignored me. Finally I went in our room and got ready for bed and got a new book I'd just started reading. I'd read about ten minutes when I heard the back door open.

Oh boy, I've done it. I got up to catch him, but decided not to. I went and looked out the window, thinking he'd be in the car, but he wasn't. *He's got a bottle hidden and was planning to drink on his day off. I fell right into his trap by getting mad at him. Now he'll try to make me think I upset him. Wow! It's taken Dr. Searchbrains so long to get me to see that.*

He drank off and on Thursday as he worked down in the south pasture on the fence. He was fine on Friday during the day but drank in the evening. Saturday, he was two hours late coming home from work; he had started drinking after he got off work at noon.

As he was coming up the road, he saw the young man who had sold drugs to Wendy a few years earlier crossing over the fence into our pasture. He walked in and yelled, "Wendy!"

Seeing he was mad and drunk, I went over to the door and said, "Why do you want her?"

He walked past me and went through the dining room and into the living room and yelled, "Wendy!" She came downstairs looking frightened.

"I just saw the young man who brought you drugs and I ordered him to stay off this place."

"Jake, Wendy hasn't seen him. Their dogs were in the pasture. He was probably going to get them."

Jake kept ranting. I reached in my pocket and got my car keys, went over and stood by Wendy and put them in her back pocket.

"Jake, she didn't do anything wrong. She's been home doing her chores." I took him by the arm and said, "Let's go have some coffee," then I mouthed to Wendy, "Go to Lisa's."

He turned around still saying, "I'll call the authorities if that young man shows up at our place."

As he slept in his chair that afternoon, I went through the house thinking, *I'll take this. No, I'll leave it and take this.* I wanted to have it all decided on so I could move fast when I would finally be able to leave the bottle.

Jake slept the rest of the afternoon but drank off and on during the weekend.

Tuesday after Bible study, Donn, asked how Jake was and I told him I was afraid he was headed for a binge.

"I'll call him about going to lunch Saturday."

"That will be good."

Saturday morning when Donn called I knew Jake would decline the lunch invitation. I knew he was headed for a binge.

"Donn, I sure appreciate your invitation to lunch. I'd like to take a raincheck on that."

When he finished talking to Donn I said, "Jake, I really need you to come home on time. Wendy has a date and I'd like for you to be here. Also, we need to go to the parade tomorrow."

"I'll be fine, Honey."

At 11:00 a.m. Jake called to tell me not to expect him for lunch.

"Jake, I'm not going to beg you not to drink—we both know that doesn't work— but you need to stay off the road if you're going to drink."

Wendy's date, Max, came about 1:00 p.m. We were both relieved her dad didn't drive up before they left.

I found myself wanting to stay close to the phone, so Roxie and I stayed at home. Her little friend came up and they played in the barn.

At 3:00 p.m. Donn called and said, "Mel, I ran in to call you. I was on my way to a couple's house. I saw Jake's car next to mine. When I got close, I saw he was in bad shape. I talked to him a little bit and asked if I could take him home. He said 'No, Donn, I came to tell you I'm not a Christian.' Then he said, 'I've got to go.' I told him to wait and I'd be back. When I got to the door to come call you, he left. I shouldn't have left him. I didn't know what to do."

I thought Donn's voice sounded a little shaky.

"Donn, you've never seen him like that, have you?"

"No, Mel, it was like I was seeing and talking to someone else. I'm so afraid he'll have a wreck."

"I know. I've tried to keep keys from that man for ten years."

"As soon as I've finished with my appointment, I'll call you. We've got to get this man acquainted with the Lord."

Wow! Finally a Christian man is burdened for Jake's soul.

About 5:00 p.m. Jake called. He was in a motel. Someone from a bar had taken him. He didn't know what room he was in.

I checked at the motel office and got the room number. Jake was waiting for me. "Who drove you, Jake?"

"A woman drove my car and her husband followed her."

I went over to where he was and said, "Stand up, Jake, and let me look in your pocket."

He got to his feet and staggered back against the dresser. I checked his pocket. All of his money was gone.

That evening when I got Roxie settled for the night, I called Jake's office manager to see when Jake had left the office. He'd left shortly after he'd called me.

"Mel," Jewell said, "when Doctor doesn't come in and I don't have another doctor scheduled to take his place, it really creates a problem."

"Oh, I know it does, Jewell."

"My girls say they are tired of lying."

"Jewell, why don't you tell him you can't run this office without him and that you and the girls are tired of lying?"

"That's not going to get him to come in."

"Why don't you talk to all four of your girls and see what they think about just going home when he's not there? I'll make sure they are paid. He'll be willing to do that because he won't take the chance of losing them."

The next morning I let him know about the money being gone. I'd gotten the Jim Beam he had in the car and poured it out, knowing he could get more. I liked pouring it out as much as he liked drinking it.

"Honey, I need a drink."

"Jake, I came to get you last night from the motel, but if you start in on me, I'll take you back. You know," I became louder, "I don't want to be around you anymore at all when you're drinking. If you're going to drink today, I'm not coming home after church. The girls and I will go on to the parade and leave you here. If you're going to drink, you need to go on back to the motel and give us peace."

"I know I'm a trial."

"Yes, you are!" I yelled. "And I'm sick of it." Just then our little seven-year-old girl walked in the room.

"Come over here, Honey, and sit by your daddy," Jake said, patting the side of the bed where he sat smoking. "Your mama's mad at your daddy for misbehaving yesterday."

I walked out of our room as mad as a hornet, wanting to explode. *He's talking about misbehaving like it's okay, except that it upsets her mama—like there must be something wrong with me.*

I whirled around and went back to the door of our room.

"Hey, Mister, let me tell you something. That statement was a poor excuse for accepting responsibility for your actions."

He sat there so calm with his arm around Roxie, talking to her like he did when she was two. Then he said with the sweetest voice, "Come on over here, Mombala, and watch cartoomers with us."

I turned around and when I got to the kitchen door said, "Oh, I'd like to kill that man." I walked in to see Wendy standing at the sink.

"Well," I said, "Maybe before I commit murder I should go to church and the parade."

Wendy smiled and said, "Well, I think maybe you should." The strain showed on her face, but she was doing better in school, and was doing more with her friends.

"How was your date with Max?"

"Okay. He'd like to come to dinner next week if that's okay."

"What night were you thinking about?"

"We wondered about Tuesday—if Dad's not drinking."

"Pastor Donn called last night. He will eat with us tomorrow night before Boy Scouts. Maybe since he'll be here Monday night, your dad will be sober by Tuesday."

As we sat at the dinner table on Monday night, Jake said, "Donn, this time of the year, with party after party and people drinking—man, it's hard to stay off that stuff."

"Oh, it won't be so bad this year. We've got the Prime Timers' party coming up. You'll be a part of that. It won't hurt you to give up some of the other ones. The only party Mel said you really needed to go to was your medical party and you'd sit with the non-drinkers. This sounds like a good way to get in control. Choose not to go to the places of temptation, Jake," he continued. "You told me Saturday you knew you weren't a Christian. The Lord is waiting with open arms."

Later in the week, Jake announced that we would skip the social events where there would be a lot of drinking. We became busier with our new friends at church and some of our non-drinking friends invited us to parties. We also spent some time with my cousins Ike and Ellen.

The boys were home for Christmas, and we celebrated with Zach and Lynne. Donn spent time out at the farm, too.

Thank you, Lord, for answering my prayers for Christian friends for Jake and me.

1974
A PLAN TO BREAK FREE

When Jake called one January evening to tell me he had stopped at a bar, it wasn't an act when I let him know I wasn't upset. When Wendy heard me say, "Drink until your heart's content," she smiled while she was mashing potatoes. I knew I was turning a corner after eleven years; someday I'd be free of the bottle. My enabling days were on their way out.

My worry about Jake coming home with a bottle wasn't as intense as it had been. The women in the Tuesday morning Bible study were a real support system. It was a wonderful open group. My being able to read and understand what I read was making such a difference in my life.

One day as we were taking prayer requests in Bible study, one of the girls got upset and started crying. A friend's husband had drowned and left the young woman with three small children. All of a sudden it became the pain of everyone in the room. Donn listened and said, "Hey, this is real Koinonia."

Joanne said afterward, "Mel, you can be open with those gals. They'll hurt with you and they aren't gossipers."

"I was in a group like that in Nebraska in the fifties but I haven't experienced that for years," I said.

"Because of their concern, that group will never be the same," Joanne said.

Each Tuesday someone opened up and shared struggles they couldn't cope with alone. On the way home one day, I told Joanne that I was beginning to feel safe in that church.

One day, I was making cinnamon rolls and I started to panic. What if Jake comes home drinking? He's been so restless lately. I started to sprinkle cinnamon sugar on the dough and the phone rang.

Oh, what if Jake is calling to say he won't be home on time.

I hated to lift the receiver.

I heard the cheery voice of my friend Sharon, who had given her heart to the Lord on my back porch. "Hi, Mel. I've been praying for you. You've been on my mind all day. You know, you told me the other day sometimes you thought you'd drown in your troubles. Well, I don't know much about the Bible, but listen to what I read in Psalms 93, verses 3 and 4. 'The floods have lifted up, O Lord, the floods have lifted up their voice; the floods lift up their waves.' That verse means you're about to drown, doesn't it?"

"Sounds like that's where I am."

"Well, listen to verse 4. 'The Lord on high is mightier than the noise of many waters, yea, than the mighty waves of the sea.'"

"Oh, wow!" I said.

"See, Mel, you won't drown. I've got to run but I just had to read that to you."

When I returned to my cinnamon rolls, I was calm and feeling like I was going to make it. I remembered the chorus of "Got Any Rivers" that we used to sing at family camp. *I have rivers that I think are uncrossable and mountains I can't tunnel through. But, yes, God specializes in things thought impossible and does the things others cannot do.*

Wendy was happier and I was enjoying her company more and more. Sometimes on Saturday morning she would come to my room and talk. I always loved that. One morning she was sitting on the bed while I was at the closet checking her dad's suits, when I felt a tender spot under my partial plate. My mind went back to the seven-year-old Wendy who had hidden my partial plate.

"Wendy, do you remember hiding my partial plate?"

"Yes! I wonder if it's still there."

"Well, go see."

She hurried out of the room, through the house and up the stairs. Just a few minutes later, she started down the steps holding something very black out in front of her between her thumb and index finger.

"Where was it?"

"In the shower drain."

We laid it on a paper towel and looked at it. It was covered with eleven years of dirt and was unrecognizable.

"Wow, Wendy, just look at that."

One night Jake came home and surprised me. "You know, Melissa Ann," he said as he took his tie off, "I want to take you to Europe."

"Where in Europe?"

"Oh, France, Germany and Switzerland."

"When?"

"Oh, March."

"Jake, it's the middle of February already."

"You and Joanne like to shop. It won't take you long to get ready."

We made arrangements for the girls, Jake got a radiologist to take care of the office and we flew to Paris. We saw the sights in that beautiful city and enjoyed delicious food. I laughed at Jake trying to talk to the people.

We took the train through Germany and into Switzerland. We spent several days in Zurich seeing the sights and dining. The food was excellent and the trip was a spectacular time for Jake and me. It was so much more than a country girl like me could ever have expected.

And if that wasn't enough, later in the spring, Jake announced that there was a medical meeting in London and that we should go after Wendy's graduation and take both the girls.

Wendy graduated on May twentieth. She was all smiles. The next day we were to leave for London. Jake and I were up at the crack of dawn picking strawberries.

"Honey, let's just leave these. You're going to be worn out by the time you get on the plane."

"Jake, if we aren't going to take care of this stuff, we shouldn't plant it. I never dreamed there was a human in the world who'd have an acre and a half of garden just for the fun of working in it when it was convenient, but leave it to rot if they wanted to go flying off somewhere."

He came over, put his arm around me and said, "Happy eleventh anniversary."

"I forgot all about it."

"I've never kissed a girl in the strawberry patch before."

We had a wonderful time seeing sights in London. Jake and Wendy made arrangements for her to spend the summer there working as a nanny. We would all miss her but were glad for this opportunity for Wendy.

Back at home, we were met with beans ready to pick and the news that my friend Sharon from Bible study had suffered an aneurysm, and that Jane and John were moving to Illinois in a few weeks.

All of the girls at the Bible study the next Tuesday were crying and praying for Sharon, as well as still praying for the widow whose husband had drowned a few months earlier. I remembered hearing as a teenager that when one member of the body suffers, they all suffer. "Now I know the meaning of that," I told Joanne, as we were on our way home that day.

Most of all, I was certain I was in a group of women who knew how to hurt with one another. It was still hard for me to be open about Jake's alcohol problem, but mainly because Jake didn't choose to discuss it. Several of the girls knew it and were a great encouragement. I just didn't discuss it in a group. I knew, however, that no one in the group would be critical.

Neil had finished his program in Scouts and came home on Saturday for his Boy Scout Eagle ceremony Sunday afternoon. That was a big day for all of us. Jacob came home. We had a reception afterward for Neil. Russ and Lynne, Ulma and her husband, the office staff, and people who'd known Neil as a boy showed up and, of course, all the Scouts and their families.

Neil has done well, I thought as we drove him back to his school.

He was driving; his dad was in front with him. "I'm really glad I finished," he said.

"I'm glad too, Neil; I'm very proud of you," Jake said.

When Neil and I had a minute alone after we walked up to his room, I said, "Neil, I know a lot of the campouts were very difficult, but you made it, and I'm very proud of you."

Shortly after Neil's school was out, he and Jake flew out to San Diego on Friday night for a short meeting. When they got home on Sunday night, Jake had been drinking. That was the start of several slips.

One Wednesday when Jake started to work, I said, "Jake you've been drinking in the evenings all week. If you plan to drink tomorrow, go to a motel."

"Melissa Ann, I'm not going to a motel."

"Okay, Jake, I'm not staying around answering the phone. I'm like Jewell and her girls. I'm tired of lying. So just know before you start drinking, don't answer the phone unless you want people to know. I've done that for you but I'm sick of it."

That night he came home plastered. I put the foam rubber mattress in the station wagon and Roxie and I slept out in the pasture below the barn, far enough away that if he called for us, I wouldn't hear him.

He was unable to go to work on Friday. Roxie and I spent time helping Jane and John get ready to move. They tried to get us to stay at their place but even though I hated to be around Jake when he was drinking, I worried about him burning down the house.

Saturday night I took the phone off the hook and Roxie and I went to our bed in the station wagon. I couldn't stand hearing him fall and I refused to pick him up.

"Out of sight, out of mind," I told Betty when I called her just before we left the house.

But it never worked out that way. Jake was always on my mind.

The strain was getting the best of Roxie also. She awoke early on Sunday morning and said, "Mama, can we go see about Daddy?"

"He's okay, Honey. Let's rest a while."

She started to cry, so I put my arm around her and said, "I'm glad you love your daddy so much. I love him, too."

I drove the station wagon to the back door and we went in with a dread hanging over our heads that only alcoholic families understand. Jake was sitting on the side of the bed. When we went to the door of our room, he said, head hanging to one side and slurring his words, "Oh, I'm glad to see you."

"Do you want some breakfast, Daddy?"

"No, Honey, I just want you and your mama to stay here."

"Jake, we don't like to look at you when you're drinking."

"You don't have to see me as long as I know you're here."

"Can we please stay, Mama?" Roxena Lynne asked when we went into the kitchen.

"Yes, Honey, we'll go upstairs. You get everything you may want so we won't need to come down except for meals."

About 10:30 a.m., John showed up. He was dressed for church.

I thought I'd slip down and get his attention to tell him we were upstairs. I got to the kitchen and heard him and Jake coming. I slipped in the dining room around the corner.

"Do you want me to fix you some breakfast, Jake?"

"No thank you, John. I just need to find my woman. Oh, there you are," I heard Jake say.

I'd forgotten all about the mirror on the wall of the dining room. He'd seen me from the kitchen. He came in the dining room and said, "Oh, am I ever glad to see you."

John said, "Jake, I'll spend the day with you. Let's get you some breakfast."

"John, I'm so sorry you're missing church," I said.

"That's okay. Jane has been trying to get you and the line was busy. She got worried."

"I'll call her when I think she's back from church," I said and slipped out of the room.

Roxie could smell bacon and eggs through the register and felt very at ease that John was there caring for Jake.

As soon as I thought Jane would be home from church, I called to tell her we were okay and that John was taking good care of Jake.

"Mel, someone needs to take care of you. My friend Doris is here and she's helping me get a great meal. Come eat some of her cooking."

I burst into tears. "Jane!" I yelled, "I've been sleeping in the station wagon out in the pasture for three nights, and am too tired to take a bath. You should see my oily hair."

"That won't make Doris any difference."

"Well, it makes a difference to me. I'm so sick of living this way. I can't wait to get the bottle behind me."

"Mel, try to get some rest while John is there."

When we hung up, I knew I hadn't been kind, but Jane seemed okay. She never said, "I love you," she just always did love me; there never was a doubt. She was no relation, but nonetheless, a true sister. I didn't have to worry about what I said or how I acted with Jane. My biggest worry that day was that they would be gone in a few weeks. How would I manage? We had been so close for so many years; I hated to see them go.

~

One fall weekend after Wendy went away to college and Neil was back in school, Jake went duck hunting with a doctor friend.

My brother Stan had called to invite us to go with him to a birthday party for one of our older cousins, two hours east of St. Louis. It was a crisp fall Saturday afternoon when he drove up. He wrapped his arms around me in his own loving way and I was so glad to see him. The next morning Stan, Roxie and I went to the birthday party. All the way home, Stan talked about all the cousins that were there, how long it had been since he'd seen them and all about their lives. We stopped for gas and Stan got out to fill the station wagon. When Roxie knew no one could hear us, she said, "Mama, do you think Daddy will be drinking?"

"Honey, I don't know. I hope not, but if he is, you and I won't have to stay around him."

She sat up and put her arms on the back of the white leather seat and said, "We won't have to sleep in the station wagon, will we, Mama?"

"No, Honey. We'll go upstairs and let Daddy have the downstairs."

Jake called on his way home. I could tell he wasn't drinking. I told him Stan was spending the night and he was very pleased. The next day, Stan and I picked Kentucky Wonder beans for Anita to put in the freezer. We had so much fun out in the garden. It had been a delightful weekend.

Donn had scheduled a speaker to come for a preaching mission at River View Community. I asked him if he'd like for me to give a dinner for the speaker and the church staff. He was delighted and I started baking and putting food in the freezer.

On Friday, I was polishing the silver. Ulma had come through with her sweeper and in her fun way was complaining that I wasn't baking a pie since the dessert for the party the next night was already in the freezer. She leaned over and rested her arms on the cabinet and was telling me about how one of her teenage boys had eaten some of the cinnamon rolls we'd baked and she was saving for a special breakfast. We were laughing and the phone rang.

"Hello, Honey. I just got a call from your boy's school," Jake said. "They've found some drugs in Neil's belongings and they are sending him home until second semester. He'll be waiting in front of C Company in two hours. Can you pick him up?"

"Well, yes, but I'll never be ready for our party, Jake."

"I'll help you and I'll pick up chicken for dinner. We'll work on your party plans tonight."

"Okay. I'll go right away."

"Ulma, Doctor told me 'my boy' needed to be picked up at school. I've got to go. I'll be back to take you home."

She lifted up her sweeper and smiled her beautiful smile and said, "The child always belongs to Mama when he's in trouble."

Neil was sitting outside his dorm alone when I went to pick him up. He put his things in the car and got in.

Sounding like his dad, he looked at me and said, "Hello, there."

"Hi, Neil."

I told him about the guest speaker coming to the church and about the dinner party for twelve the next night.

He was quiet. *Maybe he is dreading to see his dad.*

The school had sent his lesson assignments home with him.

"Neil, I'll need your help," I said as we carried his things from the car. "I'd hoped to be about ready for the party by now." He put his things down and turned on the TV. "We won't have time for TV, Neil. Go get everything put away and I'll let you take Ulma home."

He was very quiet as he turned off the TV, picked up a load in both hands and started through the living room.

He's not going to want to do anything to help me get ready for the party but I'll need help to make up the time I lost today.

I called Jake and told him I had hamburgers that I could fix for supper; he didn't need to stop for anything.

"How's your boy?"

"My boy is quiet, and I'm afraid, unhappy that we're having a party."

"Oh, no, Honey. He's unhappy that he got caught."

Yes, Doctor, you should know.

"You'll have to give him jobs, Jake, or I'll never get done. I didn't mind going to get him, but I'm behind."

"We'll help you." He was always good about helping, but I was feeling pushed. Then I had to remind myself that Jake was sober and enjoying our giving this party for Donn.

When dinner was over that evening, Jake and Neil sat down with his school-work and Jake made out a schedule for Neil's studies Monday through Friday. Neil got even quieter and I worried how this was all going to work out. When they finished with their talk, Jake said, "Many hands make light work. Let's get busy and help Mama. Come on, Neil, let's put the leaves in the table." Neil had started watching TV, but slowly walked into the dining room. He and his dad worked together to put the leaves in the oak table but he was still very quiet.

Everyone was busy on Saturday. Roxie and I set the table with a handmade Swiss tablecloth that Jake had bought me in Europe. The centerpiece arrived in mid-afternoon and everything in the dining room was in order.

Jake had promised Donn we would have pheasant, but I knew some of the people wouldn't eat it, so I browned pheasant and capon, and cooked them in a cream sauce in a slow oven. Everything except the pheasants and wild rice was from the farm. After the meat was in the oven, I opened the Kentucky Wonder beans and took the corn from the freezer. Neil got the job of cranking the ice cream to go with the strawberries Jane and I had frozen in May.

The first couple came about thirty minutes early and she and I finished the last-minute things. Neil and Roxie had gone out for pizza.

Donn and the guest speaker got there about ten minutes before everyone else arrived. Donn was so pleased to be having dinner with the speaker and his staff. He always felt very much at home at our place.

I was in the kitchen fixing a tray of hot drinks from a recipe Lynne had given me. Donn and Jake came in to see if they could help.

I handed Jake a tray and I took the other and the three of us went to the living room.

Jake was the perfect host. I watched him during dinner. He was enjoying every one of the guests. Donn was the only one of the group who knew he was an alcoholic.

Oh, thank you, Lord, that he can host this party. This is the true Jake.

Monday morning at 8:00 a.m. Neil started his assignments at the dining room table. At the end of each week, they were to be mailed to the school.

He wasn't seeing Dr. Fox anymore. I felt he needed to see someone but I preferred he see Dr. Smith. Neil's silence was getting to me. I'd say something to him and he wouldn't answer. Jake gave him afternoon chores that kept him busy part of the time.

One afternoon he was to rake leaves in the yard. I called upstairs and reminded him and he didn't answer. After a while I went upstairs and he came out of his walk-in closet. I said, "Neil, what are you doing up here when your dad has asked you to do the yard?"

He walked past me and never answered. I wondered why he was spending so much time in his closet.

Betty told me I was taking it too personally.

One day I asked him if he had carried some things from the car to the basement for his dad. We were both in the kitchen and he just walked out of the room. I followed him and said, "Neil, tomorrow you go with your dad and study at the office." *This may cause his dad to drink. The tension is so bad but I refuse to take the blame as I have in the past.*

When Jake got home, I was still upset. "Jake," I said, "in the morning Neil will go with you and study in the extra room."

"No, Honey, he needs to be here to do his studies," he said as he sat down.

"Jake, he doesn't answer me when I speak to him. He's going with you. If you don't tell him, I will. I've had it," I said, leaving the room.

I was restless all night. The next morning after breakfast, Neil sat down to study at the dining table. Jake was pouring himself a cup of coffee and I walked to the dining room door. "Neil, get ready to go with your dad and study at the office."

"Why?" he said, looking at me defiantly.

"Because you ignore everything I say."

He got up from the table and said, "I'll get worse."

"Well, I can't keep that from happening, but part of the time, you'll be with your dad."

I went back to our room, and when Jake came to say good-bye, I was drying my hair on a towel.

"Honey, I wish you'd reconsider."

He's restless and drinking is just around the corner, but I've had it. I continued with my hair.

"I don't know what to do," Jake said, leaning against the bedroom door.

"Well, why don't you go get a bottle!" I said, slinging the towel past him and watching it land on the floor. "This time, don't stop with a pint; get a gallon, because I've just thrown in the towel." I turned to walk down the hall and saw Neil standing at the door, ready to go with his dad.

Oh dear. He looks like he's lost his last friend. I went back in the bathroom feeling so defeated, hating what I'd said to Jake and that Neil had heard it, and hating that Neil was so unhappy.

"Neil," I heard Jake ask, "why do you resent Mel so?"

"Because if it wasn't for her, you and Mom would be together."

I couldn't believe my ears. *This kid has carried this belief for years,* I thought.

Then I heard Jake say, "Oh, no, Neil. She had nothing to do with that. The divorce proceedings were started before I even met her. I'm sorry, Neil. I thought all you kids understood that."

I couldn't stand it any longer. My heart started to melt as I heard them close the door behind them. I hurried to catch them. They were ready to get in the car when I went outside.

"Neil, I heard what you said to your dad," I said, going to his side of the car. "Maybe we could start over. Come back in and we'll go to the mall and Christmas shop and you can pick out everything for Jacob. If it's okay with your dad, we'll shop this morning and you can study this afternoon."

"That sounds like a winner!" Jake said as Neil started back in the house.

Neil didn't have a lot to say but I could tell he was no longer mad at me. *He really is a good kid. Life has been very hard for him.*

The next day I went up to put some clothes away in Neil's closet. In the back I saw a skinny rod sticking out behind his clothes. I pulled back some of his shirts and found a small TV. *Where did he get that? He has no extra money. Things are better with his attitude toward me; I'd better let his dad handle that.*

When the kids had gone upstairs that night, Jake said Neil told him he had saved money from his summer job and bought the TV.

I thought about that and it didn't seem right. I believed that he had already spent the money from his job. I remembered the cash Jake had brought home for me to put away for an emergency. I'd left it in my dresser drawer a few days before. When I looked, a one hundred dollar bill was missing. I decided to wait until it was time for Neil to go back to school to talk to him about it.

We decided to go to a long weekend meeting in Boston. Jake worked his usual day off and we flew to Boston that week on Thursday evening.

I was both excited and apprehensive, excited that we were going to see the historical sites in Boston and apprehensive because Jake had let a close friend from medical school know that we'd be in town. The friend had called back and asked that we have dinner with them on Friday evening. Jake had talked about Glen a lot and I knew they drank together in medical school.

"Over there on the left is the old North Church," the tour guide said Friday morning as other doctors' wives and I looked out the windows. *I wonder if any of these other women are worried about their husbands drinking on this trip? Maybe I should talk to Jake. No, this is going to be his decision. I've always watched after him, controlled as much as I could and enabled him to be weak when it came to deciding to do the right thing.*

The bus pulled up into a restaurant for lunch. I dined with a lady from Minnesota. We talked about the antique shops we were to go to shortly after lunch.

"What are you going to look for?" she asked as we were seated.

"Oh, I'm not looking for anything. I'm having problems keeping up with what I've got. But you're much younger than I, maybe you'll find something special."

"I'm looking for some brass candlesticks but I don't know when something is authentic," she said.

"One thing to check is the weight. If they are heavy, that's a good sign."

That afternoon, we found her brass candlesticks. Another radiologist's wife asked what I thought of a cut-glass vase. It was beautiful. It was shaped a lot like one I had that had been Jake's great aunt's that she'd gotten in Europe in the late 1800s.

As my two new friends were paying for their purchases, I realized I had really enjoyed the past few hours. *I'm learning to see that I'm something more than just an alcoholic's wife. I'm your child, Lord, and today you've given me peace. I can go to that dinner tonight and not try to be in control of whether or not Jake drinks.*

Jake and I were ready when Glen and Norma came to pick us up. Norma and I sat in the back seat. She was very easy to visit with. I loved her eastern accent.

Glen was a surgeon and needed to stop by the hospital to see a patient. He and Jake left Norma and me in the car. We watched as the two men walked toward the hospital. They were talking and laughing so comfortably.

"Jake has been looking forward to seeing you and Glen again."

"Oh, we have been so excited. We used to see Jake a lot when he was in Washington, D.C., years ago. We thought of several things we could do tonight but we decided on a late dinner at home so we'd have time to drink and visit."

Maybe I should tell her. No, I must let go. If he drinks it will be his decision and if he doesn't, he'll know I had nothing to do with it. He's got to learn and there's no time like the present.

"We have some wonderful wines that we'll have tonight."

Now what do I say, "Oh, that's lovely?"

"How long have you lived here, Norma?"

"We came just after Glen finished his surgery residency in 1952."

"How far are we from Stowe, Vermont?"

"About two hundred miles."

"I read Maria Von Trapp's book and I'd love to go spend a week at their lodge."

"I've never been to the lodge but I understand it's a busy place. There Glen and Jake are now. We can go home to drink and relax," she said as Jake and Glen came near the car.

Jake got in, turned around and said, "Did you ladies have a nice visit?"

"Yes, we did," I replied. "Norma went to Smith College."

"Now remind me, Honey, who did you know that went to Smith?"

"Dicky's mother and sister. I have a book written by one of the professors."

"My wife starts reading at four a.m. each morning when we're at home."

"Who are your favorite authors?" Glen asked.

"Oh, I don't know, Catherine Marshall, Dale Oldham, Corrie ten Boom, Keith Miller..."

"I know about Catherine Marshall," Norma said.

"Norma, she reads every book she can get her hands on," Jake said proudly.

"Do you read much, Jake?"

"No, Glen. I read the journal to keep up and I get <u>Mother Earth News</u> and several other magazines I try to keep up with."

Glen entered the drive of a beautiful, white New England two-story house. We walked into an elegant living room, decorated in soft ivory with flowing drapes. The dining room was to the right. The table was beautifully set with white linens and a fresh bouquet of cut flowers. But what caught my eye were the glasses; the crystal water goblets were accompanied by two different sized wine glasses.

"Now," Glen said, "Jake, what would you and Mel like to drink?"

Oh, good. He gets to do all the answering. I can't believe I'm not fit to be tied. Lord, I think you are beginning to get through to me to let go.

Then I heard Jake say, "Glen, just bring us Cokes."

"Cokes? You're kidding." He sounded shocked and Norma looked shocked. "What's this thing with Cokes? How about you, Mel, you'll have something more than a Coke, won't you?"

"No thank you, Glen, a Coke will be fine."

"Jake, have you gone religious?"

"No, no, no, although we do go to church."

Be out with it, Jake, I thought as I saw Norma standing very proper, holding her hands in front of her, waiting to go for drinks. Then she looked over to her husband and said, "Glen, I'm not sure what to do. I planned our drinking and visiting time until about eight."

"Norma, eight is fine," Jake said. "We're looking forward to visiting."

Glen and Norma went to get the drinks and came in with Cokes for us and stronger drinks for themselves.

We were standing at the French doors, looking out at their large lawn and rose garden.

"Who takes care of your roses?" Jake asked. "Do you, Norma?"

"Oh, no, we have a gardener. Do you have a flower garden, Mel?"

Before I could answer, Jake said, "We have an acre and more of vegetables and strawberries and an orchard. We have a few flowers, but not many."

"What do you do with the fruit and vegetables?"

"I can the beans and put a lot of other vegetables in the freezers."

Glen looked shocked. "Did you say freezers? How many do you have?"

"We have three," I said. "Jake likes to plant things. I was raised on a dairy farm and it's the natural thing for me to preserve food. I enjoy doing that."

"Well, let's sit down," Glen said. "Jake, I want to know why you aren't drinking. Do you just practice medicine and farm? Do you two socialize any?"

"Oh, sure, we do a fair amount of socializing, but we really enjoy the farm."

"Do you have a problem with drinking, Jake?"

Now we're getting somewhere.

"I have a problem stopping as soon as I should and I've got to be sharp for that meeting tomorrow. I'm on the panel so I need to stay off the booze."

"Well, tell me about the meeting," Glen said.

The next several minutes were spent with the men talking about medicine. Then Glen got up and said, "Mel, do you want another Coke?"

"Yes, please."

"Jake, one drink with an old buddy isn't going to keep you from presenting your information."

"Thanks, Glen, but I will just have another Coke."

He'll know what he's made of by the time we get through this night, I thought as our host went to get drinks.

We visited for half an hour more and then Norma got up to put dinner on the table.

I offered to help. She said it would just take her a short time. I wondered if she had help, but hadn't heard any noise from the kitchen. By now I was starving.

We went into the dining room and stood at our places. Norma came in with a bottle of wine and said, "Oh, dear, I really have a problem. I've planned this whole meal around these fine wines. Jake," she said, coming to our side of the table, "Won't you have a glass of wine?"

"Yes, Norma, I'll have a glass of wine."

Shortly after we started eating, Glen looked across the table and said, "Where did you two meet?" I looked at Jake and saw that he was waiting for me to answer.

"We met while I was working for a doctor."

"Mel, are you religious?" Glen asked, resting his fork on his plate.

I swallowed and said, "I wouldn't say I'm religious but I'm a Christian. I gave my heart to the Lord when I was fifteen."

"Oh, so Jake, has Mel influenced you and have you taken up religion? Is that why you're not drinking?"

"Oh, I go to church but then I've always done that. But, yes, Mel has been a great influence on my life," he said looking over at me. All was silent, and everyone was looking at me, but I felt very confident.

We continued visiting and Norma didn't fill the after-dinner wine glasses. I was surprised. At that point, it really didn't make much difference. Jake had slipped and I figured a binge would follow. There had been only a few times since I'd known him that he'd stopped with one drink.

We visited another hour after dinner and they took us back to the hotel.

Jake was up and down all night. *If anyone doubts that alcoholism is a disease, they should see him now, after spending an hour turning down drinks and then drinking one glass of wine.*

We were both awake at 5:00 a.m. I ordered coffee and juice early. I was reading my Bible when Jake came out of the bathroom.

He sat down on the bed and said, "You seemed so confident and not a bit embarrassed when you told Glen you gave your heart to the Lord when you were fifteen."

"I didn't say it to make them uncomfortable. I was just answering their questions and I am comfortable about that information."

In his "Ozark talk," he said, "You done good."

"Jake, I worked out something with the twenty-third Psalm the other day that has helped me a lot. Do you want to hear it?"

"If you worked it out, I'll listen."

"'The Lord is my Shepherd; I shall not want.' He's a perfect provider.

"'He maketh me to lie down in green pastures; He leadeth me beside the still waters.' He gives perfect rest.

"'He restoreth my soul; He leadeth me in the paths of righteousness for his name's sake.' He is a perfect guide.

"'Yea, though I walk through the valley of the shadow of death, I will fear no evil for thou art with me; thy rod and thy staff they comfort me.' He is a perfect comforter.

"'Thou preparest a table before me in the presence of mine enemies; thou anointest my head with oil; my cup runneth over.' Perfect fulfillment.

"'Surely goodness and mercy shall follow me all the days of my life; and I shall dwell in the house of the Lord forever.' He provides a perfect dwelling place."

Jake just looked at me.

"I'm glad I got to tell your friends I gave my heart to the Lord. I just didn't want to be dogmatic."

"You weren't." He poured another cup of coffee and said, "Man, I wish I could have gotten past that drink."

That evening Jake reported a good meeting and we went to dinner at the hotel's restaurant. I thought Jake might drink but I wasn't going to say a word. I had finally gotten to the place that I could give him full responsibility. *If he drinks and gets out of control, I'll get up and go to our room.* He didn't drink. He was his charming self all evening.

Our flight left Sunday just before noon but we had an hour layover in Chicago. Jake was looking at the paper and laid it aside and stood.

"I think I'll walk around a little while. Can I bring you a Snickers bar?"

"No, thank you. It's not my birthday or Christmas, so I can't indulge," I said in jest, as he walked toward the restroom.

Go with him. No, let go. If I don't go, he'll start drinking, but it will happen sooner or later anyway.

I was visiting with an elderly lady who had sat with us on the first flight. It was almost time for us to board the next flight when I saw Jake coming. Sure enough, his face was red and he had that look of false confidence.

When the drinks were passed on the plane, he ordered another. When we got to St. Louis, he stopped by the bar for another drink. I waited. I wanted him to see the new me. I was finished trying to control him. I wouldn't say anything about leaving as soon as Neil got in college, but when I got home I'd start planning to do that.

The drinking continued each evening.

On Wednesday night, three weeks before Christmas, Jake came home plastered. All day Thursday he drank.

I went into the dining room and said, "Neil, I told your dad if he started drinking, I wouldn't stay around. I want the three of us to go somewhere and just let him have the place by himself. I'll put the phone back on the hook and let him answer it drunk if he wants to."

"I don't want to go anywhere."

"I know, I really don't either," I paused. "Okay, maybe my cousin Ike will come out here and help me get him sober."

Late Thursday afternoon, I called Jewell and told her there would be no way he could be to work the next day.

"Jewell, I've given this a lot of thought," I said. "If I were you, tomorrow I'd not go to the office except to cancel patients. Give your girls time off until Doctor is ready to come back to work. When he's sober, call your girls back in and I'll come with him, and you girls tell him that you will only be there when he's sober. You won't lie or make excuses anymore. In the meantime, I'll do the same thing at home. Dr. Searchbrains tells me when we make excuses and take on his responsibilities, we are enabling him to stay in the gutter. It will take a lot of tough love but we can do it, Jewell. What do you think?"

"I think it sounds good. I know the girls will go along with it."

"Tell them they'll be paid. We don't want to lose them."

As soon as we hung up, I called Ike and explained everything. "I need you. Could you and Ellen come for supper and see if Jake will agree to taper off?"

"We'll be right out. Now that I'm retired, I don't have anything to do that's as important as helping you."

I hurried and called Betty and told her about my conversation with Jewell.

"Oh, Melissa, that's great. He never has to bear any of the pain of his binges. You and his office staff do all the explaining and covering up. Maybe he'll get a taste of what it's like."

"Oh, Betty, I hope I can stick with this."

"You will, Melissa. If you get weak, call me. I'll help you figure out what to do." I always felt so loved by Betty.

When Ike and Ellen arrived later that afternoon, I opened the door and then just lost it. They weren't huggers, but I threw my arms around them both and sobbed. Ellen had her arm around me and Ike patted my shoulder and said, "Now, now. If we have a crisis, we'll take care of it."

"No, I just saw you and I couldn't stand it."

They chuckled good-heartedly and Ike went down the hall to see Jake.

The kids and Ike watched the news while Ellen and I made dinner.

"I'm sorry to put you to work," I said as she put the gravy in a bowl.

"With all your food canned and in the freezer, it's easy to cook with you."

Jake woke up and staggered in just as we were finishing dinner.

"Come sit down, Jake," Ike said, standing and pulling out a chair.

"Thank you," Jake said, trying to hold his head straight and be polite.

I fixed him a plate of small portions. He ate just a few bites.

"You about ready to get off that stuff?" Ike asked.

"Need to do that," Jake replied.

"Yes, you do," I said. "Your girls aren't going back into the office until you're there."

Ike motioned for me to be quiet. I got up to clear the table. Ellen, Roxie and I carried the things in the kitchen and started doing the dishes.

"Why don't we start tapering you off, Jake? The girls can go home with Ellen. Neil and I will take care of you."

"Now, no offense," we heard him say, "but no, sir, I'm not ready to quit drinking."

I marched into the family room. "Jake, what about your office?"

Holding his head to one side he said, slurring his words, "I'll take care of that."

Ike gave me a nod to go back in the kitchen. I went back in and said to Ellen, "I can't help myself. I'm sick of living like this."

"You three go to our place until he sobers up," Ellen said as she washed off the cabinet.

"Mama," Roxena Lynne said, coming to stand by me, "Will Daddy be okay if we leave?"

I put my arm around her and said, "I think so, Honey."

I heard Jake get up to go back to our room. Ike went with him.

We had the kitchen cleaned when I heard Ike say to Neil, "Come into the kitchen, son. Let's have a family conference." Neil had his hands in his pockets as he slowly came in the door, but he had a lot of regard for Ike, so I knew in the long run he'd do what Ike thought best. Ike waited until we all were perfectly still, then he leaned up against the cabinet and folded his arms. I heard the grandfather clock chime 6:30.

"He's not ready to stop drinking, and until he is, we can't do anything about it. If it gets more than you think you can stand, you three can come to our place. But we can't help him until he wants help. What do you want to do?"

"I don't know, Ike. I have so much to do and I'm so exhausted. Roxie has school tomorrow. If he continues to drink, maybe we can come after school tomorrow."

"Whatever you think. We'll get him on his feet. As soon as he's ready, I'll take over. I'm tough."

"I can't wait."

Ellen and Ike laughed, but my kids weren't laughing.

We walked them to the door, and as soon as they were gone, I said, "Kids, let's go upstairs and turn off the lights down here so no one will drop by." Neil looked like he thought I was crazy.

"Mama, what if Daddy falls?"

"He'll be okay, Honey. He was walking better."

The kids helped me turn out the lights. I took the phone off the hook and we went upstairs.

I heard Jake stagger into the wall in the middle of the night. I lay in the bed getting my plans lined out for the next day. *I feel so pressured by so many people. The girls at the office need me. My kids need me. I need to write to my mama. I don't know what to say to her. I need to call Wendy at college, yet she doesn't need to have to worry about her dad. Maybe all four of the kids have tried to get me while the phone has been off the hook. Lord, I need you so much*, I thought as I lay in the bed in the big room that we called the sleeping porch. I lay there until I heard the grandfather clock strike 1:00 a.m. Shortly after that, I heard the train go by on the backside of the farm. I remembered watching and waving at the passengers when we were first married, wondering if any of them were as happy as I.

The next morning, I called Dr. Smith's office. He could see me on his lunch hour.

Jewell was waiting for me and the office phone was ringing when I went into the office at 10:00.

"The phone is ringing off the hook this morning but I haven't answered it."

"Jewell, I've spent over eleven years, and you've spent almost that many, taking care of Doctor and all his business. He doesn't have to answer any of the questions at home, I do it. He doesn't suffer when he's coming off of a binge. I lock the doors, hide the cars, take the phone off the hook and taper him off. He doesn't have to answer to the doctors and patients; you and your girls do. I've given this a lot of thought. According to Dr. Searchbrains, we're enabling Jake to stay on what I've begun to think of as white-collar skid row. The kids and I are going to go to my cousin's. I'm not taking the phone off the hook. I'm letting whoever calls know that he's drunk if he answers. He refuses to go to a motel and I'm not staying to enable him."

She closed the file cabinet and sat down at the desk as the phone rang. We counted eleven times.

"These people are going to want to know why we were closed."

"Well, why don't you just say, one moment please, and give it to Doctor."

"Oh my," she laughed. "I've answered that man's phone calls for ten years."

"That's right. He feels no pain from his binges but you and I do."

"I'll try, but he may fire me."

"It's not likely."

"So what do I do today?"

"Go home and stay until Jake will meet with us. If he calls, tell him you can't run an office without a doctor, you and the girls have run out of answers and you can't be untruthful any more."

The phone rang and she reached on the shelf to get her purse. "Let's get out of here, Mel. That phone is driving me crazy."

We hurried down the back steps, hoping not to be seen.

We paused behind our cars. "Jewell, I really appreciate you."

"I appreciate you, too. Let me know when to have the girls come in and we'll give it our best shot."

"Okay. I think we should have done this years ago."

"Sounds like we should have."

We said our good-byes and went our separate ways. I had enough time to eat lunch and get a sandwich for Dr. Smith.

He came to the waiting room of his office with a big smile on his face and a tray with coffee. I followed him to his office.

"Dr. Searchbrains," I said as I sat down in my chair, "I have an announcement to make."

"I'm anxious to hear it because you don't have that defeated look."

"I understand that I've been enabling Jake to stay in his alcoholism and Jewell and I are going to try a new way of dealing with it."

When I finished telling him the plans, it was time to go. He stood smiling, put his hand on my shoulder and said, "You, young lady, are making great strides and I believe Jake Bell is about to get the shock of his life."

Jake was in a deep sleep when I got home. I helped Ulma finish the house. Since I didn't do my usual Friday baking, we were finished by the time Roxie got home from school.

I felt guilty going off on Friday night. Both kids should have been going somewhere or having company but this was the way we lived. The bottle often dictated what we did or didn't do, especially on weekends. Neil said he'd be fine at home, but I wouldn't leave him with that responsibility. Plus, Jake was going to have to want to get off the stuff on his own.

The kids seemed to have a good time with Ike and Ellen. Ike and Neil watched TV and Ellen cut out a blouse for Roxie.

I got my Bible and went downstairs to a small sitting room. I lay my head against the back of the chair and thanked the Lord for several things: friends from the Tuesday morning Bible study who were praying for me; a church where the Word was taught and the congregation was excited about studying; and Pastor Donn who'd go out the next morning to see Jake. I thanked the Lord for Zach and Lynne who were always there when I'd call.

Then I raised my head up and opened my eyes. *Oh dear, I haven't called Zach and let him know Jake is alone.* I got up and started to the phone then stopped. *No, if Zach goes out and rescues him, it won't be any different than if I stayed, and Jake will be expecting Zach to be there. Or when he wakes up, he'll wonder why he hasn't been there. Maybe he'll begin to see he's on his own and his getting sober is up to him.* I went back and sat down in the chair, my mind starting to run wild. *What if some of my family calls and he answers the phone? What if he starts a fire with a cigarette? Let go. Let God. Oh, Lord, I wish I could do that. I remember singing that song at the family camp, sitting close to the front with my best friend, Joy. I thought all I had to do was just make up my mind to let go and let God have His wonderful way. I didn't know it could be this hard. But I have taken my own way for so long and made a mess of things. Now, Lord, I feel so guilty and I doubt that You'd want to clean this mess up.*

Then I remembered Betty saying, "Melissa, isn't that what your God specializes in?"

Lord, I don't feel like I'm letting go. I'm very anxious, but with Your help, I'm staying away from my home, at least for the night.

The next morning, I went into the kitchen and sat down at the table.

Ike turned around from making coffee and said, "Good morning! Did you have a good night?"

"No. I can't handle being away from Jake like this; but he's going to have to face the pain of a binge. I've always protected him. I've been wrong in doing so and I've got to let go."

He sat down across from me. He looked so much like my dad.

"I think the old boy is going to be ready for help in a few days."

"I can't help him, Ike. I make it too easy and Dr. Searchbrains tells me I'm enabling him to stay in his alcoholism."

He leaned across the table and took one of my hands in his, "You just leave him to me. I'm tough. I was as bad as he is once upon a time. When he gets ready for help, I'll take over."

"Oh, thanks, Ike. I'll be forever grateful but I worry about him. What if something happens to him?"

"You can't control him all the time. He doesn't have access to a car and so you don't have to worry about that." He poured me a cup of coffee.

Ellen came in and he poured her one too. "Sit down here, Mom. I'm going to get breakfast for you girls." He put bacon in the skillet, poured us each a glass of juice and said, "One of these mornings I'm going to be cooking breakfast for the good doctor."

About 11:00, I got a call from Pastor Donn. He'd been out to check on Jake. He was gone. Donn had looked all around the farm and he was not on the place. He and Ike both thought he'd called a cab and gone to a motel. I wasn't sure. He never wanted me to take him, but I was beginning to understand that as long as I was around to wait on him, why go to a motel?

Ike and Neil ran some errands. Ellen made the blouse she'd cut out for Roxena Lynne. She always enjoyed doing things with her.

I couldn't settle down. I baked an oatmeal cake but kept wondering if I should start looking for Jake.

Finally, late in the afternoon I called Lynne and asked her if they'd heard from Jake. They hadn't.

That evening Zach called me. He had checked with the motels near the farm and he wasn't registered.

"Zach, do you think I was wrong for leaving him on his own?"

"No, you did just fine. If you think that might help him see what it's like to be on his own, then I'm for however you want to handle it."

"I'm going to church tomorrow. I've got to go by home for clothes. Maybe he'll be there."

Mid-afternoon, Ellen saw my sad mood so she got us a cup of coffee and a piece of cake and asked me to come to the kitchen.

I was looking down at my cup with all kinds of emotion about to surface.

Ellen, in her quiet way said, "I remember times like you're going through. You'll make it. He'll show up or you'll hear from him."

"Ellen, sometimes I'm so worried I can't stand it. Then there're times I wish he'd hit a bridge." She didn't look shocked, just laughed. "Did you ever feel that way?"

"Lots of times."

Sunday morning, Neil stayed with Ike and Ellen. Roxie and I went home to get ready for Sunday school and church. All the way home I had a dreadful feeling as to what I might find or not find.

Roxie followed me to my room. The bed was unmade with a coffee cup on the bedside stand and an empty bottle in the trash basket.

"Where is Daddy, Mama?"

"Honey, I think he's gone to a motel until he decides to quit drinking."

We got ready and went to Sunday school and church. In church I sat by one of the young women from the Tuesday morning Bible study. Just before the service started, I whispered, "Pam, I don't know where Jake is. He's gone and we can't find him."

"Has he ever done this before?"

"Not since I've been married to him."

Just then the organ started to play and the choir started to sing. I listened and heard the words of the song "No Place Drives Him Away".

I sat there wondering where Jake might be. In a hotel room? Is he even alive? Then I thought, *Wherever he is and whatever is happening, no place or thing will drive the Lord away.*

After church, Roxie and I went by the house again. While she was upstairs changing her clothes, I went in and knelt by my bed. In a little while, I was aware of my eight-year-old by my side. I prayed a little while longer, and when I started to get up, she said, "Mama, you have a big, salty tear in your eye."

I hugged her and said, "It helps to pray."

Ellen had a wonderful meal ready for us when we got back to their house. When Roxie went to wash her hands, Ike met me in the hall and said, "What do you think?"

"I'm really worried, Ike. Zach hasn't heard from him. Not a soul has heard."

Ike just looked down. I could tell he was worried, too.

Soon after lunch, he came in the kitchen where Ellen and I were finishing up the dishes. He sat down at the back of the table and said, "Why don't you girls sit down with me? We need to talk." Ellen and I sat down and Ike looked at me and said, "Melissa, I don't want you to take care of Jake. I'll do that, but you need to be home in case he calls."

"Ike, I don't want to answer the phone. What if it's another doctor looking for him?"

"Well, if they call, you just tell them he isn't there. They've all known him for years. They know when he's drinking. It's time we face this head on."

"When you offered to help me, I made up my mind to do just what you think is best."

"Good, go on home and answer the phone when it rings. He'll be calling for you to come get him. When he does, you call me and I'll go, and you and Roxie can come stay with Ellen. I'll stay and take care of Jake. Neil can do his studying at home."

All the way home I thought, *Maybe letting Ike make the decisions is part of the process of letting go, Lord. I don't know how to let go, but You've provided help through Ike. I mustn't take over; I must go with the plan.*

We were carrying our things in the house, and as we were going through the back door, a cab turned into the drive.

"I bet that's Daddy, Mama." Roxie was excited, but I was worried yet relieved.

"Yes, Honey, I think that's right."

"Well," Neil said, "never a dull moment."

We went in the house and I went to the kitchen phone and called Ike as I watched Jake trying to pay the cab driver.

"We didn't figure that just right, but I'll be right out. You put your things back in the car and be ready to come back out here when I get there," Ike said.

Neil and I got Jake in the house and to his bed. Roxie and I got our things together to go back to Ellen's. As soon as Ike drove up, we left.

It was wonderful to have someone that I knew would handle things right.

"Your daddy will be okay now, Honey, with Uncle Ike there." I could see less strain since she knew her daddy was safe.

Monday afternoon, Ike called Ellen. *Oh, he must be better,* I thought as I anxiously waited to hear how Jake was doing.

Ellen still had a smile on her face when she hung up.

"Has he started tapering off yet?"

"Yes, he announced in the middle of the night that he was going to quit. Ike gave him a big dose of castor oil and he said it really cleaned him out."

"Where did he get the castor oil?"

"He stopped and got it on his way to your place."

"I should have been putting it in his drinks! Oh, Ellen, it's so good to have this refuge."

On Tuesday afternoon, Ike called again.

"Hi, Ike. How is your patient doing with his castor oil?"

"I cleaned him out. He's had it rough, but he's eating and hasn't had a drink since 2:00 a.m. Monday."

"That's good."

"He wants to go to work tomorrow."

"Does he know the office is closed?" I asked.

"He called this morning and no one answered. He called Jewell. She agreed to go in and schedule patients if he'd come with you early in the morning for a conference with all the girls."

"Why didn't he call and tell me this himself?"

"Well, you've got him a little worried. He keeps saying, 'I sure hope Mel sticks with me.'"

"I love seeing him squirm." We both laughed. I told him I'd drop Roxie off at school and call Jewell to see when we should be there.

We decided that we'd all meet at 8:30 a.m. I'd come in with Jake.

Wednesday morning, I met Ike on my way to the farm. I knew Jake would be waiting at the door. I drove up and started unloading my things.

"Hi, Honey," he said, coming down the back step and reaching for my suitcase.

"Hello," I said. *He looks better than I feel. Maybe it was the castor oil.*

"Honey, I know you don't want to help me out of my tight spots anymore, but Jewell wants you to come in with me this morning."

"Okay. I'll take the other car."

"No, go with me and pick me up for lunch. I'll drive myself after today."

"If that's how you want it. But I'm no longer controlling what you do or where you go or helping you out of your tight spots." I leaned against the wall by the back door. "Jake, when you choose to drink, I do not choose to be around you."

"I know, Mel. I just need you to hang in there with me today."

Jewell and the girls were having coffee in the lounge. When we walked in the back door, she met us and said, "Hello, Chief." All the girls stood and moved toward the front desk.

Jake and I stopped where they were standing. I'd never seen Jake nervous around his staff before. "Now, I understand from Jewell that none of you want to be here when I'm off misbehaving."

"That's right, Dr. Bell. We all love working for you but we won't be here when you're drinking," Jewell said.

Then Dixie added, "Doctor, you and I go way back. I've worked for you nearly twenty years. I'm tired of lying; I'll never do it again."

"I understand. I won't ask you to." Then he said, "Let's get all the complaints out. Anyone else want to say anything?"

The secretary said, "I don't want to be here when you're not here because of drinking."

"I agree," said one of the other techs.

Sue, the newest employee said, "So do I, Doctor. I love working for you, except when you're not here and we have to answer questions about why."

"Thank you all; I'm going to try. I can't promise that it will never happen again, but I'll try."

"Doctor, we just want you to know that unless we have a doctor in the office we won't be here," Jewell said.

"I get the picture. You'll all be paid for the days I've been away," he said. I winked at Jewell.

She said, "Yes, sir, thank you."

The phone rang and everyone started to their places of work. Jake poured himself a cup of coffee.

I said, "Bye, Jake, I'm going Christmas shopping."

"Bye, Honey. Thank you. Come by and I'll take you to lunch."

I said my good-byes to the girls and went to see Dr. Smith.

"The things I want to tell you, Doctor, are: I no longer plan to be near Jake when he's drinking; I've no desire to help him stay away from the bottle and no desire to help him stop drinking. Also, this is the first time after a binge that I'm not dreading going out in public."

"You shouldn't hate to go out in public. You haven't been on a binge, have you?"

"As my dad used to say, 'That's the idea, exactly.'"

It was hard to shop after I left Dr. Smith's office. I couldn't get my mind off the events of the past few days.

Finally, I decided I would get the life-sized doll Roxie had seen while we were shopping together the week before. When I got back to the toy department, there was only one left. I took it and thought, *My, I'm glad they still had one left. This will probably be the last year she'll show any interest in a doll.* I walked to the car, opened the back door and started to put it in the back seat when I realized I hadn't paid for it.

Wonder what Dr. Jake Bell would say if I were arrested for shoplifting? I thought as I started back through the far end of the store, where the toy department was located.

<hr />

Our two college kids came home for Christmas. We received a good gift from Candy that day when she gave us the news that we'd be grandparents again in July. Jake was very pleased.

On Christmas Day, one of Betty's sons came with his family to show us their new baby. When they got ready to leave, I asked Roxie to go down and get a pecan pie from the freezer for them to take home. She came upstairs with the pie and said, "Mama, the freezer door was open."

We said our good-byes to the family and I ran downstairs. Some of the meat and pies were thawing. All of a sudden I felt so exhausted and angry. I came up to the kitchen and yelled, "Who left the freezer door open?" Jake and Jacob came into the kitchen and watched as I completely came unglued.

"Why doesn't someone admit it," I yelled, knowing Neil and Wendy were gone and couldn't answer for themselves.

"Here is all this work I've done, just ruined."

"It's not ruined, Honey, we'll salvage it, and we'll give some to Ellen and Ulma. It will be used."

"That's okay for you to say. You weren't the one to peel all those apples and peaches," I said, still crying with six eyeballs glued on me. "Also, you did almost nothing to help get ready for Christmas. You've been sober only one week and working every day to catch up at the office. I've had everything to do. Now look at this."

"Can I help you, Mama?" Roxena Lynne asked, bringing me back to reality.

"I don't know what to do, Honey," I said, just wanting some room and relief from the stares. "Please give me thirty minutes," I said as I walked toward the bedroom.

I am so exhausted, I thought. *If only I could stay away from the Christmas dinner we are going to tonight with all of Jake's cousins. How am I ever going to pull myself together?*

Jake came in; he'd been down to the freezer and taken out what he thought we needed to do something with.

"Honey," he said, sitting down on the bed, "You're exhausted. I've told the kids you're to take it easy for several days."

"I dread going to another Christmas dinner."

"Now you don't need to worry about me starting to drink."

"I'm not, because if you do, I'm out of here until you're sober. And after Neil's in college I'm out of here period, if you drink."

"I hear you."

"I'm not sure about that," I said leaving the room to go back to the thawed food.

We had a good Christmas dinner. I was surprised that I could relax after the drama of earlier that day. I had apologized for my actions. Jake responded, saying I would never have ulcers, but I almost gave him one.

Mid-afternoon on Saturday after Christmas, Donn called. His voice was always upbeat but he sounded extra happy.

"Good afternoon, Mrs. Bell. If you and the good doctor are going to be home right now, I want to bring someone by to meet you."

"Oh, wow! Do I know her?"

"You know about her. We've prayed for her a lot in our Tuesday group. It's Evon White, whose husband drowned." I could hardly believe my ears. "She started to our singles Bible class last summer, and then we went to hear Corrie ten Boom in October together. We've been going very slowly. Her late husband hasn't been gone a year yet and she's gone through a horrible ordeal."

"So that's why you didn't have Christmas dinner with us."

He laughed and said, "Maybe next year."

"Well, hurry and bring her out."

When I told Jake, he asked me what I thought she'd be like.

"She's a dedicated Christian from what the ladies in the Tuesday group say about her when they ask for prayer."

"Anyone at home?" Donn called from the back door. Jake and I both left the kitchen in a rush.

At the door stood Donn, holding hands with a very nice and intelligent-looking young blonde. She captured our hearts right away.

"Come in, Donn," Jake said.

They stayed about an hour. She told us about teaching part-time and about her three children. Donn and Jake laughed and talked as usual. When the couple left, Jake said, "What did you think?"

I was so impressed with Evon, I said, "Oh, Jake, she's the one."

He laughed and said, "I know you're best when you're in charge, Melissa Ann, but I'm afraid you're not in charge of this. I do believe she's quality, though."

That Saturday we attended one last Christmas party at the home of a couple from our Koinonia group at church.

When the party was over and we were back at home, I lay thinking about how I had prayed so long for a Christian couple to be our close friends after Jane and John moved.

Thank you, Lord. We are becoming friends with Christian couples in our group more and more as time goes by. The New Year looks bright.

1975
THE FINAL ACCIDENT

The first Sunday of January, Jake was getting ready to take Neil back to school. Roxie had a friend over for the afternoon so I didn't plan to go. This was a new thing for me to not even worry about Jake going alone.

When it was time for Jake and Neil to leave, I met him at the door and said, "Neil, I know you well, and I know you're not happy when you are dishonest. So while you and your dad are alone, why don't you just tell him where you got the money for your TV." He didn't say anything, just looked down. I put my arms around him and said, "Bye, Neil. We'll be at your parade in two weeks."

"Okay, bye," he said, returning the hug.

Shortly after Jake got home, he came into the kitchen and sat down with a cup of coffee.

"Your boy told me where he got the money for the TV."

"Did he just volunteer to tell you?"

"No. When we got on the interstate, I looked over at him and said, 'Neil, where did you get the money for the TV?' He said, 'I took one hundred dollars from Mel's drawer.' I said, 'Now, Neil, it's good that you told me, but you'll feel much better about yourself if, this summer when you get a job, you pay Mel back the hundred dollars.' He didn't reply, but he'll pay you back."

We got back in the routine of going to the parades and saw Neil about every other Sunday. He was doing well in his studies and the teachers were glad to have him back.

We started going out once a month with Zach and Lynne again when things slowed after the holidays. Jake and I went to an adult class on Wednesday night while Roxie went to choir practice. We started having family dinners at the church before choir and class. I could see Jake loving the visits and study. *Thank you, Lord. I see You answering prayer. For so long I've wanted this kind of fellowship.*

Joanne and I were still attending the women's group. One day we were coming home and she said, "Mel, I've never seen you as relaxed as you are. Do you think Dr. Bell has quit drinking?"

"You know, Joanne, I don't think about it that much. It doesn't rule my life anymore. He knows that and if he drinks after Neil goes to college, I'll move out."

"Are you going to divorce him?"

"No, I told the Lord if He'd give me that man, I'd never divorce him, but the bottle doesn't rule me as much anymore."

"That's wonderful. It's taken a long time."

"When I got a tutor and could read and retain what I read, I read the Bible and so many good books, and started attending Bible studies. I'm filling a lot of vacant spots."

We had a lot of snow in February, but we had a wonderful Valentine's party at the church. Jake was so charming and we had a great time at the table with our friends from the Koinonia group. As we visited, I realized it had been days since I'd thought about the bottle. I remembered the advice Dr. Oldham had given the lady who had come to see him about her husband. I'd taken his advice and started reading the Bible. It was a great source of my strength.

I heard that the average person could read the Bible in fifty-eight hours. So I decided I should be able to read it through in a year. I had started in January and was in the book of Ruth. Other books like Guilt & Grace by Paul Tournier helped me very much, as well. When I discussed the different books with Dr. Smith, he said it was very important for the enabler to replace the problem of enabling with something positive to occupy her life. Study was a wonderful tool.

On Good Friday, Jake prepared a place for me to plant lettuce, radishes and onions. I watched as he went the length of the garden with his large, red tiller. *He looks so relaxed. Oh, I hope it lasts.*

When he finished, he came up to me, lit a cigarette, and looking over what he'd just done, said, "The first time you took me to meet your folks and your dad was showing me the place, he said, 'I like to work that dirt.'"

"You do too, don't you?"

"Oh, yes, it's so peaceful out here."

A young woman from my Bible class had asked if she could help us when we got ready to plant, so Jake told her to come by at 2:00 p.m. on Saturday. She came out with coffee for both of us.

Jake stopped his tiller, and as he took the cup she offered him, said, "Hi, Ginge. Hey, aren't you the one!"

When he started another row, she said, "Mel, as I was coming up, I watched you out here. You were laughing and really enjoying yourselves. I think what is so neat about you and Jake is that you really like one another."

"Yes, we do," I said.

"Do you ever fight?"

"Oh, yes, I hope you never see it, but when he gets desperate to drink, he will do anything to get my goat."

She dropped beans in the row, took a step and said, "That's hard to imagine. He's one of the sweetest men I know."

It was getting close to summer break. Wendy wanted to go to summer school. She would take a sociology class and spend most of the summer in New Mexico on an Indian reservation. Jacob planned to get a job in his college town so he could be close to his bride-to-be, a sweet young woman named Carmen. Neil would graduate in June and go to college in the fall. On Saturday before Mother's Day, I went down to his school for the Mother and Son Tree Planting. It was a special time, holding the tree and Neil putting dirt around it.

The graduation services at the military parade were beautiful. When the graduates tossed their caps in the air, I wanted to shout, "He made it!" Neil had made good grades the last semester. I was very proud of him. He hadn't mentioned the hundred dollars he'd taken since his dad had talked to him, but he had a sweet attitude and I was encouraged. Jake said he could tell a big difference in Neil also.

Neil started looking for a job on Monday morning after graduation, but his school closed a week later than public school, so it was slim pickings. He found a job selling for the blind, however, and his dad gave him the job of painting the board fences around the barn, orchard, yard and the out-buildings. Each evening, he was gone three or four hours selling. I asked him a few questions about his job but I never asked what he was doing with his money.

I was loading the dishwasher one evening in late August when Neil came into the kitchen. I didn't think anything about it but I noticed he was standing by me. I looked up and he had a handful of money. He held it out for me to take. I said, "What's that for?"

"It's the hundred dollars I took from your drawer."

"Oh, wow, Neil." I took it and hugged him. "I'm proud of you."

He walked into the family room and got the evening paper. I stood there crying, holding a stack of money. There were two tens, some fives and the rest were ones. I counted it and there was the hundred dollars he'd told his dad in January that he had taken.

Late summer was busy with weddings and departures.

Evon and Donn were married the end of July. Jacob and Carmen were married in the small chapel on their college campus. Wendy came home from New Mexico just in time for the wedding, then left again for college a week before Neil had to leave for school.

On Sunday afternoon of Labor Day weekend, Jake, Neil, Roxie and I got into a loaded station wagon and started for Neil's first year in college. He had chosen a school an hour's drive from the farm. After we got him settled in, we drove to Stan and Anita's home. It had been fourteen years that weekend since I had taken Jake to Stan and Anita's for the first time.

That evening Stan and Jake were visiting in the living room while I helped Anita clean up the kitchen. We could hear them laughing and talking and I said, "Anita, you'd never know now that fourteen years ago Stan was against my seeing Jake."

"Stan likes Jake very much. We're both pleased that you have him."

I wonder what they'd think if they knew the whole story.

My friend Joanne and I started back to Bible study on Tuesday morning. Some of the ladies had been to a Marriage Encounter weekend and thought it was great. They described how from Friday night to Sunday afternoon, husbands and wives had to be together and spend a lot of time communicating with each other. Joanne was going to sign up her and her husband for the next available weekend.

That evening, I told Jake about it. "We'd go to the big monastery that we went by the other day. It's a lock-in until Sunday afternoon."

I called the next day and they had an opening for mid-October. That night when I told Jake, he laid down the evening paper and just looked at me. He finally said, "Are you sure you want to do this? Our marriage isn't in trouble, and it seems like a waste of time."

"Oh, it's not for troubled marriages. It makes good marriages better."

"I don't know if I want to be locked up in that place with you for a weekend or not."

The next day he called me from the office and told me the calendar was clear for that weekend and for me to set it up. I immediately made the reservations.

One week before the Marriage Encounter, Roxie's friend Sarah spent the night. On our way to take Sarah home the next day, we took them to McDonalds for lunch.

As we drove, Roxie said, "Daddy, when do you and Mama go on your weekend?"

Jake looked in the rearview mirror and said, "Next weekend I have to be locked up with your mama."

I think he's looking forward to this. I hope we come home really feeling good about our marriage.

Sunday night, we were just turning off the evening news when the phone rang. Jake answered while I started turning back the bed covers. I held the spread in mid-air when I heard Jake say, "Sure, Charlie. I'll go pheasant hunting with you."

I could feel that sick, hopeless feeling that I knew so well.

Be calm about this. Don't let yourself be reduced to tears. Let him see the new you, I thought as he hung up.

"Well, that was a pleasant surprise," he said as he hung up the phone. "I'm going with Charlie pheasant hunting next weekend."

Trying to sound casual, I said, "This time it's not that easy. You have a lock-in date at a monastery with your wife. Call and tell him quick before he goes to bed."

"We can go to Marriage Encounter anytime, but this is pheasant-hunting season. Charlie and I always go. Call them tomorrow and cancel."

Don't blow your stack, Mel, but hold your ground and don't cry. I walked over to my purse, got out the phone number and handed it to Jake.

"Jake, I want us to go, but if we cancel, you need to make the call," I said.

All of a sudden I knew what I'd do. I'd make some calls about an apartment, and if he drank, I'd do as I'd planned—I would leave.

I called Jane and John, who now lived three hours away, and told Jane what was taking place. She invited Roxie and me to come there for the weekend. Jake and Charlie planned to leave with two other friends on Thursday at 11:00 a.m. and return Monday evening. I hadn't said anything more to Jake. Knowing the other children were settled took a lot of pressure off of me. I had begun to believe that I could let the bottle be Jake's problem.

When Betty and I were talking on the phone Wednesday morning, I said, "Betty, I can take Roxie and leave the bottle behind. I have no intention of enabling him to drink anymore."

"That's wonderful—as long as you're sure you can handle it, in case he continues to drink."

"I'll face whatever I have to, because I'm sick of the bottle. Remember you told me not to let the bottle rule my life. I don't have to do that. I can look after Roxie and let Jake be on his own." It was really a relief to know that I was going to get out from under it.

There were things I worried about. What if he had a wreck and killed himself or someone else? Then I'd tell myself that he knows that is a possibility before he ever takes a drink. So as I hashed these thoughts out in Dr. Smith's office, I felt sure that I could live with whatever happened after I left and not feel it was my fault.

Thursday morning, I didn't say anything as Jake loaded his things in the car. That was new for me and Jake would look at me every once in a while as though he was expecting me to try to talk him out of going.

We left for Charlie's early so we'd have plenty of time for breakfast.

When we got to the restaurant, I started to feel anxious. *This is for real. What if he just accepts my leaving and continues to drink?* The waitress brought menus and poured us each a cup of coffee. I felt Jake's eyes on me as I was trying to decide what I wanted. I continued to say nothing and he continued looking at me.

After our food arrived I said, "Jake, you've arranged for time off already. Joanne would keep our daughter and we could spend the weekend alone, maybe go to a nice motel for a couple of nights. Charlie has others going with him. He won't care if you tell him you've changed your mind."

He sighed then put down his fork, reached across the table and took my hand.

"Mel, you're afraid I'm going to drink, aren't you?"

Is he hoping I will beg him not to go? Is this more game-playing?

"No, I'm not afraid, because I've been waiting for all the older kids to be settled, and now that they are gone, if you drink, I'm gone. So I'm not afraid. I've worked on this decision for two years. I can do it now."

Jake glanced down at his plate and tears burned my eyes. "I love you, Jake."

He looked up. "I love you, Baby." We finished our meal in silence.

287

Charlie was outside loading his car as we drove up. He came over to say hi while Jake was putting his things into Charlie's car. I was having a hard time controlling my tears.

Charlie leaned over, looked at me and said, "Mel, if you're worried about Jake drinking, he won't drink while he's with me."

I just looked at him. We both knew that if Jake decided to drink, he wouldn't listen to anyone.

That night, Roxie had gone to bed and I was reading Psalms. *It's hard to think, Lord, with Jake gone. Down deep inside, I know he's drinking.*

I grabbed the phone on the first ring. "Hello, Darling," he said, with a slight slur in his voice. It was all too familiar. I knew without a doubt he'd been drinking.

Friday, Roxie and I drove to Jane's house. It was so good to be in Jane's company again. After breakfast on Saturday morning, we were cleaning up, and I stood by the dishwasher and sighed heavily.

"That sigh tells me you're worried," Jane said, rinsing out her dishcloth and hanging it up. "Come, sit down."

"Jake had already been drinking when he called last night."

"Are you sure?"

"Yes, and I told him if he drank on the trip, I'd be gone when he gets back."

"Did he admit that he was drinking?"

"No, but I could tell. I didn't ask him."

"Well, now," she said in a quiet way, "You don't want to give the impression that you're a frantic housewife jumping to conclusions. Maybe you ought to get him to admit that he was drinking and then leave as you said you would."

"Oh, Jane, you are so level-headed. That's how I'll do it."

I knew if I asked Jake, he'd tell me the truth. I also knew I'd be moving when I got home. I felt very sad, but ready to make the move and face whatever came.

On Monday morning, I did laundry and got groceries early. I wanted to leave food for Jake and have everything done. Joanne said she would help if I needed her.

About 9:30 a.m. the phone rang. I felt weak as I lifted the receiver and said, "Hello."

There was that familiar silence then, "Hello, there. We're leaving; the hunting's been great. I'll be home tonight."

"Jake, when you called Thursday night I could tell you'd been drinking. I need to hear it from you."

"Yes, I was, Honey, but I'm not now, and I won't be when I get home. You don't need to worry."

"Jake, I won't be here. Once you start, you don't stop. I meant what I said when you left. I'll never live with the bottle again. It's behind me."

"Now, Honey, don't you do that. As soon as I got out of town Thursday, I wished I hadn't gone. We should have gone to the Marriage Encounter, I see that now. It was a mistake to make this trip."

"Yes, it was," I said, trying not to cry, "But you did and I'm not living with the bottle."

"I'll be home tonight, Honey. You be there."

My hands were trembling when I hung up the phone. It was so hard to be firm with Jake and not just give him one more chance. I got the list of numbers I'd written down and called a nearby apartment building. They could have an apartment ready early afternoon.

Before I left to see the apartment, I called a moving company. They could send three men after lunch. *Things are falling into place*, I thought as I drove out of my drive to check out the apartment.

The two-bedroom apartment was small, but would be fine for Roxie and me.

I hurried back home and as I parked my car, I saw Joanne drive in. We loaded our cars with clothes and bedding. She made us sandwiches, and we were deciding what to take from the kitchen, when the moving truck pulled up at the back door.

I started crying and said, "Oh dear, I wish I had another choice."

I left our room in order and only took my clothes. I took the washstand in the back hallway. *This is where Jake will start to lay his things when he comes in the door*, I thought as the movers carried it out.

No one asked me any questions, for which I was grateful, but when the last thing was loaded in the truck, the man in charge came to me and said in a low tone, "Mrs. Bell, I don't know anything about your business but I wouldn't move away and leave all those antiques."

Later, I told Joanne, "I'm not worried about this stuff. I can get what I want when I want it. The thing that's foremost in my mind is I'm leaving the bottle. I'm sure I'm doing the right thing."

"I see that," she replied as we started our cars.

I had moved most of Roxie's things. Joanne made her bed in the new apartment and her room looked good.

I went back to the farm to meet Roxie after school. When she came in, she started to put her books on the washstand but it wasn't there. I hurried right away and reminded her that I'd told her daddy that if he drank on this trip we'd move out. "We have a neat little apartment and your room is all ready for you."

"Oh, boy, but can I take Queenie?"

"No, Honey, we'll leave your dog at the farm, but we'll come each day after school and take care of her."

She began to cry. I put my arms around her, knowing she was crying about leaving her daddy.

I got everything that we still needed to take in the car and sat down to write Jake a note.

I want to make this short and to the point. I must not repeat myself or preach or blame. Lord, I need help here, I thought. All of a sudden, with real peace, I wrote, "Dear Jake, I have left the bottle, never to live with it again. I love you, Mel."

I looked at the note. It sounded so final, but I had to stick with the decision, even though I loved that man as much as any woman has ever loved a man.

That night I lay in bed wondering about Jake. *I wonder if he's home. What did he do when he saw the washstand and mirror gone? He knows we've left. He's probably checked our room and started through the house to see what we took. He probably has a bottle hidden somewhere, but when he goes to bed, he'll see my note.*

There was no school Thursday and Friday, so I told Roxie she could invite her friends Sarah and Jill, who were sisters, to go to Silver Dollar City in Branson. The sisters' Grandma Wright would go with us to keep me company.

I took my car by the farm to trade for the station wagon for the trip. All the way there I dreaded what I would find. I could hardly unlock the door. Jake was fully dressed, unshaven and had a red face. He was in a deep sleep that would tell almost anyone that he was drunk.

I called Jacob and gave him the girls' grandfather's number in case any of the kids might need to get in contact with me while I was gone.

After a fun day at Silver Dollar City, the girls, their grandmother, Roxie and I were in good spirits. Sarah was dancing around in the room, stumbled into one of the beds and fell on the floor. She jumped up with blonde curls down over her eyes and laughingly said, "I'm acting like a drunk man."

I looked at Roxena Lynne and she had a look of horror on her face. I rose up and took her hand as the flood gates opened in her green eyes. We went in the bathroom and closed the door. I put my arms around her and said, "Honey, you're worried about your daddy, aren't you?"

She nodded.

"I'm worried about Daddy, too. Let's pray right now and ask Jesus to protect your daddy." So standing in the middle of the bathroom with our arms around one another, I said, "Dear Jesus, we don't know where Roxie's daddy is right now. If he's out in the car, will You send one of Your angels to protect him so he won't be killed? Wherever he is, we'll leave him in Your hands."

I had never asked the Lord to send an angel before, and I paused to contemplate that. I glanced at my watch; it was 10:15 p.m.

Roxena Lynne and I stood there until she calmed down. We washed her face and joined the others.

Saturday morning, we went back to Silver Dollar City, went on a cave tour, ate lunch, then went to a little chapel and enjoyed looking out the window into the hills.

The girls asked if they could go get some ice cream just a little ways from where we were. I said, "Yes, if you'll stay together and come straight back here."

They were gone a while. I began to worry and got up and said, "I think I'll go see about the girls."

Grandma Wright said, "I'll go with you."

We started down the street and soon saw Roxie and Sarah coming our way without Jill. I ran to meet them. "Where's Jill?"

"We thought she came back to the church," Sarah said.

"No, she didn't." I turned around and said, "Grandma, wait for us at the church and we'll go find her."

Sarah started to cry, but just then we looked down the street and there came Jill.

Still sniffling, Sarah hugged her and walked back to the church with her arm around her. I heard her say in a broken voice, "Jill, if you ever get lost, run to the church."

We went back to the chapel and sat quietly for a few minutes to regroup after the scare.

I sat there reflecting on what Sarah had said, "If you ever get lost, run to the church." *I had begun to feel so out of place and had so many feelings of guilt, and then we started to Riverview Community Church. There we got involved in the Koinonia group and the Tuesday Bible study. After reading Dr. Oldham's book, I read the Bible regularly. And so today, even though I don't know what is going on with Jake, I feel at peace. Sarah's advice to Jill was very good. I know our church friends are there for us.*

The girls' grandmother suggested we drive back to her place that afternoon and stay there for the night so the girls could continue their vacation together a little while longer.

When we pulled in the driveway, Mr. Wright came out of the house and started toward us. *Oh no, something has happened to Jake.*

I said, "Mr. Wright, has something happened to my husband?"

"Yes, your son Jacob called and said he's had an accident. He has a broken leg. He'll be okay but may lose his leg. It was a one-car accident. The doctors in the ER called his brother since they couldn't get you. He called Jacob and told him they'd been in surgery all night."

I stood on the sidewalk feeling numb, and then I remembered praying with my daughter.

"What time was the wreck?"

"Between 10 and 10:30 last night."

Roxena Lynne and I had prayed at 10:15.

Now I needed to pray again and think. I wanted to rush to the hospital and tell Jake I loved him and make sure he was all right, yet I was sick of living with the bottle and the results of the bottle. I couldn't separate the two. I knew if I called Zach and Lynne I'd get caught up in the emotions of it all. But I needed to know how Jake was. I called Dr. Smith. He had seen him. The break was in the knee and they were still afraid he could lose his leg.

I told Dr. Smith that since I'd left, I also wanted to break the pattern of running to hold his hand and do everything for him.

"Doctor, he has told me, 'I know when I get in a tight spot, Mel will think of something.' If I don't go, he'll get the picture that getting out of this will be his responsibility."

"I believe Jake Bell is going to be a little surprised," he said in his English accent.

"Also, I don't want the kids to think that when he chooses to drink and something happens, they should drop everything and run to him. Do you think this weekend would be soon enough for them to come?"

"Oh, yes, and if that's a problem, they can call him."

I called all the kids. The girls would call their dad. Jacob and his wife would come late Wednesday afternoon, so I invited them to dinner. Neil would come next weekend.

I called Lynne to let them know I was back. I apologized for not telling them that I was going out of town, but, I added, I was completely through with the bottle. "I'm sorry Jake was hurt, but he knows something bad may happen before he ever buys a bottle. I hope he doesn't lose his leg, but my trying to keep him out of trouble hasn't helped, so I'll not be a part of that again."

"You should see the picture of the car."

"I don't want to see it. It's totaled because he was drinking. I may have kept that from happening if I hadn't left, but it would happen sometime. It's all so unnecessary and I no longer want any part of the bottle or the results of it."

Roxie and I went to the farm to take care of her dog, and while we were there, Jake called. Jake mistook my presence there to mean I had come back.

"Oh, I'm so glad you're back home. I need you to come see me," he said.

"We came down to take care of the dog and will continue to do that until you get out of the hospital."

"Honey, I'm hurting so badly. I've really got myself into a mess. They may have to take this leg off. Will you please come to see me?"

"No, there's no sense of you being in this mess. You chose to drink and this is what happened. I have no desire to come and see you after you've had a wreck because you were boozing."

"The wreck was a big one. Apparently I hit a pole. A man pulled me out. No one knows where he is. You have to see the picture of that car."

Could it really have been the angel we prayed for?

"I'm really not interested in how you smashed up the car and got your leg in a mess. You're brilliant, Jake. You can do anything, but I won't accept the bottle and its messes anymore."

After Roxie talked to her daddy, she started crying and wouldn't stop. Finally I got down in front of her and said, "Roxie, Honey, Mama had a big cry, but your daddy is going to be okay, and I just can't cry all the time. I've stopped crying; now you stop crying. Here, take this tissue and dry out those green eyeballs."

She took the tissue and dried her eyes. We locked the farmhouse and went back to our apartment.

Tuesday morning, Joanne and I went to the ladies Bible study. There was such concern in the class for Jake. Everyone gathered around me and prayed. There was lots of weeping. I remembered what Sarah had said to her sister at Silver Dollar City. "When you find yourself lost, run to the church."

When Roxie talked to her daddy, she gave him our phone number. He kept calling, asking that I come see him. I really didn't want to, but finally I said I'd think about it. That evening Roxie and I had just eaten and Jake called to see if I would come over at seven. "I need to talk to you and I can't do that if you don't come see me."

I said I would come.

I had barely walked into the room when Zach showed up in a good mood.

"Hello there, Jake. I told you I'd be here by seven, and for once, I'm not late." He laid some papers from the office on Jake's table.

Oh boy, Jake got me to come when he knew Zach was going to be here and he wouldn't have to talk to me seriously.

I said, "Jake, we'll talk business another time. You have company now. I'll be going."

"Oh, no, Honey, don't go," Jake said.

"Bye, Zach," I said, going toward the door.

"Oh, Melissa, don't go," Zach said, running after me. "I'll just be here a few minutes."

We were in the hall by then, so I turned around and said, "Zach, he wanted us both here so he didn't have to get serious, but I'm not staying around for small talk."

The next day when I talked to Lynne, she said Zach had gone by to talk to Jake about work and that he didn't mean to interrupt. I explained that Jake had asked me to come when he knew Zach was going to be there so he wouldn't have to talk about my leaving.

The next time I saw Dr. Smith, he helped me to see that through the years, Lynne had waited for Zach and seen him come home exhausted many times after helping Jake. Also, they had always come when I had asked them to. Someone was always there to take care of Jake's every need after a binge, and I, for one, had broken the pattern. But I hadn't kept Zach and Lynne informed on my progress and they were very surprised at the change in me. I should have asked Zach and Lynne to be at the meeting when the office staff told Jake they couldn't lie for him anymore. It would have been smart for all of us who were enabling Jake to work together.

When I got through spilling all my thoughts to Dr. Smith, I was ready to face the world with a new look on life.

That day when I talked to Betty, she said, "You know, Melissa, I'm not religious, but ever since you've been reading, I'm seeing a change in you. You keep getting up early and reading your Bible, because I honestly believe that's what is working for you."

Roxie called her daddy each evening as soon as she came home from school. He always asked to talk to me. One evening he said, "Be thinking about coming back to see me. I'll make sure no one else is here."

I told him I'd think about it. Early the next morning when I got up to read my Bible, I was looking out the window just as daylight was coming.

Lord, what do I do about going to see Jake? Then sitting there by the window I began to tell the Lord all my fears—how I was afraid Jake would talk me into going back to the farm and I'd not be ready, or I wouldn't know that the bottle was behind us. After a long while I turned to Proverbs. It was the 11th of November, so I started reading Proverbs 11. When I got to verse 14, I stopped. "Where no counsel is, the people fall: but in a multitude of counselors there is safety."

Maybe that's my answer, Lord. I should have Dr. Smith there when I go. I lay my head back in real relief. *I can do that and not worry. Dr. Smith is convinced that I'm not going to live with the bottle and he'll back me up. Oh, thank You, Lord. I can hardly wait to tell Betty that I got my answer from Your Word. And Lord, I can never thank You enough that I can read without a struggle.*

In spite of my problems, the Lord was very real to me that morning.

When Jake called and asked if I would visit, I suggested that he arrange a time when Dr. Smith could be there. "Because," I said, "our relationship can't stand anymore game-playing."

"I'll call your Dr. Searchbrains right now."

I was waiting in the hospital lobby for Dr. Smith when he arrived. We started down the hall and I said, "Doctor, I'm so nervous."

"Oh, Mel, why are you nervous? You've made an important decision not to live with the bottle. I'll help you get that across to Jake."

"I just want to make my case and leave," I said as we neared Jake's door.

We found Jake propped up in bed with his left leg in a full cast. He looked thin and had shadows under his eyes. I wanted to run over to his bed and throw my arms around him, but I held back.

I stood there with Dr. Smith by my side and said, "Hello."

"Hi, Honey. My, I'm glad to see you. Thank you for coming. I'm putting my head on straight and I'm ready to eat crow."

"Jake, I didn't come expecting you to eat crow. I came to make sure that you understand my position. I've been planning this break for two years. The reason I waited was I wanted to see Neil in college. I've given this a lot of thought. I don't want to live with the phone off the hook and the lights off. If I ever go back to you, I will never look under the car seat or anywhere for another bottle. I will never taper you off or take care of you when you're drinking. I will never lie about your whereabouts. The only way for that to happen is for me to stay gone, or for you to decide to stay off the bottle."

He reached down and moved his leg over a little, then looked up to me. "I'm sorry I didn't take you on the Marriage Encounter weekend, Honey. You wanted to do that very much."

If he gets me talking about that, he will try to keep me from talking about his drinking. I won't play that game anymore. I had my say; I need to leave him with Dr. Smith.

"This isn't about the Marriage Encounter; this is about your drinking and I just came to make sure you understand, until you decide to stop drinking, I won't go back to the farm."

"When I decide not to drink, it will be just because I'm through with drinking, not to get you to come home."

"That's the idea. When you make that decision, let me know."

I looked over in the chair where Dr. Smith sat. He looked pleased. I turned back to Jake and said, "Jake, this is all up to you. I've never been in love with anyone but you, and I love you with my whole heart, but the games are over. I will never live with the bottle again." I turned to go.

Dr. Smith got on his feet and walked toward Jake's bed. When I got to the door, I heard him say, "Jake Bell, she knows you like a book and my friend, she's serious."

The next day I went to hear Jill Briscoe speak to the women at our church. Shortly after the luncheon, she read to us a Christmas program she had just written. The name of it was "A Time for Giving". The part that caught my attention was when Jesus was twelve and went to the temple. His parents missed him after being on the road three days. They then had to retrace their steps. While I was driving home, I finally understood that in my long journey, I'd lost my close relationship with the Lord. It was clear to me that I needed to retrace my steps—to go back and see where I'd lost touch. I pulled over on the busy interstate, and while cars whizzed by, I asked the Lord with a broken heart to forgive the impatience, anger, deceit and bitterness that had built up in me, like the dirt and grime on the partial plate that Wendy had hidden in the shower drain. Then I could take Christ home with me, as Mary and Joseph had done.

Dr. Oldham had said in his book that the lady's husband had not changed, but she had.

I knew I would never live with the bottle again but only I could be responsible for my change.

Jake didn't call for a few days and I was planning for Wendy and Neil to be with us at the apartment for Thanksgiving.

About 2 p.m., a few days before Thanksgiving break, Jake called.

As soon as I said, "Hello," I recognized that silence.

Then Jake said, "Hello, Honey."

"Hi, Jake."

"Mel, I want our family back together by Thanksgiving. I know you can't trust that I won't drink. I'm not going to promise that I won't, but I'll promise to give it my best shot. I'll also promise you this: If you'll come home and I start drinking, you won't have to move out of your home, I will."

Wow, I can't believe what I'm hearing. "Jake, would you tell me that with Dr. Smith or Donn?"

"Yes, Donn is coming tonight. Will you meet with us?"

"Yes."

"Boy, I'm glad to hear that."

That night, Jake explained what he had told me and that he would stick with his word.

"Hey, that's great," Donn said.

He told us how much our marriage had meant to him before he married Evon. "You two," he said, "like one another." That's what I ask young couples when they come to me to marry them. I know they're in love, and they always tell me they are, but when a couple likes one another and enjoys one another as you two do, they have a lot going for them."

While Donn was with us, I told Jake I'd be at the farm the day before Thanksgiving when Jake would be dismissed.

Roxie and I moved our personal belongings home after school Tuesday.

I was baking pecan pies when Neil came just in time for dinner. It was snowing heavily. About 9:00 p.m., Wendy called and said the storm was so bad they were stopping for the night. I told her I thought that was wise, and that when she did arrive, she should come back to the farm.

"Oh, good," she said. I was also glad I was back.

Jake was to be dismissed late Wednesday morning. Neil cleaned the snow off the back steps and driveway and went to pick up his dad.

I looked out the kitchen window and saw Wendy coming up the drive with a suitcase in both hands. Roxie and I ran out to meet her and helped her with her things. Her smile was so beautiful and I was so glad she was home.

Just as we got lunch ready, we heard the car horn and the girls went to the back door to wait for their dad.

We were all grateful that Jake was alive and home, but to show a lot of excitement wasn't what we usually did in a time like this. We'd been through too many crises from drinking.

Neil came behind his dad while he walked up the steps on his crutches and through the door Wendy was holding open. He was breathing a little hard from the effort but greeted Wendy and Roxie with a hug.

I was standing back. We just looked at one another for several minutes. He walked to his chair, sat down and put up the leg rest.

"Lunch is about ready," I said, and went in the kitchen. The kids and their dad were talking but I felt numb and empty of emotions. I made the hamburgers and fixed a tray for Jake. "Come on, kids, and get your plate; we'll just sit by the fire."

"It will just be us for Thanksgiving and we'll keep it simple," I told Wendy as we worked in the kitchen Wednesday afternoon. "We won't open the big table. We'll have a buffet and eat in the family room."

Jake and I were both exhausted and went to bed early. We hadn't mentioned the wreck or anything about the missing furniture that I hadn't moved back yet.

In bed, Jake put his arm around me. "I'm glad we're home, Honey. You've been a little quiet."

My heart was full and all of a sudden I started crying.

"You won't be disappointed about coming back," he reassured me.

We talked for an hour. I lay beside him in the darkness in the circle of his arms and cried it all out. He didn't make big promises, just mostly listened.

Finally, I felt at peace and a lightness of spirit that promised a new beginning.

I didn't know what was ahead. I did know I'd never live with the bottle again. Long after Jake went to sleep, I lay awake. He looked so tired and it was hard for him to get comfortable with the cast. He finally settled down on his left side. I put my hand on the back of his head. *The bald spot is bigger than it was when we married. This is how we've slept for twelve years. Some things are just like they were,* I thought, as I listened to his breathing.

Usually the farm was a noisy place. You could hear the cows or one of the horses, chickens or guineas. Often I would listen to the whistle of the train at the edge of the farm. That night there were no sounds.

Everything was still, peaceful and quiet. That was how I felt. All the old anxious feelings were gone. The change was beginning in me. I lay peacefully beside my husband, free of fear, anger and dread, and I knew the bottle was behind me. We could start over. I loved being Jake's wife but I was no longer his enabler.

With the Lord's help and the love we have for one another, we will grow and continue to recover.

EPILOGUE

Did Jake's leg heal? Did he ever drink again? If so, how did I handle it? Did any of the children become alcoholics? Below are some highlights from 1975 to the present that will answer these questions.

1976 – On the plane ride home from the Mayo Clinic, Jake had a drink but wasn't drinking when he came home. Dr. Smith and I agreed as long as he didn't bring a bottle home or stop for a drink, I should let it go. Jake assured Dr. Smith he would cooperate. This year, I spent more time working on this memoir that I had started in 1974.

1977 – Jake's leg was operated on a second time. He began to wear a brace.

1980 – Jake semi-retired and we moved to a rural area. He served as the radiologist for a small hospital.

1981 – I started working on this memoir a second time.

1982 – My brother Stan was diagnosed with cancer. Jake was the family's rock during this time. After Stan's funeral, Jake left for a meeting. On his way home he started drinking and spent the night about one hundred miles from home. When he called and told me, he said, "Don't do anything crazy now, Honey. I'll be fine when I see you." He was.

1984 – We started attending a wonderful country Church of God. The pastor and his wife, Wilbur and Anita Hunter, became our close friends. He and Jake fished and shared stories of their drinking days, and Wilbur told him how the love of the Lord turned his own life around. Jake always looked forward to doing things with the Hunters.

1985 – In July, all six children and grandchildren from five different states came home for a family reunion. It was a wonderful time. Jake and I were having dinner the day after everyone left, and he looked over at me and said, "Honey, it's so wonderful to know that none of our children are alcoholics. And it's also wonderful to live in a dry county and not have to see advertisements for liquor on the way home from work."

We planted a pink rose hedge along the edge of our front yard, and several colors of roses in front of the house. Each afternoon or early evening, Jake, without mentioning it, went out and picked one rose bud and put it on my night stand in a bud vase he'd taken from the China cupboard. He never failed to do that each spring and summer.

1986 – March 3rd, Jake had another operation on his leg. This time a rod was inserted in the entire length of his leg. He was back on crutches for a while, but later was able to walk without support.

In August, Jake went to a three-day meeting, and when he called the night before he came home, I could tell he was drinking. I was in the kitchen when he came home. He came over and kissed me. "Honey, I'm not going to try to keep anything from you. I drank while I was gone."

"I know. I talked to you last night."

"Man..."

"No, Jake," I interrupted, "Don't tell me how desperate you are. That kind of conversation ended in 1975 and isn't to be in our home again. Go get ready for dinner."

The next day I could tell he was desperate for a drink, but I had real peace about not getting caught up in the drinking and the results—I just knew if it continued, he would move out.

The next day was Saturday and I had plans to visit the Hunters before shopping. When I told Jake where I was going, he said, "Honey, I don't want to interfere with your plans, but I'd love to go with you."

Some of the Hunters' family was visiting, so I planned to only stay for half an hour. However, Anita had seen our husbands talking and said, "Mel, Jake is asking Wilbur about the Lord. You need to plan to stay for lunch." We spent the entire day. Wilbur gave Jake some of the same scriptures I'd given him in 1961. He kept reassuring him how the Lord's love and forgiveness was for him, personally.

The next morning at church, Jake went to the prayer room and gave his heart to the Lord. When we got home, he tried to call all six children. After talking to the ones he could reach, he called our former pastor at Riverview Community.

"Donn, this morning I gave my heart to the Lord. Remember we used to argue about tithing? Well, Donn, from now on, I'm going to tithe."

This is for real, I thought. *I didn't expect to ever hear him say that.*

1987 to 1992 – We attended medical meetings and took several trips to see the kids, as well as having the kids and grandchildren at our home a lot. We had extended visits from grandchildren during the summers and lots of visits with Zach and Lynne and my family.

I continued trying to write this memoir.

In 1992, Wendy's daughter, Erin, spent extra time with us that summer while Wendy was finishing college. When Wendy came home to pick Erin up, we had great talks. I told her things I regretted and I think she felt free to express herself for the first time. In one conversation, she said something that made so much sense to me: "Mel, you were rescuing the captain while the ship was sinking."

1993 – In July, our world was shaken when Jake diagnosed himself with lung cancer. He called each of the children and told them he had cancer and would be gone by Christmas. All the children came home and spent time with him. The four youngest and their families were close enough to come periodically. They spent long weekends with us and helped me take care of their dad. Never have I seen more love from a family to a parent. Rev. Wilbur and Anita Hunter were there often. We became very close friends with our pastors at that time. Jake always looked forward to the visits. Zach and Lynne also came often. They were the same source of strength during that time as they had always been. Additionally, my brother Doug (now deceased), his wife Marilyn and my sister-in-law Anita were particularly helpful.

Lots of people gave Jake special care during his illness: Ruth Ann, a nurse who had worked with Jake, our church congregation and our neighbors, Mr. and Mrs. T. and family. Once during an ice storm when no one could get to us by car, Mr. T. walked over to see about us and then walked back home to get oranges because Jake thought he would be able to drink some fresh orange juice. Two young women who had been very close to us each drove long distances to see Jake; Ginger came from Dallas, and Mary from Kansas City. My friend Ada, who had a love for the Lord and a ministry to cancer patients and their families, was a real sunshine during our storm. The doctors from the hospital where Jake had been the radiologist came to check on him at least every other day, even though it was almost an hour's drive. And our hospital's home health gave excellent care.

Jake died at home January 25, 1994.

1995 – My friend Betty was diagnosed with cancer. I would have liked to take care of her in her illness, but I couldn't because I was caring for my own mother in my home. Betty passed away in 1996 and Mama in 1997.

1997 to 2003 – During these five years, I took a few trips, went to special events for grandchildren, and spent a lot of time with Aunt Roxena, who lived to be 98 years old. I also did some speaking for women's groups, and with encouragement from my pastor, became involved with LIVE Ministries (Lay People in Vital Exchange)—a wonderful part of my life.

2003 – A writer friend of mine suggested I should start writing my story, so I started rewriting it from the beginning. I had many stops—one was for selling my home and relocating.

Our story is true and I have told it as I remember it. It was important to Jake that I write our story. After he became ill, he said, "Mel, I want you to finish that book. It may help straighten someone out. Don't worry what anyone may think or say, just spell my name right."

Well, I have finished the book. Instead of spelling his name correctly, I changed it.

If our story will help one alcoholic and his or her family, my family and I will be blessed.

**More Quality Books from The Quilldriver and On My Own Now
Ministries** Free Shipping on all orders through www.OnMyOwnNow.com

Purity's Big Payoff/Premarital Sex is a Big Rip-off is a collection of 17 first-person narratives about successfully waiting for marriage to have sex – or not – and the consequences of those decisions.
978-0-9791639-8-2, Softcover, 116 pp. ~~$14.95~~ $12.00 at OnMyOwnNow.com
Also in Spanish! *La Gran Recompensa de la Pureza/La Gran Estafa del Sexo Prematrimonial.* Free e-book at www.VivaLaPureza.info

On My Own Now: Straight Talk from the Proverbs for Young Christian Women who Want to Remain Pure, Debt-free and Regret-free By Donna Lee Schillinger
This compact collection of quirky vignettes, based on gender-reversed Proverbs, is great for daily devotions, affirmations, confessions, benedictions and many other religious "tions," all with the goal of keeping you on the yellow brick road. After all, you're not in Kansas anymore – you're on your own now.
978-0-9791639-5-1 Softcover, 288 pp. © 2008 ~~$14.95~~ $10.95 at OnMyOwnNow.com; Abridged Audiobook (MP3 download) $9.95; Kindle edition $4.95
Also in Spanish: *Por Mi Cuenta Ahora: Una Conversación Directa de los Proverbios para Mujeres Jóvenes Cristianas que Quieren Permanecer Puras, Libres de Deudas y Arrepentimientos* Por Donna Lee Schillinger
Free e-book at www.VivaLaPureza.info

Walking Man: A Modern Missions Experience in Latin America By Narciso Zamora
Winner of the 2008 Next Generation Indie Book Award, this odyssey of a Peruvian delinquent's winding and treacherous path toward finding his calling in missions recounts a literal journey of 10,000 miles.
978-0-9791639-0-6 Softcover 208 pp. ~~$12.95~~ Only $9.95 at OnMyOwnNow.com
Abridged audiobook in MP3 format and CD $9.95; Kindle edition $4.95
Also in Spanish: *Caminante con Dios...en apuro mas no desesperados: El Trabajo Misionero en América Latina* Por Narciso Zamora
978-0-9791639-1-3 Softcover 186 pp. ~~$12.95~~ $9.95 at OnMyOwnNow.com

In the Care of Angels: God's Work Through Adoption (both Physical and Spiritual) By Dorothy Grace Manning Kennedy
A tender story of a selfless act that addresses critical issues for those considering adoption. Softcover, 86pp. $9.95